# ANTI-OPPRESSIVE SOCIAL WORK

# ANTI-OPPRESSIVE SOCIAL WORK

## Ways of Knowing, Talking, and Doing

**Gary C. Dumbrill • June Ying Yee**

OXFORD
UNIVERSITY PRESS

# OXFORD
## UNIVERSITY PRESS

Oxford University Press is a department of the University of Oxford.
It furthers the University's objective of excellence in research, scholarship,
and education by publishing worldwide. Oxford is a registered trade mark of
Oxford University Press in the UK and in certain other countries.

Published in Canada by
Oxford University Press
8 Sampson Mews, Suite 204,
Don Mills, Ontario M3C 0H5 Canada

www.oupcanada.com

**Library and Archives Canada Cataloguing in Publication**
Dumbrill, Gary Corneleus, author
Anti-oppressive social work: ways of knowing, talking, and doing
/ Gary C. Dumbrill, June Ying Yee.
Includes bibliographical references and index.

Issued in print and electronic formats.
ISBN 978-0-19-902371-4 (softcover).–ISBN 978-0-19-902372-1 (PDF)

1. Social service.  2. Social service—Moral and ethical aspects.
3. Social work education.  4. Social work with minorities.  5. Oppression
(Psychology).  6. Marginality, Social—Psychological aspects.  7. Equality.
I. Yee, June Ying, author  II. Title.

HV11.D85 2018                    361.3                    C2018-901870-4
                                                          C2018-901871-2

Cover image: © rondale/123RF; Cover design: Sherill Chapman; Interior design: Laurie McGregor

Text Credits: Page 35: Excerpt from *I'm Not the Indian You Had in Mind*, Director's statement.
Copyright © 2007 Thomas King. With permission of the author. Pages 170–71: Republished with
permission of Taylor & Francis Ltd.; permission conveyed through Copyright Clearance Center, Inc.
Page 284–6, 293–4, 304–5: Extracts reprinted with permission of *Child Welfare Journal*. Pages 287–91, 302–4:
Extracts reprinted with permission of the Ontario Association of Children's Aid Societies.

Oxford University Press is committed to our environment.
This book is printed on Forest Stewardship Council® certified paper
and comes from responsible sources.

Printed and bound in the United States of America
2  3  4 — 22  21  20

# Contents

## Thinking Critically about Power and Politics  58

 ## Whiteness: What It Is and Why We Have to Understand It  87

## Isms and Intersectionality Part One: Racism and Sexism   117

## Isms and Intersectionality Part Two: Heterosexism and Cissexism, Ableism, and Sanism   145

# From Colonization to Decolonization  170

# The Problem of Poverty, Class, Capital, and the Social Order  199

**13** **Where to from Here: Innovations and Hopes for the Future   337**

# Preface

We are going to tell you lots of stories in this book. Every chapter starts and ends with a story. Each story tells you about something we have seen or experienced in life that relates to the topic in that chapter.

We start chapters with stories about life, rather than theory, because the point of social work is to understand and engage with life. Of course, to understand life one needs theory—and that is the point of our stories. Our stories are intellectual puzzles that pose questions about what is really going on in life, how we make sense of it, and what we can do about it.

Each chapter gives you the theoretical knowledge to understand the story at the start of the chapter, and to unravel and answer the intellectual puzzles the story poses. All of these stories, and the puzzles they pose, relate one way or another to oppression and anti-oppressive practice. This is also true of the other stories we populate the chapters with. Each time you come across a story in this book, remember that it is always purposive: We challenge you to look past the storyline to find its meaning and relevance for anti-oppression. At the end of every chapter we will help you pull these meanings and lessons together.

A caution about looking for meaning in our stories. We are somewhat private people. We each have differing thresholds in terms of how much we share about ourselves, oftentimes arguing that the other needs to share more in the text. Consequently, if in places you hear one of us speak more than the other, this does not mean that one of us wanted to speak more. It means that one of us wanted to speak less. As well, when you read the stories, if you think the story is about us (i.e., June or Gary), read a little deeper because you may be missing the point. The stories are not intended to be about us—they are intended to be about the world we live in.

Another important feature of this book is that you will find no formulas or recipes for doing anti-oppressive practice. We wish we could give you formulas and recipes, but we cannot because they do not exist. Indeed, what a worker does in one moment that is anti-oppressive can be oppressive the next, depending on the context and a complex array of social variables. As a result, social workers have to create anti-oppression in the moment, in partnership with those they serve, and with a deep understanding about society and the power relationships that impact everyday life. In this book we attempt to give you the conceptual and theoretical tools to do just that—to grasp the nuances and potential meanings of the stories and events you will encounter in your work—and to create anti-oppressive practice in those moments.

Below is a brief overview of what to expect in the chapters to come. The book comprises thirteen chapters.

**Chapter 1** begins by defining oppression and anti-oppression, because if we are going to engage in anti-oppression, we must understand what oppression and anti-oppression are, and what they are not. A core concept in this chapter is the way oppression treads down and holds back specific groups of people and at the same time lifts up and pushes forward other groups. In other words, there is a direct relationship between the oppression some groups face and the advantage other groups enjoy. In **Chapter 2** we examine ways to think critically about what we know and how we know it. This is because critical thinking is at the heart of anti-oppression. Without thinking critically, there is no anti-oppression. In **Chapter 3** we use what we have learned about critical thinking to examine issues of power. Understanding power is essential, because without power, oppression would only be a nasty social attitude with no ability to tread some down and lift others up.

In **Chapter 4** we begin to examine specific forms of oppression and what drives them. We start with Whiteness and White supremacy, which form the bedrock on which many forms of oppression encountered today rest. We move on in **Chapter 5** to examine various isms and how they are resisted. We start with racism, including anti-Black racism, anti-Jewish racism, and anti-Muslim racism. We also discuss sexism and intersectionality. In **Chapter 6** we consider heterosexism, cissexism, ableism, and sanism. We also introduce the concept of performativity and the way it shapes society and people's lives. In **Chapter 7** we expand our focus to consider colonization, and in **Chapter 8** the problem of poverty, class, capital, and the social order.

The chapters above ought to give you the knowledge needed to create anti-oppression in the practice moments you encounter. In **Chapter 9** we start to examine how that can be done. Here, we situate anti-oppression as "the social work dream," because it is the dream of any helping occupation to tackle the root causes of troubles rather than simply treat symptoms. In **Chapter 10** we contend that social work can never realize the dream of doing anti-oppression unless it is done in partnership with service users and also draws on service users' knowledge and theory. In **Chapter 11,** drawing on service users' knowledge and theory, we start to become much more specific about how to do (and create) anti-oppression when working with individuals, families, and communities. In **Chapter 12** we consider how to do this same work at organizational and policy levels. Finally, in **Chapter 13**, we consolidate these lessons and think about your story of anti-oppression, and where you take this work from here.

In each chapter we provide numerous exercises to help you engage with ideas, and we provide Key Concept boxes to highlight key ideas and their practical implications. Whenever we use a technical word or concept in the text, on first use (or in the sentence immediately after), we put the word or concept in bold, and provide a definition immediately after the bold text. These terms are also defined in the Glossary. As well, at the end of each chapter, we provide discussion questions, activities, and additional resources.

Many of the exercises and activities in the book require following links to various websites and forms of multimedia. We have provided URLs that are current at the time of printing. If you find a "dead" link, simply search for the new location by using the descriptions we have provided.

We hope you enjoy reading this book as much as we have enjoyed writing it. Our hope is that by the end of the book you will have the ability, or will have strengthened your existing ability, to recognize and name oppression, to know exactly how it is operating, and to have an array of strategies you can build into your social work practice to address oppression.

—Gary C. Dumbrill and June Ying Yee

## A Note on Language

Throughout the book we use what we believe is the most progressive language to refer to people and concepts. Language, however, is always contested (for good reason), so in a number of places we will provide and explain language alternatives that you may encounter.

One decision about language we ought to explain at the start of the text, lest it create confusion, is the language we have adopted regarding race. In the past "people of colour" has been an umbrella term used to refer to those who are on the receiving end of racism. More recently the term "racialized" is emerging as the preferred word choice. We adopt the term "racialized," but in doing so we do not want to mask the fact that White people are "racialized" too. Unlike people of colour, White people tend to be racialized into a position of unearned privilege and race advantage. As a result, when we use the term "racialized," keep in mind that we do not imply that White people do not gain from the racialization process, but instead we use the term exclusively to refer to the process of marking or categorizing (i.e., racializing) a person in a manner that causes them to be subjected to racism. Although we use the term "racialized" in this way, at times we revert to the term "people of colour" when we refer to an original source, or where to do otherwise might cause confusion.

# Acknowledgements

We thank Oxford University Press, especially Stephen Kotowych and Leah-Ann Lymer, for making this project happen. We thank McMaster University and Ryerson University for sabbaticals that sped this project along.

We thank the peer reviewers, both named and anonymous, whose ideas have strengthened this work, and whose comments and encouragement have energized us and kept us moving forward: Tracey A. Bone, University of Manitoba; Derek Chewka, MacEwan University; Debashis Dutta, Renison University College and Conestoga College; Jacinta Goveas, Sheridan College; Brigette Krieg, University of Regina; Felice Markowicz, George Brown College; Mallory Neuman, University of Manitoba; Olufunke Oba, University of Regina; Cristine Rego, Sir Sandford Fleming College; Si Transken, University of Northern British Columbia; and Miu Chung Yan, University of British Columbia.

We thank the following friends and colleagues for reading select chapters or sections, for talking over ideas and making suggestions: Cyndy Baskin, Michelle Brait, Liza Choi, Juliana Chooi, Laurence Cutner, Rebecca Dumbrill, John Gabriel, Luwam Ghebreslassie, Saara Greene, Julie Inngs, Randy Jackson, Winnie Lo, Zack Marshall, Dale Moorcroft, Susan Silver, Raven Sinclair, Christina Sinding, Mark Sinke, Steven Solomon, Aubrey A. Thompson, Samantha Wehbi, Danielle Wong, Helen Wong, and Yuk-Lin Renita Wong.

We thank all of the research participants and service users who have taught us how to do social work and anti-oppression.

We thank all of our ancestors and relations, and all the writers we have read whose ideas have inspired us, and whose shoulders we stand upon.

We dedicate this book to Gary's grandmother, Emma Dumbrill (nee Ellis), often known as "Nanny Rue" (1900–86), and June's mother and father, Ma Yee and Ba Yee.

# 1 What Are Oppression and Anti-Oppression?

## In this chapter you will learn:

- What oppression and anti-oppression are and how they are defined
- How oppression operates at an individual level through personal prejudices
- What your own prejudices are and how they may cause you to have biases
- How oppression operates at systemic and cultural levels
- How to identify whether oppression is occurring and how to justify your position

## Introduction

June was teaching a class where she repeatedly mispronounced the name of a student of Pakistani-Canadian heritage. The student eventually told June that the continual mispronunciation of her name was racism—a form of oppression. Was June being oppressive?

A few weeks later Gary was presenting at an event where the person introducing him mispronounced his last name "Dumbrill" as "Bumbrill." Everyone laughed, including Gary. Was the mispronunciation of Gary's last name oppression? Was this the same as or different from June mispronouncing the student's name? By the end of this chapter, you will be able to answer this question, and you will be able to justify your position. You will also have an understanding of anti-oppression and will know why it is important that social workers operate from this perspective.

## What Is Anti-Oppression?

The nature of **anti-oppressive practice** is evident from the phrase itself. "Anti" means it opposes, "oppression" is what it opposes, and "practice" is the context in which it operates. Anti-oppressive social work, therefore, opposes oppression through the practice (everyday activities) of social work.

The definition in Figure 1.1 appears simple, but its practice is complex, because there is no fixed formula that describes how social workers can oppose oppression. In fact, depending on context and an array of personal, social, cultural, and

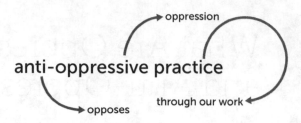

**Figure 1.1** Anti-oppressive practice

historical variables, what is anti-oppressive one moment might be oppressive the next. Anti-oppression, therefore, has to be created in the moment by basing action on a careful analysis of the context and events occurring in that moment. To undertake this analysis, we need to understand what oppression is and what it is not.

# What Is Oppression?

The word **oppress** has Latin roots that means to press down. Oppression is exactly that; it is the process of pressing and keeping a person down. It attempts to stop someone flourishing, refuses to let them get ahead, tries to prevent them from reaching their potential, stifles and keeps them underfoot. Everyone has probably felt oppressed in this way at some point: a falling out with a friend who begins to backstab in an attempt to bring one down, or a disagreement with someone at work who retaliates by spreading gossip in a way that is harmful to one's career. Although such events are "oppression" in the dictionary sense of the term, the sort of oppression that "anti-oppression" addresses has a slightly different meaning.

## How Social Workers Understand Oppression

In anti-oppressive social work we reserve the term "oppression" for acts or processes that repeatedly target the same people for harm just because they are members of a particular group. Of course, social work is interested in helping people harmed by all manner of unfair acts no matter what group they are from. But when social workers use the word "oppression" to refer to someone's troubles, it is because these troubles result from a pattern of pressing down and holding back that affect an entire group or category of people. Groups commonly pressed down in this manner include, *but are not limited to,* **racialized** people (those who face oppression because of their race); women; Indigenous peoples; people with disabilities; people who are lesbian, gay, bisexual, transsexual,

## Key Concept

When social workers use the word "oppression" to refer to someone's troubles, it is because these troubles result from a pattern of pressing down and holding back that affect an entire group or category of people.

transgender, intersex, queer, questioning, two-spirited (LGBTTIQQ2S); social work service users; people living in poverty; the very young; and the very old.

Stating a list of oppressed groups, like the one above, is fraught with problems that have dogged anti-oppression from its earliest days (Joseph, 2015; Williams, 1999). Indeed, Williams (1999) suggests that attempting to categorize oppressed groups based on identity is a "folly of reductionism" (p. 221) because it assumes that groups are fixed and do not change, and also because it feeds into seeing someone as either oppressed or an oppressor depending on the group they are in.

We agree that a list of oppressed groups is problematic, because reality is always much more complex than a list of oppressed groups can ever imply. But sometimes a little simplification is needed to grasp a topic, after which its nuances can be more readily understood. Reductionism does not necessarily dumb down a topic. Instead, it can provide an entry point for a much deeper understanding of an issue that would not otherwise be possible.

The sociologist Max Weber popularized a form of reductionism as a means to gain a deeper understanding of an issue. Weber constructed what he called **ideal types,** which were models of reality, not built as an empirical representation of reality, but as a heuristic device abstracted from parts of reality to represent the way society works (Bullock & Trombley, 2000; Kim, 2012). A **heuristic device** is equivalent to the small models architects use to represent buildings they are about to construct. These devices are useful because they demonstrate the way reality appears, but they can never accurately represent the realities of size, volume, weight loads, and other variables that every architect understands are part of the real world they are modelling. A **Weberian ideal type** is the same: a conceptual model that represents key characteristics of a social issue for analysis.

There is certainly enough empirical evidence to show that any conceptual model of oppression must include the groups we listed above. For example, we know that women are underrepresented in positions of leadership (Cook & Glass, 2014), as are racialized people (Block & Galabuzi, 2011). We know that until recently people in same-sex relationships were denied the right to marry (Woodford, Newman, Brotman, & Ryan, 2010), and not too long ago their attraction for each other was considered a mental illness (Pomeroy & Parrish, 2012). We know that Indigenous people have had their land taken and their languages largely destroyed (Qwul'sih'yah'maht & Kundoqk, 2015), and that the state continues to take their children from them in disproportionate numbers (Sinha, Trocme, Fallon, & MacLaurin, 2013).

All groups on the list above face disadvantage. In later chapters we will explain the fluid and intersecting nature of these categories, along with the impossibility of defining people as simply an oppressor or oppressed. At this point, however, we do not want these complexities to obscure our explanation of the mechanisms through which oppression operates, or to obscure the undeniable fact that people in these groups face oppression.

## Anti-Oppression and Human Rights

Patterns of oppression in society are so predictable that human rights legislation is needed to protect those commonly singled out for oppression. In Canada, this protection is provided through federal, provincial, and territorial human rights legislation. For instance, the Nova Scotia Human Rights Act prohibits discrimination on a number of grounds, including those listed below. (Review the human rights code in your jurisdiction and compare it with the list below):

- Age
- Race
- Colour
- Religion
- Creed
- Sex
- Sexual orientation

- Gender identity
- Gender expression
- Physical disability or mental disability
- An irrational fear of contracting an illness or a disease

- Ethnic, national, or Aboriginal origin
- Family status
- Marital status
- Source of income
- Political belief, affiliation, or activity

The Nova Scotia code also includes discrimination on the basis of an "individual's association with another individual or class of individuals having characteristics referred to [above]".

Canadian human rights legislation builds on the principle that all people have equal rights without distinction (United Nations, 1948). Such legislation is needed because there is a history and an ongoing pattern of denying rights to people on the grounds above. Human rights legislation attempts to ensure that people known to face these patterns of oppression enjoy the same rights and freedoms as everyone else.

There is an overlap between the way human rights legislators understand discrimination and the way social workers understand oppression, but doing anti-oppressive social work is not the same as enforcing human rights legislation. Social workers may sometimes address oppression based on individual complaints of code violation, but more often social workers unravel and address oppression embedded in the troubles people and communities face in broader systemic ways. Human rights work focuses more on the rights of the individual rather than a being systematic examination of the inequalities that prevent those rights from being realized (Crawford & Andreassen, 2015).

Both human rights work and anti-oppression go beyond the notion of equality to examine equity. The term **equality** is usually understood as things being equal, of everyone being treated exactly the same. The term **equity** is based on the recognition that people are not the same, people have unique needs, and so treating everyone the same is not always just. To achieve **social justice** (a fair society) people have to be treated according to their needs. Another related term used for this concept is **social inclusion** (enabling people to participate in society). To be included within society people have to be treated in accordance with need, otherwise they will face **social exclusion** and will not be able to take part in or enjoy events and activities that most others take for granted. Figure 1.2 demonstrates the concepts of equality and equity. Equality is shown on the left along with the exclusion caused by treating everyone the same; equity is shown on the right along with the social inclusion and participation that this brings.

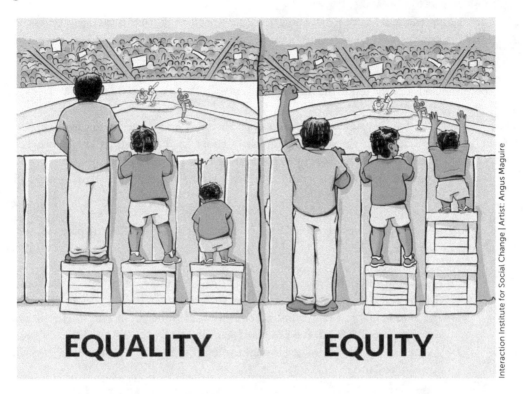

Interaction Institute for Social Change | Artist: Angus Maguire

EQUALITY    EQUITY

**Figure 1.2** Equality vs. equity

## How Social Workers Use the Term "Oppression"

Social workers should be careful to only use the term "oppression" when they are sure oppression is occurring, otherwise the concept of anti-oppression will become meaningless. Mullaly explains that:

> Not everything that frustrates or limits or hurts a person is oppressive. . . . What determines oppression is when a person is blocked from opportunities to self-development, is excluded from full participation in society, does not have certain rights that the dominant group takes for granted, or is assigned a second-class citizenship, not because of individual talent, merit, or failure, but because of his or her membership in a particular group or category of people. (Mullaly, 2010, p. 40)

Said differently, for something to be considered "oppression" in the way social work understands this term, it must result from the "holding back" or "pushing down" of *a class or group of people* in society. Unfair or unkind acts that limit or frustrate people may feel the same as oppression at a **micro** (individual) level, but what distinguishes these from oppression is that in oppression these acts felt at a micro level form a discernible **macro** (society-wide) pattern that consistently targets the same class or group of people time and time again.

Determining whether someone's troubles result from oppression is never straightforward. Consider the following individual events:

- A Black male youth is repeatedly stopped in the street for questioning by the police.
- An Indigenous parent who is unable to afford food for their child is referred to child protection services for neglect rather than to a food bank for help.
- A female student is discouraged by her school teachers from following a career she desires in engineering.

These micro interactions could all be oppression, because the following patterns exist at a macro level:

- Police stop and question Black youth on the street more often than White youth (Equity and Human Rights Commission, 2015; Rankin, Winsa, Bailey, & Ng, 2013).
- The state tends to remove Indigenous children rather than offer their parents support (Strega & Sohki Aski Esquao [Jeannine Carriere], 2015).
- Women are underrepresented in engineering (Eccles, 2007; Walton, Logel, Peach, Spencer, & Zanna, 2015).

One might conclude that because of these patterns, all of the individual examples we gave above are forms of oppression. But what if the Black youth is known to police as a gang member? What if the Indigenous parent really is neglecting their child? What if the female student actually has no aptitude for the math and science involved in engineering? Would these examples still be oppression? Perhaps not, but perhaps so—this question is hard to answer without more information.

One way to determine if oppression is at play is to consider what might happen if the individual being impacted were not a member of a group we know faces oppression. In other words, ask what would happen if the person were not a member of what Mullaly calls a second-class citizenship group, but instead was a member of what we might call a first-class citizenship group. Would a White male gang member be stopped in the same circumstances? Would a non-Indigenous parent be referred to a food bank rather than child protection services? Would a male student intent on engineering but weak at math be sent to tutoring instead of being discouraged by teachers?

Asking these types of questions may not lead to a definitive conclusion that oppression is occurring because class, geography, disability, and many other variables can easily subject White, non-Indigenous, and male students to second-class citizenship too. Although considering whether the treatment would change if the identity of the person were different may not lead to conclusive answers about whether oppression is occurring, it is a good first step in unravelling whether oppression may be at play.

Oppression is identified by examining not only the way it harms the oppressed, but also the benefits it affords dominant groups. The presence of a dominant first-class citizenship group is central to the definition of oppression—a group with the power to subjugate "others through the use of physical, psychological, social, cultural, or economic force" (Henry & Tator, 2010, p. 383). Identifying and categorizing this group is even harder than categorizing those subjugated by oppression.

## Key Concept

Oppression is identified by examining not only the way it harms the oppressed, but also the benefits it affords dominant groups.

One might think that a definition of the group that engages in oppression is the mirror opposite of oppressed groups. Sometimes it is, but sometimes it is not, which makes any attempt to understand the oppressed and the oppressors as binary opposites futile. Consequently, we define the **dominant group** in somewhat simplified terms as those who control most of society's capital, resources, and assets, and have the ability to set society's norms and values. So the term "dominant group" refers not only to social, economic, political, and cultural elites, but also to all of us, in as much as we fit within, benefit from, and identify with dominant norms and values.

Another way oppression can be identified is through the mechanisms it uses. Oppression operates through an array of processes embedded in our personal attitudes, social systems, and culture. These three levels are often referred to as personal, systemic, and cultural oppression (Henry & Tator, 2010). We describe these below and, although we have separated them for explanatory purposes, keep in mind that they overlap and merge into each other. The power of oppression is not derived simply from these three separate parts, but from the ways they merge into each other and operate together as a whole (Mullaly, 2010).

## Oppression through Personal Prejudice

Oppression operates at the personal level through discrimination and prejudice. To **discriminate** means to act on the basis of difference. For instance, an employer advertising a job will want to hire the candidate who is able to undertake the advertised work. To achieve this goal, the employer will have to discriminate on the basis of the skills and knowledge that the job requires. There is nothing wrong with this type of discrimination, because it is the way we make good decisions. **Prejudice**, however, means to prejudge without being aware of facts; it is to discriminate based on one's personal biases. For instance, if an employer is prejudiced against women or racialized people, and rejects applicants based on their gender or race rather than their ability to undertake the work a job requires, this would be gender or racial discrimination. Another term used for these forms of discrimination is sexism or racism. The suffix **ism** has origins in the Ancient Greek language and is used to refer to either an **ideology** (a way of thinking and set of beliefs), such as atheism or theism, or a form of action or doing, such as plagiarism or criticism (Andrews, 2010). Ideas and action are components of any form of prejudice; we will explore this later when we discuss other isms such as heterosex*ism*, age*ism*, able*ism*, and so on.

The "isms" that anti-oppression addresses begin with a prejudicial idea, which moves into action that pushes someone down or holds someone back. Sometimes the term "discrimination" is used on its own to refer to this type of prejudicial act, but when it is used this way keep in mind that, from an anti-oppressive perspective, it is not discriminating between alternatives that makes this a problem; the problem is discriminating on the basis of prejudice (Lee, Sammon, & Dumbrill, 2014).

Prejudice is sometimes divided into two forms: intended and unintended (Sue, 2010). Intended prejudice is often easy to identify; neo-Nazi and similar hate groups are usually open about their prejudices. **Unintentional prejudice** is more difficult to deal with, because by definition it involves persons being unaware that they are discriminating. The term **microaggression** is used to describe some of the unintended acts of well-intentioned individuals that emerge from such prejudice, which Sue explains take the form of "brief, everyday exchanges that send denigrating messages to certain individuals because of their group membership" (Sue, 2010, p. xvi).

Although microaggression is an important topic that we will return to later, we are skeptical about these and other forms of oppression being *unintentional*. Our skepticism was reinforced in a conversation over dinner at a social work conference with Dr Raven Sinclair (Associate Professor of Social Work at the University of Regina).

"I don't think there is such a thing as unintentional oppression," Raven stated.

Gary looked at Raven, puzzled, and asked, "How can that be so?"

Raven explained that to be unaware of the way one is oppressing another, one has to make a conscious choice not to examine one's own biases and attitudes, and one must deliberately decide to ignore the impact of one's comments and actions on others. In other words, "unintentional" oppression cannot exist, because it can only result from an "intentional" decision to opt out of awareness of oneself in relation to others, and an intentional decision to not examine one's **unearned privilege** (unfair advantage) or power in relation to others.

Of course, Raven was right; surely all personal human interaction includes tuning into the impact one has on another and picking up subtle cues about what pushes someone down and what lifts them up. Why is it that, in relation to certain groups of people, these cues are not being picked up? Why are the adjustments people ordinarily make to their behaviour in relation to these others not occurring? Does "unintentional" oppression really exist, or has this idea become popular simply because it makes it easier for people to feel comfortable about their own prejudices by providing a claim to innocence?

The desire for innocence is easy enough to understand. Most people don't want to be thought of as an oppressor, but the hard truth is we are all implicated in oppression one way or another. It is certainly true that a part of the human condition is to have prejudices that result from being socialized into certain ideas and attitudes toward various groups of people, and these inform our choices at a pre- or subconscious level (Banaji & Greenwald, 2013). But another part of the human condition is the work of becoming aware of oneself and one's prejudices in relation to others. If you do not think that this self-examination work is for you, and think you do not have prejudices, you can take a test to determine if you do. Project Implicit has been providing online testing to identify personal bias for several years (Nosek et al., 2007; Roithmayr, 2014). This project was founded by scientists from the University of Washington, Harvard University, and the University of Virginia who developed reliable and valid instruments to measure a number of implicit attitudes and biases (that we refer to as prejudices). These instruments are available online. Take one or more of these tests in the exercise below.

## Exercise 1.1

### What Are Your Prejudices?

Be sure that you have at least 30 minutes to spare before you begin this exercise. Go to Project Implicit at https://implicit.harvard.edu/implicit/. Go to the Social Attitudes section and, if you agree with the terms, select "take a test," and select the Race IAT test. Note that the test is American, so it uses the terms "African American" for Black and "European American" for White.

1. Before you begin, make a note in your journal about whether you think you have an automatic preference for Black or White people.
2. Complete the test and compare your result with the result you anticipated and wrote in your journal.
3. If your result is different from what you anticipated, try to explain why in your journal.
4. Repeat the above with as many of the other tests as you wish at the Project Implicit website.

If you showed no bias on your tests, congratulations; perhaps you have no prejudices at all. If you did show biases in either direction, congratulations too, for having had the courage to take the test. Your results do not mean you are a bad person; they simply mean you are like most people, someone who has adopted biases. Now that you are aware, or have been reminded, of your biases, you can begin, or continue, to take steps to do something about them. Jot down in your journal a few notes on steps you might take, and compare these with the ideas we will suggest later in this book.

Although we said above that most people do not want to be thought of as prejudiced, and the Project Implicit exercise (Exercise 1.1) focuses on biases and prejudices that we are not aware of, we do not want to lose sight of the fact that prejudice can also be open, overt, and deliberate. This fact ought to be obvious in the era of Donald Trump, whose presidential campaign and presidency have been marked by overt **misogynist** (anti-women), racist, anti-immigration, and anti-LGBTTIQQ2S sentiment (Ilc, 2017; Murray, 2017; Peña, 2017).

It would be easy to see Trump as a social and political anomaly, as a person whose attitudes do not reflect those of the general public. This view would be a mistake, because almost 63 million Americans voted for him, which, although only 42.2% of the popular vote and less than his main rival, Hillary Clinton, received, meant enough Americans supported his policies for him to win the election (Krieg, 2016).

It would be a mistake, however, to see racism and the other attitudes attributed to Trump as something unique to his presidency. Trump is not the cause of the problem; he is simply exploiting the racism and other forms of oppression that have been embedded in American "democracy" since the founding of the republic (Ilc, 2017).

Another mistake one could make is to think that such racism and oppression are a uniquely American problem. They are not. Take racism in Canada as an example. *Maclean's* magazine examined outcome data linked to systemic and other forms of racism, such as income level, infant mortality rates, life expectancy, and rates of dropping out of school. *Maclean's* compared these rates for Indigenous people in Canada and African-Americans in the USA, and found that "by almost every measurable indicator, Canada's Aboriginal population suffers a worse fate and more hardship than the African-American population in the U.S." (Gilmore, 2015). *Maclean's* concluded that racism is worse in Canada than in the USA. To understand this and other types of racism in Canada and around the world, we have to examine the way oppression works not only through our personal prejudices and biases, but also through systems.

## Oppression through Systems

Personal prejudices can become embedded in societal structures and institutions. Not everyone's prejudices become embedded in this way, because to embed prejudices in a system one must have some form of power and control over that system. Consequently, it is primarily the prejudices of dominant groups that become embedded in systems, and when this occurs we call it **systemic oppression** (Allan & Smylie, 2015; Roithmayr, 2014; Yee & Dumbrill, 2016). Once this type of oppression is at play, systems produce biased outcomes in favour of the dominant group, and less favourable outcomes for non-dominant groups. But how does systemic oppression produce unequal outcomes? We give an example from education but, as we work through this example, keep in mind that education is only one system. What makes systemic oppression so powerful and so systemic is that multiple systems become infected with the exact same biases, and all these systems oppress simultaneously.

## An Example of Oppression through Educational Systems

Gary is White and British; he grew up in a working-class council estate (government-owned housing) in the suburbs of London, England. Gary did poorly at school. His teachers were not surprised—few from Gary's neighbourhood did well academically. The catchment area of Gary's school included some middle-class neighbourhoods where people owned their own homes. Parents in these neighbourhoods ensured their children were tutored to make up for the lack of individual instruction they received in the large classes at school. Gary noticed, however, that these children already gained more teacher help than most. These children were expected to do well, and with extra teacher attention and tutoring, these children had a double academic advantage.

When Gary and his school friends turned ten years old, the school began to prepare them for an exam called the "11-plus." Gary asked if the exam was important. He was told not to worry because he "would not be in trouble" if he failed. Despite this assurance, Gary suspected there might be something to worry about because middle-class children were receiving even more extra tutoring for the exam. These children now had a triple advantage.

Gary failed the exam, which meant he was streamed into a secondary modern school, which was the lowest rung on the British educational ladder at that time and designed to prepare students for a future in the trades or blue-collar work (Gillard, 2008; Hart, Moro, & Roberts, 2012). Those who passed the exam were streamed into well-resourced Grammar Schools, which prepared students for university and white-collar jobs. These children now had a quadruple advantage. Gary, however, was relieved by his exam results; he was not sure what a university was, and he had always been told that the best thing a boy could do was learn a trade, so Gary thought he was on the advantaged track.

## Was Gary Oppressed?

Was Gary oppressed? He did not feel disadvantaged—quite the opposite; even at this early age, Gary recognized that he had many advantages in life as a White male. Gary was also a naturally slow learner and always the last to understand any topic in class. His teachers constantly told him that he needed to work harder, so he thought that not working hard enough explained his lack of academic success.

Although Gary was not feeling oppressed, and even now is reluctant to claim this, an analysis of British educational outcomes at that time shows that working-class children were failing and middle-class children were succeeding in a pattern so great that it could not be random nor explained by one group being naturally smarter than the other (Hart et al., 2012; Sumner, 2010). It was a *systemic* problem, which means that children rose to the top and were pushed to the bottom not on the basis of talent and hard work alone, but by inbuilt systemic biases that promote the success of some and hold back others. This does not mean we can conclude that Gary's lack of academic success was caused by oppression—one cannot infer from the general to the specific in this way. But Gary certainly fell within a category of children known to be disadvantaged by that system. Although Gary did poorly in the school system, in later life he gained entry to university through a program designed to give those systemically held back another chance at education.

## Looking Deeper into Systemic Oppression

The example above requires several qualifiers. We do not tell Gary's story to imply that everyone should choose a university education, or that there is something wrong with working in the trades. The issue is not that university is a "better" choice. The issue is the right to choose based on one's interests and talent, rather than having the choice made by prejudicial and biased systems. Neither is the problem the fact that middle-class children tend to succeed; we do not object to middle-class children succeeding. We object to working-class children with the talent and desire to succeed being systematically held back from doing so.

Finally, we are not suggesting that the oppressed have no agency and no ability to overcome the attitudes and systems that try to hold them back. Of course, the oppressed can fight and "win," just like a football team can win playing uphill on an uneven field if they fight and struggle hard enough, but expecting them to do so hardly makes the game fair.

## Key Concept

Oppression does not mean that the oppressed have no agency and cannot overcome the forces that push them back. The oppressed can fight and "win," just like a football team can win playing uphill on an uneven field if they fight and struggle hard enough, but expecting them to do so hardly makes the game fair. Anti-oppression is about making the game fair.

Gary's story is not simply past history. The UK has since merged grammar and secondary modern schools into a comprehensive system to overcome the class barriers Gary describes but, despite this effort, class biases remain (Miller, 2014). Gary's story is also one-dimensional; he only experienced the disadvantage of classism. If Gary had also faced racism or some other form of oppression, his disadvantage would have been compounded. In fact, a small number of elite grammar schools remain in the UK and they still determine entry by an 11-plus exam, and not only does a very clear systemic class bias remain, but a clear race bias remains too (Miller, 2014).

## Buying Even More Advantage

Our examples from educational systems above only address systemic oppression in schools for the general public. When we consider the private schools that upper-class children attend, the biased outcomes become even greater (Ryan & Sibetia, 2010). Elite private schools exist in most nations (Weis, 2014), and well-known examples in a Western context include Upper Canada, Lakefield, and Appleby Colleges in Canada, Trinity School and Exeter Academy in the USA, and Eton and Harrow in the UK. These and similar schools are based on a British education model (McCarthy & Kenway, 2014) of private schools that operate apart from state schools, a separation that has been described as a "Berlin Wall" (Paton, 2014). Indeed, the annual fees of such private schools are usually higher than the average annual take-home salaries in their respective nations. Some of these schools do offer means-tested assistance to bright children from poor backgrounds, so it is not just the children of the elite who attend, but it is predominantly so (Paton, 2014).

These elite private schools provide an almost direct route to elite universities and global leadership positions. For instance, Upper Canada College boasts a 100 per cent university acceptance rate for its students and highlights the success they gain at top-ranking universities, and the subsequent success the college's "Old Boys" gain in global leadership positions (Upper Canada College, 2016). In the USA, *Forbes* magazine refers to the ability of American elite private schools to ensure that their students are accepted in elite universities as the "Ivy/MIT/Stanford pipeline," with the top schools scoring much higher admission success than non-private schools (Weis, Cipollone, & Jenkins, 2014). Similar rates exist in Britain where the top five elite schools send more students to Cambridge and Oxford than all the other 2000 schools (excluding technical and trade schools) across the nation (Laneri, 2010; Vasagar, 2011).

Given the resources of these elite schools, one would expect their exam results to produce academic success, and for the most part they do; but the success rate of these schools in funnelling their students into elite universities cannot be explained by academic exam results alone (Koh, 2014; Maharaj, 2015; The Sutton Trust, 2007). If one controls for population differences, the quality of education in state schools outperforms private schools (Lubienski & Lubienski, 2014). The success of elite schools is not that they take the brightest and enable them to become the best, but that they take children of the world's most powerful people and pipeline them through a process that ensures these children are prepared for similar power and dominance as their parents. As Koh (2014) observes, "Those who enter and exit elite schools have an elite destination and pathway carved out for them. . . . They are prepared for power" (p. 197). As mentioned before, a few poor children may also go through this system and some of them will enjoy success; and some privileged children will go through this system and will fail. Attendance guarantees nothing, but it affords students an astronomical advantage. An Internet search of the alumni lists of any elite school reads like a list of the world's rich and powerful. In the UK, Eton's alumni list reads like a "who's who" of British leaders dating back to the fifteenth century, and because Britain colonized the world, it includes a "who's who" of the men who have dominated the world over the past 600 years.

Education is only one example of the way privilege and oppression operate at systemic levels. What makes oppression so powerful is the fact that almost every other system simultaneously pushes the same groups forward and holds the same groups back. It used to be said that the **old school tie**, a euphemism for attending an elite school, opens doors. The old

"Just one old school tie would have done."

**Figure 1.3**    The old school tie

school tie certainly does open doors, but the advantage is not bestowed by the school, but by the broader societal attitudes and systems. These attitudes and systems ensure that the advantages of an elite school, or some other similar advantage, usually leads to another and then another advantage, and with each advantage the distance between those pushed forward and those held back by the system increases.

# Oppression through Culture

**Cultural oppression** is the dominant group using their social influence to "gain cultural power, which is a privileged status based merely on [that group's] cultural identity" (Dermer, 2010, p. 326). For instance, in the run up to the Canadian 2015 general election, Stephen Harper said that if re-elected, "his government would consider banning public servants from wearing the niqab" (Barton, 2015). The niqab is a type of veil or face covering worn by some Muslim women. Some years earlier the Harper government had already attempted to ban the niqab being worn by women taking part in Canadian citizenship ceremonies (MacCharles, 2015). Earlier, in 2013, the Quebec government went further by proposing the Charter of Quebec Values (Charte de la laïcité or Charte des valeurs québécoises), which would have prohibited public employees wearing any religious headwear or displaying other religious symbols (The Canadian Press, 2013).

Such bans treat everybody equally, but they are not equitable, because they lock the culture of one group of Canadians into Canada's major institutions, and lock out the culture of other groups. If the ban in Quebec had been successful, anyone whose culture is expressed through wearing a religious symbol would have to give up that part of their identity to take part in society. If the Canadian ban had been successful, Canadian Muslim women who choose to follow the cultural practice of wearing a niqab would have to give up this part of their identity to participate in society.

These attempted bans failed, at least in the moments referred to above, because at that time Canadians seemed to be saying that these attempts (at what we consider oppression) were not acceptable. Since then, however, in October 2017 Quebec's National Assembly passed legislation that states, "Niqab-wearing Quebec women who want to ride the bus, visit the library, go for a medical check-up or meet with their child's teacher are now legally required to uncover their faces while receiving provincial and municipal government services" (Hamilton, 2017). At the time of writing it remains to be seen how this law will be resisted and whether it will be amended or repealed.

In the past, the idea of laws banning the niqab and other head coverings were resisted by some very creative statements made by those within Canadian institutions. For instance, Figure 1.4 shows how Lakeridge Health responded to the 2013 attempts to ban religious head coverings. They produced a recruitment poster showing a doctor wearing a hijab, along with a caption that said, "We don't care what's on your head. We care what's in it" (Mendleson, 2013).

In some ways we see the Lakeridge Health poster as anti-oppressive, because it pushes back at the forces that attempt to push particular groups down. The only caution we have regarding the poster is that to engage with its message one looks into the face of someone who many consider "different" from mainstream culture. In this instance, this works well, but mainstream Canada cannot understand how cultural oppression works by looking at someone who represents what it considers as cultural "difference"; mainstream Canada has to look hard in a mirror to see its own cultural "sameness" and the way that this sameness dominates. We will be looking into this mirror throughout this book.

## June's Experience of Oppression

Cultural oppression is seen and felt not only in blatant acts like attempts to ban the niqab or other religious symbols but also in many of the other ways society operates—even in the way we construct and decorate our important buildings.

June felt this type of oppression when attending an event in Toronto, Ontario, hosted by provincial politicians and a representative of the Crown. The event was held at a great building constructed in a Romanesque style that reflects a European architectural history traced

**WE DON'T CARE WHAT'S ON YOUR HEAD.**

**WE CARE WHAT'S IN IT.**

We're Lakeridge Health, a leading hospital in the Greater Toronto Area. Our focus is on safety and quality, and we're looking for people like you to join our team of health professionals. Check us out: www.lakeridgehealth.on.ca

FOLLOW US: @LAKERIDGEHEALTH
LIKE US: FACEBOOK.COM/LAKERIDGEHEALTH

**Lakeridge** Health

Design by Aaron Lazarus and Kathleen Rose. Reprinted with permission of Lakeridge Health.

**Figure 1.4**   We don't care what's on your head

back to Ancient Rome. Of course, the building is not that ancient—it is young by European standards—built perhaps 150 years ago on ancient First Nations land. June noticed how the architectural style emulated the grandeur of a European past and created the illusion that the building had stood there much longer. An uninformed observer might think it had always been there.

Inside the building, art adorned the walls—mostly antique paintings of important-looking older White men in regal clothes. The arrangement and serving of lunch followed formal Western rules of etiquette. June felt uneasy and knew exactly why. It was not because she was unfamiliar with the rules and cultural customs of this place; she was born and raised in Toronto and knew how to dress, when to sit and stand, and which of the vast array of knives, forks, and spoons to use with each dish. A racialized woman sitting next to June glanced at her and gestured to the art and architecture and said, "Colonization." June found it reassuring that someone else felt it too; this was confirmation that there was nothing wrong with her; there was something wrong with this place. June had learnt the subtle lessons at school about the hard reality that she and people like her did not belong in places like this.

June remembered that when she told friends and family that she wanted to become a university professor, they laughed and seemed to doubt that this was possible. "Tell us one Chinese professor you know?" they asked. At that time, June knew none. June's friends and family were not trying to hold her back or push her down, they were trying to be realistic; they knew that June would have to fight uphill against classism, racism, and sexism to achieve that goal. June did work uphill through Canada's best universities, and had now been invited to this government event in her role as a university professor. But June knew she did not fit in, not in the same way as the White men in the paintings on the wall or those who looked like them at the dinner. June wondered: Who designed this building? Who put those paintings on the wall? Who made the rules about which knife and fork to use? Not her or her ancestors, that's for sure! June turned to the woman next to her and nodded. "Colonization," she softly repeated. The woman smiled. They both understood, and in that mutual recognition there was a moment of quiet victory. June felt satisfied with her unease, because although she was invited to this place, her feeling of not belonging told her that she had not given up who she was and where she came from along the way.

## Key Concept

If you are from a marginalized position and in a mainstream dominant institution and you feel like an outsider who does not fit in, it might be a sign that you have not given up who you are and have not forgotten where you came from.

## Colonization: A Part of Oppression

We will address colonization in more depth in Chapter 2, and in considerable detail in Chapter 7, but in simple terms **colonization** entails conquering, occupying, and controlling a people's land or territory, or controlling the way they think and act. The part of colonization that impacts thinking can cause people to lose touch with who they are and where they come from, and not giving up who you are and what you understand is an important part of resisting colonization. We suspect that refusing to give up a part of oneself is why British poet and Black activist Benjamin Zephaniah turned down the offer of a prestigious Order of the British Empire (OBE) from Buckingham Palace. Zephaniah explains his stance in his poem "Bought and Sold" (Zephaniah, 2003).

## Exercise 1.2

### Bought and Sold

If possible, undertake this exercise in groups.

Read Benjamin Zephaniah's poem "Bought and Sold" at http://benjaminzephaniah .com/rhymin/talking-turkeys-4/. Consider the following questions:

1. What point is Zephaniah making and why?
2. What does his point and the poem make you feel, and why?
3. Describe the point he is making in your own words?
4. If you were offered an OBE, what would you do and why?

In answering the above questions, search on the web for more about Zephaniah, the reasons for his decision, and the history and events that informed it.

One of the things to be careful with in taking up Zephaniah's ideas is jumping to the conclusion that people who are oppressed "sell out" by working within the system. We have no issues with Zephaniah raising this possibility, or with him personally challenging individuals he may know for accepting government awards, but that does not make it appropriate for us to criticize these people too. The oppressed have already been judged and pressed down by the system, so we are not going to press them down with our judgment too. If someone from an oppressed group thinks that getting an award and using that prestige as leverage for change will make a difference, we do not judge them for that. Indeed, we believe that working for change within the system can be an important form of resistance and a proven strategy for change—not everyone does resistance in the same way.

## The Basis of Oppression

Mullaly (2010) refers to **difference** as the "basis for oppression" (p. 34). In other words, when oppression operates at personal, systemic, and cultural levels, it does so on the basis of difference. All groups and people who experience oppression do so because in one way

**Figure 1.5**    Where are you from?

or another the dominant group considers them different. Sometimes the term **Other** (with the first letter capitalized) is used to refer to this group. The cartoon in Figure 1.5, "Where are you from?" by Simon Kneebone speaks to the issue of difference. If people are found floating in an overcrowded raft at sea, what happens to them depends on where they came from. The cartoon poignantly demonstrates how ridiculous this is—we all come from the same planet—but where on the planet those on the raft are from is about to determine whether they are rescued or turned away (Champion, 2015). In these and similar circumstances, who we are and where we or our ancestors are from determine whether those with monopoly on power and control of the earth's resources will let us live or die.

All acts of oppression boil down to the way difference results in some demarcation of "them and us." Addressing oppression requires us to understand where those boundaries are and how they are constructed. One would think that such a boundary and its corresponding oppression would be easy to recognize and stop, especially if it were life threatening, but it is not. The current and ongoing "refugee crisis" and similar events in history reveal how sometimes the most obvious forms of injustice and oppression go unaddressed. For instance, consider the Holocaust in which Nazis killed about 6 million Jewish people and numerous members of other oppressed groups. If you lived in those days, would the oppression inherent within the Nazi regime be obvious to you? And if, at absolutely no risk to yourself or others, you could prevent people from being sent to a Nazi concentration camp, would you? If you answered "yes," your response is unlike that of many Canadians who lived in that era.

In 1939 Hitler allowed a number of Jewish refugees to leave Nazi Germany on an ocean liner called the M.V. *St Louis*. The passengers were set free to sail anywhere they chose, but the world was unwilling to give them refuge (Abella & Troper, 2012; Aretha, 2001). To fully understand the *St Louis* incident, we have to begin the story one year before the ship sailed.

On 9 November 1938, an evening that became known as Kristallnacht (the night of broken glass), Nazi Storm Troopers enacted a pre-orchestrated methodical attack on Jewish homes, businesses, schools, and synagogues throughout Germany and parts of Austria (Abella & Troper, 2012). Prior to the attack, Gestapo chief Heinrich Müller ordered the entire German police force to ignore what was happening and not defend Jewish people, telling them that "these [assaults] are not to be interfered with" (Aretha, 2001,

p. 123). In the two days and nights that followed, tens of thousands of synagogues, Jewish homes, and Jewish shops were attacked; 92 Jewish people were killed; and approximately 30,000 were apprehended and sent to concentration camps (Gilbert, 2006). The atrocities of Kristallnacht received international condemnation (Gilbert, 2006), with Canadian Prime Minister McKenzie King noting, "The sorrows which the Jews have to bear at this time are almost beyond comprehension" (Abella & Troper, 2012, p. 39). It was seven months after this event in May 1939 that Nazi Germany decided to allow 937 Jewish people to leave Hamburg on the M.V. *St Louis* to seek refuge anywhere they could find to go.

The *St Louis* escaped across the Atlantic and arrived in Cuba, but only 29 refugees were allowed to land. The others were told to leave. Before departing Havana, some of the refugees aboard so feared a return to Germany that they committed suicide (Aretha, 2001). The *St Louis* then sailed north along the eastern seaboard of the United States hoping to find refuge, but it was denied. Looking farther north they asked Canada for help, but Ottawa responded in an official communiqué saying that "none would be too many" (Abella & Troper, 2012). The harsh wording of this rejection was telling; it did not say, "Sorry, we do not have space," or "Unfortunately we have just emerged from a recession and do not have jobs for you," but instead was couched in words with a clear message that no Jewish people were welcome. Without hope for freedom in the Americas, the *St Louis* returned to Europe. Eventually, England, France, Holland, and Belgium agreed to take some of the refugees; the rest returned to Nazi Germany where they faced death in concentration camps.

If you said "yes" when we asked whether you would be willing to prevent someone from being sent to their death in a Nazi concentration camp, what explains the difference between you and those who said "no" in 1939? Perhaps you believe that you and others today are more likely than the 1939 generation to stand against oppression. Yet this argument does not explain why many of those who denied refuge to the *St Louis* in 1939 went on to give their lives in a war to end the Nazi regime. We cannot, therefore, dismiss the 1939 rejection of refugees as that generation being less willing to stand against oppression than people today; another explanation is needed. We suggest the following sentence can help to explain the inaction of 1939.

pEoplearesoMetimessocAughtuPintHeirown
eVerydaylivesthattheydOn'tlooKforoRseeopPreSsion
anDiftheYdon'TlookfororseEoppRession
theywilLneVerfiGureoutiFtHeyarEdoinGit
anDifthEycAn'tFiGureoUtheyarEdoinGittHeywilLnever
sTOPiT

The sentence above is hard to read because there are no gaps between words and we have deliberately set the capitalization to obscure meaning. Unless you examine the sentence very closely, all you see when you read—or hear if you listen on an audio-reader, or feel if you read in Braille—is a mass of letters. Life is like this sentence: events blur into each other and people hardly understand what they mean, and sometimes the media and others present materials in a manner that deliberately obscures what is occurring. The sentence is easier to read when the words are correctly spaced and the capitalization is removed.

> people are sometimes so caught up in their own
> everyday lives that they don't look for or see oppression
> and if they don't look for or see oppression
> they will never figure out if they are doing it
> and if they can't figure out they are doing it they will never
> STOP IT

Because life is more like the first sentence than the second, we must look deeper and think harder about what we see and experience if we are to recognize oppression in society, in our culture, and in ourselves. The mistake of 1939 was not looking or thinking critically enough at what was occurring in that moment. We do not suggest that this "mistake" absolves anyone in those days from responsibility about the *St Louis,* nor do we suggest that everyone in those times was oblivious to what was occurring and did not resist, because a number of people did understand and resist (Michman, 1998). But those with the power and means to provide refuge to the Jewish people on the *St Louis* failed to act. This failure surprises and embarrasses us today, but it was entirely anticipated by the Nazi regime, because they knew that anti-Semitism extended across the Western world. In fact, the voyage of the *St Louis* can be seen as a Nazi propaganda exercise to demonstrate this point.

If people failed to recognize and act against an emerging holocaust, what similar events are we not recognizing today? Also, if it is difficult to recognize and act against a holocaust when it occurs, how much harder is it to recognize and act against the more subtle forms of oppression that anti-oppression usually focuses upon?

## Naming and Challenging Oppression

To challenge oppression one has to not only recognize it, but also name it. For example, when Gary led a public anti-oppression workshop for social workers and activists, Gary asked participants to decide whether the events described in the case scenarios he presented were oppressive. After considering the scenarios, an exercise participant stood up and said that all the scenarios were racist and sexist. Gary agreed, and asked the participant to say why. The participant said, "Because as a woman of colour I say so and that is the only explanation you need." The participant sat down and the people in the workshop fidgeted nervously.

June relates to this participant's experience. As a racialized woman herself, she is routinely asked to explain to those oppressing her why she thinks they are being oppressive. Expecting a person who is oppressed to explain why this is so places the oppressed person, rather than the process of oppression, under scrutiny. Srivastava and Francis

(2006) contend that in these situations, listeners, who are usually the oppressors, place themselves in the position of a judge with the power to decide whether something is truly oppressive or not. This makes the participant's response to a White male trainer quite understandable, because providing any explanation reinforces race and gender dynamics that place the White male trainer in the dominant position of deciding what is true.

To counter this dynamic, a principle we employ in anti-oppression is that those who benefit from oppression have the responsibility to understand, and those pushed down by oppression do not have the responsibility to explain. But this rule does not apply to social workers or other community professionals engaged in anti-oppression. If it is your job to address oppression, and/or if you are paid by public funds to identify oppression, you have an obligation to explain the position you take. For this reason, at the end of this chapter we are going to ask you to complete an exercise where you decide whether oppression is occurring, and we will ask you to justify your position. First, however, we will provide you with some practical tools to help you in this task.

We have already explained that oppression presses people down and holds them back just because they are members of a particular group of people. For a working definition of the process that enables this to occur, we say that prejudice and bias plus power equal oppression. We base this definition on Pat Bidol's statement of 1970 that "Power + Prejudice = Racism," which was later popularized in the anti-racist work of Judy Katz (1978, 2003).

There are several limitations with this original formula. It deals only with racism, it does not speak to the nuances of prejudice or systemic and cultural power we have addressed above, and it makes no effort to explain the causes of oppression. But with these limitations in mind, the formula is useful for the beginning stages of identifying oppression.

As can be seen in the equation below, we have adapted the definition by replacing "prejudice" with "prejudice and bias," and we ask that you keep in mind that this includes not just personal prejudice but also prejudice and bias at the structural and cultural levels. We replaced the word "racism" with the broader term "oppression" (which includes racism, but many other "isms" too). We kept the term "power" at the centre of the equation, because without power, prejudice and bias are no more than nasty social attitudes and systemic annoyances. But when combined with power, prejudice and bias move from being an annoyance to becoming something that presses people down and holds them back.

**Oppression: A Working Definition**
**PREJUDICE & BIAS + POWER = OPPRESSION**
Source: Adapted from Pat Bidol's statement cited in Katz, 1978 & 2003.

## Understanding Opression in Practice

We said at the beginning of this chapter that there is no formula to determine what anti-oppression is; neither is there a formula to determine what oppression is. To determine whether oppression is at play, the equation above may help, but you will also need to consider all of the ideas of this chapter (and other ideas in the book). With these qualifications in mind, we demonstrate with the following case example how the formula above and the ideas of this chapter may help you to begin to explore whether something is oppressive.

## Exercise 1.3

### Is This Oppression?

If possible, undertake this exercise in groups. Try to complete the exercise before reading our analysis of the case below, and then compare your analysis to ours.

A child protection worker apprehends a five-year-old from an Indigenous family living in poverty because the child was being left unsupervised, and because the conditions in the family home were a serious health hazard. The parents say that their child is being removed because of oppression and a racist child protection system.

1. Is it oppression, and if so why?
2. If it is not oppression, what is it, and why?
3. Regardless of what it is, if you were the worker, how would you deal with it, and why?

## Gary and June's Response to the Scenario in Exercise 1.3

There is a pattern of Indigenous children being overrepresented in state care (Sinha et al., 2013), so the possibility exists that the child's removal is oppression. To decide whether oppression is at play, we need to consider whether personal or cultural prejudices have shaped the conclusion that the child is at risk of harm. Do the conditions of the home really place this child at risk, or are the conditions simply different from the way this worker expects homes to be? Was this child really unsupervised, or is this a tightknit community where neighbours and relatives watch children without being asked so that the child was never actually left unsupervised? If the latter in either of these possibilities is occurring, oppression may be at play.

To identify whether oppression is at play, we also need to determine whether power is present. Clearly it is, because the worker has the power to remove the child against the parent's wishes and also has the power to provide or deny resources that might prevent the need for this to occur. When considering the issue of power in this instance, the race or culture of the worker makes no difference. The worker could be Indigenous themselves, but in their role as a child protection worker, they represent the Crown and hold the power of the state.

If the worker has used power inappropriately and based the decision to remove the child on some form of prejudice rather than the child being at risk of harm, the courts might interrupt the removal of the child by denying the worker's protection application

(application to bring the child into state care). This denial, however, is unlikely, because if the worker's prejudices reflect those of the dominant society, one can expect them to also be built into the structural systems and cultural values employed by the courts.

## Key Concept

If someone's personal prejudices reflect those held by the dominant society, one can expect those prejudices to be backed up and supported by other individuals in society, by societal institutions, and also by society's cultural norms.

In the circumstances above, if there were no real risks to the child at home, we would agree with the parents and consider the removal to be oppressive. But what if there were real risks to the child? What if the assessment were not prejudicial and there was no doubt that the child would be seriously harmed unless some form of immediate action was taken? Even in these circumstances, one could not rule out oppression until one had ensured that other alternatives to removing the child were considered. But let's suppose all these alternatives had been considered: suppose the worker had contacted the Band Office and extended family and yet no ideas to prevent removal were presented; suppose a White middle-class family would have had their child removed in the exact same circumstances; suppose the worker had access to funds for in-home supports and for help addressing the health hazards in the home, but for some reason none of these would remedy the problem. Even then we may not be able to rule out oppression being at play.

Indeed, social work is an occupation that addresses problems by identifying the micro (individual level), **mezzo** (neighbourhood and small to medium-size groups level) and macro (society-wide) origins of the problem, and also considers these in a historical context. It is almost inconceivable that the troubles this family face are not connected one way or another to the history of residential schools, the Sixties Scoop, and colonization. While this history may not absolve the parents of responsibility for whatever is occurring that places the child at risk, it does begin to explain the situation. Consequently, any worker who denies the parents' claim that this child is "being removed because of oppression and a racist child protection system" denies the impact of history, fails in their responsibility to connect the micro to the mezzo and macro, makes a fool of themselves and their profession, and indicates to the parents and community that they face great risk from this worker's ineptitude.

Given the above, if the child *really* is at risk of harm and there are no safe alternatives other than removal, what is the anti-oppressive social worker to do in this case and others like it? We will return to that answer in Chapter 11, but for now, let's consider what the worker should *not* do. First, the worker should not deny that racism and other forms of oppression have played a role in creating the current circumstances. Next, if there are no remedies to keep the child safe at home, the worker should *not* leave the child in the home. Leaving the child to be harmed is also oppression, because the child is not being provided with the protection that any other child would be given. This places the worker in a dilemma because whatever is chosen will be oppressive. This dilemma is sometimes difficult to grasp. Our experience is that people believe that if they think hard and long enough they will always be able to find an anti-oppressive alternative in any situation they encounter, but this is not the case. Sometimes the choice a worker faces is between two bad alternatives. This lack of choice is disappointing, but if anti-oppression were as simple as identifying and having access to a perfect remedy, then we would all be doing it and there would be no oppression.

Continually considering multiple variables when trying to decide whether anti-oppression is at play, and then not finding an immediate anti-oppressive remedy, can be extremely frustrating. It would be much better, especially in an anti-oppressive text like this, if we as authors could simply say what oppression is and say what one has to do in order to be anti-oppressive. But anti-oppressive social work has no pre-set answers, and even using the formula we provided above to help identify oppression often raises more questions than it provides answers. This is the nature of social work and especially anti-oppression, and it is important to recognize that it is not the ability to learn quick and snappy answers about what oppression is and what to do about it that makes a good anti-oppressive social worker, but instead it is learning to live with the discomfort of dealing with hard questions and not having easy answers.

## Key Concept

There are no pre-set formulas to identify oppression. The anti-oppressive social worker will have no quick and snappy answers about how to identify oppression or what to do about it. Instead the anti-oppressive social worker will see the nuances in every situation, will be able to sit with the discomfort of hard questions that have no easy answers, and will be able to carefully craft custom-made anti-oppressive options that fit the circumstances and context of the situation they are addressing.

## Chapter Summary

In this chapter, we provided an overview of oppression and anti-oppression in broad strokes. We introduced some of the concepts of oppression and anti-oppression at a basic level. (We will discuss and explore these in more depth later in the book.) We have defined oppression as the holding back and pushing down of entire groups of people within society, which is matched by a lifting up and a propelling forward of other groups that gain advantage from oppressive processes. We have explored how oppression operates through personal prejudice, systemic discrimination, and culture. We named some of the groups who are advantaged or disadvantaged by these processes, but discussed how any definitive attempt to divide people into oppressor or oppressed groups is impossible. We emphasized attention to context and power dynamics when evaluating whether oppression is at play.

At the start of this chapter we told you a story about June mispronouncing the name of a student of Pakistani-Canadian heritage. As mentioned in the Preface of this book (be sure to read the Preface explanation of why we use stories), we use stories not to tell you about us (Gary and June), but to tell something about the way oppression and anti-oppression operate in everyday life. These stories provide you with a means to think about the ordinary and everyday ways any one of us might encounter, understand, engage with, reinforce, or resist oppression. With that in mind, the question we asked at the start of the chapter was whether you thought June repeatedly mispronouncing the name of the student of Pakistani-Canadian heritage was oppressive. After reading this chapter you should have the conceptual tools to form an opinion about this (and similar situations of this nature). The student whose name was being mispronounced thought it was oppression and June agreed with her. June reflected on how she is able to learn complex names for theoretical concepts used in social work literature and memorize the awkward long names of European scholars and theorists important to social work. So why had she not taken time to learn to say this student's name? June recognized that, although a racialized woman herself, she was in a position of power in relation to this student, and therefore in a position to oppress. In addition, June realized that the student had undoubtedly faced many instances of being held back and told she did not belong. June realized that her mispronouncing the student's name in class was doing the same. June apologized to the student, acknowledged that this was oppressive and inappropriate, and took time to learn the student's name.

We also asked at the start of this chapter whether the person who mispronounced Gary's last name as "Bumbrill" was being oppressive. We suggest that they were not. Gary might have the right to consider the mispronunciation rude and to take offence (though he did not), but he could not claim that the mispronunciation was oppressive. On the surface the mispronunciation of Gary's name and June mispronouncing the student's name may appear the same, but they are different. It is important to understand this difference, because doing something about oppression starts with knowing what oppression is and what it is not. As a result, conclude this chapter by discussing the following questions.

## Discussion Questions

Discuss the following questions in a group, or if working individually reflect on these questions alone and note your answers in your journal. Draw on the concepts we have discussed in this chapter to formulate and explain/justify your answers.

1. Do you agree with June and Gary that June mispronouncing the student's name is oppression? Explain and justify your position.
2. June was not deliberately mispronouncing the student's name. Does this fact influence your answer to question 1 above? Explain and justify your position.
3. Do you agree with June and Gary that the mispronunciation of Gary's name is not oppression? Explain and justify your position.

## Activity

If you agree with June's and Gary's analysis of the mispronunciation of the names, retell this story to a friend, and explain to them why one mispronunciation is oppression (racism) and the other is not. Do not worry about whether your friend agrees with the point you are making. This activity is not about changing the way your friend thinks; the activity is to find out whether you understand the arguments of this chapter enough to articulate them to a friend.

If you do not agree with the mispronunciation example June and Gary gave, develop your own example that illustrates the difference between an unfair or offensive act that is not oppression in the way social workers understand the term, and an unfair or offensive act that is. Explain this to your friend. And of course be sure to also assure your friend that social workers will deal with any unfair or offensive act whether it is oppression or not. Social workers distinguish what is not oppression from what is oppression, not to decide which one to address, but to understand the different origins and solutions for both.

## Key Concept

Keep in mind that social workers distinguish what is oppression from what is not oppression, not to decide which to address, but to understand the different origins and different solutions for both. Always remember the goal of social work is to help people, whether they are being oppressed or not.

## Suggested Resources

Sing Hey! Love, struggle and community with Janice Jo Lee on rabble.ca podcasts. Retrieved from http://rabble.ca/podcasts/shows/awl/2016/01/sing-hey-love-struggle-and-community-janice-jo-lee

"All the times you were silent" by Janice Jo Lee from the album "Sing Hey" (featured in the Podcast above). Retrieved from https://janicejolee.bandcamp.com/track/all-the-times-you-were-silent-2

Wehbi, S., & Parada, H. (Eds). (2017). *Reimagining anti-oppression social work practice*. Toronto, Canada: Canadian Scholars' Press.

Mullaly, B., & West, J. (2018). *Challenging oppression and confronting privilege: A critical approach to anti-oppressive and anti-privilege theory and practice (3rd edn)*. Toronto, Canada: Oxford University Press.

## References

Abella, I., & Troper, H. (2012). *None is too many: Canada and the Jews of Europe, 1933–1948*. Toronto, Canada: University of Toronto Press.

Allan, B., & Smylie, J. (2015). *First peoples, second class treatment: The role of racism in the health and well-being of Indigenous peoples in Canada*. Discussion Paper. Retrieved from http://www.wellesleyinstitute.com/wp-content/uploads/2015/02/Summary-First-Peoples-Second-Class-Treatment-Final.pdf

Andrews, J. (2010). *The Economist book of isms: From abolitionism to Zoroastrianism*. London, UK: Profile Books.

Aretha, D. (Ed.). (2001). *The holocaust chronicle: A history in words and pictures*. Lincolnwood, IL: Publications International Ltd.

Baines, D. (2002). Storylines in racialized times: Racism and anti-racism in Toronto's social services. *British Journal of Social Work, 32*(2), 185–99.

Banaji, M.R., & Greenwald, A.G. (2013). *Blindspot: Hidden biases of good people*. New York, NY: Delacorte Press.

Barton, R. (2015, October 6). Niqab ban for public servants would be considered: Stephen Harper. *CBC News*. Retrieved from http://www.cbc.ca/news/politics/stephen-harper-niqab-ban-public-servants-1.3258943

Block, S., & Galabuzi, G.E. (2011). *Canada's colour coded labour market: The gap for racialized workers*. Retrieved from http://www.wellesleyinstitute.com/wp-content/uploads/2011/03/Colour_Coded_Labour_MarketFINAL.pdf

Bullock, A., & Trombley, S. (Eds). (2000). *The new Fontana dictionary of modern thought* (3rd edn). London, UK: HarperCollins.

Champion, M. (2015). The cartoon that sums up the world's "migrant crisis." *indy100 from Independent*. Retrieved from http://i100.independent.co.uk/article/the-cartoon-that-sums-up-the-worlds-migrant-crisis--g12atJpSWZ

Cook, A., & Glass, C. (2014). Women and top leadership positions: Towards an institutional analysis. *Gender, Work & Organization, 21*(1), 91–103. doi:10.1111/gwao.12018

Crawford, G., & Andreassen, B.A. (2015). Human rights and development: Putting power and politics at the center. *Human Rights Quarterly, 37*(3), 662–90. doi:10.1353/hrq.2015.0053

Dermer, S.B., Smith, S.D., & Barto, K.K. (2010). Identifying and correctly labeling sexual prejudice, discrimination, and oppression. *Journal of Counseling & Development, 88*(3), 325–31. doi:10.1002/j.1556-6678.2010.tb00029.x

Eccles, J.S. (2007). Where are all the women? Gender differences in participation in physical science and engineering. In S.J. Ceci & W.M. Williams (Eds), *Why aren't more women in science? Top researchers debate the evidence* (pp. 199–210). Washington, DC: American Psychological Association.

Equity and Human Rights Commission. (2015). *Stop and think again, towards equality in police PACE stop and search*. Retrieved from https://www.equalityhumanrights.com/en/publication-download/stop-and-think-again-towards-equality-police-pace-stop-and-search

Gilbert, M. (2006). *Kristallnacht: Prelude to destruction*. New York, NY: HarperCollins Publishers.

Gillard, D. (2008). Us and them: A history of pupil grouping policies in England's schools. Retrieved from http://www.educationengland.org.uk/articles/27grouping.html

Gilmore, S. (2015, January 22). Canada's race problem? It's even worse than America's. *Maclean's*. Retrieved from http://www.macleans.ca/news/canada/out-of-sight-out-of-mind-2/

Hamilton, G. (2017, October 18). Quebec passes bill banning niqab, burka while receiving public services: The controversial law is the Liberal government's answer to a decade-long debate over the accommodation of religious minorities in the province. *National Post*. Retrieved from http://nationalpost.com/news/politics/quebec-passes-bill-62

Hart, R.A., Moro, M., & Roberts, J.E. (2012). *Date of birth, family background, and the 11 plus exam: Short- and long-term consequences of the 1944 secondary education reforms in England and Wales*. Retrieved from http://dspace.stir.ac.uk/bitstream/1893/6612/1/SEDP-2012-10-Hart-Moro-Roberts.pdf

Henry, F., & Tator, C. (2010). *The colour of democracy: Racism in Canadian society* (4th edn). Toronto, Canada: Nelson Education.

Ilc, B.V. (2017). Racism and the crisis of political representation in the American Republic — from its constitution to the Trump phenomenon. *Teorija In Praksa, 54*(1), 17–37.

Joseph, A.J. (2015). Beyond intersectionalities of identity or interlocking analyses of difference: Confluence and the problematic of "anti"-oppression. *Intersectionalities: A Global Journal of Social Work Analysis, Research, Polity, and Practice, 4*(1), 15–39.

Katz, J.H. (1978). *White awareness: Handbook for anti-racism training*. Norman, OK: University of Oklahoma Press, Norman Publishing Division.

Katz, J.H. (2003). *White awareness: Handbook for anti-racism training* (2nd edn). Norman, OK: University of Oklahoma Press, Norman Publishing Division.

Kim, S.H. (2012). Max Weber. In *The Stanford encyclopedia of philosophy*. Retrieved from http://plato.stanford.edu/archives/fall2012/entries/weber/

Koh, A. (2014). Doing class analysis in Singapore's elite education: Unravelling the smokescreen of "meritocratic talk." *Globalisation, Societies and Education, 12*(2), 196–210. doi:10.1080/14767724.2014.888308

Krieg, G. (2016, December 22). It's official: Clinton swamps Trump in popular vote. *CNN Politics (online)*. Retrieved from http://www.cnn.com/2016/12/21/politics/donald-trump-hillary-clinton-popular-vote-final-count/index.html

Laneri, R. (2010, April 29). America's best prep schools. *Forbes*. Retrieved from http://www.forbes.com/2010/04/29/best-prep-schools-2010-opinions-private-education.html

Lee, B., Sammon, S., & Dumbrill, G.C. (Eds). (2014). *Glossary of terms for anti-oppressive perspectives on policy and practice* (2nd edn). Toronto, Canada: CommonAct Press.

Lubienski, C.A., & Lubienski, S.T. (2014). *The public school advantage: Why public schools outperform private schools*. Chicago, IL: University of Chicago Press.

MacCharles, T. (2015, October 6). Niqab ban for public servants would be considered, says Stephen Harper. *Toronto Star*. Retrieved from http://www.thestar.com/news/federal-election/2015/10/06/niqab-ban-for-public-servants-would-be-considered-says-stephen-harper.html

Maharaj, S. (2015, April 6). Do private schools provide a better education? *Toronto Star*, p. A15.

McCarthy, C., & Kenway, J. (2014). Introduction: Understanding the re-articulations of privilege over time and space. *Globalisation, Societies and Education, 12*(2), 165–76. doi:10.1080/14767724.2014.893188

Mendleson, R. (2013, September 12). Oshawa hospital uses Quebec controversy as recruitment tool. *Toronto Star*. Retrieved from http://www.thestar.com/news/gta/2013/09/12/oshawa_hospital_uses_quebec_controversy_as_recruitment_tool.html

Michman, D. (Ed.). (1998). *Belgium and the Holocaust: Jews, Belgians, Germans*. Jerusalem, Israel: Yad Vashem.

Miller, F. (2014, September 16). State pupils doing worse in 'tutor-proof' tests: Buckinghamshire's new 11-plus was meant to cut stress and improve access for poorer children, so what happened? *The Guardian*, p. 37.

Mullaly, B. (2010). *Challenging oppression and confronting privilege: A critical social work approach.* (2nd edn). Toronto, Canada: Oxford University Press.

Murray, M.J.D. (2017). Intimate choices, public threats—reproductive and LGBTQ rights under a Trump administration. *The New England Journal of Medicine, 376*(4), 301–03.

Nosek, B.A., Smyth, F.L., Hansen, J.J., Devos, T., Lindner, N.M., Ranganath, K.A., & Banaji, M.R. (2007). Pervasiveness and correlates of implicit attitudes and stereotypes. *European Review of Social Psychology, 18*(1), 36–88. doi:10.1080/10463280701489053

Paton, G. (2014, February 5). Eton College to admit pupils irrespective of family income. *The Telegraph*. Retrieved from http://www.telegraph.co.uk/education/educationnews/10620461/Eton-College-to-admit-pupils-irrespective-of-family-income.html

Peña, L.G. (2017). Judgment day in the D.R.: Recent events in the Dominican Republic and the U.S. reveal the deepening links between anti-immigrant xenophobia and anti-Black racism. *NACLA Report on the Americas, 49*(1), 76–80. doi:10.1080/10714839.2017.1298252

Pomeroy, E., & Parrish, D.E. (2012). The New DSM-5: Where have we been and where are we going? *Social Work, 57*(3), 195–200.

Qwul'sih'yah'maht, & Kundoqk. (2015). Indigenous children in the centre: Indigenous perspectives on anti-oppressive child welfare practice. In Sohki Aski Esquao [Jeannine Carriere] & S. Strega (Eds), *Walking this path together: Anti-racist and anti-oppressive child welfare practice* (2nd edn, pp. 25–41). Black Point, Canada: Fernwood Publishing.

Rankin, J., Winsa, P., Bailey, A., & Ng, H. (2013, September 28). 'Devastating. Unacceptable'; Toronto police board chair appalled by Star findings that show a stubborn rise in the number of citizens stopped and documented by our police officers—with black males heavily overrepresented. *Toronto Star*, p. A1.

Roithmayr, D. (2014). *Reproducing racism: How everyday choices lock in white advantage.* New York, NY: New York University Press.

Ryan, C., & Sibetia, L. (2010). *Private Schooling in the UK and Australia.* Retrieved from http://www.ifs.org.uk/bns/bn106.pdf

Sinha, V., Trocme, N., Fallon, B., & MacLaurin, B. (2013). Understanding the investigation-stage overrepresentation of First Nations children in the child welfare system: An analysis of the First Nations component of the Canadian Incidence Study of Reported Child Abuse and Neglect 2008. *Child Abuse Neglect, 37*(10), 821–31. doi:10.1016/j.chiabu.2012.11.010

Srivastava, S., & Francis, M. (2006). The problem of 'authentic experience': Storytelling in anti-racist and anti-homophobic education. *Critical Sociology, 32*(2–3), 275–307.

Strega, S., & Sohki Aski Esquao [Jeannine Carriere]. (2015). An introduction: Anti-racist and anti-oppressive child welfare practice. In Sohki Aski Esquao [Jeannine Carriere] & Susan Strega (Eds), *Walking this path together: Anti-racist and anti-oppressive child welfare practice* (2nd edn, pp. 1–24). Halifax, Canada: Fernwood Publishing.

Sue, D.W. (2010). *Microaggressions in everyday life: Race, gender, and sexual orientation* Hoboken, NJ: Wiley.

Sumner, C. (2010). 1945–1965: The long road to Circular 10/65. *Reflecting Education, 6*(1), 90–102.

The Canadian Press. (2013, August 25). Pauline Marois: 'Charter of Quebec Values' will help unite province. *Huffington Post*. Retrieved from http://www.huffingtonpost.ca/2013/08/25/pauline-marois-charter-of-quebec-values_n_3814367.html

The Sutton Trust. (2007). *University admissions by individual schools.* Retrieved from http://image.guardian.co.uk/sys-files/Education/documents/2007/09/20/Strust.pdf

United Nations. (1948). *Universal Declaration of Human Rights.* (Adopted and proclaimed by General Assembly resolution 217 A III of 10 December 1948). New York, NY: UN General Assembly. Retrieved from http://www.refworld.org/docid/3ae6b3712c.html

Upper Canada College. (2016). *Success at UCC and beyond.* Retrieved from http://www.ucc.on.ca/wp-content/uploads/2015/09/UCC_WhereHaveTheyGone_2015-16_final.pdf

Vasagar, J. (2011, July 8). How many pupils from your school go to Oxbridge? A report out today highlights the division between schools and applications to Oxbridge. Find out how many pupils from schools in England get accepted. *The Guardian*. Retrieved from http://www.theguardian.com/news/datablog/2011/jul/08/school-applications-oxbridge-selection

Walton, G.M., Logel, C., Peach, J.M., Spencer, S.J., & Zanna, M.P. (2015). Two brief interventions to mitigate a "chilly climate" transform women's experience, relationships, and achievement in engineering. *Journal of Educational Psychology, 107*(2), 468–85. doi:10.1037/a0037461

Weis, L. (2014). A comment on class productions in elite secondary schools in twenty-first-century global context. *Globalisation, Societies and Education, 12*(2), 309–20. doi:10.1080/14767724.2014.899130

Weis, L., Cipollone, K., & Jenkins, H. (2014). *Class warfare: Class, race, and college admissions in top-tier secondary schools.* Chicago, IL: University of Chicago Press.

Williams, C. (1999). Connecting anti-racist and anti-oppressive theory and practice: Retrenchment or reappraisal? *British Journal of Social Work, 29*(2), 211–30.

Woodford, M.R., Newman, P.A., Brotman, S., & Ryan, B. (2010). Northern enlightenment: Legal recognition of same-sex marriage in Canada. *Journal of Gay & Lesbian Social Services, 22*(1–2), 191–209. doi:10.1080/10538720903332677

Yee, J.Y., & Dumbrill, G.C. (2016). Whiteout: Still looking for race in Canadian social work practice. In A. Al-Krenawi, J.R. Graham, & N. Habibov (Eds), *Diversity and social work in Canada* (2nd edn, pp. 13–37). Toronto, Canada: Oxford University Press.

Zephaniah, B. (2003, November 27). "Me? I thought, OBE me? Up yours, I thought." *The Guardian*. Retrieved from http://www.theguardian.com/books/2003/nov/27/poetry.monarchy

# Thinking Critically about What We Know and How We Know It

## Introduction

June's love for reading began when she was very young. She excitedly read every book she could find, and recounted for her parents everything each book said. One day June's father cautioned her, "If you are going to believe everything in books, you had better not read."

Gary, on the other hand, did not read much while growing up, but he received a similar caution from his parents, "Believe half of what you see and nothing that you hear." Perhaps you received similar advice. But how does one know what to believe or not believe? This chapter tries to answer that question.

Questioning what to believe is essential in anti-oppression, because the personal prejudices, societal biases, and dominant culture we spoke of in the previous chapter become embedded in texts, movies, advertisements, the things people say, and the ways we treat each other. These influences infiltrate thinking, which means if "left to itself . . . [our thinking will become] biased, distorted, partial, uninformed or down-right prejudiced" (Paul & Elder, 2006, p. 4). As a result, we cannot leave thinking to itself; we have to question the way we think and also the things that shape it. In other words, we have to think critically. As social workers it is especially important to think critically, because the way we think defines the way we help. It shapes the problems we see and the remedies we imagine. By the end of this chapter you will be able to use critical thinking to help you determine what to believe or not believe. You will also be able to use this thinking to identify the ideas and assumptions that social work policy and practice are based upon. This thinking will help you to recognize and name oppression, which is a prerequisite of doing anti-oppressive social work.

# What Is Critical Thinking?

Critical thinking is not putting people or their ideas down, nor being deliberately rude, negative, or finding fault with everything. Critical thinking is questioning everything and never accepting anything at face value. It involves questioning our beliefs, attitudes, and responsibilities. It requires us to scrutinize the logic and reason for the theories we are using, the assumptions underlying these theories, the way these frame service users' troubles, and the meanings and remedies that this framing and these theories imply and exclude (Brookfield, 2012; Facione, 1990; Mathias, 2015; Paul & Elder, 2006).

Critical thinking must not be confused with looking up facts in books or the Internet to oppose statements one disagrees with. Of course critical thinking is embedded in bits and bytes of information, but the essence of critical thought is understanding how information is threaded together to make meaning, and questioning why it is threaded together in a particular way.

Some people think Socrates was the first person in history to think critically and use reason to question ideas; this is certainly the conclusion one would come to after a quick Internet or literature search on these topics (see for instance Spitzer & Evans, 1997; Šulavíková, 2014; Wikipedia, 2015c). This conclusion is one of those things that you read but should not believe. Socrates was a philosopher who lived about 2500 years ago in Greece, and while it is true that some modern wisdom can be traced back to Ancient Greece, not everything that scholars claim originated in Ancient Greece actually did. We personally find it hard to believe that when Socrates figured out how to think critically and use reason, people had not already been doing this elsewhere during thousands of years of previous human history. Indeed, the Chinese philosopher Confucius, who pre-dates Socrates, was a critical thinker who demanded reason and rationality from his students (Kim, 2003), and we suspect he was not the first.

Confucius also argued, "学而不思则罔，思而不学则殆" (Soothill, 1968, p. 165), which translates, "Learning without thinking is a vain effort. Thinking without learning is a dangerous effort" (translation cited in Kim, 2003, p. 81). In other words, if you learn facts without thinking, or think without grasping meaning, you are not really that smart! Said differently, "Knowledge is not the accumulation of information. Knowledge is *understanding* what information means."

## Exercise 2.1

### Critical Thinking

If possible, undertake this exercise in groups. Reflect on and discuss the following:

1. Given that Confucius was a critical thinker, why do you think that the roots of critical thought are said to be located in Ancient Greece rather than China (or some other non-European location)?

2. Think *critically* about this issue and note your thoughts in your journal.
3. Pay attention to your feelings when considering the questions above. Does questioning whether certain ideas were first thought of in the East or West evoke feelings for you? If so, why?
4. We will discuss question 3 later in the chapter, and at that point ask you to compare your thoughts and feelings about this issue with ours.

In Exercise 2.1, we asked you to consider your feelings because thoughts are connected to feelings, and both help produce understanding. Just like thoughts, feelings cannot always be trusted, so we need to critically think about what our feelings are trying to tell us. A text like this one, which asks you to think about oppression, social norms, attitudes, values, and beliefs, can be expected to evoke a broad range of emotions including anger, frustration, anxiety, delight, relief, joy, etc. Which feeling you experience, and when, is likely to depend on whether the ideas we share confirm or challenge your own values and beliefs (MacFadden, Herie, Maiter, & Dumbrill, 2005).

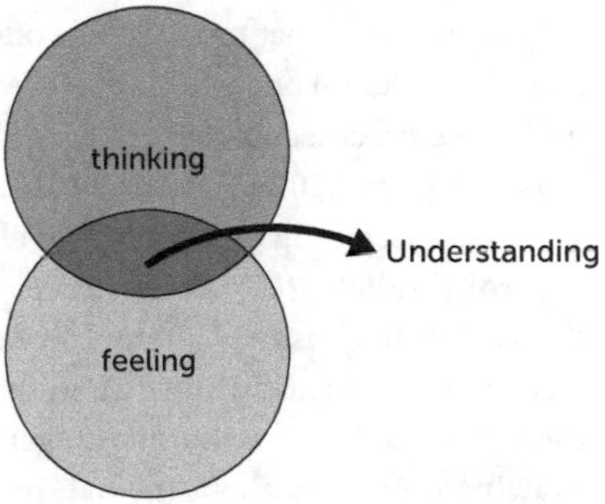

When this text evokes feelings, pay attention to these moments—perhaps note them

**Figure 2.1**   Thinking, feeling, and understanding

Source: Adapted from http://www.forbes.com/sites/jessicahagy/2012/10/04/40-things-to-say-before-you-die/5/. Reproduced with permission of Jessica Hagy.

in your journal—because in these moments your feelings are trying to teach you something. Think critically about why certain feelings (positive or negative) arise at a particular moment. Perhaps in these moments your feelings will be alerting you to an unjust bias we have inadvertently written into our text that you should challenge and not believe, or perhaps your feelings will be alerting you to an unjust bias you have in your thoughts that you need to challenge and not believe.

## Theory and Understanding in Social Work

When we develop understanding and make meaning, we are using and producing theory. **Theories** are sense-making mechanisms. All helping rests on theory. Even non–social workers use theory when they offer help. Imagine a friend trying to help someone with a problem. Most likely the friend will begin by asking what is wrong. Next the friend will do or say things based on a hunch or theory about what might help and why; maybe sympathy will help the person feel better, maybe supporting them to think through options will help them make a good choice, maybe telling a joke will take their mind off their trouble for a few moments and lift their spirits. It is good to have friends who help in this way, but when someone comes to a social worker for assistance, it is usually because their trouble has moved beyond the help friends can offer.

When someone comes to a social worker for help, there is an expectation that the social worker will develop a precise understanding of the person's trouble and emotional condition, and will have a fairly good idea about the corresponding action most likely to help in the person's circumstances. There is also an expectation that if the social worker does not know how to help, they will be capable of finding out how, or they will refer the person to someone who is able to offer the help needed (Cournoyer, 2014; Hepworth, Rooney, & Larsen, 2013).

Social workers attempt to ensure that the professional help they offer goes beyond the helping hunches that most friends offer each other. Workers usually do this by basing the help they offer on practice that research has shown to be effective. In this process, workers will make precise and deliberate use of sound theory and good evidence (see for instance Stoker & Evans, 2016; F. J. Turner, 2017).

Theory contains the following elements, **description, explanation, prediction**, and **control** (Mullaly, 2010; Payne, 2005, 2015). When social workers address a problem they *describe* it; they usually attempt to *explain* and understand it; they then attempt to help resolve the problem by implementing an approach that they believe will enable or support the service user or community to gain some kind of *control* over the issue. In addition to drawing on theory about the nature of problems and the ways to resolve them, workers will simultaneously draw on theory about the use of self and the best ways to engage with communities and service users in the helping process (Gladstone et al., 2012).

When social workers use theory, they are imposing on service users a way of understanding and making sense of a service user's troubles. They are also imposing a set of possible remedies. Social workers, therefore, need to think critically about the theories they use, about the assumptions that underlie these theories, and about the assumptions that underpin any research that has produced evidence for or against the effectiveness of a particular helping theory. Said differently, workers need to question the science that their helping is based upon. The type of science that informs social work is called **social science**, which is a branch of science that studies human and social relations, and includes disciplines such as psychology, sociology, politics, social policy, economics, law, and many more.

## Understanding Assumptions That Underlie Theory

Theory rests on assumptions that are embedded in the way we view the world. These assumptions can be divided into ontological and epistemological beliefs. **Ontology** refers to beliefs about the nature of the world and its realities. It deals with the question of what it means to exist (Chilisa, 2012). **Epistemology** refers to beliefs about the way things can be understood. It deals with questions about *how* we can know, like "What are the sources of knowledge?" "How reliable are these sources?" "How does one know something is true?" (Chilisa, 2012, p. 21). Our ontologies and epistemologies shape the things we believe, the questions we ask (and the questions we do not think of asking), and the help we offer (and the help we do not think of offering).

The concepts of ontology and epistemology have roots in Ancient Greek philosophy and the European enlightenment . . . or do they? If you do an Internet search on the term "ontology," it will lead you to a Wikipedia page where you will find an image of an Ancient Greek White man called Parmenides, along with the claim that he was "among the first to propose an ontological characterization of the fundamental nature of reality" (Wikipedia, 2015b). A similar search on the word "epistemology" leads to a Wikipedia page with details about the Greek origins of the concept, along with images of three White European men: Plato, Kant, and Nietzsche (Wikipedia, 2015a). Do not be fooled by these sources. They are more examples of things we should not believe, because although the words *ontology* and *epistemology* have European origins, the concepts pre-date European history (Chilisa, 2012). Our critique here is not of Wikipedia; in fact these particular Wikipedia entries have excellent references and are reflective of the dominant literature. Our critique is of something else—something that dominates the literature and scholarly thinking: the problem of dead White men (Pett, 2015). A **dead White man** is a "writer, philosopher, or other significant figure whose importance and talents may have been exaggerated by virtue of his belonging to a historically dominant gender and ethnic group" (Oxford Dictionaries, ND).

We personally have nothing against dead White men. We have nothing against most living ones either, but we do have something against the way ideas are traced back to mostly White European men even if they were not the first to think of them. This is the same misrepresentation of ideas and history we asked you to think about in relation to Socrates and Confucius earlier. Such misrepresentation creates a way of thinking that is problematic. It not only cuts us off from a whole range of non-European ideas and thinkers, it also enables some to and prevents others from seeing and thinking about themselves in the good parts of history, of recognizing their contribution to history, and imagining themselves (and others like them) in important places in the present and future. In this manner the dominance of White European ideas and ways of being become embedded in our ontologies and epistemologies; knowledge becomes associated with what White European men say. As well, important ideas are not associated with non-Europeans. We refer to this process and this thinking as the problem of *dead White men*. Confucius, therefore, could never be defined as a critical thinker who used rationality and reason, because to do so would challenge the dominance of dead White men.

## Key Concept

Exaggerating the importance of White European ideas limits our imagination and cuts us off from a whole range of important non-European ideas and thinkers. It also enables some to and prevents others from seeing and thinking about themselves in the good parts of history, from recognizing their contribution to history, and from imagining and thinking about themselves in important places in the present and future.

It is the problem of dead White men that caused June's father to warn her about books. He was not only worried about her believing things written on the lines, he was also worried about the way the dominance of White European thought was written between the lines. White European men were written into history and ideas, while people with bodies like June's were written out. June's father knew that books written by White people (along with movies, comics, and school and university curricula) might prevent June from feeling a sense of belonging in stories, ideas, or history.

For Gary the perils of reading were different. Any aspirations he had to one day become a "dead White man" were much more likely to be realized. But there are other perils in these texts too, which is why so many parents, aunties, uncles, and grandparents have undoubtedly warned their children, relatives, and friends about resisting other things found in texts, such as heterosexual, ableist, male, cisgender, and other types of normative thought. We will speak more about all of these issues and normativity and resistance later, but for now by **normative** we mean a "standard" White male European dominance written in texts, and by "resistance" we mean thinking critically and not buying into the belief that these are the only ideas and that this is the only way of thinking and being that matters. June's and Gary's parents also considered these issues when cautioning them about what to believe. It was a caution not only about not believing thoughts and ideas that might exclude them, but also about their own normative positions that might cause them to think and act in ways that exclude others. Often this lesson came in the simple idiom "live and let live," which means you can be the way you want to be but don't impose your way of being on another.

So what are we to do about all these dead White men? By now we hope you recognize that it is not White men, whether dead or living, who are the problem (breathe a sigh of relief if you are male and White). Instead, the problem is the way White ideas dominate how we think and what we do today (take back that sigh of relief if you are male or White because you are implicated in this—in fact we are all implicated no matter what race or gender—each of us has to think about what we do today in relation to these issues).

The problem of dead White men cannot be overcome by refusing to cite White thinkers, by pushing them out of the narrative of history, or by banishing White thinkers from the ideas of today. Chilisa (2012) speaks of how Western and Indigenous knowledge must co-exist in the present. In other words, if we are interested in the fullness of human knowledge, we cannot throw out one form of knowledge and knowing and replace it with another. If we are interested in undoing domination, we cannot throw out one form of domination and replace it with another. The knowledge and ways of thinking of *all* peoples have to be present for us to be complete as a planet. Consequently, the remedy for dead White men is for us as writers to think critically about the text we produce both on and between the lines (the way we are doing now), and for you as a reader to think critically about your own thinking and the ways you take up the text on and between the lines (the way we hope you are doing now).

## Key Concept

If we are interested in the fullness of human knowledge, we cannot throw out one form of knowledge and knowing and replace it with another. The knowledge and ways of knowing of *all* peoples have to be present for us to be complete as a planet.

## Exercise 2.2

### What Do You Have in Mind?

If possible, undertake this exercise in groups.

1. Reflect on and discuss the things you have read since childhood, and also consider movies, comics, and other forms of knowledge that have shaped your thinking. Consider who has been included and excluded in these, and in what roles or forms (positive, negative, hero–villain, rescuer–rescued, actor–acted upon).

   Begin to think through the implications of your answer for "what you have in your mind." (The questions below will explain the meaning behind the phrase "what you have in your mind.")

2. Once you have done question 1, watch the video produced by Thomas King (2007a) "I'm Not the Indian You Had in Mind" at http://www.nsi-canada .ca/2012/03/im-not-the-indian-you-had-in-mind/.

3. Read and discuss King's explanation (quoted below) about what he sets out to achieve in this poetry. Reflect on how developing an awareness of what you have in mind is the beginning of critical thought.

   "I'm Not the Indian You Had in Mind" challenges the stereotypical portrayal [of] First Nations peoples in the media. This spoken word short offers an insight of how First Nations people today are changing old ideas and empowering themselves in the greater community.

   > The actors, in business suits, jeans, and typical urban attire are juxtaposed against the loincloth-wearing, tomahawk wielding Natives of yesterday's spaghetti westerns.
   >
   > Through the use of stock footage, language, and common artifacts like a cigar store Indian, the viewer is encouraged to examine the profound role that these one-dimensional media representations have played in shaping their perspectives of an entire group of people. The man living next door, the woman working in the next cubicle, or the stoic wood carving in front of the cigar store — which Indian did you have in mind? (King, 2007b)

The things we "have in mind" interact with, shape, and become part of the ontologies, epistemologies, and theories that govern the social work we do. Because the theories of social work are based on scholarship and research in social science, we can sometimes think that the knowledge and practice they produce are based on pure truth about things that are absolutely so. But what science produces is shaped by "what we have in mind." Indeed, all the theories science produces and the practices these lead to are based on deep ontologies and epistemologies that we need to question. We need to question science and the ways we use it.

## The Problem of Science

The problem of science is that it has been used to colonize. There are several types of colonization. **Political colonization** involves conquering, occupying, and controlling a people's land or territory. **Scientific colonization** involves the colonizer imposing their ways of knowing and thinking on the minds of those whose territory has been colonized (Chilisa, 2012). Political and scientific colonization have to be understood together, because they interact, with one process supporting the other.

### Science and Imperial Dreams

European political colonization was driven by **imperialism**, which is the process of governments and private companies building empires by taking over nations and the lives of the people who live there. Europeans did not invent imperialism; it existed long before Europe had empires. Europe perfected and expanded it, however, to cover almost every corner of the globe. An example of European colonization is the work of Cecil Rhodes, a leading British imperialist who was involved in colonizing Africa. For Rhodes, dominating this planet was not enough, he once lamented that the stars were out of his imperialist reach, and asserted that, "If I could, I would annex other planets" (S. R. Brown, 2009, p. 4).

It seems that the grandiose nature of Cecil's vision of ruling the universe did not go unnoticed by his peers. Figure 2.2 is a cartoon by *Punch* showing Cecil Rhodes dominating Africa when he proposed a telegraph to connect the North and South (Adler & Pouwels, 2014). His pose is reminiscent of the Colossus

THE RHODES COLOSSUS
STRIDING FROM CAPE TOWN TO CAIRO.

Punch Limited

**Figure 2.2**  Cecil Rhodes stands on Africa, which he helped colonize

of Rhodes, a statue of a Greek Titan god that stood at Rhodes harbour, which was once regarded as a wonder of the Ancient World.

The image of Rhodes standing like a self-proclaimed god on a map of Africa created strong feelings for us. Gary felt anger and sadness. June also felt anger—she described feeling this anger as a pain tearing through her body. We *thought* about why we were *feeling* this: it is because of the arrogance of this man standing on Africa, where millions of lives were trod down and destroyed by him and others like him in a process of accumulating vast personal fortunes.

These feelings helped us better *understand* why many people want statues that honour Rhodes removed from university campuses (Hall, 2015; Khomami, 2015; Princewill, 2015). It is not simply because he is a *dead White man* who trod people down in the past, but because the treading down he helped to start continues today (Mnyanda, 2015). (Note: You can follow recent development in the Rhodes debate by searching social media using the hashtag #rhodesmustfall).

We almost did not include the image of Cecil Rhodes in this text because of the strong feelings it evoked for us and the feelings it might evoke for readers. We decided to include the image, however, because this history sets the stage for oppression today. *Thinking* about the *feelings* this image and this history evoke can lead to a deeper *understanding* of contemporary issues, and it can lead to a deeper understanding of ourselves. Do you have feelings about the Rhodes image? They may not be the same as ours, but whatever they are, or even if the image and these issues evoke no feelings for you, these feelings or the lack of them are trying to teach you something. Consider reflecting (as we have done) on what that might be.

## Science and the Tools of Colonization

Science provided the technologies and weapons Europe used to conquer, and also the factories and machinery used to turn the raw materials and labour of the colonized into wealth for the colonizers. Europe also used a softer science, particularly social science, to justify and enact political colonization and imperialism. Using their own "scientific theories" about race, Whites considered themselves superior and entitled to rule and enslave non-Europeans (Hall, 1996; Stevenson, 2015). Europeans did not use only science to justify colonization; they covered all of their ideological bases by also using religion. A quote sometimes attributed to Archbishop Desmond Tutu, and other times to Jomo Kenyatta, an African activist and former prime minister and president of Kenya, summarizes the role European missionaries played in this conquest.

> When the white man first came here, he had the Bible and we had the land. Then the white man said to us, Come let us kneel and pray together. So we knelt and closed our eyes and prayed, and when we opened our eyes again, lo!—we had the Bible and he had the land. (Battle, 1997, p. 31)

We are not suggesting that religion or science are inherently oppressive, but we are suggesting that at times the ways they are taken up are. As well, one should not take the quote above to mean that Europeans were the first to bring Christianity to Africa. Christianity came to Africa long before White European men or European colonization came to Africa (Ngulu, 2016). The point remains, however, that when White Europeans came to Africa, they used religion and science to colonize. As social workers, we need to pay attention to this, particularly to the ways science can be used to colonize, because science is a part of modern social work, and we want to avoid taking it up in a way that makes our practice colonizing.

## Key Concept

Social workers need to pay attention to the way science has been used to colonize, because science is a part of modern social work. We must be on guard against taking up social work and science in a way that makes our practice colonizing.

## The Problem of Positivism

A form of science called positivism has been particularly damaging because it comes with an inbuilt potential to colonize. **Positivism** only accepts the observable as real (so it recognizes no form of spiritual world), and breaks things into small elements to understand them (so it does not usually look at things in a holistic way). Positivism views all truths as absolutes waiting to be discovered (Green, 2016). To achieve discovery and define truth, positivism has an *ontology* and *epistemology* based on separating things into small parts.

This positivist way of knowing is different from other ways of knowing, especially Indigenous knowing, which is based on connection and examining things in a more holistic manner (Chilisa, 2012). As well, unlike positivism, Indigenous knowing has an emphasis on spirituality that "embodies an interconnectedness and interrelationship with all life . . . [in which] everyone and everything (both "animate" and "inanimate") are seen as equal and interdependent, part of the great whole and as having a spirit" (Baskin, 2016, p. 171).

Positivism, along with broader Western thinking, was imposed on Indigenous peoples in a way that separated them from the ontological and epistemological truths and knowledge that they had accumulated over thousands of years. Separating peoples from their distinct ways of knowing is one of the most effective ways to subjugate them.

## A Story of Conquest

A few years ago we were in a Tim Hortons coffee shop where we were working on some preliminary ideas for this book. An elderly lady who overheard our conversation asked us, "Want to hear a story?" "Sure," we replied. "A story for our book?" The elderly lady nodded and began:

Long ago there was a land where every village was a small nation, and every nation had its own way of understanding music and singing songs. The songs were connected to the land; there were songs for the forests, mountains, rivers, and songs about every kind of place in that land.

Singing the songs reminded people who they were and where they came from. Some of the songs were so old that they contained tunes that once helped sing the forests, mountains, and rivers into existence, and singing them kept the land healthy.

Even though the land was strong and beautiful, sometimes people went through troubles and even wars, but the people learned that if they came together, there were so many different ways of singing that they could always find a way to solve every problem with a song.

But then a ruler in a country across the sea decided he wanted everything in that land, so he sent armies to conquer it. Soon all the land was his, but the people were unhappy because they did not like someone taking the land and telling them what to do. The ruler knew that one day the people would figure out a way to take back their land from his armies. The ruler thought hard about what to do, and realized that the best way to keep the people conquered was to take away their songs. So he made a law that banned all the singing and music different from his own. He sent out the police to punish those who sang the old songs and thought in the old ways; he sent out teachers who taught only the ruler's new songs.

Pretty soon the police were no longer needed because the people policed themselves; the old songs were forgotten, people were unhappy but they could not remember why, and they could not think of what else to do because they could only think in the songs the ruler had given them.

We have never seen that lady again and do not know what land she was talking about, maybe Africa, Australia, New Zealand, or Turtle Island (now known as "Canada"), or perhaps a place we have never heard of and nobody can remember. Europe used this colonizing formula in many places, including Turtle Island. They conquered by taking Indigenous land, by resettling Indigenous communities on reserves, and by taking and placing Indigenous children in residential schools where they tried to subjugate them by breaking their connection with the land and making them forget their traditions and languages (Dumbrill & Green, 2008).

## The Problem of Ongoing Subjugation

Minds were subjugated not only by the lessons that Europeans taught about things (which all led back to White European men inventing everything of importance), but also in the ways Europeans taught about how to think. European ways of knowing became *the* way of knowing. European truths became *the* truth. European history became *everybody's* history. Indigenous connections to knowledge of family, community, land, language, tradition, and ceremony were broken. Europeans reasoned that if they took away the traditions that make a people a nation, the nation could no longer resist, because they would no longer be a nation. That of course was the genocidal plan (MacDonald & Hudson, 2012; Smith, 2010), but Indigenous peoples survive and exist to tell the tale—resistance is never futile!

Science is not only used to colonize Indigenous peoples, it is also used to colonize other people, including White Europeans who do not fit the normative position of the White male archetype. We use the term "archetype" because we refer to a position rather than a real person. The term is a little bit like an ideal type, in that the person (the White male archetype) may not be real, but the position certainly is. The closer a person is to the White male archetype position, the more they are pushed forward by dominant biases, systems, and culture. The further a person is away from that position, the more they are pushed down and held back by these same forces.

The White male archetype position is linked to the way the West sees itself in relation to Others. Edward Said explains this in the context of **Orientalism**, which is the way the West views the East in a patronizing or demeaning manner—in a way that views the East as inferior to the West. Said argues that the West justifies colonizing the East by imagining itself as the opposite of the East (Said, 1979, 1994). Seidman (2013) explains Said's argument, "before there could be an era of European colonization there had to be an idea of 'Europe' or the notion that there is a social and geographical space called the 'West' in contrast to the 'East'" (p. 258). The West imagines itself as the centre of scientific thought and reason, democracy, and freedom (Said, 1979, 1994; Seidman, 2013)—a place where the men are rational, ambitious, and smart, and the women are "wholesome" and bake apple pie! The West imagines the East as the exact opposite; we will not list these opposite attributes because frankly many of them are offensive. Said brings our attention to the offensiveness that the West imposes on the East.

Said's arguments not only apply to the way the East and West are imagined, but also to the way the North and South are imagined, and to the way people pushed down by racism and other forms of oppression within the West are imagined. This is why Thomas King said that he was "not the Indian you had in mind" (2007a). King knows that colonization has infiltrated people's minds, so the way they imagine "Indian" people is not necessarily the way "Indian" people are.

Science, therefore, has been used as an instrument of colonization and imperialism; it provides the tools and thinking needed to conquer and subjugate. But science does not have to be taken up this way. Science has a potential to help us see things the way they are, and in social work it also provides the means to bring anti-oppressive change.

## The Potential of Science in Social Work

In its simplest form science is beautiful; it is critical thinking mixed with the never-ending curiosity of wondering why something is so. Consider a child wondering why ice floats in water; this is the beginning of scientific thought. Toddler curiosity might be satisfied with the explanation that ice floats because it is lighter than water, but curiosity will eventually ask more critical questions. If ice is water, how can it be lighter than water? Answers now demand explanations of density, polarity, the hydrogen bond, and kinetic energy. Those whose curiosity is still not satisfied will ask even more critical questions; some may go on to become natural scientists whose job description requires them to *go beyond everyday explanations* and *unravel the workings of the physical world* and *question the rules* that we believe explain the way things are. It is exactly the same for social workers. Their job description requires them to *go beyond everyday explanations* and *unravel the workings of the social world* and *question the rules that we believe explain the way we are*. Science helps social workers in this unravelling.

## Key Concept

Science is beautiful when taken up as critical thinking mixed with curiosity and a never-ending questioning about what we believe and why things are so. It is exactly this type of science that anti-oppressive social workers need to take up, because undoing domination requires the ability to ask critical questions about why the social world is the way that it is, and the ability to imagine the possibility of it being different.

We are fans of this type of science. This science is not the rigid detachment of positivism, but is a more fluid, context aware, less certain, and more critical science. Most science today is more fluid than the types of positivism we described above. Even in the physical sciences the positivist pretense of detachment and truth has given way to a post-positivism where, although scientists believe that truth exists, they are never certain whether they have found it (Chilisa, 2012; Ponterotto, 2005). Modern scientists, at least the type of scientist we are referring to, are never convinced that they have achieved detached objectivity; they are always questioning their own assumptions, the way they are conceptualizing the issue, and whether the ways they have gathered and made sense of data might be incorrect. At an ontological and epistemological level, even if this type of science is taken up in a Western and non-Indigenous manner, its tentative claims on truth mean it can be taken up in ways that do not colonize.

Within this type of more critical, less rigid post-positivism there has also been a shift from **verification**, which means trying to prove that one's ideas and conclusions are correct, to **falsification**, which means trying to prove one's ideas and conclusions wrong (Ponterotto, 2005). The process of falsification is a part of critical thinking. It helps us avoid **confirmation bias**, which is a tendency to look for evidence that proves one's ideas right. Discover the need for this yourself. Undertake the following exercise and try to discover the "scientific" rule behind this sequence of numbers: 2, 4, and 8.

## Exercise 2.3

### Figure Out the Scientific Rule

If possible, undertake this exercise in groups.

1.  Make sure you have 20 minutes to spare. Go to *The New York Times* interactive puzzle on "TheUpshot" website: http://www.nytimes.com/interactive/2015/07/03/upshot/a-quick-puzzle-to-test-your-problem-solving.html.
2.  On that site, you are presented with a sequence of three numbers that follow an unnamed rule. Your task is to uncover the rule. The site allows you to conduct a scientific experiment: You can enter your own sequence of three numbers and you will be told whether these conform to the rule. Continue entering numbers until you figure out the rule.
3.  When you think you know the rule, write this rule down, then select "I think I know it." The site will allow you to determine whether your rule is right.
4.  After this exercise (not before), go to the YouTube channel "Veritasium: An element of truth" and watch the same experiment conducted and explained: https://youtu.be/vKA4w2O61Xo.

Reflect on the significance of this exercise for social work.

## Debunking Fake Science and Dodgy Claims

Critical thinkers also make sure that science gets things right in a range of other ways. These include looking for gaps in data that suggest things are being hidden, and examining the methods of a study to tell whether data supports conclusions that researchers or others claim.

The ways to critically appraise research are beyond the scope of this book to explore; they are taken up in research texts and courses. Although outside the scope of this book, the skill of recognizing bad science is essential in anti-oppression. Ben Goldacre explains how epidemiologists do this in his popular TED Talk and in his easily readable texts (Goldacre, 2010 , 2011, 2012). Similar approaches are used by social workers.

## Exercise 2.4

### Recognizing "Dodgy Claims"

If possible, undertake this exercise in groups. Make sure that you have 20 minutes to spare:

1.  Watch Ben Goldacre's TED Talk on "Battling Bad Science" at https://www.ted.com/talks/ben_goldacre_battling_bad_science.

2.  Reflect on a newspaper, magazine, or website article you have read over the past week that has made scientific claims.
3.  Drawing on Goldacre's thinking, consider how you would find out whether these claims can be trusted.

Testing one's own position, arguments, and data is not only important for the sake of winning arguments. It is also essential for the sake of truth. We consider truth more important than winning arguments. We use the term *truth* cautiously, not only because one should always be open to revising what one considers true, but also because what people regard as truth is often the product of power rather than the revelation of an absolute reality (more about that in Chapter 3).

With these cautions about truth in mind, we contend that some absolute truths do exist, especially in relation to oppression. We explained in the last chapter that oppression forms patterns in society. Scientific methods are very good at capturing **quantitative data** (measurable data often represented numerically) about these patterns, and these hard data are an especially powerful tool for social justice.

## Why Hard Data Can Be Beautiful

The importance of hard quantitative data in anti-oppression can be seen in the work of Cindy Blackstock, Executive Director of the First Nations Child and Family Caring Society of Canada. Blackstock used quantitative data to take the Government of Canada to court under the Human Rights Act (Blackstock, 2011).

Blackstock alleged that Government provision of First Nations Child Welfare is discriminatory because there is **disproportionality** (a pattern of First Nations children over-represented in state care) and **disparity** (a pattern of First Nations children and families receiving less child welfare services and resources than other families and children). In court, an array of government lawyers and statisticians set out to prove Blackstock's data wrong. They failed. In fact, government lawyers in the end confirmed that Blackstock's data was correct (Blackstock, 2015). Of course after one establishes disproportionality and disparity as facts, one then faces arguments about what these facts mean, so the case is not won on the basis of data and facts alone. But workers who present inaccurate data or facts are thrown out of court, lose credibility, and fail the communities they serve before debates about meaning begin.

Governments are scared of hard quantitative data in the hands of competent social workers and social activists. The Canadian government under Stephen Harper prohibited scientists employed by the government from sharing the findings of their publicly funded research, and cut the long-form census so that less social demographic data was available (Turner, 2013). Other governments have done the same in what has become known as a "war on science" (Kolbert, 2015). Governments and other powerful groups also try to skew data that is available and we, like most academics, have received calls from government ministries to submit proposals for research that *fit strategic government policy directions.* This type of activity produces evidence only within the parameters defined by government policy. As a result, "research" and "science" produce "evidence" that is linked to government policy, political ideology, or other regimes of "truth" (Holmes, Murray, Perron, & Rail, 2006). But a social worker trained in research methods and equipped with critical thinking has the tools and skills to critically appraise the "truth" such studies proclaim.

Even when the findings of a study can be believed, the anti-oppressive social worker asks *whose truth* the research represents. Research, especially at a quantitative level, rests on statistical analysis that often relies on means or norms; it is looking for what occurs at the centre of the bell curve. We learned in the previous chapter that the dominant society situates itself as the norm; as a result we need to know whether the study simply captures and reproduces normative ideas. Also, if a study uses a randomized sample of "average" people, and policy and practice are based on those "average" people, who gets left out of the "truth" being measured and the services being developed? We are not saying that all research misses the realities of those on the margins and fails to identify the best ways of helping such groups, but we are saying that this is a question that needs to be asked when basing policy and practice on evidence. When reviewing research evidence, always ask, "Whose story it has the potential to tell . . . whose story it will hide . . . why, for whom, and with what consequence" (Strega & Brown, 2014, p. 6). Answering these questions takes us into the realm of politics.

## Politics, Paradigms, and Self-Reflection

Political perspectives are like **paradigms** (Payne, 2015). A paradigm is a worldview. It is similar to the way ontological and epistemological perspectives mix to form understanding. In the strictest sense of the term, a paradigm is like a big box that contains all the worldviews or ways of thinking about a topic that exist within an entire discipline at a particular point in time (Kuhn, 1962). Another way to think of paradigms is, instead of a single big box, to imagine many "small box" paradigms constantly coexisting. This small box definition better fits our experience of political perspectives, because it seems to us that sometimes those with differing political views understand the world so differently that they can hardly understand each other.

The power of paradigms over our thinking and understanding is explained by Kuhn (1962) in the example of Copernicus. In ancient times astronomers had a **geocentric** paradigm, which means that they thought the planets and sun rotated around the earth. Copernicus changed all of this by discovering, sometime in the 1500s CE, that the planets rotated around the sun and as a result a paradigm shift to a **heliocentric** (planets rotate around the sun) model occurred.

Copernicus's discovery is an excellent example of a paradigm shift, but in the spirit of critical thinking we want to be careful of what this example writes between the lines. As far as we can tell, Copernicus deserves credit for a paradigm shift to a heliocentric model of the solar system in Europe during the 1500s, but we are aware of others who may have made the shift before him; certainly the Greek astronomer Aristarchus of Samos suggested a heliocentric model in 270 BCE, and outside Europe the Indian astronomer Aryabhata in 500 CE and the Persian astronomer Abu Rayhan Biruni in 1000 CE may have done so too. Copernicus, therefore, through no fault of his own, may be another one of those "dead White men."

The above historical issues aside, Kuhn's point is important: a paradigm shift creates profound change in human understanding and a huge leap forward in knowledge. After Copernicus (and the other astronomers before him) explained that the planets in our solar system were moving around the sun rather than the earth, people would look up at the same night sky to see the same old stars they had always seen, but now everything had new meaning. Quite literally, the entire universe had shifted.

Change of this nature invariably causes upset. Copernicus knew that his discovery was likely to annoy some very powerful people. Leaders of the Christian church had built theology, and astronomers had built reputations, around geocentrism. A paradigm shift threatened the authority and power of these groups (more about authority and power in Chapter 3). Copernicus realized that these groups, especially the church, were not going to give up their versions of truth easily. Copernicus understood that he was likely to be labelled a heretic and executed for his ideas, so he kept relatively quiet about his discoveries until shortly before his death. Even then it took a while for his ideas to be accepted, and later thinkers like Galileo who adopted the new paradigm were imprisoned (Glenberg, 2015).

Just as paradigms shape the way we see the stars, they also shape the way we see society, and they shape our politics. Mullaly (2010) divides politics into **conflict** and **consensus** perspectives, Payne (2015) refers to these as **socialist** and **liberal** paradigms, and these loosely correspond to **left** and

Copyright 2001 Leigh Rubin
Creators Syndicate, Inc.

"This is pure heresy! Everybody knows that the Earth revolves around *us*!"

**Figure 2.3**   Changing paradigms can cause upset

**right political perspectives** (sometimes called left wing and right wing). The political concept of left and right originates in France where, during the Estates-General of 1789, "some aristocrats and the low clergy occupied the seats on the left [of the king], whereas most aristocrats and the high clergy sat on the right" (Rosas & Ferreira, 2013, p. 4). The same designations are used today. We use the term "left" for those informed by socialist ideas, who believe that the playing field is tilted toward corporate and other elites and needs to be adjusted, and who think that competition favours the rich. We use the term "right" for those who tend to be conservative, who believe that the playing field is level and that people can get ahead through hard work, and who think that competition is the key to fairness and efficiency.

The left–right political binary is an oversimplification of politics, because people can sometimes be left on one issue and right on another. In addition to many right and left positions, there are centrist positions. There are also ideas about how much liberty and freedom people should have compared to how much authority the state should have that do not fit neatly on a linear left-and-right scale (Rosas & Ferreira, 2013). Despite the over simplicity of the left–right binary, these notions are useful because, although not a perfect model of political paradigms, the left and right positions do represent the major political divide in the world.

Literature on anti-oppression is embedded almost entirely in the perspectives of the left. We think this is a mistake. Oppression existed long before Europeans invented the left and right, and we have seen regimes from both the left and right oppress, so how can either of these European perspectives offer human liberation? We think an entirely new form of politics is needed for liberation to occur: a form of politics that bridges difference, including the difference between the right and left. *You* can contribute to that process, but to bridge political difference and create something new, you first need to know where you currently stand. You cannot begin to think outside your political box unless you know where that box begins and ends.

Understanding your political paradigm requires **critical self-reflection** (Rosin, 2015) and **reflexivity,** which Moore (2012) describes as the process of uncovering our social unconscious. You have been engaging in critical self-reflection already in the "test your implicit attitudes" exercise in Chapter 1, and also in many other reflective exercises we have suggested. In this next exercise, David Nolan, an American social activist, has developed a "political compass" that enables you to identify your political leanings. In this instrument, Nolan includes a horizontal "left" to "right" spectrum, and also a vertical spectrum from "authority" (views on how controlling the state should be) to "liberty" (views on how much freedom the state should give) (Rosas & Ferreira, 2013). The compass position of "liberty" however, in the form of **libertarianism**, not only advocates a minimal role for the state in controlling and regulating citizens, it also sees a minimal role for the state in providing social work, social security, or supports for citizens.

The political compass may be an oversimplification of political views, but it is a good place to begin when thinking about your own political perspectives (see Exercise 2.5).

## Exercise 2.5

### Recognizing Your Politics

If possible, undertake this exercise in groups. Go to the Political Compass website (https://www.politicalcompass.org/). Read the description of the project, look for the link that says "take the test," complete the test, and consider the following questions:

1. Do you agree with the results? If so, why?
2. Do you disagree with the results? If so, why?
3. How does your political compass compare with any other compass you use to find your way in the world?
4. Finally, do you notice anything missing from the political compass?

We are not suggesting that a box can be drawn around your score on the chart to define your political perspective, nor do we suggest that any perspectives the political compass test in Exercise 2.5 identifies the answer to oppression. We suggest that you use this exercise to reflect on the political views that shape the way you see the world, and help you to think through the way that these views shape the help that you offer to service users.

Another thing to notice in the political compass exercise is that no matter which direction the compass points, it points to a perspective embedded in Western thought. This is another example of the problem of dead White men. This is not to say that the compass is not a useful tool or a valid measure of the range of political options open to people. But we suggest that if we are to imagine a new politics of liberation, it may need to be imagined outside the world portrayed by this compass.

## How Does All This Relate to Everyday Social Work Practice?

We sometimes hear students and practitioners say that politics, paradigms, ontologies, epistemologies, and theories are not relevant in the real world of social work practice. They say that what matters in the real world is what social workers do, not the deeper conceptual issues the academy concerns itself with. What real-world social workers do, however, always rests on theory, and theory rests on epistemology, and epistemology rests on ontology. All these deeper levels of thought are linked to distinct political paradigms and agendas, which in turn are linked to the ways social workers make sense of and address issues. Even **practice wisdom**, where practitioners develop ways of working from the experience of what they find effective, is a form of theory and is based on assumptions about people, problems, and remedies. Consequently, workers who think they are simply doing practice without theory become a mindless cog in the wheel of someone else's political agenda. Such workers will have no hope of practising anti-oppressively, and will ultimately fail clients and perpetuate oppression.

## Guarding against Embedding Oppression in Caring

The caring professions have a long history of not only perpetuating oppression, but also of committing crimes against humanity. Medical professionals once claimed that Black slaves running away from their White masters were suffering from a mental illness called drapetomania, which they defined as an irrational desire for freedom (Bowman, 2014; Singy, 2015).

During the 1920s social workers provided well-off White people with therapy while poor families struggled to afford food (Woodcock, 2012). In Nazi Germany social work co-operated with scientific racism, acted as an agent of Nazi social control, and co-operated in genocide (Barney & Dalton, 2006; Evans, 2015; Woodcock, 2012). In the United States during WWII social workers helped to force Asian-Americans into internment camps (Woodcock, 2012). We previously mentioned the attempted destruction of Indigenous Nations and peoples by removing their children; this too was undertaken by social workers and is now recognized as a form of genocide (MacDonald & Hudson, 2012).

Also, until the 1970s social work and psychiatrists regarded gay, lesbian, and bisexual people as mentally ill and offered "cures" (Bingham & Banner, 2014). Social work gets drawn into such practice and even into supporting crimes against humanity by political ideology (Woodcock, 2012), which we referred to above as political paradigms. Barney and Dalton (2006) say these crimes were caused when "social workers substituted their technical and specialist knowledge for their moral responsibility" (p. 56). Consequently, if a social worker is thinking only of the technical and specialist aspects of social work, and not thinking of the ideas these rest on and what their approaches to practice are asking social workers to do, they may right now be repeating such crimes. Indeed, the Canadian and Australian prime ministers apologized for crimes the state (and social workers) committed against Indigenous peoples. What crimes are we committing today that tomorrow's prime ministers will apologize for? Remember the lesson of the M.V. *St Louis* in the previous chapter. Unless we are looking closely we may not know we are engaging in oppression. Critical thinking at paradigmatic levels is one of the ways we look closely at our practice in an effort to guard against it becoming oppressive.

## Understanding the Deep Thinking behind Practice

Figure 2.4 represents a social worker engaging in practice. The social worker formulates interventions based on a practice approach, which, as noted earlier, rests on theory, epistemology, and ontology. We describe each of these levels on the right of the triangle

**Figure 2.4** The hidden determinants of practice

diagram the social worker stands upon. To the left we list some of the assumptions and political ideas that may be associated with each level. Everything the worker says or does at the top of the triangle emerges from these deeper levels of thought.

To think critically about what the social worker is doing in this figure, we focus on the worker's practice approach and the theory it is derived from. We mentioned at the start of this chapter that theory comprises three elements, *description, explanation,* and a third element composed of two parts: *prediction* and *control* (Howe, 1987; Mullaly, 2010). This conceptualization of theory is somewhat positivist, especially as intervention (control) rests on an explanation of the problem or issue. Nevertheless, social work assessments almost invariably follow this formula and have a *description* of the problem to be addressed, an *explanation* of why the problem is occurring, and some *prediction* or idea about what might help *control* or remedy the problem. Table 2.1 shows how to think critically at each stage of this process.

*Description* is the first step in any social work assessment. Always question descriptions. Is it the service user or community who is defining the problem or is it someone else? Who stands to lose or gain from this description? For instance, when escaping slaves were described as a problem, this was not because slaves regarded the desire and ability to escape as a problem; it was because escaping slaves posed a problem for slave owners. A more recent example is the "problem" of gender identity. When children who are gender

**Table 2.1** Social Work Theory: A Critical Thinking Matrix

| Component | What This Means | Critical Thinking Tasks |
|---|---|---|
| **Description** (gathering information and naming issues) | Social work intervention usually begins with a description of the problem (a trouble or issue) that the social worker is being asked to address. Describing the problem sets the stage for understanding the problem and the issues to be addressed. | Who is defining this as a problem?<br><br>Who is this a "problem" for?<br><br>Who stands to gain or lose because of the ways this problem is defined?<br><br>If I accept this definition of "the problem," whose agenda am I buying into?<br><br>Whose power is being used to define this problem in this way and why? Who lacks power and is not being heard in this situation? |
| **Explanation** (understanding) | Explaining the problem means trying to *understand* the problem and its causes. What causes the problem and why?<br><br>What would need to change for this to no longer be a problem? | Does the problem explanation fit the cause? Is this a political problem misrepresented as someone's personal failing, or is this a personal problem misrepresented as a political problem or societal issue?<br><br>Is my explanation of the problem different from service users'? If my explanation is different, why and what does this mean? Have I discussed this difference and the implications with the service user or community I am serving?<br><br>Whose power is being used to explain the problem and why? What ways of explaining this problem are not being considered and why? What is the implication of adopting the explanations being suggested? Are my own biases shaping the way I understand this problem? |
| **Prediction/ Control** (action) | What is likely to happen and for whom if we do nothing?<br><br>What things can be done to address the problem, and what are the likely outcomes of the various solutions?<br><br>Who will these potential outcomes benefit? | What approach to helping might address or remedy this problem? Does my approach locate problems in the relationships, attitudes, and thinking of individuals involved, or in the attitudes, structures, and culture of oppression? What are the implications of this approach at the personal and political levels for those involved and also for wider society?<br><br>What assumptions does my helping approach rest on and are they appropriate in this case?<br><br>Have I discussed any concerns I might have about intervention with the service users involved, and have I asked them if they have any concerns? |

| Are there any potential unintended consequences of the proposed help/intervention? | Am I imposing my solutions or politics on service users in the remedies I am offering? |
| --- | --- |
| | Have I discussed, with the service users involved, the potential benefits and harms of the proposed intervention? Have we discussed who in the long run benefits and loses as a result of the plan? Have I been given consent to proceed? |
| | Whose power is driving this intervention approach and is that appropriate? |

Source: Adapted from Howe, 1987; Payne, 2005, 2015

non-conforming are taken to psychiatrists for help, is this because the child has a problem, or because society has a problem with the child not conforming to a gender norm? Who has the power to make their definition of the problem prevail? Whom does this definition harm, and whom does it benefit?

*Explanation* is the next step in an assessment. When psychiatrists explained that slaves desiring freedom did so because they were ill, psychiatrists supported slavery and oppression. When social workers and psychiatrists explain that children who are gender non-conforming have a "condition" that requires "treatment," social workers and psychiatrists are supporting the idea that there are only two genders, and that people must conform to one or the other. Of course children who do not conform may have personal troubles at school and in society that result from them not conforming to gender expectations. Such trouble is not because these children are ill or confused; it is because dominant society is confused about gender. This problem may have a personal impact on people who do not conform to society's gender expectations, but this is a political problem with a social cause.

*Prediction* and *control,* also known as an intervention plan, are the next steps in an assessment and in the social work process. Psychiatrists controlling escaping slaves by treating them for an illness became the same as slave traders. These psychiatrists were no different from those who put people in chains and sold them to members of the White ruling elite. Social workers and psychiatrists who treat gender non-conforming children for their "condition" are doing something very similar; they are taking away the freedom of gender expression. Sometimes we hear people justify treatment of such children by referring to the troubles they will face in society by not conforming. Escaped slaves would also undoubtedly face a whole host of problems in a society intent on keeping them captive, but this does not justify psychiatrists treating them as if they were ill. Of course social workers may want to help gender non-conforming children deal with the problems they face in society, but "cures" should be firmly reserved for the confusion society has about gender, and not for the child.

## Critical Thinking in Practice

The critical thinking matrix in Table 2.1 helps to identify the way oppression may shape practice and gives clues about how to intervene anti-oppressively. Keep in mind that the critical thinking matrix is not comprehensive. You may want to add questions of your own or adapt it to better fit your practice context. The critical thinking matrix is also not fool-proof. It is after all a box and formula, and once critical thinking relies on a formula it is no longer critical. The critical thinking matrix can assist in casework, community action or development, and policy work. It is also useful in a school context when critically appraising theory or ideas being taught. We will operationalize the critical thinking matrix in an exercise based on a clinical casework referral.

## Exercise 2.6

### A Problem of Motivation?

If possible, undertake this exercise in groups. Imagine you are a social worker at an agency that offers a range of services including clinical counselling. Another agency in the community refers a service user to you for counselling. The referring agency *describes* the service user's problem as being unemployed and having trouble finding work. The referring agency *explains* that this problem arises from the service user's "loss of motivation to find work." The referring agency suggested to the service user that they seek counselling for this motivation problem. The client agreed, hence the referral to your agency.

1. Using the critical thinking matrix, what questions would you ask in this case and why?
2. Be sure to complete this exercise before reading our analysis of the case below. Once you have completed this exercise, read our analysis below, and compare our analysis to yours.

### June's and Gary's Analysis of the Scenario in Exercise 2.6

The referring agency *describes* the problem as the service user not finding work. We never accept descriptions at face value, so we want to verify whether this is the case. Consequently, after the usual intake preliminaries (Hepworth et al., 2013), we want to know how the service user understands the problem and its causes.

Is the service user not having work a problem, and if so is this a problem for the service user or for someone else? Maybe the service user not having work is a problem for an employment officer who wants the service user off benefits and off their caseload. Or maybe the service user not having work is a problem for an insurance company looking for ways to deny some payment or reduce a settlement, or for a probation officer looking for ways to send the service user back to jail for breaching a parole condition that requires the service user to actively seek employment. We will not know if any of these or some other factor is at play unless we explore the problem description with an open and critical mind.

As we explore the problem *description*, we also question the *explanation* that the referrer provides. Has the service user really lost motivation to find employment, or perhaps they simply want a break from work because they are unwell, or perhaps they cannot work because they are responsible for the care of an elderly parent or sick child. Any of these or similar *explanations* change the nature of the problem and its remedies.

If reasons like those above are preventing the service user from seeking employment, perhaps they felt unable to share these with whoever referred them, or perhaps these reasons do not fit the categories employment officers, insurance companies, or probation officers recognize as valid reasons to be out of work. If any of these explanations are so, the problem *explanation* switches from something located within the service user (such as a lack of motivation) to something embedded in societal structures (such as a lack of services for those too unwell to work, or lack of community supports and options when family members need home care).

If we *explain* the problem as a lack of motivation when one of these other factors is the cause, not only will our intervention be unhelpful, we might be buying into an employment agency, insurance company, or probation system's agenda to find grounds to cut benefits, stop paying some settlement, or send the service user to jail. In these circumstances our records might be subpoenaed to a hearing to confirm that we "diagnosed" the problem as a "lack of motivation to work." In this manner we become a part of the system that pushes this service user down.

But suppose the service user confirms that the referral information is accurate; they are willing and able to work, but they have been unable to find work, and as a result they have begun to lack motivation to seek work, and they want help with this issue. In these circumstances we might offer intervention to help motivate them in their job search, but we have more critical questions to ask first. What if the service user is facing racism, has disabilities, or faces discrimination on these or other grounds in hiring processes? In other words, what if oppression is contributing to their problem finding work? Of course the service user may still lack motivation, because being consistently pushed down by oppression and systemic inequality can be demoralizing, but in these circumstances if we *explain* the problem as a lack of motivation and do not *explain* the role structural inequalities play, we become a part of the problem the service user faces. Our records and our thinking will have turned the political and social problem of prejudice in hiring processes into the personal problem of the service user lacking motivation. In this circumstance, if an employment officer, insurance company, or probation officer is looking for ways to cut benefits, settlements, or send the service user to jail, our thinking and our records will provide them with the means to do this.

Of course if racism, ableism, or some other oppression were playing a role in the service user not being able to find work, we would not deny the service user motivational counselling if they believed this would help, because to deny the help the service user is asking for would be another form of oppression. We would, however, be very clear with the service user and in our records about the structural nature of this problem, and the fact that the service user being unable to find employment cannot be explained simply by a lack of motivation. In addition to counselling, we might, in partnership with the service user, engage in advocacy and social action around the issue of discriminatory hiring processes, and we might try to engage the employment office, insurance company, or probation system in this too. Indeed, we might ask these other service providers if there is a pattern of this problem occurring with certain service users. If so, we might ask these organizations what attention they have paid to the impact prejudicial hiring processes have on their service users, what the consequences are, whether anyone has documented these patterns, and if so what they are doing about it.

## Chapter Summary

At the beginning of this chapter we spoke of June's father telling her, "If you are going to believe everything in books, you had better not read," and Gary's parents telling him, "Believe half of what you see and nothing that you hear." We have described the reasons for this advice and the way critical thinking can help us determine what to believe or not believe.

We have shown that social workers need critical thinking skills to identify the politics and agendas that shape the ways they understand problems and provide help. We argued that without critical thinking, social work will fail to address societal inequalities, will reinforce oppression, and may even engage in crimes against humanity. We have explored ways to think about and utilize science, "objective" knowledge, and subjective realities to proclaim "truth" and seek social justice, and we have made connections between political perspectives and understanding. We have also asked you to critically reflect on your own politics, the way you think, and what is in your mind when you engage with others in the helping process.

Thomas King (2007a, 2007b) helped us understand the importance of what we have in our minds. Perhaps King got this wrong for you and maybe he was exactly the Indigenous person you had in mind, or maybe he was not. Either way the key issue is to know what is in your mind and where it comes from. If you do not have this understanding, you will not be able to see things for what they are and will be of little assistance to service users.

## Discussion Questions

Think of a time when you saw a social issue one way, but later were able to see the issue differently, and as a result you changed the way you understood the issue. Discuss the following.

1. What caused your original understanding of the issue?
2. What caused you to see things differently and change your mind about the issue?
3. Does anything in this chapter speak to the processes that created your original view or your ability to change your mind and see things differently?

## Activity

Listen to or read Helen Knott's (2014) spoken word poem, "your eyes they curve around me," which is about murdered and missing Indigenous women at:

> Video: http://nationtalk.ca/story/featured-video-of-the-day-your-eyes-they-curve-around-me-spoken-word-poetry
> Text: http://www.ourcommons.ca/DocumentViewer/en/41-2/IWFA/report-1/page-18

Consider sharing the spoken word poem with a friend, and discuss what "structural giants" are and the types of issues they can cause people's eyes to "curve around."

## Suggested Resources

A Tribe Called Red—"The Virus Ft. Saul Williams, Chippewa Travellers" (Official Video). Retrieved from https://youtu.be/4_5VAKdHMek

"Microfilm: A Tribe Called Red." Retrieved from https://vimeo.com/23970949

Lavell-Harvard, D.M., & Brant, J. (Eds). (2016). *Forever loved: Exposing the hidden crisis of missing and murdered Indigenous women and girls in Canada*. Bradford, Canada: Demeter Press.

King, T. (2003). *The truth about stories: A native narrative*. Toronto, Canada: House of Anansi Press Inc.

Parada, H., & Wehbi, S. (Eds). (2017). *Reimagining anti-oppression social work research*. Toronto, Canada: Canadian Scholars' Press.

## References

Adler, P.J., & Pouwels, R.L. (2014). *World Civilizations: Volume II: Since 1500* (7th edn). Stamford, CT: Cengage Learning.

Barney, D.D., & Dalton, L.E. (2006). Social work under Nazism: An analysis of the "profession-in-the-environment." *Journal of Progressive Human Services, 17*(2), 43–62. doi:10.1300/J059v17n02_04

Baskin, C. (2016). *Strong helpers' teachings: The value of Indigenous knowledges in the helping professions* (2nd edn). Toronto, Canada: Canadian Scholars' Press.

Battle, M. (1997). *Reconciliation: The Ubuntu theology of Desmond Tutu*. Cleveland, OH: The Pilgrim Press.

Bingham, R., & Banner, N. (2014). The definition of mental disorder: Evolving but dysfunctional? *Journal of Medical Ethics, 40*(8), 537–42. doi:10.1136/medethics-2013-101661

Blackstock, C. (2011). The Canadian Human Rights Tribunal on First Nations Child Welfare: Why if Canada wins, equality and justice lose. *Children and Youth Services Review, 33*(1), 187–94. doi:10.1016/j.childyouth.2010.09.002

Blackstock, C. (2015). *Reconciliation: The children's version*. Keynote Address: McMaster School of Social Work Field Forum. McMaster University, Ontario, Canada.

Bowman, S. (Ed.). (2014). *Colour behind bars: Racism in the U.S. prison system*. Santa Barbara, CA: Praeger.

Brookfield, S. (2012). *Teaching for critical thinking: Tools and techniques to help students question their assumptions*. San Francisco, CA: Jossey-Bass.

Brown, S.R. (2009). *Merchant kings: When companies ruled the world 1600–1900*. New York, NY: Thomas Dunne Books, St. Martin's Press.

Centre for Addiction and Mental Health. (2015). *News Release: CAMH to make changes to Child and Youth Gender Identity Services*. Retrieved from http://www.camh.ca/en/hospital/about_camh/newsroom/news_releases_media_advisories_and_backgrounders/current_year/Pages/CAMH-to-make-changes-to-Child-and-Youth-Gender-Identity-Services.aspx

Chilisa, B. (2012). *Indigenous research methodologies*. Thousand Oaks, CA: Sage.

Cournoyer, B. (2014). *The social work skills workbook* (7th edn). Belmont, CA: Brooks/Cole.

Dumbrill, G.C., & Green, J. (2008). Indigenous knowledge in the social work academy. *Social Work Education: The International Journal, 27*(5), 489–503.

Evans, R.J. (2015). *The Third Reich in history and memory*. New York, NY: Oxford University Press.

Facione, P.A. (1990). *Critical thinking: A statement of expert consensus for purposes of educational assessment and instruction. Findings and recommendations*. Retrieved from https://eric.ed.gov/?id=ED315423

Gladstone, J., Dumbrill, G.C., Leslie, B., Koster, A., Young, M., & Ismaila, A.A. (2012). Looking at engagement and outcome from the perspectives of child protection workers and parents. *Children and Youth Services Review, 34*(1), 112–18. doi:10.1016/j.childyouth.2011.09.003

Glenberg, A.M. (2015). Few believe the world is flat: How embodiment is changing the scientific understanding of cognition. *Canadian Journal of Experimental Psychology, 69*(2), 165–71. doi:10.1037/cep0000056

Goldacre, B. (2010). *Bad science: Quacks, hacks, and big pharms flacks.* New York, NY: Faber and Faber Inc.

Goldacre, B. (2011). Battling bad science *TEDGlobal 2011.* Retrieved from https://www.ted.com/talks/ben_goldacre_battling_bad_science

Goldacre, B. (2012). What doctors don't know about the drugs they prescribe. *TEDMED.* Retrieved from https://www.ted.com/talks/ben_goldacre_what_doctors_don_t_know_about_the_drugs_they_prescribe?language=en

Green, T.L. (2016). From positivism to critical theory: School-community relations toward community equity literacy. *International Journal of Qualitative Studies in Education, 30*(4), 370–87. doi:10.1080/09518398.2016.1253892

Hall, M. (2015, March 25). The symbolic statue dividing a South African university. *BBC News, 2015,* BBC. Retrieved from http://www.bbc.com/news/business-31945680

Hall, S. (Writer). (1996). Race, the floating signifier. In S. Jhally (Producer): Media Education Foundation.

Hepworth, D.H., Rooney, G.D., & Larsen, J.A., Strom-Gottfried, K., & Rooney, R.H. (2012). *Direct social work practice: Theory and skills* (9th edn). Belmont, CA: Brooks/Cole.

Holmes, D., Murray, S.J., Perron, A., & Rail, G. (2006). Deconstructing the evidence-based discourse in health sciences: Truth, power and fascism. *International Journal of Evidence Based Health Care, 4*(3), 180–86. doi:10.1111/j.1479-6988.2006.00041.x

Howe, D. (1987). *An introduction to social work theory: Making sense in practice.* Aldershot, UK: Ashgate.

Khomami, N. (2015, December 22). Oxford students step up campaign to remove Cecil Rhodes statue. *The Guardian.* Retrieved from http://www.theguardian.com/education/2015/dec/22/oxford-students-campaign-cecil-rhodes-statue-oriel-college

Kim, H.-K. (2003). Critical thinking, learning and Confucius: A positive assessment. *Journal of Philosophy of Education, 37*(1), 71–87.

King, T. (Writer). (2007a). I'm not the Indian you had in mind. In L. J. Milliken (Producer). Winnipeg, Canada.

King, T. (2007b). I'm not the Indian you had in mind: Director's statement. Retrieved from http://www.nsi-canada.ca/2012/03/im-not-the-indian-you-had-in-mind/

Knott, H. (2014). Preface to *"Invisible women: A call to action – A report on missing and murdered Indigenous women. Report of the special committee on violence against Indigenous women".* Retrieved from http://www.parl.gc.ca/HousePublications/Publication.aspx?DocId=6469851&File=18

Kolbert, E. (2015, May 6). The G.O.P.'s war on science gets worse. *The New Yorker.* Retrieved from http://www.newyorker.com/news/daily-comment/gop-war-on-science-gets-worse

Kuhn, T.S. (1962). *The structure of scientific revolutions* (2nd edn). Chicago, IL: Chicago University Press.

MacDonald, D.B., & Hudson, G. (2012). The genocide question and Indian Residential Schools in Canada. *Canadian Journal of Political Science/Revue Canadienne de Science Politique, 45*(2), 427–49.

MacFadden, R.J., Herie, M.A., Maiter, S., & Dumbrill, G.C. (2005). Achieving high touch in high tech: A constructivist, emotionally-oriented model of web-based instruction. In R.L. Beaulaurier & M. Haffey (Eds), *Technology in social work education and curriculum: The high tech, high touch social work educator* (pp. 21–44). New York, NY: Haworth Press.

Mathias, J. (2015). Thinking like a social worker: Examining the meaning of critical thinking in social work. *Journal of Social Work Education, 51,* 457–74. doi:10.1080/10437797.2015.1043196

Mnyanda, S. (2015, March 25). "Cecil Rhodes' colonial legacy must fall—not his statue." *The Guardian.* Retrieved from http://www.theguardian.com/world/2015/mar/25/south-africa-rhodesmustfall-statue

Moore, W.L. (2012). Reflexivity, power, and systemic racism. *Ethnic and Racial Studies, 35*(4), 614–19. doi:10.1080/01419870.2011.630097

Mullaly, B. (2010). *Challenging oppression and confronting privilege: A critical social work approach.* (2nd edn). Toronto, Canada: Oxford University Press.

Ngulu, J.M.J. (2016). Is Christianity in Africa a fruit of colonialism? *Human Dignity Journal/Roczniki Teologiczne, 63*(10), 95–110. doi:10.18290/rt.2016.63.10-12

Oxford Dictionaries. (ND). Dead white European male. *Oxford Living Dictionary.* Retrieved from https://en.oxforddictionaries.com/definition/dead_white_European_male

Paul, R., & Elder, L. (2006). *The miniature guide to critical thinking: Concepts and tools.* Dillon Beach, CA: The Foundation for Critical Thinking.

Payne, M. (2005). *Modern social work theory* (3rd edn). Chicago, IL: Lyceum.

Payne, M. (2015). *Modern social work theory.* (4th edn). New York, NY: Oxford University Press.

Pett, S. (2015, May 8). It's time to take the curriculum back from dead white men. *The Conversation.* Retrieved from http://theconversation.com/its-time-to-take-the-curriculum-back-from-dead-white-men-40268

Ponterotto, J.G. (2005). Qualitative research in counseling psychology: A primer on research paradigms and philosophy of science. *Journal of Counseling Psychology, 52*(2), 126–36. doi:10.1037/0022-0167.52.2.126

Princewill, V. (2015, December 22). It was racism at Oxford, not a statue, that made me buckle. *The Guardian.* Retrieved from http://www.theguardian.com/commentisfree/2015/dec/22/statue-racism-oxford-university-cecil-rhodes-must-fall-black-student

Rosas, J.C., & Ferreira, A.R. (2013). Left and right: Critical junctures. In J.C. Rosas & A.R. Ferreira (Eds), *Left and Right: The great dichotomy revisited* (pp. 2-20). Newcastle upon Tyne, UK: Cambridge Scholars Publishing.

Rosin, J. (2015). The necessity of counselor individuation for fostering reflective practice. *Journal of Counseling & Development, 93*(1), 88–95.

Said, E.W. (1979). *Orientalism.* New York, NY: Vintage Books.

Said, E.W. (1994). *Culture and imperialism.* New York, NY: Vintage Books.

Seidman, S. (2013). *Contested knowledge: Social theory today* (5th edn). West Sussex, UK: John Wiley & Sons, Ltd.

Singy, P. (2015). Power, knowledge, and laughter: Forensic psychiatry and the misuse of the DSM. In P. Huneman, G. Lambert, & M. Silberstein (Eds), *Classification, disease and evidence: New essays in the philosophy of medicine* (pp. 131–45). Dordrecht, Netherlands: Springer.

Smith, A. (2010). Heteropatriarchy and the three pillars of white supremacy: Rethinking women of color organizing. In M. Adams, W.J. Blumenfeld, C.R. Castañeda, H.W. Hackman, M.L. Peters, & X. Zúñiga (Eds), *Readings for diversity and social justice* (pp. 66–73). New York, NY: Routledge.

Soothill, W.E. (1968). *The analects of Confucius* (2nd edn). New York, NY: Paragon Book Reprint Corp.

Spitzer, Q., & Evans, R. (1997). The new business leader: Socrates with a baton. *Strategy & Leadership, 25*(5), 32–8. doi:10.1108/eb054599

Stevenson, B.E. (2015). *What is slavery?* Cambridge, UK: Polity Press.

Stoker, G., & Evans, M. (Eds). (2016). *Evidence-based policy making in the social sciences: Methods that matter.* Bristol, UK: Policy Press.

Strega, S., & Brown, L. (2014). Introduction: From resistance to resurgence. In L. Brown & S. Strega (Eds), *Research as resistance: Revisiting critical, Indigenous, and anti-oppressive approaches* (2nd edn, pp. 1–16). Toronto, Canada: Canadian Scholar's Press.

Šulavíková, B. (2014). Key concepts in philosophical counselling. *Human Affairs, 24*(4), 574–583. doi:10.2478/s13374-014-0250-9

Turner, C. (2013). *The war on science: Muzzled scientists and wilful blindness in Stephen Harper's Canada.* Vancouver, Canada: Greystone Books Ltd.

Turner, F.J. (Ed.). (2017). *Social work treatment: Interlocking theoretical approaches* (6th edn). New York, NY: Oxford University Press.

Wikipedia. (2015a). Epistemology. *Wikipedia, The Free Encyclopedia.* Retrieved from https://en.wikipedia.org/w/index.php?title=Epistemology&oldid=693369314

Wikipedia. (2015b). Ontology. *Wikipedia, The Free Encyclopedia.* Retrieved from https://en.wikipedia.org/wiki/Ontology

Wikipedia. (2015c). Reason. *Wikipedia, The Free Encyclopedia.* Retrieved from https://en.wikipedia.org/wiki/Reason

Woodcock, R. (2012). Knowing where you stand: Neoliberal and other foundations for social work. *Journal of Comparative Social Welfare, 28*(1), 1–15. doi:10.1080/17486831.2011.595077

# Thinking Critically about Power and Politics

| In this chapter you will learn: |
|---|
| • Why it is important for social workers to understand power |
| • How to conceptualize and understand power |
| • How power operates in social work |
| • How to think about and navigate power in social work |
| • The power of love and why this is important in anti-oppression |

## Introduction

When Gary was a social work student he was assigned the case of Mr Jones, an elderly man who was emotionally distraught over several recent losses. Mr Jones's partner had left him, he had been forced into retirement, his pet cat had died, and because of a change on his rental agreement he was about to lose access to the small garden he had tended for the past 25 years.

Gary's social work program and placement specialized in psychodynamic casework, and Gary was expected to work with Mr Jones from this perspective. Gary met with Mr Jones and formulated a plan: counselling for the issues of loss and advocacy to try and retain Mr Jones right to his garden.

Gary's supervisor said that the plan seemed good, except the advocacy part, which did not address the issue of Mr Jones's loss. Gary objected, but his supervisor insisted that advocacy would not help Mr Jones with his distress, and she said that if Gary's work did not help Mr Jones with his loss, Gary might not pass his placement.

Several forms of power are at play in this situation. By the end of the chapter you should be able to name them all, you will be able to identify the way power operates in social work, and you will have developed strategies to address this. At the end of the chapter June will share how she would have approached issues of power in this placement and in the Mr Jones case if she had been Gary's field site advisor.

We focus on power in this chapter because power is central in almost everything that happens in the social world. Bertrand Russell said, "the fundamental concept in social science is Power, in the same sense in which Energy is the fundamental concept in physics" (Russell, 1996/1938, p. 4). If a social worker is unable to see where and how power operates in the issues they are addressing, they will fail to understand much of what is occurring.

We have already spoken about power. In Chapter 1 we talked about the way power turns prejudice into oppression, and in Chapter 2 we explored the power of ideas. But what is power and how does it operate? If you do not know, you will not be able to recognize, resist, or use power; your social work abilities will be compromised; and you will fail to understand much of what is occurring in the social world. This chapter helps you understand power and what it is.

## Key Concept

Power in the social world is the same as energy in the physical world—nothing happens without it. Power is the ability of someone or some group to get their way, even when opposed by others.

## The Machinery of Power, Influence, and Control

Max Weber developed one of the first sociological definitions of power, which he defines as "the ability of an actor or actors to realize his/her/their will in a social action, even against the will of others" (translated from original German by Roscigno, 2011, p. 350). Said differently, power is the ability of someone or some group to get their own way, even against opposition.

Weber saw power as either coercive or authoritative, with both being exercised top down and enacted through some form of leadership. Weber saw **coercive power** as getting one's own way through the use of threat or force, and **authoritative power** as getting one's own way by persuading others of one's **legitimacy**, which is having others accept one's right to rule or be in charge. Legitimacy is usually established through either a charismatic leader whom people follow because of their personality, a traditional leader such as a monarch whom people follow because it is taken for granted that they should rule, or a rational-legal leader whom people follow because they agree to a social contract such as parliamentary democracy. These leadership models are "ideal types" (a concept we explained in Chapter 1), so keep in mind that they are caricatures of leadership and in reality each type of leadership blurs into another, as do coercive and authoritative power.

Weber's work on power has been complemented by the work of several other theorists. We review below some of those theories, focusing on those that we believe best explain the way power operates in social work and in society. We begin with Lukes (1974, 2005), who expanded Weber's ideas by seeing power operating in three dimensions.

## Lukes's Model of Power

Lukes's **first dimension of power** is exercised through coercion (see Table 3.1). When this power is used, the person or group with the ability to cause negative consequences for others uses this ability to make others do something they would not ordinarily do, or prevents them from doing something that they want to do. The most obvious example of this power is enforcing laws through policing. When this power is used, the person being forced knows that coercion is being used and that they are on the receiving end of somebody else's power. This form of power is visible, and it has to be, because it operates through constant reminders that non-compliance will bring some form of sanction. Uniformed police officers and security guards are a reminder of such power. This type of power is not always a bad thing. The police are there to "serve and protect," but in part they are also serving and protecting those with power by keeping in place the type of social order that those with power determine should be so.

Lukes's **second dimension of power** is exercised through manipulating agendas and decision-making processes. When this power is used, people are either completely excluded from decision-making forums and meetings, or if they are invited and included, it is to address an agenda or choose among options that those with power have set in advance. Another way that this type of exclusion occurs is by those with power not inviting the people they wish to exclude, or if they do invite them, ensuring that they do not have the information they need to participate or are not given the opportunity to speak.

When people are excluded in this manner, they are usually aware that power is being used to exclude them. Sometimes people accept the use of this power. For instance, people know that they cannot take part in most parliamentary debates, government cabinet meetings, or company board meetings. People tend to accept being excluded from making decisions in such forums because they accept the legitimacy of the state to rule

**Table 3.1** Lukes's Three Dimensions of Power

| Power Dimension | Description of Power |
| --- | --- |
| 1. Coercion | A group or person has the ability to cause a negative outcome for others and they use this to force others into compliance. Those being forced know that power is being used over them. |
| 2. Controlling agendas | A group or person has the ability to control agendas and exclude others from decision making. Those being excluded know that power is being used to exclude them. |
| 3. Controlling the way others see the world | A group or person has the ability to control the way others see the world, and they use this to ensure that people only think and imagine in ways that the controlling person or group determines. Those being influenced in this way are unaware that power is being used and that they are being controlled. |

and boards of directors to make company decisions. If people try to question this authority by shouting opinions from the public gallery in Parliament, trying to force their way into a cabinet or board meeting, or engaging in public protest, they may find that the second dimension of power quickly resorts to the first.

Lukes is best known for his **third dimension of power**, in which those with power control the way others see the world (Lukes, 1974, 2005). This type of power causes people to voluntarily think and do what those with power want, because those being controlled do not

"I questioned authority, and then authority questioned *me!*"

**Figure 3.1** When the second dimension of power becomes the first

even imagine acting in any other way. This is the ultimate form of power, because it is completely invisible. There is no need to coerce, control agendas, or to exclude anyone from decision making. Indeed, those with this kind of power can simply hand over agendas and decisions to the people, because the people will pursue only the possibilities that those with power allow them to imagine.

## French and Raven's Model of Power

Lukes's ideas about power are complemented by French and Raven, who developed a taxonomy that describes six sources of power (Feather & Boeckmann, 2013; Smith & Fink, 2015). French and Raven's ideas are more complex than Lukes's, but we feel compelled to include them because their model has dominated the way organizations and social scientists have conceptualized social power for over 50 years (Elias, 2008).

French and Raven initially identified five bases of power (French & Raven, 1959): coercion, reward, legitimacy, expert, and reference; later they added a sixth dimension, informational power (Raven, 1965). French and Raven argue that these six forms of power constitute the elements of social control, which is "the process by which members of a social entity are influenced to adhere to values and principles of proper behavior deemed appropriate for that social entity" (Raven, 1999, p. 162). In other words, these forms of power explain why people comply with governments and other forms of authority, why they follow social norms, and why people are reluctant to rise up in revolution even when trod down. Table 3.2 is our interpretation of these dimensions.

French and Raven's model and Lukes's model overlap and complement each other. Lukes's first dimension is similar to French and Raven's concepts of coercion and reward. French and Raven's concepts of legitimacy, expert, and reference overlap Lukes's second

**Table 3.2** French and Raven's Bases of Social Power

| Power Dimension | Description of Power |
| --- | --- |
| 1. Coercion | A group or person has the ability to cause a negative outcome for others and they use this to force others into compliance. Those being forced know that power is being used over them. |
| 2. Reward | A group or person has the ability to cause a positive outcome for others and they use this to cause others to comply. Those being controlled in this way are usually aware that power is being used over them. |
| 3. Legitimacy | A group or person causes others to believe that they have a right to be in charge. People accept this and the power this affords the group or person who has taken charge. People are aware that they are being controlled, but give up control voluntarily. |
| 4. Knowledge | A group or person causes others to believe that they hold superior knowledge and should therefore be in charge. People accept this proposition and allow the person or group to make decisions. People are aware that they have given control to this person or group but think this is best, because the individual or group with power knows best. |
| 5. Reference | A group or person causes people to identify with them, and people follow them because of this identification. People are aware that they follow the group/person, but do so because they believe in the group/person or the cause that group/person represents. |
| 6. Informational | A group or person holds power that people need, so people comply because they need access to the information. This is somewhat like knowledge power; people comply because they rely on access to the information that a group or person provides. |

and third dimensions of controlling agendas or controlling people's consciousness. Which of these it falls within depends on whether the person being controlled unconditionally accepts the control they are under, or whether they recognize and question the legitimacy, expertise, and information being used to control them.

Although Lukes, and also French and Raven, separate power into multiple types, in reality these types of power overlap. Consequently, when looking for the way power is operating in a situation, one should not only look for the distinct ways these forms of power operate independently from each other, but also look for the ways they interact and reinforce each other.

## Power Over, Power To, and Power With

Power, especially when used by social workers, is sometimes divided into three types: power over, power to, and power with. These conceptualizations do not focus so much on the mechanics of power and where it comes from, but instead on how it is used.

## Power Over

**Power over** is usually thought of as a negative form of **domination** (rule or control) over those who are subordinate (Holms, 2000). Power over, however, is not always negative. At times power over can be used in a way that stops domination, for instance, the police stopping a murder, or the corrections system keeping a violent rapist behind bars and off the streets. Even in less dramatic situations, power over can liberate. For example, when we drive on the roads or walk on the sidewalk, the police using the negative power of coercion to stop reckless or speeding motorists gives us all the positive freedom to remain safe when we travel. Although power over is appropriate in these and similar circumstances, in other situations it is not, especially when it holds mechanisms of oppression in place.

## Power To

**Power to** involves someone with power enabling another person to do something that they would not ordinarily be able to do. Power to has some characteristics of power over, because the person with power usually holds some kind of authority over the person they are helping; however, instead of using that power to hold the person back, the power is used to move them forward in a way that is productive and transformative. Swartz (2007) uses the example of the teacher-and-student relationship. This could be viewed as a relationship of domination because the teacher instructs the student who is dependent on the teacher for knowledge. But when *power to* is used, the teacher's power becomes productive and transformative. The student grows intellectually and personally and becomes able to do things that they would not have been able to do without the teacher's help.

## Power With

**Power with** is a form of power that is non-hierarchical, co-operative, collaborative, and relational (Berman & Buren, 2015; Whipps, 2014). This way of conceptualizing power became popular in social work after Mary Parker Follett (1868–1933), an American social worker, demonstrated how it helps avoid an overdependence on power over by using power organically in the moment (Berman & Buren, 2015; Whipps, 2014). In power with, there is no winner on either side and there is also no compromise, since it enables new values and desires to emerge based on the differences created from the influence of each actor's view. The integration finds a new resolution where the desires of the different parties are not only met, but also come together to work as a whole (Whipps, 2014). This type of power is important in social work because the oppressed usually lack voice in society, but when power with is at play, social workers ensure that "all parties come to the discussion as equals in terms of responsibility, voice and authority. The power develops together as they take action together" (Whipps, 2014, p. 416) in a way that creates genuine participation by all (Berman & Buren, 2015).

## How Power Operates in Social Work

All of the models above help us identify some of the ways power operates in social work. For instance, Mr Jones (the case we began the chapter with) was forced to retire and was barred from having access to his garden. As a result, Mr Jones faced what French and Raven, and Lukes, would describe as coercion. Indeed, under the legislation at that time, Mr Jones's employer had the power to force him to retire because he was over 65 years old, and the housing authority had the ability to change, without his consent, the rental agreement that gave him access to his garden.

Mr Jones was also impacted by other forms of power. Mr Jones was excluded from decision-making processes (Lukes's second dimension). The most obvious decisions Mr Jones was excluded from were decisions about the age of retirement and decisions about the rules governing rental agreements. But there were other less obvious decisions Mr Jones was being excluded from too. Mr Jones was given no say in the nature of the social work services he was receiving. Mr Jones had agreed with Gary's basic plan, but he had no access to the decision-making meeting of Gary's supervisor or the agency that set the parameters of that plan. Here power through *exclusion from decision making* was overlapping with the power of *expert knowledge*. Indeed, Gary's supervisor, and those who set the type of social work the agency delivered, believed that they knew best what service users need. All of these forms of power play a role in excluding service users from decision making (Kemp, 2012).

Also interwoven in the Mr Jones case, several forms of power were unfolding in Gary's relationship with his supervisor. Gary believed that his supervisor was using what Lukes, and also French and Raven, would describe as *coercion* to force him to abandon the advocacy plan (i.e., change your plan or you may not pass your placement). Intermingled with the threat of this negative consequence was the offer of what French and Raven would call *reward* (change your plan and you are more likely to pass your placement).

Although Gary believed power was being used over him in the form of coercion, his supervisor saw this differently. From the supervisor's perspective, she was using *legitimacy* and *expertise*, and there was an expectation that she would use these and other forms of power to ensure what she believed were in the best interests of Mr Jones. Did Gary really think he knew better than his supervisor? Perhaps the clinical expertise and experience of the supervisor meant that she knew best. Was Gary's supervisor exercising *power over* him, or *power with* Mr Jones? Perhaps as a teacher she was using *power to* enable Gary to become a competent social worker.

## Key Concept

Just because power is at play, do not automatically assume that it is a bad thing. Even *power over* someone might be *power with* someone else. The question is not whether power is at play, because power is always at play. The question is who is using power, and for what purpose.

Our analysis of power in Mr Jones's case is focused primarily on power at a micro level between individuals, combined with some mezzo analysis of the power Mr Jones's workplace and the housing department have over him. These forms of power exist in a broader macro political context that shaped Mr Jones's life, his present circumstances, and the role the various actors in Mr Jones's life were playing. As social workers, you must grasp these larger political contexts. We need to ask who governs the rules that Mr Jones and the rest of us live by, how these contributed to Mr Jones's predicament, and also how they shaped the social work he received.

# Power and Ruling Relations

Mr Jones is being dominated. That is why he has to retire and give up his garden. But where there is domination there is always the potential to act and have agency (Haugaard, 2010). The term **agency** means the power to do something. In this instance it means not giving in to housing departments or retirement policies, but to grasp power and resist—to push back at the system and initiate change. The potential of this type of power is always present, because if there were no power to resist, there would be no need for the power to dominate.

But just how accessible is the power to push back at the system? Surely we all have access to this power because we live in a **democracy,** which is a political system in which we all get to have a say in who rules and how they govern (Haugaard, 2010). But how "democratic" is democracy, and who really governs what we regard as democratic societies? This question interests us as social workers because, if we are going to use *power to* or *with* service users, we need a basic understanding of the way power operates in political contexts.

## Who Governs?

The question of who governs has troubled social scientists for years. In what is now regarded as a classic debate within political science, Robert Dahl (1961), a political theorist at Yale University, claimed that there were many powerful groups in society who compete to influence government. This system is called **poliarchy**, which means rule by many people. Because rule operates through many people (through interest groups), a form of **pluralism** operates, which means that a constant push and pull among competing interest groups attempting to influence government ensure that no one group dominates, and in this manner democracy works, and tyranny is prevented (Son, 2015). In other words, the will of the people shapes government decisions through the power of interest groups.

C. Wright Mills, a sociologist at Columbia University, claimed that Dahl got this wrong. Mills claimed that America was governed by an anonymous **power elite** who operated behind closed doors using what Lukes (1974, 2005) would later describe as the second dimension of power, which is domination through controlling agendas (Mills, 1956). Mills did not refer to the power elite as a ruling class, but a number of Marxist scholars at the time considered this elite to be a ruling class in the Marxist sense (Barrow, 2007).

## The Ruling Class

Marx referred to the **ruling class** as the **bourgeoisie**, which is a French term originally used to describe middle-class manufacturers and owners of industry. According to Marx, the bourgeoisie were initially friends of the oppressed, because they led a revolution in France that overthrew the feudal system in which kings and lords ruled over land and exploited the serfs and peasants who worked for them.

The bourgeoisie certainly helped usher in a new system, **capitalism**, where industrialization and a free market enabled wealth to be produced by factories and industry (Felluga, 2015). This meant that the bourgeoisie became the new ruling class, because they owned the means of production, and pretty soon they were exploiting those who worked for them. Exploitation was possible because the **proletariat**, which is a French term used to describe the working class, could only survive by selling their **labour power** (work) to the ruling class, who made profit from their **surplus labour**, which is profit from the goods they produced. The pushing down of workers and the inflation of the cost of goods is also caused by value being distorted through **commodity fetishism**, which is a replacement of human relationships with the value of money and commodities.

Marx predicted that the proletariat will one day revolt against the bourgeoisie, just like the bourgeoisie did against the aristocracy (Ypi, 2014). Marx not only predicts this future, he also explains the past; as such his ideas form a grand theory (Aakvaag, 2013). The term **grand theory** was coined by C. Wright Mills (1959, 2000) to describe attempts to explain all human history and the entire social order. Marx does exactly that; he attempts to explain the evolution of societies and political systems throughout the ages. Marx's ideas are on the left of the political compass we examined in Chapter 2, and also toward the authoritarian position, because Marx envisions that, after the revolution in which the proletariat takes power, a new state will play an active role managing the economy on behalf of the people. Marx, however, also anticipates after an initial period of leadership, a **communist society** emerging, in which there is no longer a need for any form of authoritative state control.

Although Marx's ruling class is similar to what Mills calls a power elite, they are not the same. Mills deliberately stepped away from a Marxist class analysis to recognize that it is not simply those who own the means of production who rule, but military leaders, bankers, politicians, and others also rule through interwoven interests and power within existing systems of social relations. In more recent language, those who benefit the most from these ruling relations are called the 1%, and the context they operate in is referred to as neo-liberalism and globalization.

## Ruling Ideologies: Neo-Liberalism and Globalization

**Neo-liberalism** is defined by McKenzie and Wharf (2015) as an "increased reliance on the free market over government programs and regulation, reduced public expenditures, particularly for social programs, and the expansion of free trade agreements with provisions that include disproportionate benefits for multinational corporations" (p. 20).

Neo-liberalism is located toward the right and libertarian position of the political compass discussed in Chapter 2. Neo-liberalism influences societal attitudes and views toward those who are in need of support, because the idea of neo-liberalism is that minimal government intervention and a free market produce an efficient and fair society. As a result, a neo-liberal view is that individuals and families should be self-reliant and any support from the state should be a last resort (McKenzie & Wharf, 2015).

**Globalization** is the way in which nation-states around the world are politically, economically, and socially interconnected in a worldwide market so that any decision made in one nation-state will have an impact on others. The effect of globalization is that governments respond to the demands of corporations, because it is no longer simply the working class, but also nations and the world economy, that depend on those who own the means of production. From this perspective, it is not governments that have the power to rule, but global corporations (Rice & Prince, 2013).

Despite these theories, it seems to us that it is not simply corporations that rule, but an idea or an ideology, which in this context means a set of ideas about how social relations, politics, and economics ought to operate. In a sense, an ideology is a close relative to a paradigm, but with an emphasis on doing rather than thinking. The ideology that rules is neo-liberalism, and the doing part of this ideology is anything and everything that maintains the conditions in which corporations can thrive in a global context. These conditions are ensured by enacting doctrines, which we consider to be similar to an ideology, but are more formal statements of these beliefs, such as a free market and government intervention to ensure the well-being and continued profitability of the corporations on which they depend. We will return to examine neo-liberalism in Chapter 8 when we discuss poverty, the world order, and ruling relations.

## Key Concept

It is not simply corporations that rule, but an idea or an ideology that benefits corporations. In a sense, the primary product of multinational corporations is an ideology.

## A Challenge to the Ruling Elite: We Are the 99%

Very few benefit from the existing economic and political system. Inequality and disparity in wealth is increasing at an extraordinary rate. *The Guardian* reports that the top 1% of the world's population owns more wealth than the other 99% (Elliott & Pilkington, 2015). *Fortune* magazine contests this 1% vs. 99% ratio, but admits that disparity of wealth is so great that the "statistics that describe the magnitude of economic inequality are stark" (Matthews, 2015). In a bizarre act of journalistic illogic, even though this *Fortune* article is analyzing the Occupy Wall Street Movement, it claims that the 1% vs. 99% ratio can't be right, otherwise Americans would be "taking to the streets" (Matthews, 2015). If the Occupy Movement was not Americans taking to the streets, what was it?

The **Occupy Movement** took to the streets to protest these inequalities. Occupy began in 2011, after the world financial crisis of 2008 when governments spent billions of tax-payer's monies to bail out the bankers who helped create the crisis, and to bail out the industries that were suffering from it (Congleton, 2009; Herbst, 2013). This bailout drew attention to the way governments provide financial support to the rich and very little to the poor. This is a form of **corporate welfare,** which Harrington (1997) refers to as social-ism for the rich (government intervention to help the fate of the rich) and capitalism for the poor (letting the market decide the fate of the poor). In a growing discontent about this situation, a Tumblr post that coined the term "we are the 99%" sparked the Occupy Wall Street protests in New York City's Zuccoti Park that soon spread to over 80 countries around the world, including Canada (Chou, 2015).

We have some issues with the idea of "occupy"; it is a poor choice of words for a social justice movement in a North American context where Indigenous land is already occupied by settlers (Thomas-Muller, 2013). But aside from a lack of attention to this type of imper-ialism, the movement drew attention to key issues such as growing income inequality and shrinking opportunity (Stiglitz, 2011), the fact that there is a direct relationship between the wealth of the top 1% and the poverty of the 99% (Northridge, 2012), and the injustice inherent in governments meeting the needs of the 1% at the expense of the 99% (Chou, 2015). The movement also developed new ways of thinking about democracy (Chou, 2015) and began to enact this as they thought through issues about alternate ways power can be used and how leadership can emerge from the grassroots.

Many of the issues raised by the Occupy Movement were discussed by Russell Brand in his BBC interview with Jeremy Paxman (2013). We do not agree with everything Brand says, and we take exception to some of his comments, but there is something to be learned in some of the points he makes. Review this interview and the points Brand and Paxton make in the following exercise.

## Exercise 3.1

### Russell Brand and Jeremy Paxman on Politics and Power

If possible, do this exercise in groups. Make sure you have 30 minutes to spare.

Comedian and actor Russell Brand was asked to be the guest editor of an issue of the *New Statesman* political magazine (Brand, 2013). He was subsequently inter-viewed by BBC journalist Jeremy Paxman about his political ideas. While we do not agree with all of Brand's ideas, he does debate many of the ruling relation ideas we have addressed above, and he argues that voting in elections makes us complicit in oppression.

1.  Watch the Paxman-Brand interview at https://youtu.be/3YR4CseY9pk.
2.  Discuss Brand's proposition that voting makes us complicit in oppression. What is your opinion on this issue and why?
3.  If Brand and others we discussed in the text preceding this exercise box are correct that the current political system is a façade that operates in the interests of a corporate elite or a ruling class, what form of power do you think holds this in place?

## The Power to Shape the Way the World Is Understood

It strikes us as odd that many people did not know what the Occupy Movement aims were, because these aims were clearly articulated, and the Occupy Movement's claims about growing societal inequity were backed by considerable empirical data. Several forms of power were used to silence the message of the Occupy Movement.

Coercive power was used to stop and silence protestors. An inquiry into the Occupy Wall Street protests by law schools at NYU, Fordham, Harvard, and Stanford universities found that the New York Police Department broke American and international laws in their attempts to suppress the protest, which included excessive and inappropriate use of force and surveillance that violated the private lives of protestors (Friedersdorf, 2012). Such power not only shuts down protest, it also stops protest from beginning or taking hold. June and Gary considered going to the Occupy Toronto event but were concerned about being arrested simply for showing up. Gary did attend, and though the Toronto police did not engage in the overt suppression of protest that had been evident in New York, a number of Canadian protestors were clearly concerned about this. Some carried signs such as "I have class on Monday . . . please don't arrest me," and "peaceful protester." We wonder how many people want to raise concerns about unfairness in the existing social order, but do not because they fear the consequences.

In addition to coercive power being used to stop the message getting out, another type of power was used to stop the message being heard. As mentioned above, *Fortune* (Matthews, 2015) refused to recognize that the Occupy Movement was "America taking to the streets" about an issue of inequality. How could so many people in the USA, Canada, and all around the world protest, while media outlets like *Fortune* refused to acknowledge that this was people "taking to the streets"? And how could so many people and institutions claim that they did not understand why this was happening?

We suggest that Lukes's (2005) third dimension of power, the power to control the way people see the world, explains why the Occupy Movement was misunderstood. Lukes's ideas are not Marxist, but to some extent Lukes explains the power behind **false**

Both photos by Gary C. Dumbrill

**Figure 3.2** Occupy comes to Canada

Reprinted with permission of Jim Morin and Morintoons Syndicate.

**Figure 3.3** Occupy: What do you stand for?

**consciousness**, which is a concept Marx used to explain the way the oppressed fail to understand their own oppression. There is a false consciousness when a group (class) of people oppressed by an unfair system do not recognize that the system is unfair. The opposite of a false consciousness is class consciousness. According to Marx, when people develop a **class consciousness**, they recognize that they are oppressed as a group (class), and revolution becomes possible.

Clearly those occupying Wall Street had a consciousness about their shared oppression—maybe not a singular "class" consciousness in the classical Marxist sense, but certainly an understanding that the existing social order is not fair. Those with this consciousness who were protesting were subjected to coercive power in Lukes's first dimension, with the police trying to shut down the protests.

One might speculate that those who did not understand the Occupy protests had no class consciousness. One might argue that they were subjected to Lukes's third dimension of power that limits the way they think. Alternatively, one might argue that instead of being subjected to power, those who claimed they did not understand the Occupy Movement were actually exercising power. Indeed, perhaps those "claiming" to not understand the Occupy Movement did grasp issues of class but deliberately refused to acknowledge and name these issues. Refusing to name issues, or to even acknowledge that Americans, Canadians, and others around the world had "taken to the streets" in protest, suppresses the development of ideas about the need for change. As such, refusing to name issues prevents the type of full-blown revolution that might occur if the entire 99% ever gained a class consciousness about inequality.

## Postmodernism and Power

Another way of understanding power is the way it is understood within postmodernism. The term **postmodern** means "after modern." It is a rejection of the ideas of **modernity,** which emerged in the Enlightenment and emphasized the importance of rationality, individualism, reason, and a belief that science will eventually answer all questions and make human progress inevitable (Sim, 2011).

In contrast to modernism, postmodernism contends that there is no absolute truth. Postmodernists contend that we do not consider things to be truth because they represent some immutable reality, but because people with power cause us to regard them as true (Fillingham, 1993). For the postmodernist, power is not simply held and wielded by a power or class elite, but instead power is everywhere. From a postmodern perspective, power emerges in a **discursive** process, which is the act of creating a **discourse,** which is a term used to refer to the way "we make meaning of and construct our world through the language we use (verbal and non-verbal) to communicate about it" (Fook, 2012, p. 72). It is through discursive power that dominant reality comes into being. From this perspective, power is exercised and maintained through a **dominant discourse**, which is the meanings that predominate within society and the things we accept as truth.

When people do not conform to dominant meanings, they are nudged back into compliance or normativity either gently by friends and family, or by the "treatment" and intervention of social workers and psychiatrists. If these measures fail, discipline occurs through coercion from the police, by "correction" or containment by the justice system, or in some nations and states by execution. Although these more coercive forms of power are available and are often used, such as police brutality toward Occupy Movement protestors, people often engage in self-discipline by not attending such events. Alternatively, as mentioned above, people do not even grasp the reason such protests are occurring, or if they do they suppress this form of truth. For example, this may be why *Fortune* seemed to suppress the truth that Americans had taken to the streets, and in this manner the magazine helped maintain the dominant discourse that claims all is well within society.

We are not suggesting that all dominant meanings are bad, that all power is negative, or that to correct someone or something is always wrong. "Beneficial power" is also embedded in societal systems and the way we organize society (Crawford & Andreassen, 2015). But at the same time, social systems have jailed people for opposing some of the unjust ways we have organized society. Boxing champion Muhammad Ali and British writer Bertrand Russell were jailed for resisting war, and Nelson Mandela, Mahatma Gandhi, Rosa Parks, and Dr Martin Luther King Jr, were jailed for seeking civil and political rights. We could list hundreds of others who were also jailed for seeking human rights. Of course, these people were jailed not because they sought human rights, but because they broke laws. For instance, Rosa Parks was jailed because she broke a law that forced Black people to sit at the back of the bus. With history now on the side of these activists, and with us benefiting from hindsight, most people today can see why these laws and jailing these activists were wrong. But would you have seen it at the time they were jailed? Or would you have bought into the dominant discourse that jailed them as criminals? We believe that if you combine the critical thinking we discussed in the last chapter and the understanding of power this chapter provides, you will see through the dominant discourse and grasp what is right, and know when to take a stand for justice. Put it to the test. Do you understand Occupy, or is the reason the Occupy Movement claimed society was unfair and unjust a mystery to you? Not only is understanding these points essential in becoming an anti-oppressive social worker, it is essential if you want to be on the right side of history.

## Key Concept

Do not automatically assume that all dominant meanings are bad, that all power is negative, or that to correct someone or something is always wrong. These things may be oppressive, but they may not be. To understand if they are oppressive, social workers have to look deeper and think harder about the specifics.

# Pierre Bourdieu's View of Power

An additional view of power is that of Pierre Bourdieu, whose theories began to find popularity in social work about 10 years ago (Garrett, 2007a, 2007b). Dr Winnie Lo, an assistant professor of social work at Algoma University, introduced us to Bourdieu's work about five years ago. Winnie specializes in using a Bourdieuian framework to understand oppression, particularly the mechanisms through which exclusion operates. We asked Winnie to help us better understand the way Bourdieu thinks about power. Winnie explains:

> Bourdieu is interested in the less obvious forms of power. These forms of power are more resistance-proof, because by being less obvious, they are harder to resist. One way of power escaping resistance is if it is "misrecognized," (see for instance Lovell, 2007) so that even though people see it, they do not think of it as power, and do not resist it.
>
> An example of obvious power is economic power—Marx spoke of this as capital—owning a factory or a multi-national corporation. If you own a large company and if workers and even the wealth of nations depend on the industry you own, you obviously have power. To get your own way you can coerce (threaten people or states that you will move your production plants away), reward (promise people or states that you will move production to their regions and create jobs), control agendas, and even use advertising and perhaps the media to get people to see things the way you want them to.
>
> Bourdieu agrees that capital is a source of power, but he speaks of capitals in the plural not just the singular, and the things he considers to be capital are not just material. Bourdieu named several capitals: economic, cultural, social, and symbolic.
>
> **Economic capital** includes owning corporations, money, stocks, and other material assets. **Cultural capital** is a source of power based on cultural assets that include things like academic credentials that help us get ahead, and the clothes, manners, and hobbies (like golf or polo) that help us fit into elite environments. **Social capital** is any social connection (with an individual or institution) that has prestige and power. All of these forms of capital are converted into **symbolic capital** (more about symbolic capital in a moment), which is further converted into a range of material benefits (i.e., we can buy goods and services) and relational benefits (we are seen and are accepted into elite groups who hold power).
>
> All these forms of capital are mutually convertible and reinforce each other. For instance, money (economic capital) buys the type of club memberships, clothing, cars, and houses that signal wealth and prestige (cultural capital). These capitals enable access to the type of elite schools that give students the credentials, interests, and ways of acting and being (more cultural capital) that open doors to the type of careers that bring even more money (economic capital). At the same time, the elite schools, careers, club memberships, and so on enable one

to seamlessly fit in and establish friendships, relationships, and networks (social capital) with the world's rich and powerful.

All these forms of capital are symbolic—this part of Bourdieu's work can be difficult to understand. One can begin to understand capitals without understanding that they are symbolic, but if one can grasp how capitals become symbolic, one begins to see the distinct contribution Bourdieu makes to the understanding of power. In brief, capitals have power because of their capacity to *symbolize* and signal social hierarchy. This is perhaps best explained through an example.

Imagine that you hire a law firm, and the firm sends a junior law associate to represent you on an issue. A discovery meeting is set up with the opposing lawyers to review your case. Imagine your lawyer, the junior associate, attending the meeting wearing an "off the peg" $100.00 polyester suit, a Casio wristwatch, a goose down parka, and an Edmonton Oilers toque. Now imagine that the opposing lawyer, who is a managing partner of one of the nation's top law firms, arriving at the meeting wearing a $50,000 bespoke business suit, a cashmere overcoat, a $200,000 Rolex watch. This lawyer is followed into the meeting by several immaculately dressed junior associates who are assisting on the case. This opposing lawyer then mentions that they can spend only an hour in the meeting, because they have a lunchtime appointment with Prime Minister Justin Trudeau! Of course none of these things mean that this lawyer is better or more powerful than your lawyer, but if at this point you are feeling a little nervous about your case, then you are beginning to grasp what symbolic capital is.

Bourdieu's capitals operate in overlapping and interacting fields. A **field** can be a geographic region like a city or nation, or it can be a discipline like the legal profession, politics, the military, social work, or the corporate world. What gives you power in one field may not give you power in another. For instance, imagine the two lawyers we mentioned above coming to present in a social work class. In this field, the polyester suit and Casio watch of the junior associate might carry more capital and prestige than the lawyer's exhibition of conspicuous symbols of extravagant wealth, especially if the junior associate has a record of human rights work and pro-bono work for those who cannot afford to hire top law firms.

A final concept from Bourdieu that shapes power is **habitus**, which is the way we internalize what various capitals symbolize or mean in any given field. Habitus does not mean that we simply internalize and passively conform to any given field. The idea of habitus is that we also shape and influence fields, so that what the various capitals symbolize and mean in a given field shifts over time and from context to context.

Bourdieu helps us to go beyond the simplistic view Marx has of capital and a binary power struggle between two groups. Bourdieu also helps us see how power is embedded in several forms of capital, and how the power of any given capital depends on the field or context in which one is situated. Additionally, Bourdieu's concept of habitus helps us understand how we reflect and absorb the way power and capitals work in society, and how in turn we help create and reinforce these power mechanisms too.

## Key Concept

The anti-oppressive social worker needs to be able to think outside of simplistic binaries to develop a more nuanced understanding of power struggles. Bourdieu helps us do that by examining multiple types of capital and contextualizing them in fields.

Bourdieu's ideas are complex, but the world is complex, and Bourdieu's ideas are becoming increasingly important in helping social work understand that world. So if you can learn even a part of what Bourdieu is saying, this will help you make sense of the world and especially how power operates. We will return to some of these ideas in Chapter 8 when we consider the social order, but for now if you grasp that power is capital, and that capital can take many forms, this is a good point from which you can start to use Bourdieu's ideas to gain insights into the way power operates within society.

## Social Work Ruling Relations

Social work is a field that has its own capital and habitus, its own political ideologies and doctrines, and its own power mechanisms that hold these in place, sometimes at the expense of those social work serves. In many ways social work capital is made up of theory, knowledge, and practice. These are just like commodities, because they are produced and consumed by social workers and society. Careers are made, salaries paid, and billions in grants and government funding are spent on our industry.

In the same way capitalism exploits workers to produce commodities for consumption, social work can find itself exploiting people's troubles and stories by producing ideas, analysis, and intervention models for consumption. Social work academics gain prestige and promotion by producing theories and models. Social work practitioners use theories and models to explain and shape service users' lives, to gain professional prestige, and to gain the expertise to progress in their careers. Social work as a discipline and profession enjoys the privilege of being funded to speak about and address social troubles. We as social workers, therefore, need to look not only at the way governments and corporations use power to promote their own interests, we have to look at ourselves too. We do this by asking if the theories, ideas, and interventions we develop really make sense and have relevance in the world of service users.

## Theoretical Stories Social Work Tells

As much as we love theory, we have a hard time believing some of the ideas that social work produces, especially the way social work explains the origins of oppression. For instance, Mullaly (2010) contends that the structures of oppression were "originally established by and for the most part are still dominated by a particular social group—bourgeois, Christian, heterosexual males of European origin" (p. 24).

"Bourgeois, Christian, heterosexual males of European origin" certainly benefit the most from oppression today, but oppression did not "originate" with them. For instance, as mentioned above, the bourgeoisie have not always held the power to oppress, and when they gained power this was used to end the power of feudal masters. Consequently, the bourgeoisie may oppress now, but they certainly did not originate oppression.

The same is true of Christians. Christians in Western nations may benefit from the way oppression operates today, but when Christianity was founded some 2000 years ago, Christians were persecuted by the state and faced jail and execution because of their spiritual beliefs (Gwynn, 2015). Consequently, Christians could not have established oppression, when oppression pre-dates the founding of Christianity, and when early Christians were subjected to oppression.

Europeans did not originate oppression either. Long before Europeans emerged from their mud-huts and caves, great cities and empires already existed in Africa and Asia that in some instances were forged through conquest, slavery, and other forms of oppression (Eller, 2011). In fact, the idea that White European men originated oppression is somewhat Eurocentric. It seems that even anti-oppressive scholars buy into the idea that White Europeans invented everything—even oppression!

In clarifying this history we are not attempting to defend White, heterosexual, Christian, bourgeois men of European origin. This group dominates and drives oppression today—there is no denying that truth—but clearly this group did not "originate" oppression. Having an accurate understanding of history is important, because if one is going to base lessons on how to deal with oppression today on what happened yesterday, one has to get the history of yesterday right.

Anne Bishop (2015) also engages in analysis that oversimplifies both history and the present. Bishop draws a direct causal link between the emergence of human competition in some ancient prehistoric past that she says produced the notion of "class," which Bishop claims "is both the foundation and the result of all other forms of oppression" (Bishop, 2015, p. 35).

Bishop argues that once class emerged in pre-history as a result of competition, this led to ideas of separation and a hierarchy, which produced the idea of private property. These ideas resulted in people conquering other nations, to seeing animals and plants as separate from the large ecological system, to men seeing women as "things" whom men have the right to rape and force into servitude, and this then led to the destruction of gay and lesbian people. We find these linkages hard to believe. Bishop presents no evidence for this historical chain of causal events, and although we agree with Bishop about the condition we find ourselves in today, we have some difficulty buying into her grand theory of events that she claims brought us here.

## The Importance of Getting History Right

Despite our critique of Mullaly and Bishop's views of history, we value their work, and agree with much of what they say about where we find ourselves today. The problem is that errors in the stories we tell of history can create errors in the way we understand others and ourselves in the present. This becomes most evident in the way Bishop depicts Turtle Island (Canada) before colonization.

Bishop (2015) characterizes Turtle Island as a place where people "lived in peace, and each person, regardless of gender, age and ability, had the right to self-determination and everything they needed to live" (Bishop, 2015, p. 14). But this claim is not true. People had troubles in those times. The Haudenosaunee, also known as the Iroquois, tell of a time when there were "bloody wars in every village" (Porter, 2008, 274). Some say that these wars were 1000 years ago, others say 2000. Either way it was long before first contact with Europeans.

Haudenosaunee scholar Tom Porter (2008) tells how, in those times, war existed not only between the separate nations who now form the Iroquois Confederacy (Haudenosaunee), but also between the Mohawk (a part of the Iroquois Confederacy) and the Huron. In the worst of those times, a supernatural event happened: a Huron woman gave birth to a child without having sex, a child who grew to become a teacher who brought peace to the peoples (Porter, 2008). The Great Law of Peace that this teacher taught is still studied by the Haudenosaunee today (Porter, 2008). It is not our place to give details of those teachings. We tell this story to show that oppression existed on Turtle Island before Europeans arrived, and the Haudenosaunee found a way to stop it.

Portraying Turtle Island as oppression free before Europeans invaded denies the important work that Indigenous people undertook to overcome oppression in their own societies. This misrepresentation draws on the idea of the **noble savage**, an inherently racist concept that represents Indigenous peoples before European contact as childlike and living an innocent, idyllic life (Warnera & Grint, 2012). This is a little like the misrepresentation of the East by the West that Edward Said (1979, 1994) speaks of, which we referred to in Chapter 2. But instead of the West constructing itself through the misrepresentation of the East, anti-oppressive social work scholars construct their explanations of oppression by misrepresenting Indigenous peoples and the history of bourgeois, Christian, heterosexual men of European origin in order to support their own theories of oppression.

As noted above, and we cannot emphasize this enough, we *are not saying* that bourgeois, Christian, heterosexual men of European origin do not benefit the most from the way oppression operates today. We *are not saying* that social class is not an important factor in oppression. We are saying that the explanation given for why these variables count today misrepresents the past and the present for the sake of theory. We contend that in this process social work engages in a form of *consumer fetishism*, whereby it does not deal with real lives and the realities of people, but instead exploits their stories in ways that enables social work to sell its own theories as a commodity, to fuel its own ideologies, and to formulate its own texts and doctrines.

## Key Concept

Be on guard against moments when social work forgets the real lives and the realities of people it claims to serve, and instead exploits their stories in ways that enables social work to sell its own theories as commodities, to fuel its own ideologies, and to formulate its own doctrines.

Similar to capitalism, whereby the rich build fortunes by exploiting the labour of the working class to produce commodities for profit, social work exploits those trod down by oppression by producing theories about these people and their troubles that satisfy social work's own ideological, scholarly, and practice aims. We contend that a different way of conceptualizing anti-oppression is needed, a way based in knowledge and theory produced by service users themselves (more about that in later chapters). We also contend that anti-oppression needs to be driven by a politics and power based in love.

# The Power of Love

Dr Martin Luther King Jr said, "Power at its best is love implementing the demands of justice, and justice at its best is power correcting everything that stands against love" (King, 1967, p. 578). King is not talking about a sentimental or a romantic love, but about a type of caring for others that is reflected and interwoven in a number of similar teachings and philosophies from around the world. In Africa such teachings are called Ubuntu (Tutu, 2011); the Haudenosaunee call it Ganigonhi:oh, which is often translated as "a good mind" (Newhouse, 2013); the Anishnawbe refer to the Seven Grandfathers'/Grandmothers' Teachings (Baskin, 2011), also known as the Seven Sacred Teachings (Baskin, 2016); and almost every world religion has something similar to "the golden rule" (Dumbrill, 2011). We do not suggest that all these teachings and philosophies are the same. They are all quite different, but each contains a responsibility that we have toward the Other.

**Ubuntu** has definitions embedded in differing African nations and traditions (Buqa, 2015). Desmond Tutu sees Ubuntu as a way of being that he describes as "Umntu ngumtu ngabantu" (Tutu, 2011, p. 21), which Buqa (2015) translates as "a person is a person through other persons" (p. 4). Battle (1997) explains this as meaning "individuals have no existence apart from their relations with other persons" (p. 50). As such, Ubuntu places a responsibility to care for the other, and from this place of caring, community and humanity grow, without which one's own personhood does not exist (Ngcoya, 2015).

European scholars have come to similar conclusions. We are not claiming that European and African understandings of these ideas are the same. Instead we suggest that African thinkers know a universal truth about humanity that European scholars have begun to discover, or perhaps rediscover. For instance, Emmanuel Levinas argues that one does not exist apart from others (Crowell, 2015; Levinas, 1989; Levinas & Kearney, 1986). As a result, Levinas considers the responsibility to the other paramount, the first responsibility, the first ethic, which means that one's "ethical response to my fellow human being is the lens through which all other philosophical questions must be addressed" (Crowell, 2015, p. 564).

Larner (2008) explains the implications of Levinas's teaching. The "ethical response is to put the relation to the other before knowledge or theory of being. To be face to face with another person overwhelms all our concepts and theorizing, and evokes an infinite experience of responsibility" (Larner, 2008, p. 353). Larner means that because our relationship with others makes us human, our relationship with others is more important than all of our theories and ideologies. In other words, it is our relationship to other people that produces humanity, especially our relationship to people who are different from us, because otherwise the world (humanity) would just be a mirror image of ourselves.

In fact, if all the other people in the world were just like us, we would not exist as individuals. Each of us would not be unique. Consequently we owe our own sense of self and being to the Other who is not like us. Because we owe our individuality to the Other who is different, Levinas says, "To be in relation with the other face to face is to be unable to kill" (cited by Larner, 2008, p. 353). The "killing" Levinas refers to is not a physical killing, but a "killing" by denying the alterity (difference) of the Other, a killing by imposing on others what we believe is normal. This includes "killing" by misrepresenting the stories and histories of the Other in a way that denies their realities and absorbs their stories into the ontologies, epistemologies, and theories that we have developed to explain the world in a way that meets our personal or professional needs.

## Key Concept

Social workers need to remember that because it is our relationship with others that makes us human, our relationship with others is more important than all of our theories and ideologies.

We see similar ideas about our responsibility to the Other in the teachings of Indigenous peoples. Again we are not saying that all these teachings are the same, but we do wonder if all these teachings share some underlying universal truths. For instance, consider the Anishnawbe Seven Sacred Teachings (Baskin, 2016) and the Haudenosaunee teaching of the Good Mind (Newhouse, 2013), which contain values about the relation of the self and Other.

Indigenous teachings are difficult to learn outside an Indigenous context. The ideas of Levinas can also be difficult to learn unless one is already familiar with the European philosophical context Levinas works within. Ubuntu is also difficult to understand outside the African context it was developed within (Praeg, 2014). We make no claim to do justice to any of these teachings. However, it seems clear to us that all of these teachings place on us a responsibility toward the Other. We take this position as the starting point of all social work. Baskin explains how the Anishnawbe tradition takes this up:

> My understanding is that the Seven Sacred Teachings are about ethics. Love is one of these ethics, but it has a different connotation than it has for mainstream society. In Indigenous world views, love is about connectedness. In my experience, students can relate to this concept within social work and discuss it. They acknowledge that a relationship is being built between the social worker and the service user, and they acknowledge that it is okay to care about people who we are working with. (Baskin, 2016, p. 181)

While the teachings of the Seven Grandfathers/Grandmothers is not a part of our tradition, this part of the teaching Baskin shares resonates with us because we are human. We suggest that similar to us, even if this teaching is not a part of your tradition, it is likely to resonate with teaching you may know by some other name or tradition that you relate to. If your teaching is similar, and if it is centred on love, we contend that this power can be used to inform how you do social work.

Keep in mind that when we refer to "love" we are referring to a doing love rather than a feeling love. We often hear people respond to oppression by saying that "love is the answer," and then doing absolutely nothing to stop oppression other than feeling "sorry" for the oppressed. Make no mistake. Anything that stops at feelings is not love—it is an excuse for doing nothing. The love we speak knows no excuses. It is a love that always drives action.

Philosopher and anti-oppression scholar Paulo Freire makes it clear than unless love generates freedom, "it is not love" (Freire, 2012, p. 90). Freire says that "love is commitment to others. No matter where the oppressed are found, the act of love is commitment to their cause—the cause of liberation" (Freire, 2012, p. 89). Peter McLaren (2000) says that such love, "in this Freirean sense, becomes the oxygen of revolution" (p. 172). By **revolution** we mean social change, and of course the type of change we are interested in is one that ends oppression. We concur with Freire, and McLauren, that love is the key to this type of change. Commenting on the work of Freire, Darder (2017) describes this love in the following way:

> . . . a love that is never about absolute consensus, or unconditional acceptance, or unceasing words of sweetness, or endless streams of hugs and kisses. Instead it is a love without constriction, rooted in a committed willingness of struggle persistently with purpose in our life and to intimately connect that purpose with what he [Freire] called our "true vocation"—to be human. (p. 40)

We contend that without such love anti-oppression is meaningless. Revolution based on this type of love will invariably bring anti-oppression, but revolution without love will invariably replace one form of oppression with another.

# Mr Jones's Case Analysis

Having reviewed several theories of power, we return to Mr Jones's case that we discussed at the start of this chapter. What would June do if she were the field-site advisor?

Field-site advisors play a role in overseeing social work placements. The student spends time at an agency placement supervised by someone at that agency who works in the field. The placement and supervision are an opportunity for the student to put the theory and ideas they learn in school into practice. Such placements are crucial because social work is not simply a thinking academic discipline, it is also a doing occupation. Social workers are expected to combine knowledge, skills, and attitudes to help service users. The field placement is where these three elements come together in practice. The field supervisor has primary responsibility to help and ensure that this learning comes together.

A field-site advisor is usually a faculty member from the student's social work program who liaises with the student and field supervisor to ensure the placement is progressing satisfactorily, and will try to help if the placement runs into trouble. In addition, the field-site advisor usually visits the placement to make sure the student is learning the lessons they need to learn to become a qualified social worker.

For June to address this situation successfully, she would want to be aware of and navigate the types of power already at play in this situation. We have already reviewed some of the forms of power operating in the Jones case earlier in this chapter. Can you name these and any other forms of power that are operating? Do so in the following exercise.

## Exercise 3.2

### Identifying Power

If possible, undertake this exercise as a group.

1. Review Mr Jones's case. List each form of power you can identify in the case, and name the interests that this power seems to be serving.
2. When June meets with Gary and his supervisor, what power issues does she need to be mindful of?
3. Compare your answers with our analysis.

## June's Analysis

There is a potential for a power struggle to occur in the field-site meeting between Gary and his supervisor. June would try to pre-emptively defuse this by turning the focus away from Gary's and his supervisor's needs or views, and onto the needs and views of Mr Jones.

June would use this refocusing to avoid the meeting being one in which Gary or his supervisor try to "win" a debate on case direction. June would set the objective as Mr Jones being the "winner." This refocusing should be relatively easy, because the supervisory process is one that ought to already be focused on helping Mr Jones overcome whatever internal feelings or external constraints he is currently struggling with. In framing the meeting this way June would be using a *power with* perspective. She would expect Gary and his supervisor to do so too, in a process where everyone has a voice, and everyone is heard, with no winner on either side (except for Mr Jones).

Although the meeting is ultimately about Mr Jones, it needs to be noticed that Mr Jones is not present. There may be good reason to exclude Mr Jones from this meeting because the meeting focuses on the supervisory process and the issue of Gary learning to be a social worker. But as the entire purpose of the social work process is the service users' needs, we need to ask, "Where is the place for the service users' voices?"

Service users' voices are rarely heard in supervisory meetings. In these settings social workers decide what service users need and the direction that social work takes. As a result, the power at play in this process is not simply exclusion, but also expertise, with social workers knowing (or believing they know) what is best for service users. June would recognize that the absence of Mr Jones meant that the power of professional expertise was operating in the meeting. June would be careful to not let her focus on Mr Jones threaten or undermine the expert opinions and knowledge in the room. After all, the placement had been selected because the agency and the supervisors *really do* have expert skills and abilities to help, so June would want to draw on this expertise and not undermine it.

Aside from being excluded from the field-site meeting, there are several other forms of power impacting Mr Jones, such as the requirement that he retire (this is a form of ageism) and the housing authority demanding that he give up his garden. It is unclear whether forcing Mr Jones to give up his garden results from a form of oppression, or whether it is simply something that was unfair, but either way it seems unjust and this is why Gary wants to fight it through advocacy—something his supervisor opposes.

Gary is expected by his supervisor to help Mr Jones adjust to his losses by offering in-depth counselling. This is the type of service the agency offers, and this is what Gary is supposed to be learning. June would ask Gary if the idea to fight the loss of Mr Jones's garden with advocacy is Mr Jones's or Gary's agenda. June would ask where Mr Jones's voice is in this plan. If fighting is what Mr Jones wants, June would ask Gary why he had not referred Mr Jones to an agency that specialized in this work rather than taking it on himself under the umbrella of his placement agency that does not specialize in this type of advocacy. June would ask how taking on an advocacy role outside the expertise of the agency would help Mr Jones. If Mr Jones did want advocacy and not counselling, June would suggest that a referral to someone who specializes in advocacy be made, but would reiterate the question Gary's supervisor asked about how this will help Mr Jones deal with the considerable grief he is struggling with over multiple losses, especially when managing these feelings was the reason he came to the agency.

June would also ask similar critical questions about counselling and whether managing grief caused by loss was Mr Jones's agenda. If counselling was Mr Jones's agenda, June would also raise the possibility that Gary considered about whether, despite grief and loss being the primary focus, the loss of the garden might be avoided, and whether Mr Jones might be open to a referral for advocacy on this issue.

Although June would address the placement issues by examining the case that caused the issues to arise, her role as a field-site advisor is not to address cases, but to address learning. Once the case conflict is resolved, she would want to invite Gary to reflect on the lessons he learned from this process.

## Chapter Summary

In this chapter we considered how nothing happens in the social world unless driven by power. We began by exploring the machinery of power in Lukes's model, and also the model offered by French and Raven. From there we explored power at the personal and political levels and examined several theories of power as we introduced concepts such as capitalism, socialism, neo-liberalism, globalization, and competing ideas of democracy. We also introduced postmodern ideas of power, and we looked at the way Pierre Bourdieu conceptualizes power operating through capitals within a context of fields and habitus. We concluded by exploring the power of love. We do not want you to misunderstand the power of love; we are not saying all we have to do is love each other and oppression will end. The love we speak of is a call to action, based on the responsibility to the other—it is a doing love, not a feeling or sentimental love.

## Discussion Question

When Gary was a student he learned many things from the Mr Jones case about the way power operates in society and in social work. Discuss and put into your own words the main lessons you think Gary learned, or should have learned, from this case. Also, discuss the lessons *you* have learned from this case.

## Activity

We ended this chapter by looking at power in relation to a single case. Much of the chapter, however, has been on power at a political and societal level. Doing anti-oppression hinges on understanding the way all levels of power operate together, and the way what occurs for us as individuals is framed and shaped by power in a bigger political context.

Read the lyrics and listen to "revolution" by Tupac, and reflect on which ideas in this chapter resonate with his lyrics. Keep in mind that Tupac uses reclaimed words in this performance. (A reclaimed word is a word that is usually offensive or derogatory, but has been "reclaimed" and used as a form of resistance by those the word is usually used against. We will discuss reclaimed words in more detail in Chapter 6). For revolution by Tupac, see https://genius.com/2pac-revolution-lyrics.

## Suggested Resources

Buffy Sainte-Marie—"Universal Soldier." Retrieved from https://youtu.be/VGWsGyNsw00

2Pac: "Revolution" Lyrics. Retrieved from https://genius.com/2pac-revolution-lyrics

"CANADA, I can cite for you 150," by the Onaman Collective. Retrieved from https://youtu.be/Y6U9JV5-bA8

Alfred, T. (2008). *Peace, power, righteousness: An Indigenous manifesto* (2nd edn). Toronto, Canada: Oxford University Press.

Anthony, W., Anthony, J., & Samuelson, L. (Eds). (2017). *Power and resistance: Critical thinking about Canadian social issues* (6th edn). Halifax, Canada: Fernwood.

Collins, P.H. (2013). *On intellectual activism.* Philadelphia, PA: Temple University Press.

## References

Aakvaag, G.C. (2013). Social mechanisms and grand theories of modernity—worlds apart? *Acta Sociologica, 56*(3), 199–212. doi:10.1177/0001699312468804

Barrow, C.W. (2007). Plain Marxists, sophisticated Marxists, and C. Wright Mills' "the power elite". *Science & Society, 71*(4), 400–430.

Baskin, C. (2011). *Strong helpers' teachings: The value of Indigenous knowledges in the helping professions.* Toronto, Canada: Canadian Scholars' Press.

Baskin, C. (2016). *Strong helpers' teachings: The value of Indigenous knowledges in the helping professions* (2nd edn). Toronto, Canada: Canadian Scholars' Press.

Battle, M. (1997). *Reconciliation: The Ubuntu theology of Desmond Tutu.* Cleveland, OH: The Pilgrim Press.

Berman, S.L., & Buren, H.J.V. (2015). Mary Parker Follett, managerial responsibility, and the future of capitalism. *Futures, 68,* 44–56.

Bishop, A. (2015). *Becoming an ally: Breaking the cycle of oppression in people* (3rd edn). Halifax, Canada: Fernwood.

Brand, R. (2013, October 24). Russell Brand on revolution: "We no longer have the luxury of tradition." *New Statesman.* Retrieved from http://www.newstatesman.com/politics/2013/10/russell-brand-on-revolution

Buqa, W. (2015). Storying Ubuntu as a rainbow nation. *Verbum et Ecclesia, 36*(2), 1–8. doi:10.4102/ve.v36i2.1434

Chou, M. (2015). From crisis to crisis: Democracy, crisis and the occupy movement. *Political Studies Review, 13*(1), 46–58. doi:10.1111/1478-9302.12070

Congleton, R.D. (2009). On the political economy of the financial crisis and bailout of 2008–2009. *Public Choice, 140*(3/4), 287–317. doi:10.1007/s11127-009-9478-z

Crawford, G., & Andreassen, B.A. (2015). Human rights and development: Putting power and politics at the center. *Human Rights Quarterly, 37*(3), 662–90. doi:10.1353/hrq.2015.0053

Crowell, S. (2015). Why is ethics first philosophy? Levinas in phenomenological context. *European Journal of Philosophy, 23*(3), 564–88. doi:0.1111/j.1468-0378.2012.00550.x

Dahl, R.A. (1961). *Who Governs?: Democracy and Power in an American City.* New Haven, CT: Yale University Press.

Darder, A. (2017). *Reinventing Paulo Freire: A pedagogy of love.* New York, NY: Routledge.

Dumbrill, G.C. (2011). Doing anti-oppressive child protection casework. In D. Bains (Ed.), *Doing anti-oppressive practice: Social justice social work* (2nd ed., pp. 51–63). Halifax, Canada: Fernwood Publishing.

Eller, C. (2011). *Gentlemen and Amazons: The myth of matriarchal prehistory, 1861–1900.* Los Angeles, CA: University of California Press.

Elias, S. (2008). Fifty years of influence in the workplace: The evolution of the French & Raven power taxonomy. *Journal of Management History, 14*(3), 267–83. doi:10.1108/17511340810880634

Elliott, L., & Pilkington, E. (2015, January 19). New Oxfam report says half of global wealth held by the 1%: Oxfam warns of widening inequality gap, days head of Davos economic summit in Switzerland. *The Guardian.* Retrieved from http://www.theguardian.com/business/2015/jan/19/global-wealth-oxfam-inequality-davos-economic-summit-switzerland

Feather, N.T., & Boeckmann, R.J. (2013). Perceived legitimacy of judicial authorities in relation to degree of value discrepancy with public citizens. *Social Justice Research, 26*(2), 193–217. doi:10.1007/s11211-013-0183-1

Felluga, D.F. (2015). *Critical theory: The key concepts.* New York, NY: Routledge.

Fillingham, L.A. (1993). *Foucault for beginners*. Danbury, CT: Writers and Readers.

Fook, J. (2012). *Social work: A critical approach to practice* (2nd edn). London, UK: Sage.

Freire, P. (2012). *Pedagogy of the oppressed* (30th Anniversary edn). New York, NY: Bloomsbury.

French, J.R.P., & Raven, B. (1959). The bases of social power. In D. Cartwright (Ed.), *Studies in social power* (pp. 150–167). Ann Arbor, MI: The University of Michigan.

Friedersdorf, C. (2012, July 25). 14 specific allegations of NYPD brutality during occupy wall street. *The Atlantic*. Retrieved from http://www.theatlantic.com/politics/archive/2012/07/14-specific-allegations-of-nypd-brutality-during-occupy-wall-street/260295/

Garrett, P.M. (2007a). Making social work more Bourdieusian: Why the social professions should critically engage with the work of Pierre Bourdieu. *European Journal of Social Work, 10*(2), 225–43. doi:10.1080/13691450701318010

Garrett, P.M. (2007b). The relevance of Bourdieu for social work: A reflection on obstacles and omissions. *Journal of Social Work, 7*(3), 355–379. doi:10.1177/1468017307084076

Gwynn, D.M. (2015). *Christianity in the later Roman empire: A sourcebook*. London, UK: Bloomsbury Academic.

Harrington, M. (1997). *The other America: Poverty in the United States* (50th - Anniversary edition). New York, NY: A Touchstone Book published by Simon & Schuster.

Haugaard, M. (2010). Democracy, political power, and authority. *Social Research, 77*(4), 1049–74.

Herbst, M. (2013, May 28). The bank bailout cost US taxpayers nothing? Think again. *The Guardian*. Retrieved from http://www.theguardian.com/commentisfree/2013/may/28/bank-bailout-cost-taxpayers

Holms, M. (2000). Second-wave feminism and the politics of relationships. *Women's Studies International Forum, 23*(2), 253–46.

Kemp, S. (2012). Evaluating interests in social science: Beyond objectivist evaluation and the non-judgemental stance. *Sociology, 46*(4), 664–79. doi:10.1177/0038038511425561

King, M.L. (1967). *Where do we go from here: Chaos or community?* Boston, MA: Beacon Press.

Larner, G. (2008). Exploring Levinas: The ethical self in family therapy. *Journal of Family Therapy, 30*(4), 351–61. doi:10.1111/j.1467-6427.2008.00446.x

Levinas, E. (1989). Ethics as first philosophy. In S. Hand (Ed.), *The Levinas reader: Emmanuel Levinas* (pp. 76–87). Oxford, UK: Blackwell.

Levinas, E., & Kearney, R. (1986). Dialogue with Emmanuel Levinas. In R. A. Cohen (Ed.), *Face to face with Levinas* (pp. 13–34). New York, N.Y.: State University Press.

Lovell, T. (Ed.). (2007). *(Mis)recognition, social inequality and social justice: Nancy Fraser and Pierre Bourdieu*. Abingdon, UK: Routledge.

Lukes, S. (1974). *Power: A radical view*. London, UK: Macmillian.

Lukes, S. (2005). *Power: A radical view* (2nd expanded edn). New York, NY: Palgrave Macmillan.

Matthews, C. (2015, March 2). The myth of the 1% and the 99%. *Fortune Magazine*. Retrieved from http://fortune.com/2015/03/02/economic-inequality-myth-1-percent-wealth/

McKenzie, B., & Wharf, B. (2015). *Connecting policy to practice in the human services* (4th edn). Toronto, Canada: Oxford University Press.

McLaren, P. (2000). *Che Guevara, Paulo Freire, and the pedagogy of revolution*. Lanham, Md Rowman & Littelfield Publishers Inc.

Mills, C.W. (1956). *The power elite*. New York, NY: Oxford University Press.

Mills, C.W. (1959). *The sociological imagination*. Oxford, UK: Oxford University Press.

Mills, C.W. (2000). *The sociological imagination* (40th Anniversary Edition). Oxford, UK: Oxford University Press.

Mullaly, B. (2010). *Challenging oppression and confronting privilege: A critical social work approach*. (2nd edn). Toronto, Canada: Oxford University Press.

Newhouse, D. (2013). Ganigonhi:oh: The good mind meets the academy. In F. Widdowson & A. Howard (Eds), *Approaches to Aboriginal education in Canada: Searching for solutions* (pp. 391–406). Edmonton, Canada: Brush Education Inc.

Ngcoya, M. (2015). Ubuntu: Toward an emancipatory cosmopolitanism? *International Political Sociology, 9*(3), 248–62. doi:10.1111/ips.12095

Northridge, M.E. (2012). We are the 99 percent. *American Journal of Public Health, 102*(4), 585. doi:10.2105/AJPH.2012.300691

Paxman, J. (Writer). (2013). Russell Brand: "I've never voted, never will: [TV]. In *Newsnight*. England: British Broadcasting Corporation.

Porter, T. (2008). *And grandma said . . . Iroquois teachings as passed down through the oral tradition*. Bloomington, IN: Xlibris.

Praeg, L. (2014). *A Report on Ubuntu*. Pietermaritzburg, South Africa: University of KwaZulu-Natal Press.

Raven, B.H. (1965). Social influence and power. In I. D. Steiner & M. Fishbein (Eds), *Current studies in social psychology*. New York, NY: Wiley.

Raven, B.H. (1999). Kurt Lewin address: Influence, power, religion, and the mechanisms of social control. *Journal of Social Issues, 55*(1), 161–186. doi:10.1111/0022-4537.00111

Rice, J., & Prince, M. (Eds). (2013). *Changing politics of Canadian social policy* (2nd edn). Toronto, Ontario: Oxford University Press.

Roscigno, V.J. (2011). Power, revisited. *Social Forces, 90*(2), 349–374.

Russell, B. (1996/1938). *Power: A new social analysis*. London, UK: Routledge.

Said, E.W. (1979). *Orientalism*. New York, NY: Vintage Books.

Said, E.W. (1994). *Culture and imperialism*. New York, NY: Vintage Books.

Sim, S. (Ed.). (2011). *The Routledge Companion to Postmodernism* (3rd edn). New York, NY: Routledge.

Smith, R.A., & Fink, E.L. (2015). Understanding the influential people and social structures shaping compliance. *Journal of Social Structure, 16*, 1–15.

Son, K.M. (2015). A discordant universe of pluralisms: Response to Wenman. *Political Theory, 43*(4), 533–40. doi:10.1177/0090591715579516

Stiglitz, J.E. (2011, March 31). Of the 1%, by the 1%, for the 1%. *Vanity Fair.* Retrieved from http://www.vanityfair.com/news/2011/05/top-one-percent-201105

Swartz, D.L. (2007). Recasting power in its third dimension: Review of Steven Lukes, *Power: A radical view.* New York, NY: Palgrave Macmillan, 2005. *Theory and Society, 36*(1), 103–9. doi:10.1007/s11186-006-9018-5

Thomas-Muller, C. (2013, January 23). Occupy talks: Indigenous Perspectives on the occupy movement—media wrench (Toronto). *Indigenous Environmental Network.* Retrieved from http://www.ienearth.org/occupy-talks-indigenous-perspectives-on-the-occupy-movement-media-wrench-toronto/

Tutu, D.M. (2011). *God is not a Christian: And other provocations.* J. Allen (Ed.). New York, NY: HarperOne.

Warnera, L.S., & Grint, K. (2012). The case of the noble savage: The myth that governance can replace leadership. *International Journal of Qualitative Studies in Education, 25*(7), 969–82. doi:10.1080/09518398.2012.720736

Whipps, J. (2014). A pragmatist reading of Mary Parker Follett's integrative process. *Transactions of the Charles S. Peirce Society: A Quarterly Journal in American Philosophy, 50*(3), 405–24.

Ypi, L. (2014). On revolution in Kant and Marx. *Political Theory, 42*(3), 262–87. doi:10.1177/0090591714523138

# 4 Whiteness: What It Is and Why We Have to Understand It

## In this chapter you will learn:

- How domination and subjugation operate in society
- What oppression does and how it operates
- What Whiteness and White supremacy are and the role they play in oppression
- What the "racial contract" is and how it operates
- What White privilege is and its relationship to oppression

## Introduction

June and Gary led a workshop on anti-racism at a Canadian social work conference. June was the lead presenter and consequently June spoke first, she spoke more than Gary, she stood in the forward position closer to the audience, and she concluded the presentation.

At the end of a workshop, it is common for participants to come forward to talk to the presenters and ask questions. This workshop was no exception; about seven social work agency executive directors came forward, ignored June and walked around her, shook Gary's hand, congratulated him on a fine presentation, and asked if he could present something similar at their agencies.

The executive directors offered Gary an opportunity that should have been June's. The unjust nature of this should have been obvious. Gary has his own scholarship on anti-racism, but it had been made clear that the workshop just presented was June's scholarship. June wondered where things had gone wrong. The entire presentation had been about how racism, sexism, and other isms promote some people and hold others back, and now that process was occurring in front of their eyes. June wondered whether it was her race, gender, age, or maybe all of these that made the executive directors ignore her and go to Gary.

What do you think? What caused this? Why was Gary approached and not June? How do you think Gary ought to respond? By the end of this chapter, you will be able to suggest what might be occurring in this situation and will have developed ideas about how to address it.

# A Topography of Domination

The story above cannot be understood by looking at June's gender, race, age, or some other aspect of her identity. It has to be understood by examining both June's and Gary's identities in relation to the way power, domination, and oppression operate in society.

One's position in relation to societal power and domination is referred to as a social location. A person's **social location** is an aspect of their identity such as race, gender, age, class, sexual identity, ability/disability, etc. (Carniol, 2005). We all have an array of such locations. Some people identify with these and others do not, and some entirely reject the idea of having their identities labelled. We do not like defining people by social location because an individual can never be reduced to a collection of labels. Despite our dislike of the term, the concept of social location is necessary. Indeed, social locations represent the way society sees and categorizes people. We might not personally categorize people this way, but society does, and consequently if we want to understand society we have to understand these labels.

Figure 4.1 provides a **topography**, which is a map that looks down on a landscape or phenomena. Figure 4.1 maps the way domination works in relation to select social locations. This is our version of what Patricia Hill Collins (2000) refers to as the **matrix of domination** or **matrix of oppression,** which moves away from looking at singular dimensions of oppression and toward understanding a bigger context in which oppressions intersect. In our Figure 4.1, we place emphasis in the centre on the sites of domination, because these are what drive oppression. We also place emphasis on understanding the way Whiteness and White supremacy provide a context in which interlocked sites of domination hold together (more about these concepts later in the chapter).

## Separating First- and Second-Class Citizenship

The outside of the circle in Figure 4.1 represents what Mullaly and West (2018) call *second-class citizenship.* The centre of the circle represents *first-class citizenship*—we might also call this prime societal space, prime social real estate, or in Bourdieuian (2004) terms a place of economic, social, symbolic, and cultural capital. (We defined these terms in Chapter 3.)

In Figure 4.1, imagine oppression as a force that pushes outwards from the centre. The power of oppression pushes select groups of people to the margins, excludes them, and locks them out of opportunity and participation. At the same time, this power locks the dominant group into a position of first-class citizenship where they gain unearned privilege and an advantage over others. The relationship between first-class citizenship in the centre and second-class citizenship on the margins are interdependent; one cannot have a first class unless there is also a second class.

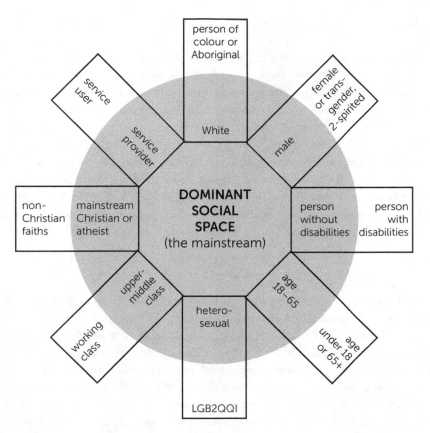

**Figure 4.1** A topography of oppression

Source: Based on Dumbrill, 2003, 2012

## Key Concept

The relationship between first-class and second-class citizenship are interdependent; one cannot have a first class unless there is also a second class. In the same way, the relationship between the centre and the margins are interdependent; one cannot have a margin if there is no centre. The problem anti-oppressive social workers pay attention to is how some groups get to reserve first-class citizenship for themselves, and how these groups manage to push others to the margins.

The social locations we name in Figure 4.1 are arguably the most common sites where the sorting of first- and second-class citizenship occurs. We have discussed all of the locations shown in Figure 4.1 in previous chapters, except one's relationship to social service delivery, and religion. We add social work service users because they tend to face marginalization and lack of voice just because they rely on services, while service providers tend to gain voice along with the ability to determine what happens to service users' lives. We will be talking more about social work's relationship to service users in Chapter 10. We have also added religion. We have placed Christians, atheists, agnostics, or otherwise secular people in the centre, with non-Christian groups on the outside. Since 9/11, Muslims in particular have been even more singled out for oppression (Geddes, 2013), but other faiths face oppression too (McClelland, 2001; Weinfeld, 2016). Many other social locations, which we could have added to Figure 4.1, are also impacted by oppression. We will give you an opportunity to think about these locations later in the chapter.

## Applying the Topography of Oppression

Figure 4.1 can help us understand what happened to June and Gary in the story at the start of this chapter. June is outside the circle in relation to gender and race, while Gary is in the centre of the circle in relation to these and most other positions too. We suspect that personal prejudices and attitudes related to gender, age, and race caused the executive directors to step around June and offer opportunities to Gary. We cannot be certain that this is the case, because not every instance of inclusion and exclusion is caused by oppression, but incidents similar to the story above have happened so many times to us when working together that it is hard to imagine that at least some of them are not caused by oppression.

It would be tempting to conclude that the executive directors walked around June and went to Gary because they were sexist and racist. But we cannot use the topography to infer from a society-wide pattern to the specific—we do not know what motivated the executive directors to walk around June and go to Gary. Consequently, keep in mind that one *cannot* use the topography in Figure 4.1 to determine whether a specific incident results from racism, sexism, or some other form of oppression. To do that one has to go through the analytical processes we outlined in Chapter 1. The topography of oppression only gives a broad overview of the shape and pattern of oppression at a societal level. Of course we know, because the topography tells us, that whatever the reason the executive directors excluded June and included Gary, their actions reinforced the pattern of racism and sexism that exists within society—or would have done if we had let them get away with it!

Also keep in mind when applying the topography of oppression that the locations inside and outside the centre are somewhat fluid and can shift with time (moment in history) and space (geographic context). For instance, in some countries Christians and atheists will be outside rather than inside the circle (Hodge, 2007). In addition, in some historic moments, those who usually find themselves in the centre can find themselves outside. In World War I (1914–1918) women publicly called out and shamed men who refused or were unable to fight in the war. In the UK, Emmeline Parkhurst, a woman's rights activist, mobilized women, in what is known as "white feather feminism," to give white feathers to men not wearing a uniform as a public accusation of cowardice (Gullace, 1997; Purvis & Brooke). In that moment, women used stereotypical notions of maleness to force men who objected to war to fight (Gullace, 1997). We consider this a form of oppression, so keep in mind that in some rare moments the locations inside and outside the circle in Figure 4.1 can reverse. In the social world one can always find exceptions to most rules, but this does not mean that the overarching pattern the rule represents does not exist. Pay attention to exceptions, but do not be so distracted by exceptions that you miss the rule, or miss the reality that groups affected by the rule face oppression day in and day out, with almost no exception.

## The Relationship between the Centre and Margins

Being in the centre of the circle does not guarantee success, nor does being outside prevent it, but predominant prejudices, social systems, and culture are predisposed to give those in the centre a hand up and those on the outside a push down. In this manner, White people benefit from racism because it usually holds racialized people back and allows White people to get further ahead. Men benefit from sexism because it usually holds women back and provides opportunities for men to get ahead. The other forms of oppression operate in a similar manner, so the more you occupy the centre of the circle the more you experience being pushed forward or lifted up into success. In most cases, to fail from the centre position you have to either work extra hard at trying to fail or have a lot of bad luck, whereas to succeed from the outside position you have to work extra hard to get ahead or have a lot of good luck.

## Key Concept

Having first-class citizenship and being a member of dominant society does not guarantee success, nor does having second-class citizenship or being in a marginalized position prevent it, but predominant prejudices, social systems, and culture are predisposed to give those in the dominant centre a hand up and those on the outside a push down.

Because the centre dominant space is comprised of multiple social locations, a person can gain domination in one location, but face oppression in another. The more locations someone has in the centre the more they are pushed forward; the more locations someone has on the outside the more they are pushed back. One cannot, however, calculate the effect of this pushing and pulling by adding up the outside and inside locations to calculate how much domination one gains or oppression one faces. One form of oppression may compound another, but in some contexts only one form of oppression counts.

For instance, the Black Lives Matter movement makes clear that the single dimension of race is often a matter of life or death (Powell, 2016). In other situations disability trumps race; for instance, building evacuation plans often stipulate that in a fire everyone who can use stairs should evacuate and leave those who cannot (such as people in wheelchairs) behind next to a stairwell or other designated location (Kecklund, Kristin, Staffan, Sara, & Elena, 2012; Scholes, 2005). In the context of a burning building, disability rather than race might decide life or death. Consequently, because oppression is context specific, one cannot determine which group is more oppressed than another.

Another layer of complexity that has to be considered when using Figure 4.1 is that each social location contains multiple internal divisions. For instance, social class is not simply a binary between upper and lower class, but is divided into many layers with differing access to power and privilege. For instance, when Gary left school and was working in construction with no academic or formal trade qualifications, his prospects for promotion and advancement in that system was nil. In contrast, trade persons qualified with a college education had prospects of promotion to a trade foreperson or even building site manager. Yet both Gary, with no qualifications or prospects for advancement, and those with qualifications and prospects for advancement, were considered working class.

Gender is another example of a social location not being a binary as portrayed in Figure 4.1. We have placed men inside the circle, and women, transgender, and two-spirit persons outside (we will discuss these social locations in Chapter 6). But it could be argued that women who are cisgender (more about this term in Chapter 6) are inside the circle relative to transgender or two-spirit persons.

## Maintaining Domination

The domination of locations in the centre of Figure 4.1 are established and maintained by power. At some point in history, those in the centre gained the power to define anyone who did not look or act like them as different (as Other), and also gained the power to push them into a position of second-class citizenship and sometimes no citizenship at all. Once attained, the power and advantage of the centre position became self-perpetuating, because members of the centre groups had access to the best schools, the best jobs, and the best resources. They ran the country, owned most of the land, and held controlling interests in the banks, industry, and all the other social institutions on which society relies.

The ongoing domination of any group in power relies on their ability to keep themselves in power and others out. This is done by the dominant group in the centre of the circle establishing, maintaining, and policing a line between themselves and those on the outside. Later in this chapter, and also in the following chapters, we will examine in some detail the specific ways this line has been established, policed, and resisted in relation to the dimensions shown in Figure 4.1. For now, however, it is important to grasp the idea that domination can only be maintained by a ruling group policing a line between themselves and those they subjugate.

## Key Concept

Oppression relies on dominant groups keeping themselves in power and keeping those they oppress out. To disrupt this process, anti-oppressive social workers have to understand how the line between the dominant groups and those they oppress is drawn and policed.

The key to maintaining any long-term system of oppression is to make the mechanisms of domination invisible. Overt blatant oppression works for a while, but risks the downtrodden majority and even some of the ruling group eventually deciding that the system is unfair and rebelling. Consequently, some of the most powerful expressions of oppression in today's society are not undertaken by such things as invading armies or state sanctioned mass slavery, but by acts embedded deep within the type of everyday personal, systemic, and cultural processes we described in Chapter 1.

When oppression is mostly covert, the ruling group can claim innocence. In our story at the start of this chapter we were left wondering whether it was oppression or some innocent misjudgment that excluded June. Even when someone notices a pattern of oppression that shows something is unfair, the ruling group can divert attention by claiming that "this is just the way the world is, we worked hard to get ahead, you have the same chance, go get an education, get a job, hard work will set you free!" Such statements are a mantra of **meritocracy**, which is a belief that what separates those who get ahead from those who do not is hard work and intelligence rather than the system the powerful group has instigated.

A problem for the ruling group, however, is that policing a hidden line between themselves and Others can never be perfect, so by luck or extraordinary effort, some Others do manage to get ahead and gain access to the resources of the ruling group. Rather than loosen the ruling group's grip on domination, this strengthens it, because these instances reinforce the myth of meritocracy. There is, however, no meritocracy, because far from being fair, the system ensures that no matter how hard the majority work, most will not get ahead. It is quite the opposite, especially in relation to class; those outside the circle work for those in the centre, so the system ensures that the harder those on the outside work, the richer and more powerful those in the centre become.

A characteristic of domination that makes it particularly hard to notice and define is that dominance is not controlled by a single **homogeneous** (identical) group of people. If there were one ruling elite, for instance if the centre of Figure 4.1 were only defined by men, or only White people, or only people without disabilities and so on, the boundary between those who dominate and those who are dominated would be obvious. But the centre is not one group; instead it is a complex array of groups whose interests and power overlap to produce a harder-to-identify similarity.

## Key Concept

The "dominant group" in society is not one group; instead it is a complex array of groups whose interests and power overlap to produce a harder-to-identify similarity.

As well, many people have locations both inside and outside the dominant centre of the circle, so who dominates whom becomes even harder to categorize. Additionally, we have only shown eight social locations of domination and subjugation in Figure 4.1, and as mentioned above, there are many more locations of dominance and subjugation. Consequently, although Figure 4.1 helps us to understand the beginning nuances of oppression, to fully understand the complexities we need to go further than the figure implies.

Before we go into this depth, we want to consider what oppression does and how it does it. This helps us understand more about who is doing what to whom.

# Things That Oppression Does

Domination is built and maintained through several processes that include, but are not limited to, annihilation, assimilation, marginalization, exploitation, and appropriation.

## Annihilation

**Annihilation** is the extermination of a people or their way of being. An example is the Nazi attempt to annihilate Jews, Jehovah Witnesses, gay and lesbians, Romany, and others (Aretha, 2001). Another term for this is **genocide**, which the United Nations General Assembly Resolution, 1946 96 (I), defines as not only murder and the denial of a right to live, but also the denial of the right of existence as a human group. Indeed, genocide often kills "a people" (distinct cultural or national groups) without killing people; the oppressor keeps persons alive but annihilates them as a distinct culture or nation. This was the strategy behind Canada's residential school system (Downey, 1999; MacDonald & Hudson, 2012).

## Assimilation

**Assimilation** is annihilation by other means; it is the process of being absorbed into something so that one's own distinctness is lost. Canada's residential school system was attempted genocide by assimilation. In a deliberate attempt to annihilate Indigenous cultures, languages, and ways of being, the state tried to "kill the Indian" within children. The state saw the ongoing existence of First Nations on colonized land as a threat to its own legitimacy, and so the idea was to destroy the language, culture, and distinctiveness of First Nations along with other Indigenous peoples, but to keep their bodies alive by absorbing them into positions where they serve the dominant culture. This absorption is not acceptance into a full belonging in the wealth and opportunities of dominant space, but instead is absorption to the margins of that space. Assimilation is not about inviting people into a circle of equal opportunity; it is about maintaining their subjugation by annihilating their nations and shared identities.

Some people see assimilation as the answer to oppression. Indeed, if difference is the basis of oppression, surely all we have to do to end oppression is have everyone become the same. Do not misinterpret Figure 4.1 and think that we are suggesting ending oppression by absorbing everyone into the sameness of the centre. Not at all. The objective of anti-oppression is not to do away with what we perceive of as human difference, but to stop those in the centre using power to construct difference in a manner that allows them to draw a line around resources that they keep for themselves. The point of anti-oppression is to disrupt the power mechanisms and processes that allow difference to be the basis of domination and exclusion. The point of Figure 4.1 is not to have all people become the same as those in the centre, but to disrupt the mechanisms that allow those in the centre to gain an unfair advantage.

## Marginalization

**Marginalization** is the process of pushing people and groups to the edges of society where they are denied the opportunities and resources that those in the centre keep for themselves (Young, 2011). Another term used to describe this pushing out process is "social exclusion," which is locking out or *excluding* people from the resources and opportunities of the centre (Lightman & Gingrich, 2013).

## Exploitation

**Exploitation** is the process of gaining resources and advantage by treating someone unfairly. This can involve refusing to pay fair wages (Young, 2011), subjecting people to slavery, stealing and settling on someone's land, dispossessing people of their nationhood, and taking their children and placing them in residential schools where they are trained to serve White masters who occupy dominant space.

## Appropriation

**Appropriation** is related to exploitation. It is taking something belonging to someone else and using it for one's own means. The most obvious example in North America is taking Indigenous land, sovereignty, and resources. A related concept, **cultural appropriation,** adds insult to the injury of having one's material resources appropriated. For instance, the injury caused to Indigenous peoples by the theft of land, sovereignty, and resources is compounded by the insult embedded in acts like football teams using Indigenous symbols and names, or White people dressing up in costumes mimicking Indigenous regalia at Halloween. A similar insult occurs when White people dress up with blackface for entertainment. Not content with taking the materials, territory, or labour of the oppressed, the oppressor also takes and enriches their own lives with the images, art, and culture of those they have trod down. This insult is made worse by the fact that those whose lands were stolen are excluded and not welcome in prime societal space, but their symbols, art, and culture are. In other words the cultural artefacts of the oppressed are incorporated into mainstream and elite culture, while those who created this art and made these symbols are locked out.

Unravelling whether something is cultural appropriation can be difficult, especially in a world where cultures are interwoven. Amandla Stenberg succinctly explains cultural appropriation in relation to hairstyles in a video titled, "Don't Cash Crop on My Cornrows." Stenberg explains:

> The line between cultural appropriation and cultural exchange is always going to be blurred. But here's the thing: Appropriation occurs when a style leads to racist generalizations or stereotypes where it originated, but is deemed as high fashion, cool, or funny when the privileged take it for themselves. (Daniels, 2015)

Hairstyle became an issue in March 2016 at San Francisco State University. A Black female student challenged a White male student for having his hair in dreadlocks; she accused him of cultural appropriation (Arewa, 2016). A video of this incident went viral on social media, along with debates about whether this was cultural appropriation. Online opinion was polarized with some condemning the man for appropriation and others condemning the woman for calling him out in the way she did. We set aside the way the interaction occurred to focus on the issue that drove it: was it cultural appropriation, and if so why?

We heard some commentators suggest that if this was cultural appropriation, "we ought to stop eating Taco Bell," because surely that would be appropriation too. Other commentators took the issue more seriously and looked for answers with questions such as: Where did dreadlocks originate? Was it Egypt? Were the Egyptians Black? Are dreadlocks **Rastafari**? (Rastafarianism is a religion/belief system developed in Jamaica with Ethiopian roots.) Was the man who seems to be White in the video Rastafarian? Can White people be Rastafarian? Did the Rastafari appropriate dreadlocks from the Nazarenes of Ancient Israel? What race were the Nazarenes?

These are important questions, but trying to answer whether something is cultural appropriation by looking at the past is a mistake; one has to look at what is occurring in the present. Today, and in recent history, dreadlocks are primarily associated with Black culture. A Black man wearing dreadlocks draws attention to his Blackness, and this is dangerous, because it is linked to stereotypes that make Black people more likely to be shot and killed by the police or armed vigilantes (Hall, Hall, & Perry, 2016). In contrast, a White man wearing dreadlocks usually risks very little, other than being considered cool and fashionable. It is this difference that makes cultural appropriation a problem.

We are not suggesting that cultural appropriation be addressed by some kind of fashion policing, but instead by honest conversations about personal responsibility. Fashion is always a personal statement. So what personal statement is a White person making by wearing Black fashion, knowing that society will regard the White person as cool for doing so, and also knowing that those they took this fashion away from are likely to be targeted and killed for looking this way? Of course, maybe the White person is trying to use fashion to **culture jam**, which is a way of disrupting mainstream ideas and subverting stereotypes. If so, this could be considered anti-oppression. Even so, our point is that when the issue of cultural appropriation arises, we need to ask what kind of statement the person who appears to be appropriating is making, and what impact that is having on those most associated with the fashion.

## Exercise 4.1

### What Is the Statement?

In this exercise we ask you to identify the meaning and consequences of an instance of cultural appropriation. If possible, undertake this exercise in groups.

### Part 1

The US government gave Osama bin Laden, who was arguably America's most hated enemy, the code name "Geronimo." The real Geronimo was an Apache military leader who lived from 1829 to 1909. When bin Laden was located and killed in Pakistan by US Special Forces, President Obama received a message from a Navy SEAL involved in the mission, "Geronimo E-KIA," in other words, bin Laden was dead.

Discuss as a group, or consider on your own, the following questions:

1. Why appropriate the name of a revered Indigenous leader and give it to America's most reviled enemy?
2. What (and whose) purpose does this appropriation serve?
3. What message does using this name give to Indigenous peoples?
4. What ideas about Indigenous peoples does it reinforce in non-Indigenous peoples?
5. What impact might this appropriation have on Indigenous peoples?
6. What impact might this appropriation have on non-Indigenous peoples?

Continued

**Part 2**

In response to this appropriation, the 1491s created a spoken word video as a form of resistance. The 1491s are a Minnesota-based Indigenous group who specialize in comedy and satire. They also engage in political commentary and resistance and this is one of those works. Engage with this work in the exercise below.

1.    Watch *Geronimo E-KIA—A poem by the 1491s* at https://www.youtube .com/watch?v=y7vKu7X4aNA, or search the web for the video using that title.
2.    Reflect and journal or discuss with your group your reactions to the video. What does the video make you feel and why? What does it make you think?

When engaging with this video, do not idealize Geronimo. If you do, you miss the objective. Geronimo lived in dangerous and violent times and as those producing the video note, he was a "product of his environment" and a human with flaws. As such his name can be appropriated and spun in many directions because, as stated in the video, he comes with "enough history that the person charged with defining who he is can shape the narrative any which way he likes."

The producers of the video add, "People chase him today, just as they did then. His story, or people's versions of it, lead us to this point where we are today. But this poem isn't about Geronimo, is it?"

In response to the question ". . . this poem is not about Geronimo, is it?" conclude this exercise by saying what you think the poem is about.

To disrupt oppression we have to understand what holds it together. We are not suggesting that we can end all appropriation, assimilation, annihilation, exploitation, social exclusion, marginalization, or similar practices. We believe there will always be individuals who try to move themselves forward by pushing others back. We may not be able to stop these individuals, but we can stop their principles from being built into the operating system of society. To do this we have to understand how that system works and how the centre of the circle holds itself together.

## Key Concept

Anti-oppression may not be able to stop every individual or group intent on oppressing others, but we can stop their principles from being built into the operating system of society. To do this we have to understand how the operating system works.

# Whiteness: The Operating System at the Centre of the Circle

For the past 400 to 500 years, the centre of the circle has been dominated by what is called **Whiteness**. You already understand much about Whiteness if you understand dominant social space, because everything we have said about dominance in the centre of Figure 4.1 can also be said about Whiteness.

Whiteness is not just about White people, nor is it just about race. It is about all locations in the centre of Figure 4.1 (Yee & Dumbrill, 2016). The idea of Whiteness, however, does have conceptual origins in the concept of race. Scholarship on Whiteness was started by African American scholar W.E.B. Du Bois (1903). In Du Bois's day, Black people were physically barred from entering the space Whites preserved for themselves and they were not allowed to cross what Du Bois called "the race line." If we understand how that line was established and policed, and is still maintained today, we not only understand how the line that excludes Black people is drawn, but we gain clues about the way lines that exclude other groups are drawn too.

The race line, the process of barring Blacks and including Whites, rests on racialization. Racialization is a sorting of people based on the notion of racial difference—and more specifically a process through which people of colour are marked as "different" and marginalized. The modern concept of race did not exist in the ancient world (Allen, 2012; Mills, 2015). In ancient times, the concept of "race" referred to kin (family group), clan, or nationality. This is different from the modern notion of race, which W.E.B. Du Bois (1903) named as "differences of color, hair and bone." Of course, kin and family groups usually share similar physical characteristics, but in ancient times these visible human characteristics were not the organizing principle behind the concept of race. This changed in the Enlightenment, when botanist Carl Linnaeus used physical characteristics to classify people into distinct "racial" groups (Müller-Wille, 2014). Blumenbach built on this idea and classified humans into five primary races (Yee & Dumbrill, 2016):

- Caucasians (the white race)
- Mongolians (the yellow race)
- Malayans (the brown race)
- Ethiopians (the black race)
- Americans (the red race)

Blumenbach's typology provided the basis for White Europeans, who at that time had gained access to global power, the ability to define themselves as superior, and to regard all others as inferior. Blumenbach's system not only classified humans, it also ranked them, and placed White people at the top.

Blumenbach's typology makes no ontological sense because the concept of race has no scientific basis. Blumenbach imagined his categories of race into existence, and this idea became a **social construction** (an idea people believe in and act upon) that provides the basis for **racialization**—sorting humans into distinct groups.

Explore for yourself in Exercise 4.2 why the idea of "race" makes no sense, and how the invention of "race" is integral in oppression.

## Exercise 4.2

### The Social Construction of Race

If possible, undertake this exercise in groups. Be sure you have at least 30 minutes to spare.

This exercise is based on The California Newsreel website developed for a PBS series about race, where they challenge viewers to sort images of people into the racial categories used by the US federal government definitions of race and ethnicity. Go to the PBS website at http://www.pbs.org/race/002_SortingPeople/002_00-home.htm.

Take the sorting test. Try to classify people based on the way race is currently conceptualized in the USA. If you are working in groups, compare your results with the results of others in your group. Explore the rest of the PBS website on race and discover explanations for your results and the ways they describe the origins of race as a concept. Reflect on and answer the following questions:

1. What does this teach you about the concept of race?
2. Can you generalize the lessons from this exercise? In other words, does this exercise have implications for the way you understand other social locations, such as gender?
3. What types of power discussed in Chapter 3 do you see at play here?

It is no coincidence that White Europeans invented the idea of race at the exact moment they were conquering the world and dividing its resources among themselves. What better way for White Europeans to justify their conquest of others than claiming that they were superior and destined to rule, and to claim that people of colour were inferior and destined to be ruled?

Once "race" was invented and the racialization of "Other" races by Whites was established, the idea of the White race and its supremacy became self-perpetuating. The more Europeans came, saw, and conquered, the more they reinforced their belief in their own superiority, and the more they thought they had a right to treat others in dehumanizing ways. With the power and resources to exploit others, Europe got richer and the conquered got poorer, and the myth of White superiority was spun. Turner reflects that this myth "legitimizes the power and wealth of White nations by making them appear self-made, worthy of emulation, and immune from claims of unjust enrichment. It also relieves Europe, Euro-America, and Euro-Australia of responsibility for 'Third World' underdevelopment" (Turner, 2015, p. 476).

As mentioned above, Whiteness is not simply about race. It is about the ability of those in an interlocked set of power positions to mark the Other as different from themselves, to draw a line between themselves and the Other, and to oppress those on the other side of this line. To achieve this, Whiteness relies on and is the product of the ways in which "societal norms are produced through visual markers of difference" (Badwall, 2016, p. 11). In this sense, **subject positions** (social locations) are personified through a set of power relations that are predicated upon notions of civility and degeneracy (Goldberg, 1993). Said differently, the process of determining which bodies are allowed inside the circle is regulated by notions of difference backed by a power that operates through personal prejudice, systems, and culture.

Although Whiteness is not only about race, it is built on the domination that White Europeans have gained over the past few centuries. Said differently, many groups may share a part of societal dominant space, but the core component in the creation of this space and the power that holds it in place today is White. The ideology, or thinking, that holds this power in place is sometimes called "White supremacy."

## White Supremacy: The Power behind Whiteness

White supremacy is not confined to the ideology of overtly racist organizations like the Ku Klux Klan or neo-Nazi groups. White supremacy is an unnamed global political system based on the belief that one's race is superior to all others (Turner, 2015). Charles W. Mills refers to White supremacy as a **racial contract** (Mills, 1997, 2015). Mills uses the term "contract" in the sense of a **social contract**, which is a shared understanding and agreement within society about the way human political relations should be structured. The racial contract is the idea that Whites should rule, or at the very least benefit the most from societal systems; as such the racial contract describes a world "written by and for whites" (Leonardo, 2015, p. 87). The racial contract rests on the invention of race, which includes the idea that Whites should be at the top, and is enforced by the power Europe gained by dominating the world over the past 400 to 500 years.

Laws that made Blacks slaves and Whites masters formed the initial racial contract. The key innovation in this process was not slavery, since this had been practised by people around the world for thousands of years. The innovation was the invention of "race" to mark people as slaveable. Overt laws forcing Black people into slavery were so obviously unjust that they were eventually abolished. But in the USA, **Jim Crow laws** (non-federal state and local laws enforcing racial segregation) enabled the racial contract to remain intact. In Canada and the UK and around the world similar laws and practices existed (Cannon, 1995; Gilroy, 1987). Today many of these laws have been abolished, but similar practices continue because the racial contract is embedded in society at the personal, systemic, and cultural levels.

Today's racial contract is not entirely overt or written. Instead it is a tacit (implied) agreement we have with each other about the way we organize our social and political world. Such contracts are a bit like the practice of inviting friends to a birthday party.

No written rule stipulates whom you can and cannot invite, but try inviting strangers and not your best friends and see how this affects your social life. The racial contract is similar; it stipulates who gets invited, who gets excluded, and who gets gifts, but on a much larger scale than a birthday party and in relation to vastly more serious life-and-death issues.

The racial contract does not benefit all Whites in a uniform manner. White women, working-class Whites, and "other marked whites" do not gain from race or racism in the same way (Leonardo, 2015, p. 87). The uneven bestowal of first class-citizenship to Whites is shown in Figure 4.1, where to be fully White (in the sense of gaining full dominance) one usually must also be male, cisgender, heterosexual, middle- or upper-class; not have a disability; fall within a certain age group; have a job or occupation; and so on. Even these attributes do not always guarantee a position in the centre. Indeed, there were times in history (and now) when people regarded as White, such as the Irish, Italians, and Jewish people, were locked out of dominance. In these moments these groups were considered Black (Brodkin, 1998; Guglielmo & Salerno, 2003; Ignatiev, 1995).

The idea that some Whites are Black seems counter-intuitive. This is because the idea of race is socialized into our intuition as an ontological reality. Once we understand that race is a social construction, new ways of looking at Black and White become possible. We see that although race is not real, racialization is, and this process does not necessarily follow the divide we perceive to be Black and White. Of course, racialization overwhelmingly sorts those perceived as White into domination and those perceived as Black into subjugation. Yet to see this as simply a Black-and-White issue oversimplifies the processes behind racism and other forms of oppression. We may use the language of Black and White to describe racism and other forms of oppression, but at a conceptual level these terms encompass a more complex reality. So keep in mind that when we use these terms, we are not buying into the fiction of distinct races, but into the reality of racialization. Said differently, even though a White race is not real, Whiteness is real, and so is the ideology of White supremacy, along with the machinery that has emerged from these ideas that maintain White dominance.

# How the Dominance of Whiteness Is Maintained

Several mechanisms hold Whiteness and White supremacy in place. These mechanisms include but are not limited to naturalization and universalization, invisibility and exnomination, surveillance and policing, and White innocence.

## Naturalization and Universalization

**Naturalization** is situating one's position as the natural or normal perspective. It is making one's own way of being and understanding *the* way of being and understanding.

Naturalization is related to **universalization**, which is the White experience being thought of as everyone's experience. Naturalization and universalization combine to form what is sometimes called the **White, male, rational subject**. In this phrase, "White" describes this position as a part of Whiteness. "Male" emphasizes the male aspect of Whiteness (because, currently and historically, White men claim to produce most of what we regard as knowledge). "Rational" refers to this position producing what are regarded as rational facts. The notion of rationality is closely associated with the age of reason and the scientific colonization we spoke of in Chapter 3.

We are not suggesting that universal truths do not exist or that there is something wrong with rationality and reason. The problem is when the subject position (one group's subjective perspective) is used to define truth and reason for everyone. For instance, take the discovery of America. If we asked when America was discovered, what would you answer?

1. 1004
2. 1492
3. None of the above

When we ask this question in the classes we teach or the workshops we run, about 50% of participants answer "1492," which is the date Columbus "sailed the ocean blue." Some answer 1004 and claim that this is when the Vikings discovered America. About 20% answer "none of the above," and say that this is because there were already people living in the Americas long before Columbus or the Vikings came, so it could not be "discovered" when the people living here already knew that it existed. Of course, one can argue that from the perspective of Columbus or the Vikings, they did "discover" America, because they did not previously know that it existed. We concur, but the problem arises when their European perspective becomes *the* perspective, when the subjective experience of White Europeans is recorded as the objective history of the entire world. Indeed, have you ever wondered why you do not hear the story about how the Indigenous people of Turtle Island (now called North America) discovered Europeans when they found a strange White man in a tin hat lost and confused on their beach? History is not told this way because the White European side of this story is naturalized and universalized as everyone's truth. Europeans are always the discoverers, the Other the discovered.

## Key Concept

A European perspective is not the problem. The problem is when a European perspective becomes *the* perspective, when the subjective experience of White Europeans is recorded and regarded as the objective history of the entire world.

## Invisibility and Exnomination

**Invisibility** (not being seen) and **exnomination** (not being named) are related to naturalization and universalization. Columbus's perspective becomes naturalized and universalized because his subject position is not seen or named. For instance, consider the concept of "diversity." Have you ever asked "diverse from what?" If not, this is because of the invisibility of Whiteness, which situates itself as an unnamed silent norm from which difference is defined and measured. We can illustrate this type of invisibility through an example of shopping at a supermarket (Yee & Dumbrill, 2016). When June goes shopping she finds her favourite Chinese food in the "ethnic" food aisle, while Gary finds his favourite fish and chips in the "regular" food aisle. Gary's tastes are not labelled "ethnic"; he and his ethnic tastes are considered "regular" or "normal." Perhaps not all supermarkets operate this way, but most of the ones we have come across do. This issue is not just supermarket aisles. If you go to buy a "regular" Band-Aid and see what colour it is, it will more than likely be a pinkish colour that matches Gary's skin. Such Band-Aids were once referred to as "skin colour," but recognizing that this was racist because it privileges White people, the name was changed to "regular." If you get the irony of the new name being called "regular," you understand the point we are making; White people tend to be regarded as "regular" and the Other as irregular or different.

The ability of Whites and Whiteness to be unnamed creates the illusion that "there is no white perspective but only the universal, impartial, disinterested view from nowhere" (Farr, 2004, p. 154). This enables a discursive technique, which is a kind of trick through language that defines the Other from a pretended place of natural, neutral, reasonable normality. Yet the position is not neutral at all, because it represents a particular standpoint or perspective that has made itself invisible. In this manner, those who come from a place of Whiteness maintain dominance because they are never under scrutiny. They invisibly set societal standards, values, and norms of our social, political, cultural, educational, and economic institutions. They name and mark the Other, but are never named or marked themselves.

## Surveillance and Discipline

**Surveillance** and **discipline** hold Whiteness and White supremacy in place. When June went to Dublin, Ireland, she visited Kilmainham Gaol, a prison (now a museum). The Kilmainham Gaol housed adults and children imprisoned for petty crimes, and also Irish freedom fighters called "the irregulars," who fought British rule in the 1920s. It reminded June of the circle we used to explain oppression in Figure 4.1, the topography of oppression.

The gaol was built using a panoptical design devised by Bentham. We have reproduced a copy of Bentham's original plans for this type of prison in Figure 4.2. Kilmainham Gaol is not a perfect circle like Bentham's schematics show, but it is based on the same idea. Figure 4.2 shows the panopticon from the side and from above.

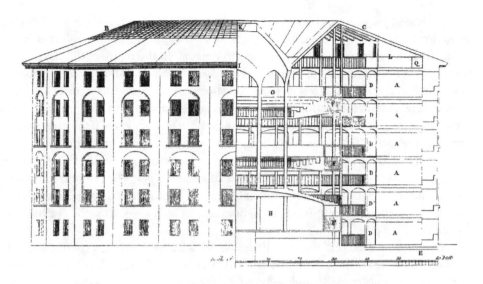

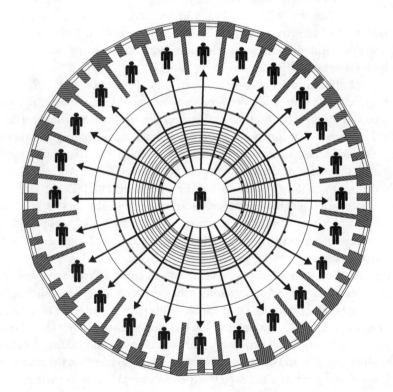

**Figure 4.2** Bentham's panopticon

Source: Adapted from https://en.wikipedia.org/wiki/Willey_Reveley

The idea of the panopticon is to use surveillance to evoke a form of self-discipline and regulation that can be used in prisons, schools, hospitals, industry, and in any other societal setting. Figure 4.2 shows the idea in relation to a prison. In the centre of the structure is a tower from which those in the cells around the edges are watched. Surveillance only goes one way, from the centre out. Shutters on the observation position enable the watcher to look out at the inmates but prevent the inmates from watching the watcher. In this manner, one person in the tower controls the entire inmate population. Inmates never know if they are being observed, so they act as if they are always being watched, which results in self-discipline.

It is no accident that the panopticon mirrors the structure we show in Figure 4.1 (the topography of oppression). Whiteness, or "normality," is in the centre from where it imposes its dominance on the Other. It enforces this domination through a supervision that "includes everything in its line of sight except its own apparatus: the eye that sees" (Leonardo, 2015, p. 91).

Across Canada, surveillance and discipline operate in part through conducting traffic stops on Black drivers in disproportionate numbers, and in Black and Indigenous people being stopped and "carded" and searched by the police in disproportionate numbers (Wakefield, 2017; Wortley & Tanner, 2004). In Toronto, race-biased "carding" practices are so extensive that in some neighbourhoods almost every single Black male has been stopped and documented by the police (Rankin, 2012), and carding rates are even higher in Saskatoon (Weighill, 2015).

This is not just a race issue or a Canadian issue. Feminists in the 1960s USA came under FBI surveillance (Johnston, 1991) for wanting equality with men. The FBI recruited women who were willing to infiltrate and spy on the feminist movement. (Recruitment was needed because at that time women were prohibited from becoming FBI agents so the FBI had no female agents who could do this undercover work.) The infiltrators reported back to the FBI that the feminist meetings were not a threat because they focused on issues like child care and who does the dishes, but the head of the FBI, J. Edgar Hoover, insisted that the undercover surveillance continue, because he regarded such talk as a threat to the security of the USA (Dore, 2014). In a similar way, Cindy Blackstock was placed under surveillance by Canadian government spies after campaigning for Indigenous children to be given the same access to social services that non-Indigenous children have (Harper, 2011). Also in Canada, the previous Harper government and current Trudeau government target charities for Canada Revenue Agency audits if they speak on issues or publish research that "irritates" the government (Smith, 2016). Such audits hardly ever show that charities have broken Canada's strict policy on political interference, so these audits serve little purpose other than to use the stress and extra workload caused by an audit to discipline and punish those who draw attention to issues that may cause people to question the status quo.

Such surveillance sends a message that people should "keep in their place" and not question the existing social order. Surveillance and discipline are backed by insidious messages in personal attitudes, societal systems, and culture that keep people "in their place." These messages become internalized as a form of self-discipline, resulting in people keeping themselves "in their place." Benjamin Zephaniah likens these disciplinary messages to listening to the "rong" radio station.

## Exercise 4.3

### The Rong Radio Station

If possible, undertake this exercise in groups.

View the video "the rong radio station" by Benjamin Zephaniah at one of the following links.

http://blackcabsessions.com/artists/#benjamin-zephaniah
https://youtu.be/oQIaU35EyVs

If you are wondering why Zephaniah is reciting the poem in the back of a London Taxi (a Black Cab), read the "about" information at the http://blackcabsessions.com. Answer the following questions:

1. Why did Zephaniah want to arrest himself?
2. What things does Zephaniah say that resonate for you and why?
3. What things does Zephaniah say that you cannot relate to and why?
4. Why does Zephaniah spell "wrong" as "rong"?

## White Innocence

Messages from the "rong radio station" help to hold those outside the circle of first-class citizenship on the margins, and help to keep those in the circle of first-class citizenship in a position of advantage. Exnomination and naturalization enable those in the centre of the circle to claim **White innocence**, which is the denial that processes of inclusion and exclusion are occurring. In fact rather than society and the media holding those in the centre responsible for oppression, those on the outside tend to get blamed for their own oppression. As Malcolm X observed, "If you're not careful, the newspapers will have you hating the people who are being oppressed, and loving the people who are doing the oppressing" (cited in Jones, 2001, p. 11).

Anyone paying attention understands there is no real White innocence because, although Whiteness has the power to make itself invisible and not be named, each of us has the power to see and name it. If we want to, we can stop blaming the oppressed and start holding responsible those who perpetuate the system. If we look and think critically as outlined in Chapter 2, the footprint of Whiteness in patterns of exclusion and inclusion are too obvious to miss; yet people do have an incredible ability to ignore, deny, or not see this footprint.

Figure 4.3 is a cartoon depicting contrasting Black and White perspectives in the **Black Lives Matter** movement. This movement began on social media in 2013 when George Zimmerman was acquitted for the killing of Black teen Trayvon Martin in Miami, Florida (Brown, 2013; Dennis, 2013). The cartoon in Figure 4.3 speaks to a later incident

**Figure 4.3**  I can't breathe, I can't see

in 2014 when a New York police officer choked to death Eric Garner, a Black man in New York, during an arrest. The slogan "I can't breathe" was adopted in protest. This slogan referred not only to this incident, but to the continual pattern of pushing down and holding back Black people, and especially the role of police violence in this process (Laughland, 2015).

The cartoon in Figure 4.3 makes the point that while Black America can't breathe, White America can't see. The cartoonist places a mask over the eyes of White America to convey that not seeing is the result of not looking. Indeed, the disproportionate killing of Blacks by the police in the USA is undeniable (Chaney & Robertson, 2013, 2015; Hall et al., 2016; Warren, Tomaskovic-Devey, Smith, Zingraff, & Mason, 2006). Racism in policing in Canada (Rankin, 2012; Rankin, Winsa, Bailey, & Ng, 2013), Europe (Pugliese, 2006) and Oceania (Medhora, 2015) is also undeniable. In the cartoon, the person who cannot (or will not) see not only fails to recognize the oppression of the Other, they also fail to see their own dominance or Whiteness.

We refuse to believe that most people would turn their backs on injustice unless something had closed their eyes to what is occurring; we contend that this "something" is Whiteness. Indeed, the racial contract is "an agreement among Whites to misinterpret the world as it is" (Leonardo, 2015, p. 92)—to deny the existence of racism and other isms. The nature of this contract is not an agreement to remember to forget, but an agreement to not process information in a way that challenges the dominance of Whiteness. The agreement is to not pay attention to racial (and other) disparity.

Although everyone should be able to recognize oppression, those who occupy the centre space can find it harder to tune into what is occurring. Indeed, feminists call the **glass ceiling** (sexism preventing the advancement of women in work places) "glass"

## Key Concept

The racial contract is not an agreement to remember to forget, but an agreement to not process information in a way that challenges the dominance of Whiteness. The agreement is to not pay attention to racial (and other) disparity.

because it can appear invisible until you bump up against it. Those not impacted by oppression have to work harder to notice it, because they do not experience it. In other words, **positionality** shapes perception. Positionality is a term coined by Alcoff (1988) to describe a relational position that arises from one's social location (such as race, gender, class, etc.). It is our place in the topography of oppression, which shapes the way we perceive others and the world around us. Given that Whiteness ensures that the world is structured around the needs, culture, and ways of being of those in the centre, the more one is in the centre of the circle, the more one is like a "fish in water." Indeed, exnomination means that many do not even know the name for the water they bask in, because their lives and likes are situated as natural or normal (universalized and naturalized). Unless those in the centre are paying attention, and that includes all of us who have some of our identity in the centre, we will not understand the extent to which we are privileged by the world being structured around our needs.

## White Privilege

Understanding privilege is crucial in anti-oppression. The word **privilege** means a special advantage. We are not against privilege when it is earned—if someone works hard to get ahead, we have no objection to them enjoying what they have earned. For us, anti-oppression is not restricting everyone to gaining the same from life, but ensuring that everyone gets the same opportunity in life. In other words, anti-oppression is not about stopping the game of life, but is about levelling the field that life is played upon.

Privilege is not a problem, but *unearned privilege* is, because it is inherently unfair when someone gains an advantage simply because of their race, gender, religion, or some similar characteristic. It is simply not fair to get ahead as a result of systems designed to push entire classes or categories of people forward and hold other classes and categories back. Nor is it fair to have the world structured according to one's own needs and likes at the expense of someone else.

Although we use the term *unearned privilege*, we have mixed feelings about using "unearned" as an adjective, because the fact is this privilege was "earned" (we are using the term "earned" satirically here) through hundreds of years of violent subjugation and the ongoing "hard work" of a vast majority refusing to accept that racism, sexism, and other isms still operate and make today's society unfair. Said differently, we do not like the term "unearned privilege" because it implies that the unfair advantage people get from it occurs by accident. There is no accident. They "earned" it (unfairly) through designing and operating an unjust system that dispossesses and marginalizes the Other.

We are not suggesting that those who benefit from the systems today are responsible for the actions of their ancestors. Even W.E.B. Du Bois (1903) said that the generation of White folks after the abolition of slavery were not responsible for slavery. We today, however, are fully responsible for the ways we perpetuate the ongoing inequalities that have roots in the early days of colonization. Every time someone denies the existence and ongoing impact of racism, colonization, and other forms of oppression, they are doing the "work" of earning unfair privilege for some at the expense of the Other. One does not have to be White to do the work of supporting oppression; people of all races, genders, and other locations inside and outside the circle of Whiteness engage in it too.

## Key Concept

Those who benefit from oppression today are not responsible for the actions of ancestors who built those systems of oppression. Those who benefit today, however, are fully responsible for the ways they perpetuate, maintain, and continue to reap the rewards of those systems.

Even though we are not entirely comfortable with the term *unearned privilege* (because it implies innocence), we use it because most people understand that it refers to gaining something that one has not earned in an honest and fair manner. Sometimes we replace the term unearned privilege with **White privilege**, because as described above the centre of the circle can be referred to as *Whiteness*. Also as mentioned above, do not misunderstand this term and conflate Whiteness with White people, or make assumptions and judge people based simply on their social location. One cannot judge people in this way; one cannot infer from the general to the specific; you cannot judge an individual based on a societal pattern. We do not use the term "White privilege" to stereotype, generalize, or judge White people, but to discuss the system of domination and subjugation as a whole. If you are reading this chapter and are judging or blaming White people, or if you are White and are blaming yourself, you are missing the point entirely. One way or another we are all implicated in Whiteness. The point is not to find someone to blame, but to find a way for each of us to  take responsibility for the part we play in oppression and for us to collectively change the system. We will talk more about how to bring change in later chapters, but first we want to explore your relationship to dominance.

## Locating Yourself

We locate ourselves by identifying our social locations in reference to the dominance shown in the centre of Figure 4.1. Our positionality within Figure 4.1 does not define who we are or what kind of person we are. Anyone who suggests that they can determine something about someone based on social location is wrong. The practice of labelling or making judgments about people based on assumptions about any of the locations they occupy inside or outside the circle is the first step in being oppressive (as discussed in Chapter 1). One cannot overcome oppression by more oppression.

We do not locate ourselves to define who we are. We do it to define our position in relation to the way power mechanisms operate at personal, systemic, and cultural levels to divide and sort people across a number of social variables. We locate not to define ourselves, but to map the way power may be defining us and the way it may be infiltrating our attitudes, thinking, and action. Locating ourselves helps us to take action to resist these forms of power by helping us to find unique points at which we can disrupt the way oppression operates.

## Exercise 4.4

### Flower Power

If possible, undertake this exercise in groups.

In the diagram of flowers on the next page, the centre of each flower represents dominance or first-class citizenship, and the petals represent social locations (gender, race, and so on). Each petal is divided into two, a part close to the centre and a part farther away. The part of the petal closest to the centre represents the same dominant space that we showed in the centre of the topography of oppression previously shown in Figure 4.1, and the outside part represents the marginalized space.

1. Make an enlarged photocopy of the flower on the left of Figure 4.4, or draw a copy of that flower on a piece of paper.
2. Using your copy of the flower, label each petal with social locations that you occupy and do not mind discussing and identifying in this exercise. These locations might include gender, race, religion, language, culture, class, etc.
3. For the petals in which you have a dominant social location, colour or shade in the part of the petal closest to the centre of your flower.
4. For the petals in which you have a marginalized social location, colour or shade in the part of the petal closest to the outside of your flower.

Once the flower is complete, the more dominant locations you have chosen to identify, the more the centre of your flower should be shaded or coloured, and the more marginalized locations you have chosen to identify the more the outside of your flower will be shaded or coloured. We have illustrated what the flower might look like for a social work manager in Ontario who identifies as a Muslim, woman of colour, whose native language is French (but also speaks English), and immigrated to Canada from Senegal, Africa.

Continued

The person in our example rates her gender, religion, and language as sites of marginality, and the remainder of sites she has chosen to highlight as locations of domination. She might change this configuration in a different context. For instance, if she moved to Quebec she might find her native French language gave her privilege, though she may find that speaking French with a Senegalese accent may not gain her the full social and cultural capital that comes from speaking French as a native Québécois.

If unsure about where to shade a petal because of these types of complexity, feel free to be creative and shade outside the lines and customize your response to represent the ways you see and experience your own position.

Discuss if you are in a group, or reflect and journal if alone:

1. Why did you choose (or not choose) specific locations?
2. Did you find yourself looking for and trying to include more marginalized locations, if so why?
3. What can you take for granted in life because of locations you have in the centre?
4. How might the locations change in differing contexts?
5. How does your flower shape the way you see and experience the world?
6. In which way do personal attitudes, systems, and culture operate to push you forward or hold you back in the dimensions you have shaded in the flower?

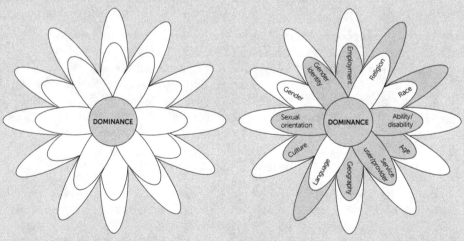

**Figure 4.4**

Source: Adapted from Lee, 1985

# Chapter Summary

In this chapter we explored the topography of oppression and what holds it in place. In particular, we examined the role of Whiteness, White supremacy, and the racial contract. We looked at how the boundary between first- and second-class citizenship is policed and maintained, we examined White privilege, and we asked you to explore your own social locations.

At the start of this chapter we told a story in which June wondered what made executive directors ignore her and go to Gary. We have seen in this chapter that this incident cannot be understood by looking only at June's social locations, but by looking at both June and Gary's locations in a broader social context of domination and subjugation.

After the incident June joked with Gary, "I want your body!" Of course June did not really want Gary's body, she was referring to the fact that Whiteness, the mechanisms of Figure 4.1, advantage some bodies over others. June was not implying that Gary had not worked to get ahead, nor that he did not deserve his success as a scholar; but the executive directors' offering him an opportunity based on her work was the perfect example of how White male privilege works. Of course June did not want this White privilege, she just wanted to get what she had earned.

When the incident with the executive directors occurred, June certainly did not want Gary to speak up for her, because June can speak for herself, and Gary knew this. Some might suggest that Gary should have spoken and used his unearned privilege to push back at oppression, but from June's perspective that would have been patronizing. And besides, the purpose is not to use unearned privilege, but to disrupt the mechanisms that cause it.

Gary paused to see if June was going to say something. It was not June's responsibility to say something, but if she wanted to respond Gary was not going to get in the way. Once it was clear that June was choosing not to speak, Gary spoke up—not for June—but for himself. Gary said to the executive directors, "June led this presentation and it is her work, so you had best speak with her." Gary then stood aside.

Stepping aside deserves no praise. It is not heroic, nor does it rest on some complex anti-oppressive algorithm. Stepping aside is just respect, good manners, and common sense. When someone offers you something that does not belong to you or you did not earn, do not take it. Instead say, "No, thanks." At least in this instance anti-oppression was easy. Or was it that easy? Consider June's and Gary's responses in the following discussion questions.

## Key Concept

The purpose of anti-oppression is not for those in a position of domination to use their unearned privilege on behalf of the oppressed. The purpose of anti-oppression is to disrupt the power mechanisms that give people privilege in the first place.

## Discussion Questions

As mentioned earlier, we still feel discomfort over the incident with the executive directors. We believe that we should have had a far better response, but even now we cannot think of what that response would be. Discuss the following questions in a group and note conclusions in your journal, or if working individually reflect on these questions alone and note your answers in your journal.

1. Why do you think Gary and June felt discomfort? In particular, what made them feel discomfort when it was the executive directors who had acted inappropriately?
2. We have always been unhappy with our response to the executive directors. Can you think of a better response than what June and Gary gave to the executive directors? Why do you think your response is better?

In developing your response, it would be easy to become angry with the executive directors involved, and shame them by calling them out publicly. Perhaps that is a legitimate response. But keep in mind that their mistake is one that many of us make one way or another at some point in time. So if your anti-oppressive response is to call out the executive directors and shame them, explain the following:

3. How would shaming the executive directors bring change (because change is the purpose of anti-oppression)?
4. Imagine others shaming you, and consider how others shaming you would help you (or not help you) change the next time you make a mistake of this nature (because sooner or later, one way or another, there are times when we all reinforce the dominance of Whiteness).

## Activities

1. Watch Kat Blaque describe the history of Whiteness in the USA at https://www.youtube.com/watch?v=bmHct5IHxrA. Develop your own explanation of Whiteness in the Canadian context and provide examples. (Do this individually or as a group.) Present your explanation to a friend or to a group, and invite them to challenge your ideas and examples (to ensure that your work is credible and robust).
2. Visit Macklemore & Ryan Lewis's website at http://www.whiteprivilege2.com and listen to their song, "white privilege II." Explore the website and their approach to addressing Whiteness.

## Suggested Resources

White millennials in Dallas, TX, talk about race: Whiteness project—Intersections of I. Retrieved from http://www.whitenessproject.org

Podcast: The Whiteness of public radio: What qualifies as a "good" radio voice? on CBC. Retrieved from http://www.cbc.ca/1.2967369

Baldwin, A., Cameron, L., & Kobayashi, A. (Eds). (2011). *Rethinking the great White North: Race, nature, and the historical geographies of whiteness in Canada.* Vancouver, Canada: University of British Columbia Press.

Salter, C. (2013). *Whiteness and social change: Remnant colonialisms and white civility in Australia and Canada.* Newcastle upon Tyne, UK: Cambridge Scholars Publishing.

Stanley, T.J. (2011). *Contesting white supremacy: School segregation, anti-racism, and the making of Chinese Canadians.* Toronto, Canada: UBC Press.

# References

Alcoff, L. (1988). Cultural feminism versus post structuralism: The identity crisis in feminist theory. *Signs, 13*(3), 405–36.

Allen, T.W. (2012). *The invention of the white race: Racial oppression and social control* (New Expanded Edition ed. Vol. 1). New York, NY: Verso Books.

Aretha, D. (Ed.). (2001). *The holocaust chronicle: A history in words and pictures.* Lincolnwood, IL: Publications International Ltd.

Arewa, O. (2016, June 21). Denim, dreadlocks and democracy: When does cultural appropriation become exploitation? *Quartz Africa.* Retrieved from http://qz.com/712556/denim-dreadlocks-and-democracy-when-does-cultural-appropriation-become-exploitation/

Badwall, H. (2016). Racialized discourses: Writing against an essentialized story about racism. *Intersectionalities: A Global Journal of Social Work Analysis, Research, Polity, and Practice, 5*(1), 8–19.

Bourdieu, P. (2004). The forms of capital. In S.J. Ball (Ed.), *The Routledge Falmer reader in sociology of education* (pp. 15–29). Abingdon, UK: Routledge.

Brodkin, K. (1998). *How Jews became white folks and what that says about race in America.* Piscataway, NJ: Rutgers University Press.

Brown, O.J.R. (2013). The legal murder of Trayvon Martin and New York City stop-and-frisk law: America's war against black males rages on. *Western Journal of Black Studies, 37*(4), 258–71.

Cannon, M. (1995). *The invisible empire: Racism in Canada.* Toronto, Canada: Random House of Canada.

Carniol, B. (2005). Analysis of social location and change: Practice implications. In S. Hick, R. Pozzuto, & J. Fook (Eds), *Social work: A critical turn* (pp. 153–166). Toronto, Canada: Thompson Educational Publishing.

Chaney, C.R., & Robertson, R.V. (2013). Racism and police brutality in America. *Journal of African American Studies, 17*(4), 480–505. doi:10.1007/s12111-013-9246-5

Chaney, C.R., & Robertson, R.V. (2015). Armed and dangerous? An examination of fatal shootings of unarmed black people by police. *The Journal of Pan African Studies, 8*(4), 45–78.

Collins, P.H. (2000). *Black feminist thought: Knowledge, consciousness, and the politics of empowerment.* New York, NY: Routledge.

Daniels, S. (2015, April 15). '"Hunger Games" Amandla Stenberg Talks Cornrows & Cultural Appropriation. *HypeHair.* Retrieved from http://www.hypehair.com/46876/amandla-stenberg-addresses-black-hairstyles-discussing-cultural-appropriation/

Dennis, D. (2013, August 15). Post-Zimmerman trial, a divided America. *The Guardian.* Retrieved from http://www.theguardian.com/commentisfree/2013/aug/15/george-zimmerman-trial-racially-divided-america

Dore, M. (2014). She's beautiful when she's angry [DVD/Film]. USA: Cinema Guild.

Downey, M. (1999, April 26). Canada's "genocide." *Maclean's, 112*(17), 56–8.

Du Bois, W.E.B. (1903). *The souls of black folk.* Chicago, IL: A.C. McClung and Co.

Dumbrill, G.C. (2003). Child welfare: AOP's nemesis? In W. Shera (Ed.), *Emerging perspectives on anti-oppressive practice* (pp. 101–19). Toronto, Canada: Canadian Scholars' Press.

Dumbrill, G.C. (2012). Anti-oppressive child welfare: How we get there from here. *The Ontario Association of Children's Aid Societies Journal, 57*(1), 2–8.

Farr, A. (2004). Whiteness visible: Enlightenment racism and the structure of racialized consciousness. In G. Yancy (Ed.), *What White looks like: African-American philosophers on the whiteness question* (pp. 143–58). New York, NY: Routledge.

Geddes, J. (2013, October 3). Canadian anti-Muslim sentiment is rising, disturbing new poll reveals: Angus Reid survey reveals a land of intolerance. *Macleans.* Retrieved from http://www.macleans.ca/politics/land-of-intolerance/

Gilroy, P. (1987). *There ain't no black in the Union Jack: The cultural politics of race and nation.* London, UK: Hutchinson.

Goldberg, D. T. (1993). *Racist culture: Philosophy and the politics of meaning.* Oxford, UK: Blackwell Publishers Inc.

Guglielmo, J., & Salerno, S. (2003). *Are Italians white? How race is made in America.* New York, NY: Routledge.

Gullace, N.F. (1997). White feathers and wounded men: Female patriotism and the memory of the great war. *Journal of British Studies, 36*(2), 178–206.

Hall, A.V., Hall, E.V., & Perry, J.L. (2016). Black and blue: Exploring racial bias and law enforcement in the killings of unarmed black male civilians. *American Psychologist, 71*(3), 175–86. doi:10.1037/a0040109

Harper, T. (2011, November 15). Tim Harper: Government spies on advocate for native children. *Toronto Star.* Retrieved from http://www.thestar.com/news/canada/2011/11/15/tim_harper_government_spies_on_advocate_for_native_children.html

Hodge, D.R. (2007). Advocating for persecuted people of faith: A social justice imperative. *Families in Society, 88*(2), 255–62. doi:10.1606/1044-3894.3623

Ignatiev, N. (1995). *How the Irish became white*. New York, NY: Roultledge.

Johnston, D. (1991, September 30). For FBI, Women's Lib spelled danger. *Toronto Star*, p. B1.

Jones, R.S. (2001). Black/Indian relations: An overview of the scholarship. *Transforming Anthropology, 10*(1), 2–16. doi: 10.1525/tran.2001.10.1.2

Kecklund, L, Kristin, K., Staffan, B., Sara, W., & Elena, S. (2012). How do people with disabilities consider fire safety and evacuation possibilities in historical buildings? A Swedish case study. *Fire Technology, 48*(1), 27–41. doi:10.1007/s10694-010-0199-0

Laughland, O. (2015, July 25). Eric Garner killing, one year on: "Sit down son, it's time for The Talk." *The Guardian*. Retrieved from http://www.theguardian.com/lifeandstyle/2015/jul/25/eric-garner-killing-one-year-on-sit-down-son-its-time-for-the-talk

Leonardo, Z. (2015). Contracting race: Writing, racism, and education. *Critical Studies in Education, 56*(1), 86–98. doi: 10.1080/17508487.2015.981197

Lightman, N., & Gingrich, L.G. (2013). The intersecting dynamics of social exclusion: Age, gender, race and immigrant status in Canada's labour market. *Canadian Ethnic Studies, 44*(3), 121–45. doi:10.1353/ces.2013.0010

MacDonald, D.B., & Hudson, G. (2012). The genocide question and Indian Residential Schools in Canada. *Canadian Journal of Political Science, 45*(2), 427–49. doi:10.1017/S000842391200039X

McClelland, S. (2001, October 22). Rising from the fire. *Maclean's, 114*(43), 56.

Medhora, S. (2015, October 29). Police abuse of Aboriginal man shows racism still rife, says Warren Mundine. *The Guardian*. Retrieved from http://www.theguardian.com/australia-news/2015/oct/29/police-abuse-of-aboriginal-man-shows-racism-still-rife-says-warren-mundine

Mills, C.W. (1997). *The racial contract*. Ithaca, NY: Cornell University Press.

Mills, C.W. (2015). The racial contract revisited: Still unbroken after all these years. *Politics, Groups, and Identities, 3*(3), 541–57. doi:10.1080/21565503.2015.1053400

Mullaly, B., & West, J. (2018). *Challenging oppression and confronting privilege: A critical approach to anti-oppressive and anti-privilege theory and practice* (3rd edn). Toronto, Canada: Oxford University Press.

Müller-Wille, S. (2014). Race and history: Comments from an epistemological point of view. *Science, Technology, and Human Values, 39*(4), 597–606. doi:10.1177/0162243913517759

Powell, K.J. (2016). Making #BlackLivesMatter: Michael Brown, Eric Garner, and the specters of black life—Toward a hauntology of blackness. *Cultural Studies Critical Methodologies, 16*(3), 253–60. doi:10.1177/15327086166347759

Pugliese, J. (2006). Asymmetries of terror: Visual regimes of racial profiling and the shooting of Jean Charles de Menezes in the context of the war in Iraq. *Borderlands E-Journal: New Spaces in the Humanities, 5*(1).

Purvis, J. (2002). Emmeline Pankhurst: A biography by June Purvis. Abingdon, UK: Routledge.

Rankin, J., & Winsa, P. (2012, March 9). Known to police: Toronto police stop and document black and brown people far more than whites. *Toronto Star*. Retrieved from http://www.thestar.com/news/insight/2012/03/09/known_to_police_toronto_police_stop_and_document_black_and_brown_people_far_more_than_whites.html

Rankin, J., Winsa, P., Bailey, A., & Ng, H. (2013, September 28). "Devastating. Unacceptable":Toronto police board chair appalled by Star findings that show a stubborn rise in the number of citizens stopped and documented by our police officers—with black males heavily overrepresented. *Toronto Star*, p. A1.

Scholes, B. (2005). Exit strategy. *The Safety & Health Practitioner, 23*(12), 50–2.

Smith, R. (2016, March 20). Canada's charity chill continues. *Toronto Star*. Retrieved from http://www.thestar.com/opinion/commentary/2016/03/20/canadas-charity-chill-continues.html

Turner, J. (2015). Reconstructing liberalism: Charles Mills' unfinished project. *Politics, Groups, and Identities, 3*(3), 471–87. doi:10.1080/21565503.2015.1050418

Wakefield, J. (2017, June 27). Black people, Aboriginal women over-represented in "carding" police stops. *Edmonton Journal*. Retrieved from http://edmontonjournal.com/news/local-news/black-people-aboriginal-women-over-represented-in-carding-police-stops

Warren, P., Tomaskovic-Devey, D., Smith, W., Zingraff, M., & Mason, M. (2006). Driving while black: Bias processes and racial disparity in police stops. *Criminology: An Interdisciplinary Journal, 44*(3), 709–38. doi:10.1111/j.1745-9125.2006.00061.x

Weighill, C. (2015, August 19). Saskatoon police do more carding than other Canadian cities: report. *CBC News*. Retrieved from http://www.cbc.ca/news/canada/saskatoon/saskatoon-police-do-more-carding-than-other-canadian-cities-report-1.3196741

Weinfeld, M. (2016). A history of antisemitism in Canada by Ira Robinson. *Canadian Ethnic Studies, 46*(1), 179–81. doi:10.1353/ces.2016.0000

Wortley, S., & Tanner, J. (2004). Discrimination or good policing? The racial profiling debate in Canada. *Our Diverse Cities* (1), 197–201.

Yee, J.Y., & Dumbrill, G.C. (2016). Whiteout: Still looking for race in Canadian social work practice. In A. Al-Krenawi, J. R. Graham, & N. Habibov (Eds), *Diversity and social work in Canada* (2nd edn, pp. 13–37). Toronto, Canada: Oxford University Press.

Young, I.M. (2011). *Justice and the politics of difference: With a new foreward by Danielle Allen*. Princeton, NJ: Princeton University Press.

# 5 Isms and Intersectionality Part One: Racism and Sexism

## In this chapter you will learn:

- What racism is and how it is understood, including anti-Black, anti-Jewish, and anti-Muslim racism
- What sexism is and how it is understood
- How multiple forms of oppression intersect
- How all the forms of oppression listed above are resisted

## Introduction

Emma, Gary's Nan (grandmother), lived off Cable Street in the East End of London, England. At that time, in the early 1900s, the East End was home to the poorest of the poor, a place for those down on their luck, a place of displaced persons, a place for the down-trodden and refugees. In those days newcomers included Ashkenazi Jews and people like Gary's Nan, the daughter of Irish immigrants.

Although there were conflicts and sometimes violence between East Enders, they were joined together by the solidarity of all being on the margins, and by the title "cockney," which was the name given to anyone who put down roots in that area of London.

In the 1930s, Sir Oswald Mosley, a member of Britain's ruling elite (Catterall, 1994), formed the British Union of Fascists (BUF), which he modelled on Mussolini's fascism (Tilles, 2015) and Hitler's Nazi ideals (Catterall, 1994). BUF members were soon making incursions into the East End to attack cockney Jews (Tilles, 2015). To further the intimidation, Mosley decided to march an army of thousands of BUF fascists (mostly in military Blackshirt Nazi uniforms) through the East End streets where the Jewish communities lived.

On the day of the march, 4 October 1936, 6000 police officers arrived to clear away anyone trying to stop the fascists (Catterall, 1994). Gary's Nan told him the story of what happened next. "Boy," she said (she always called Gary *boy*), "we were not going to put up with that. We decided, 'They shall not pass,' so we barricaded Cable Street near Tower Hill, I picked up a big stick, and I cracked some fascist heads."

It was not just Gary's Nan who took to the streets. An estimated 20,000 (Tilles, 2015) to 250,000 (Catterall, 1994) came from all over England to stop the march. In an event now known as "The Battle of Cable Street," despite mounted police baton charges, neither the police nor fascists were able to pass the community blockade.

Gary's Nan and the communities she was a part of understood something about oppression and anti-oppression that is crucial today. In this chapter and the next we will review several forms of oppression and the isms associated with them. We begin this chapter by examining racisms and sexism, and we continue in the next chapter with heterosexism, cissexism, ableism, and sanism. In this chapter we will also get into some of the complexities of racialization, including how certain White groups are sometimes racialized. In these moments we will, as mentioned in the preface, sometimes use the term "people of colour" where to do otherwise might cause confusion about the groups who are being racialized in specific situations.

At the end of the next chapter you will understand how multiple forms of oppression operate and intersect, and some of the complexities of racialization. You will also understand how to identify and name these forms of oppression, and how the story of The Battle of Cable Street

Douglas Lander/Alamy Stock Photo

**Figure 5.1** A partial image of a mural on Cable Street commemorating the battle

demonstrates how people can unite across their own differences to form effective anti-oppressive alliances. You will also understand how you can develop such alliances in your own work.

# Racism

The conceptual work needed to understand racism was explained in the previous chapter. We learned that race does not exist; it is a social construction based on a perception of human difference. We also learned that although race does not exist, racism exists. Racism is the pushing down and holding back of people who are considered racially different from the dominant group. There are many forms of racism, but one of the most predominant is anti-Black racism.

## Anti-Black Racism

The Atlantic slave trade was one of the founding events of anti-Black racism. As stated in the previous chapter, slavery has existed for thousands of years but the invention of race and the emergence of White European colonization transformed slavery into a process that designated the Black race as slaveable. No longer were people made slaves only as a consequence of debt or crime, because their nations had been conquered, or for some similar reason. Now people were made slaves and were designated as a commodity to be traded simply because of their physical appearance. The ideology that designated Black Africans as slaves still exists today and it drives modern anti-Black racism.

## Critical Race Theory

**Critical race theory** (CRT) uncovers the way anti-Black racism is embedded in modern society. CRT originates in the USA and builds on the insights advanced by critical legal studies and radical feminism movements and, more recently, can be seen applied in the social sciences, political theory, and educational and ethnic studies. A number of CRT scholars (for instance Aylward, 1999; Constance-Huggins, 2012; Delgado, Stefancic, & Harris, 2012) draw out six key points from the literature on this topic. Not all CRT scholars use these points, but these do seem to cover the core concepts of CRT. We have discussed many of these points already because they are not unique to CRT, but because of the importance of these points, we reiterate them here:

1. Racism is not simply the prejudiced views and acts of an individual, but is a part of a broader system of inequality and oppression that is not only built into the social fabric, it also routinely shapes and affects the everyday life experiences of racialized people. Since racism is so commonplace and present in society, those who hold racial privilege can choose, if they wish, to ignore the realities of racism and even pretend that they do not exist.

2. Race is a social construction that provides the basis for racialization and racism.

3. Racialization occurs in different ways for various "racial" groups and at different points in history depending on the context and in particular the extent a group's interests are (or are perceived to be) congruent with the dominant group.

4. Race is a core issue in racism, but oppression is also intersectional, which means that one oppression compounds another in unique ways along the lines of not only race, but also class, gender, ethnicity, religion, sexual identity, etc.

5. Racism needs to be countered by the storytelling and narrative-making of those who are racialized in ways that exclude them from the dominant White narrative (Parker, Ledesma, & Calderón, 2015; Leonardo, 2013). We have not discussed storytelling yet, but you have probably already noticed that we have built this book around the idea of stories.

6. The legal system, backed by the state, operates primarily in the interests of White people. We have not addressed this issue yet, though it is implicit in previous chapters and especially in the points we made about the racial contract in Chapter 4. CRT scholars, however, are quite explicit that racism is put into both the letter and process of today's laws (Bell, 2008; Delgado et al., 2012).

## Interest-Convergence

The CRT argument about law is founded on the idea that the state is "a *tool*, created, maintained, and used by whites to advance their collective racial interests . . . and as an instrument for maintaining white dominance" (Bracey II, 2015, p. 558). It may appear that laws such as the American Civil Rights Act of 1964, which banned racial segregation, was an advancement of anti-racism won through activism. CRT scholars, however, would contend that this and similar advances only occur because Whites recognized that there was something in this change for them too (Bell, 1980). This process is sometimes called interest-convergence (Bell, 1980, 2004; Parker, 2015).

**Interest-convergence** is a process in which "Black rights are recognized and protected when and only so long as [White] policymakers perceive that such advances will further interests that are their primary concern" (Bell, 2004, p. 49). For instance, one could argue that the Civil Rights Act of 1964 was less about justice for Black people and more about the interests of Whites. America had to do something about the rights of Black citizens in the civil rights era because international and domestic criticisms of America's human-rights record was undermining the nation's credibility and especially the way it positioned itself as a force for justice and freedom in the face of growing global communism (Bell, 1980). As well, desegregation helped Whites in the American South move away from a rural plantation economy toward a more industrialized and profitable one (Bell, 1980). In other words, desegregation was needed to end the "state-sponsored segregation" (Bell, 1980, p. 525) that was preventing the American South from realizing its economic potential in the global world.

Of course interest-convergence does not mean that Black people do not benefit from such change, but it does mean that change only occurs if it also benefits Whites. In other words, there will only be an advance in the rights of those outside the circle of Whiteness (see Figure 4.1) if this advance benefits those inside the circle.

# Key Concept

Interest-convergence does not mean that Black people do not benefit from advances in civil rights and anti-racist change, but does mean that such advances and change only occur if they also benefit Whites.

Interest-convergence theory can be seen in action with the abolition of slavery. Abolition should have erased the race line, yet no sooner was slavery abolished than there were new ways to maintain that line and preserve the interests of Whites. An array of Jim Crow laws (state laws segregating Black from White) and other regulations and cultural practices were used to tread down and hold back freed slaves to maintain the supreme advantage of Whites.

## Policing the Race Line

With slavery gone, how was the race line to be policed? Slavery had made things simple. Whites were free and Blacks were mostly slaves, so the race line was relatively easy to distinguish and maintain. Abolishing slavery made things more complex; without the distinction of "free" and "slave," how were Black and White to be distinguished? As shown in Chapter 4, what we label as "race" is not always easy to discern, so with the categories of free and slave abolished, how would people know who to oppress and who to privilege?

The solution was to draw the race line based on how much "Black blood" one had (Omi & Winant, 1994). Of course there is no such thing as Black or White blood, so formulas to calculate whether one was Black or White were based on ancestry. The problem is nobody could agree on a calculation formula about how many Black ancestors one needed to be considered Black (Sharfstein, 2003). As a result, some people were Black in one state and White in another. These different formulas caused all manner of absurdities. For example, given that railway carriages were racially segregated (Baker, 1901), some people would have needed to change carriages when their train crossed the borders of states that used different race formulas.

Although efforts to separate White from Black are absurd, policing the race line was serious business, because it determined who was to get ahead in life and who was to be held back. It sorted those who could exploit from those who could be exploited. Eventually efforts were made to standardize the way the race line was set with the "one drop rule" which designated anyone with any Black ancestor as Black (Sharfstein, 2003). Policing the race line was not only about deciding who to oppress, it was also about keeping the White race "pure."

## Key Concept

Efforts to separate Black from White and police the race line are absurd, because there is only one race, the human race. But policing the race line is serious business, because it determines who is to get ahead in life and who is to be held back; it sorts those who can exploit from those who can be exploited.

This policing of the race line, and the anti-Black racism it represents, remains just as alive and well today as it was in the days of slavery and in the Jim Crow era. We reviewed this in Chapter 4 when considering the drivers of anti-Black racism, which are Whiteness and White supremacy, so we will not reiterate those examples here. Keep in mind, though, that although we have focused on the history of these processes, the overrepresentation of Black children in state care (OACAS, 2016), the police carding of Black youth (Rankin, Winsa, Bailey, & Ng, 2013), the overrepresentation of Black people in the criminal justice systems (Owusu-Bempah & Wortley, 2014), the underrepresentation of Black people in positions of power and influence (Allen & Lewis, 2016), and the systematic killing of Black people by the police (Morgan, 2016) are all manifestations of anti-Black racism in today's society.

## Exercise 5.1

### Where Is Freedom?

If possible, undertake this exercise in groups. Listen to the performance of "letter to the free" by Common at https://youtu.be/KO7tVuPHOxA. (Be aware that Common reclaims words in the video. See Chapter 3 for an explanation of this language.) Reflect on and discuss:

1. What do you think this song is about? What does it communicate to you, and why?
2. What things in "letter to the free" resonate with our review of anti-Black racism in this chapter and why?
3. Why do you think Common calls this song/spoken work "letter to the free"?
4. Next, watch Common recite and explain the lyrics of this song at https://youtu.be/WKR2CULDWrg. Compare these meanings with the meanings that you noticed. Go back and watch the full music video and look for these meanings, not only in the lyrics, but also in the way they are communicated in the music and the visuals in the video. Look for echoes of these meanings in the rest of this chapter.

## Anti-Jewish Racism

Racism also impacts Jewish people. Racism against Jewish people is usually referred to as **anti-Semitism**, which is a term used for a "hostile political and social attitude towards Jews, for the sole fact of being who they are [i.e. Jewish]" (Iugu & Batin, 2013, p. 65).

The oppression of Jewish people pre-dates the term anti-Semitism. The term **Semite** was developed in the eighteenth century when biblical scholars began to use it to refer to a family of languages, such as Hebrew and Arabic, with a common historical root they traced back to the Biblical character Sem, the son of Noah (Kalmar, 2009). These ideas led to the notion of a corresponding Semite "race." The idea of a Semite race is now recognized as a social construction and the term "Semite" is no longer used outside linguistics (Wikipedia, 2017). The idea of a Semite *race*, however, locates the hatred of Jewish people as a form of *racism*.

Nazi oppression of Jewish people was based on the notion of race, and on a grand theory Hitler developed about human history being a struggle between races, with the White Aryan race being the superior race and destined to rule. Within this ideology, six million Jewish people were killed because the Nazis believed that the Semitic race needed to be eliminated in the name of human progress (Iugu & Batin, 2013).

Anti-Semitism not only shaped Nazi atrocities, it also shaped the decision of Canada and the USA to refuse entry of Jewish people escaping the holocaust on the ship M.V. *St Louis*, and the decision of Britain to rescue only a few from that ship (mentioned in Chapter 1). This ideology also drove Mosley's attacks on the Jewish communities of London's East End (mentioned at the start of this chapter).

The oppression of Jewish people predates the social construction of race. In the Middle Ages the concept of a Semite race did not exist, yet Jewish people faced **anti-Judaism**, which is a hatred and oppression of Jews based primarily on their religion. The Christian church played a significant role in this oppression by claiming that Jewish people were responsible for the killing of Jesus. Even though this belief is based on a misreading of Christian texts (Marendy, 2005), and in our opinion is based on a total misunderstanding of Christianity, the anti-Jewish acts this type of Christianity propagated over the centuries have been extensive and deadly.

Given the above, we can divide what we now call anti-Semitism into several historical waves, including "religious anti-Semitism specific to the Mid Ages, the economical anti-Semitism of the modern age, the racial and nationalist anti–Semitism specific to the first half of the 20th century and a politically driven anti–Semitism which manifested itself in the post-war and contemporary period" (Iugu & Batin, 2013, p. 65). Despite a shift over the centuries from a religious- to a race-based oppression (Marendy, 2005), we suspect that all along the exact same attitudes drove both ideologies; all that changed was the way that people attempted to justify and propagate their hatred.

Anti-Semitism is still with us. Attacks on Jewish people, synagogues, and Jewish monuments are a growing trend in Canada (B'Nai Brith Canada, 2015). Despite these trends, there have been changes, with some authors claiming that Jewish people have become White (Brodkin, 1998; Green, 2016a). In other words, Jewish people have moved from outside the circle of Whiteness (shown in Figure 4.1) and into the centrality of the mainstream. This may be so, but given that anti-Semitic hate crimes are growing in Canada, it seems that this membership in Whiteness is tenuous at best.

## Anti-Muslim and Anti-Islam Racism

Racism also impacts Muslims. We use the term "anti-Muslim" or "anti-Islam" to refer to this racism, but many call it **Islamophobia** (Garner & Selod, 2015; Perry, 2015; Taras, 2013). All of these terms refer to the "social reality—that Islam and Muslims have emerged as objects of aversion, fear, and hostility in contemporary liberal democracies" (Bleich, 2011, p. 1584).

We have an issue with the term "Islamaphobia," because *isms* that are called *phobias* makes the ism sound like an anxiety disorder related to mental illness rather than a bigotry that comes from personal, systemic, and cultural prejudices. In addition, likening any kind of bigotry to a mental illness insults Mad people (more about that in Chapter 6). We could use the term "Islam*ism*" for Islamaphobia, but that word is already taken in a completely different context to describe a political form of Islam, so we prefer to use the term anti-Muslim or anti-Islam racism.

We are also uneasy with using the term "race" because Islam is a faith of many "races," so **anti-Muslim** or **anti-Islam** (with no "racism" attached) are considered more precise terms to describe the prejudice directed at Muslims (Bleich, 2011). We, however, find that there are so many similarities between racism and the oppression of Muslims that we interchangeably use the words "racism," "anti-Muslim," and "anti-Islam" to mean the same thing, and where necessary we use the term "Islamophobia" to make our analysis complement current literature on this topic.

Anti-Muslim attitudes have grown in recent years (Geddes, 2013) and this is often attributed to the terrorist attacks of 9/11 (Perry, 2015). While one cannot understand modern anti-Muslim sentiment without understanding the post 9/11 world, Western hatred of Muslims goes back many years before this. For instance, over 1000 years ago British and other Europeans initiated a series of Crusades to rid the "Holy Land" (Palestine) and the wider Mediterranean from a growing Muslim influence (Riley-Smith, 2014). To kick-start these wars, the Pope gave anyone taking part "indulgences," which was an assurance that God would forgive any killing and murdering the Crusaders engaged in (Riley-Smith, 2014). These indulgences were soon used. The first English crusaders murdered and raped their way across Europe on route to Palestine, starting with a massacre of Jewish communities in Germany (Nerenberg, 2002). Killing peaceful Jews in Germany had nothing to do with liberating Palestine from Muslims. Instead it had everything to do with hate and bigotry toward the non-Christian *Other*, which was arguably one of the main influences that caused people to set off on this (and other) crusades.

Similar violence against the Other exists today. In Hamilton, Ontario, after 9/11, a Hindu temple came under an anti-Muslim arson attack. Of course if this had been a Muslim mosque this attack would be equally wrong, but the fact that the attackers seemed to not care what kind of Other they were attacking reminds us of the massacre of the German Jews in the First Crusade; when hate and bigotry is at play, any Other serves as a target for attack.

A term used for the hatred of the Other is **xenophobia**, which comes from the Greek words "xeno" (stranger) and "phobia" (fear); thus xenophobia means fear of the stranger. Again we do not like the notion of a phobia, but fear is certainly a part of this process, especially when fear turns into hate. Xenophobia is arguably a part of all oppression, particularly racism. In this context, the term **xeno-racism** is used for "'a non-colour-coded' racism that is based on conceptions of immigration status, culture and religion" (Fekete, 2014, p. 33). Xeno-racism takes aim at people who are different from the mainstream, particularly in religion or culture. Xeno-racism can be defined as a:

> . . . racism that is not just directed at those with darker skins, from the former colonial territories, but at the newer categories of the displaced, the dispossessed and the uprooted who are beating at western Europe's doors, the Europe that helped to displace them in the first place. It is a racism, that is, that cannot be colour-coded, directed as it is at poor whites as well, and is therefore passed off as xenophobia, a "natural fear" of strangers. But in the way it denigrates and reifies people before segregating and/or expelling them, it is a xenophobia that bears all the marks of the old racism. It is racism in substance, but "xeno" in form. It is a racism that is meted out to impoverished strangers even if they are white. (Sivanandan 2001 cited in Fekete, 2014, pp. 36–7)

Muslims are particularly vulnerable to xeno-racism because political leaders and the media consistently portray them as a threat. This anti-Muslim rhetoric was especially prevalent in Donald Trump's 2016 presidential campaign and his subsequent presidency, which has seen attempts to ban Muslims from several countries from entering the United States, a policy that has impacted Muslims in Canada too (Mulligan, 2017). Anti-Islam racism is driven in part by Muslims being portrayed as "real or potential 'enemies'" (Shyrock, 2010, p. 9). Indeed, attacks on mosques in Canada and the USA have become an ongoing reality (BBC, 2015), including an armed attack on the Islamic Cultural Centre in Quebec City in 2017 that left six people dead and nineteen injured. Charged with six counts of murder in the Quebec attack is a Canadian man described in the media as supporting US President Donald Trump (*The Globe and Mail*, 2017).

As well, the vilification of Islam and all Muslims can be partly explained by Edward Said's (1979) notion of Orientalism that we discussed in Chapter 2. Orientalism creates the conditions to allow Islamophobia to happen through a discourse of Othering that situates Islam (and as a result Muslims) as belonging to the uncivilized East (Orient), as opposed to the civilized West (Occident). Note that this applies to Judaism and Jewish people too.

Like all isms, prejudice against Muslims comes in the form of contradictory and constantly changing stereotypes, and from the many distorted views made about Islam that are routinely perpetuated by the West (Tamdgidi, 2012). Islamophobia, however, is not confined to the West; it is also a worldwide phenomenon (Shyrock, 2010). Indeed, anti-Islamic and anti-Muslim acts and attitudes are a growing issue; parts of Canada are said to be facing an "epidemic of Islamophobia" (Keung, 2016). In France there was a 400 per cent increase in physical attacks on Muslims in the first half of 2015 compared to the same time the previous year. Such attacks are also skyrocketing elsewhere in Europe (Alkan, 2016), and in the USA (Green, 2016b).

## Racism against Whites, and "Reverse Racism"

White people can be pushed down by racism too. For instance, the British Brexit referendum on withdrawing from the European Union (EU) evoked a number of racist attacks on Polish and other Eastern European people who were told to "go home." Even British people of colour took part in this racist rhetoric (Fitzgerald & Smoczyński, 2015; Spigelman, 2013). In Britain, Eastern Europeans have been racialized into a position outside the dominant circle of Whiteness, and have had the White power of the centre position turned against them. This is similar to the processes we spoke of in Chapter 4, when Irish, Italian, and Jewish people were not considered White (Brodkin, 1998; Guglielmo & Salerno, 2003; Ignatiev, 1995).

Eastern Europeans being told to "go back home" is certainly racism, and although British people of colour joined in these attacks, it does not mean that racism has been reversed. **Reverse racism** describes a process in which the power that drives racism has switched so that White people as a whole are the target of racism undertaken by people of colour who now wield systemic and cultural power (C.E. James, 2007; Stikkers, 2014). This process is not illustrated in the attack on Eastern Europeans, because although Eastern Europeans are certainly being subjected to racialization and racism, this racism is not underwritten by people of colour, but by White British nationalism. Consequently, there has been no reversal of racism, because Eastern Europeans are being targeted by the exact same White supremacy that drives all racism. All that has happened is that British White supremacy has marked White Eastern Europeans as Other, and is subjecting them to a similar form of White racism that continues to routinely exclude people of colour. Consequently, Eastern Europeans are facing *xeno-racism*, not reverse racism.

## Does Gary Face Reverse Racism?

Questions about reverse racism often come up when we teach or train on the topic of anti-oppression. We often find White people thinking that they, or their friends, have been on the receiving end of reverse racism. These stories and questions arise when people do not recognize that, for something to be racist, it has to be backed by systemic and cultural power. For instance, once in Hong Kong someone called Gary 鬼佬 (Gwai Lo), which means foreign devil or White ghost person, and several times in New York City he has been called a "honkey." These events are not *racism*, because these words are not connected to systems of power at systemic and cultural levels that push Gary down and hold him back in multiple dimensions of his life. Even in Hong Kong, rather than being disadvantaged by his social location, Gary gains advantage by being White and very obviously British. Consequently, White people may be made uncomfortable by derogatory terms, attitudes, and even harmful acts toward them because of their race, but they do not face the relentless daily powerful putting down and pushing back of personal, systemic, and cultural oppression along the lines of race. Consequently, derogatory racial put-downs and remarks toward Gary and other White people can be considered hurtful and wrong, but they can only be considered racist if they are backed by systemic and cultural oppression.

## June Faces Racism

June faces almost constant racism from systemic and cultural oppression, which give any derogatory racial comments she receives at a personal level a different meaning to any that Gary may receive. This is because derogatory racial comments reinforce the race-based oppression she faces at systemic and cultural levels. For instance, at school June used to be teased about her middle name "Ying" and was advised by friends not to use it because it made her sound "too ethnic" (Yee & Dumbrill, 2016). Gary had trouble with his middle name at school too; "Cornelius" was so out of vogue that he was constantly teased. We cannot say who felt more hurt, Gary or June, but we can say that the nature of the teasing was different. Gary was made fun of because of a name, while June was made fun of because of who she was; her name was linked to her racial identity. This meant that June's school friends were replicating and reinforcing a message that June and other Asian people face in almost every aspect of their life in Canada: a message that they do not belong. Indeed, in 2010 Canadian *Maclean's* magazine ran a front page article titled "Too Asian," which complained that "too many" Asian students were attending Canadian universities (Cui & Kelly, 2013). Also, when Canada announced the design for the new $100 bill, with the image of a Canadian woman of Asian heritage on the back, public protests arose stating that the woman was "not Canadian enough." The government quickly replaced the image with a White woman (The Canadian Press, 2012). The message was clear: June and those like her do not belong in the Canadian fabric.

Gary has never been told that he is "too British," or that he is "not Canadian enough," nor does he face a macro (society-wide) pattern of exclusion or rejection. Consequently, teasing Gary about his middle name may be hurtful and inappropriate, but it does not connect to a system of oppression based on who he is. In contrast, teasing June about her middle name does connect to systems of exclusion, which makes derogatory remarks about June's name a racial microaggression. We briefly mentioned such aggressions in Chapter 1, which are:

> . . . a form of systemic, everyday racism used to keep those at the racial margins in their place. They are: (1) verbal and non-verbal assaults directed toward People of Color, often carried out in subtle, automatic or unconscious forms; (2) layered assaults, based on race and its intersections with gender, class, sexuality, language, immigration status, phenotype, accent, or surname; and (3) cumulative assaults that take a psychological, physiological, and academic toll on People of Color. (Huber & Solozano, 2015, p. 298)

Although we understand teasing Gary and June about their middle names differently, it does not mean that either teasing was acceptable; it simply means that we understand the nature and implications of each differently. Gary faced bullying, June faced bullying and racism. Gary faced put-downs and a sense of exclusion because of his name, June felt exclusion and put-downs because of who she was.

## Resisting Racism

The primary means for addressing and resisting racism is **anti-racism**, which is a broad international social movement that began in the 1980s, comprising activists, intellectuals, practitioners, and everyday people committed to challenging racism in national and local contexts. Anti-racism needs to be broad because, as shown above, racism affects many different groups of people. There is some logic in bringing these differences together under a broad banner of anti-racism, because although anti-Black, anti-Jewish, anti-Muslim, and anti-Chinese racism (and many other racisms we could have mentioned) all manifest in different ways, the driving force behind them is Whiteness and White supremacy. The American scholar Judy Katz (2003) makes this clear in her anti-racism work—the problem of racism is not the problem of those on the receiving end of racism, but rather the problem of White people and the Whiteness that propagates racism. Of course we must also focus on the way racism impacts specific groups within society, and on the specific impact of certain kinds of racism. For instance, the Black Lives Matter movement makes it clear that we have to pay attention to the impact of anti-Black racism. Our point, however, is that to stop racism we have to focus on the people who are doing it and are benefiting from it.

Canadian scholar George Dei defines anti-racism as "an educational political action-oriented strategy for institutional and systemic change to address racism and the interlocking systems of social oppression" (Dei, 1996, p. 25). In Canada's educational and human services sector, anti-racism is used as a practical tool to challenge the often hidden and unknown White hegemonic practices operating in institutional, procedural, and everyday practices (Dei, 1996; Henry & Tator, 2010; McCaskell, 2005). Similar to the point we consistently make in this text, such work recognizes that the belief and value system that holds the entire structure of oppression together is based on White supremacy (Snyder, 2015).

## Exercise 5.2

### Canadian Anti-Racist Initiatives

If possible, undertake this exercise as a group.

The state has taken up anti-racism, particularly in the UK and Canada, in recognition that the government has a responsibility to address racism. Search for an official government department responsible for anti-racism in your province or territory. Look also for any other organizations in your area that do anti-racism work. Review the work of these departments and organizations and answer the following questions:

1. Does your province or territory have a department with the mission of anti-racism work?
2. If so, how does this department define racism, and what work is it doing?
3. What other organizations do anti-racism work in your area? What work do they do? How does this work compare or contrast with the government departments who do this work?
4. Do you think the anti-racism work of the government or other organizations in your area is compatible with what we have said about anti-oppression in this book?

Some scholars claim that anti-oppression and anti-racism are incompatible (Pon, Giwa, & Razack, 2016). We disagree. Anti-racism and anti-oppression are entirely compatible. Anti-racism prioritizes "race" as the entry point to understanding other forms of intersecting oppressions, such as gender, class, and ability. We have adopted this same strategy in this book. We use racism as an entry point to understand oppression. Our anti-oppression work has always done this. We centre race in our work because we consider it the obvious entry point for understanding the Whiteness and White supremacy that underpins all forms of oppression. We also find that unless we begin with race, anti-oppression can easily forget about racism. Indeed, research by Barnoff and Moffatt (2007) found that a number of agencies that have implemented anti-oppression have unwittingly silenced specific struggles such as racism. In other words, racism can become invisible within anti-oppression. This is not, however, a problem of anti-oppression, but a problem with the way that some people understand anti-oppression and are taking it up.

We wonder if anti-oppression sometimes forgets racism because of a flight to innocence (Rossiter, 2001). A **flight to innocence** refers to an attempt to distance oneself from one's unearned privilege and to un-implicate oneself from the way oppression operates. Racism is such an ugly phenomenon that when we teach or train on the topic we find that the very mention of it causes students and participants angst, so people gravitate to the more neutral term "oppression" as a way to avoid tough conversations about race. Also, given that racism is such a pervasive and insidious form of oppression operating in the various political, social, and economic contexts of society, there is also an institutional investment in its denial (Lipsitz, 2006). To counter this and to make anti-oppression what it was truly intended to be, we unapologetically begin our analysis of oppression with race. For us, anti-oppression has to be rooted in anti-racism.

## Key Concept

Beware the urge to take flight to innocence. If you find yourself implicated in racism or some other ism, resist the urge to protest your innocence, and instead protest against and change the system in which you are implicated.

We are not the only ones who find talk of racism resisted. Others also claim that talk about racism tends to digress to talk about the individual self and result in claims to innocence and defensive statements such as "You're calling me a racist" (Srivastava, 2009). Leonardo (2004) argues that this is because those who hold White racial privilege, or who come from the dominant societal space, fail to see how they are implicated in these institutional processes. They also fail to see the role they play in continuing the historical process of domination in today's institutional practices, policies, procedures, and decision making. To name the benefits that White people gain in power and privilege is not enough to change the systems, because not only do some White people go to a place of innocence, but they will also deny how the system gives them advantage over racialized people. More directly, Leonardo (2015) suggests that most White people fail to align themselves with the political project of anti-racism and, instead, they tend to deny complicity and responsibility in the role they play in maintaining the current racial order of inequality. Consequently, although one can take up "anti-oppression" in a way that skirts issues of racism, in our opinion that is not anti-oppression at all!

## Sexism, Women's Rights, and Feminism

Another ism addressed by anti-oppression is sexism. **Sexism** is the attitudes and processes that produce inequality for women; it pushes women out of first-class citizenship and maintains men within it. Similar to racism, sexism operates at personal, structural, and cultural levels within society.

The term *sexism* is said to have been first coined in 1965 by Pauline M. Leet, who argued that sexism is to women what racism is to people of colour (Shapiro, 1985). Of course sexism predates the word sexism and even predates racism, because **patriarchy,** which is the domination of men within society, is said to have existed since the early days of human history (Bishop, 2015).

Sexism and human rights for women are addressed primarily through **feminism**, which is a broad term that refers to "advocacy of the rights of women" (Bullock & Trombley, 2000, p. 314). Although feminism was started and is maintained by women, men can also be feminists. Canadian Prime Minister Pierre Trudeau has described himself as a feminist (Panetta, 2016). Although some men use this term, men cannot extricate themselves from the structural advantages that sexism and patriarchy give them, so some feminist men prefer to be known as **profeminist**. Originally introduced in the late 1980s and 1990s, profeminism is activism led by men, in particular to help other men recognize their male privilege. Such men look for practical actions and remedies at an everyday level to address the sexism and gender violence that they and other men perpetuate against women (Pease, 2015).

Feminism has undergone several different phases of understandings about women and their relationship to gender, race, class, sexuality, disability, and so on. These phases are often referred to as the **waves of feminism** (Gray & Boddy, 2010; Mann & Huffman, 2005; Phillips & Cree, 2014).

We have several concerns about the concept of waves. First, they misrepresent history. The first feminist wave is said to have begun in Europe during the nineteenth century, yet women challenged male patriarchy long before this and not only in Europe (Wayne, 2011). Second, the thoughts from each wave overlap with the ones before, so it is not possible to accurately distinguish one wave from another. Third, the idea of waves makes it easy for people in one wave to critique the ones before while forgetting that their own wave was only possible because of the ones before. Finally, waves tend to be taken up as categorical square boxes, and we can never shove the roundness of human experience and thought into a box or category. We are not the only ones who do not like waves (Butler, 2015; Garrison, 2005; Laughlin et al., 2010).

Although the concept of waves has problems, the idea of waves predominate the literature, and they provide a means to grasp some of the main changes that have occurred within feminist thought. They can also be used to explore the limitations and opportunities for feminism found in the narratives that have predominated at specific points in time (Chamberlain, 2016; Evans & Chamberlain, 2015). Consequently, with these cautions in mind, we use the concepts of waves to examine the way feminism has understood, articulated, and resisted sexism.

## First-Wave Feminism

First-wave feminism developed in countries such as Canada, the USA, and the UK during the nineteenth century and early twentieth century. At that time and in these contexts, women were considered the property of men and were not seen as human beings with their own legal rights. Notable first-wave feminists included the "mothers of social work" Mary Richmond (1861–1928), Octavia Hill (1838–1912), Adelaide Hoodless (1857–1910), and Jane Addams (1860–1935).

Mary Richmond developed social casework, which enhanced the credibility of the social work profession because of its foundation in the scientific method. Octavia Hill developed for the poor: housing, gardens, and playgrounds for children. Jane Addams created Hull House, the first settlement house for immigrants, and worked at the structural level to advocate politically for the rights of the poor. Adelaide Hoodless helped to found several organizations that focused on issues that impacted women, including the Women's Institute in Canada, which became an international organization that is now led from the UK (http://www.thewi.org.uk). Jane Addams also joined in the efforts to gain **suffrage** for women: the right for women to vote and to run for political office (Gray & Boddy, 2010). Gaining woman's suffrage is one of the key achievements of first-wave feminism.

Although first-wave feminism fought one form of oppression (sexism), it reinforced another (racism). First-wave feminists only gained suffrage for White women. White women gained provincial voting rights in 1916 and federal voting rights in 1918, but many racialized women did not receive federal voting rights until much later, and Indigenous women were refused voting rights until the 1960s (Crowson, 2016).

Although first-wave feminism did not support the rights of all women equally, Black women feminists were active at that time and they made a significant contribution to feminism. Their stories are often missing in the historical accounts of activism in that era. Some Black authors do tell these stories. For example, James (1999) highlights the role of historical **protofeminist ancestors,** which means those who were feminist activists before the term *feminist* had been coined. These include Maria W. Stewart (1803–1880), Ida B. Wells-Barnett (1862–1931), and Ella Baker (1903–1986). These Black women refused to adhere to White middle-class norms and, according to James (1999), could be viewed as **shadowboxers**, because they were the preshadow of Black feminist radicalism that emerged much later in third-wave feminism that we see today (Collins, 2009; hooks, 2015; Lorde, 1997).

Shadowboxers are positioned in what James (1999) calls **limbos**, because they "repudiate the gentleness of the culture of 'true' womanhood, a bourgeois construct for civility" (James, 1999, p. 41). In this moment, "African American feminisms display an agility and imaginative power in both building paradigms and trashing them" (James 1999, p. 42). Limbos can be more aptly described as "a fluid flexibility [that] allows such feminisms to bend lower and lower and with limber steps dance past a descending bar of political and intellectual dismissals" (James, 1999, p. 42). The political and intellectual dismissals were the numerous ways in which the experience and activities of Black women were not allowed to shape the women's social movement during this time, despite their active presence and existence.

## Second-Wave Feminism

Second-wave feminism emerged during World War II, which marked an increase in the number of women in the labour force, particularly doing jobs traditionally undertaken by men (who were engaged in military service). More emphasis was placed on gender because of concerns about child care, children's and women's safety, employment and equal pay, and educational and reproductive rights (Gray & Boddy, 2010).

Some argue that, similar to first-wave feminism, second-wave feminism reflected mainly the interests of White women and largely ignored race- and class-based oppression (Phillips & Cree, 2014). Some authors (Gray & Boddy, 2010; Vogel, 1991) dispute the idea of second-wave feminists ignoring race, class, and imperialism. To them, such views simplify what was occurring, because White women were active in the Civil Rights Movement, the New Left, and the anti-Vietnam War movement.

Second-wave feminism popularized the name "women's liberation" (often shortened to **women's lib**) and gave us the slogan **the personal is political**. The insight this slogan provides has become a bedrock for understanding all oppressions. Any process that holds entire groups of people back and does not give them rights that the dominant groups take for granted is political. This oppression is reflected in Figure 5.2. Failure to fit the "really good careers" mould is not simply the personal problem of the woman in this figure, but a problem all women face because of the political way we organize ourselves as a society.

**Figure 5.2** Really good careers

## Third-Wave Feminism

Third-wave feminism started to emerge in the 1970s by expanding the focus on gender oppression to simultaneously examine the way other forms of oppression operate and impact women along lines like race, ethnicity, sexuality, and class. Talk of "feminism" gave way to "feminisms" by recognizing how the diversity among women was often missing in the second-wave movement (Philips & Cree, 2014).

One of the third-wave groups that focused on this diversity was the Combahee River Collective, a group of Black feminists, who put out a statement in 1978 recognizing the simultaneity of coexisting oppressions, and the importance of taking a combined stance of being both anti-sexist and anti-racist (Combahee River Collective, 1978). This Collective advocated coalition building with other progressive organizations and movements. It also recognized that to fully understand and address how oppression operates, one has to employ analysis and practice that recognize the way systems of oppression interlock and connect to a country's history of state practices that are underpinned by White male rule and White supremacy.

Women of colour played a leading role in this movement (Collins, 1990; hooks, 2015; Lorde, 1997), with the term "third wave" coined by Rebecca Walker (1992), an African American woman who drew on **queer theory** (a rejection of traditional categories) to question the way we understand sexuality and gender. (We will speak more about this contribution of third-wave feminists, and the related idea of performativity, in the next chapter).

Third-wave feminists also coined the term **womanism** to describe the need for social change to address the everyday struggles and experiences of Black women and other racial minority women (A. Walker, 1983/2004). Within this approach, the identity of Black women was affirmed and the other systems of oppression that Black women faced were considered. Indeed, the movement critiqued earlier waves of feminism for operating on the principle of an **essentialist woman** homogenized and unified around only gender, and ignoring the differences that exist between women (Lorde, 1984/2007). **Essentialization** is the belief that someone can be defined by their race, gender, sexuality, sex, or some other category. This type of essentialization is based on the idea that human difference defines our characteristics and who we are.

## Intersectionality

Understanding differences between women, and the ways oppressions intersect, is crucial not only in feminism but in all forms of anti-oppression. **Intersectionality** is a term coined by Kimberlé Crenshaw (1989, 1991) to identify how the social locations through which one might be oppressed require a non-additive and non-hierarchical examination.

The intersectional model was a step forward from the **additive model**, which starts with a specific site of oppression, such as gender, race, class, or sexuality, and adds other variables into the mix. Patricia Hill Collins (2013) says that the additive model has two pitfalls. First, it hierarchizes one oppression over others, and makes the hierarchized oppression seem more important. In contrast, the intersectional model recognizes that multiple oppressions "intersect" to compound each other and to create unique forms of oppression for some groups. Mullaly and West (2018) demonstrate this in Figure 5.3, where they show oppression intersecting along lines of class, gender, race, and age.

To grasp the significance of the intersectional model, and the ways it differs from the additive model, one has to recognize that where the locations in Figure 5.3 intersect, one does not simply add the oppressions. For instance, one does not add racism and sexism and conclude that racism and sexism are operating together. Instead, Crenshaw explains that, at this intersection, a new form of oppression occurs that goes beyond racism and sexism. If only anti-racism and anti-sexism are employed as remedies, an **intersectional failure** occurs, which prevents the intersectional oppression from being addressed. This intersection effect is best explained by Crenshaw herself.

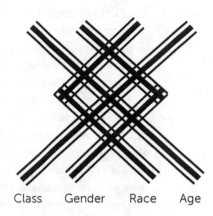

Class    Gender    Race    Age

**Figure 5.3** Intersectional model of oppression

Source: Mullaly & West, *Challenging Oppression*, Third Edition, 2018, p. 266 (Mullaly & West, 2018, p. 266). Copyright © Oxford University Press Canada 2018. Reprinted by permission of the publisher.

## Exercise 5.3

### Understanding Intersectionality

Watch Kimberlé Crenshaw's keynote presentation on intersectionality at the 2016 London South Bank "Wow" conference at https://www.youtube.com/watch?v=-DW4HLgYPlA. Alternatively, search for the video using the search term "Kimberlé Crenshaw - On Intersectionality - keynote - WOW 2016" and locate the video.

   If possible, watch the video in a group, or alternatively watch alone, and consider the following points. If you are keeping a journal, write your reflections.

1.   After reviewing the video, formulate a short statement to articulate intersectionality.
2.   Give an example of intersectionality not given in the video.
3.   Discuss or reflect on a personal experience you have had, or have encountered, of intersectionality operating.

## The Intersection of Oppression, Power, and Privilege

Not only oppressions, but power and privilege, intersect. We addressed this intersection in the previous chapter, and portrayed it in Figure 4.1 (the topography of oppression). Privilege and oppression can mix; a person may experience several sites of oppression intersecting in their life and several sites of power and privilege doing the same. How these play out is context specific, which means that oppression plays out in a complex mix of intersecting oppressions and interlocking privileges. In this mix there are few pure victims or oppressors (Collins, 2000). To reflect this fact, some authors speak of a web of oppression (Mullaly, 2010; Sisneros, Stakeman, Joyner, & Schmitz, 2008). Patricia Hill Collins (1990) developed the matrix of domination to identify and challenge categories from a binary of either/or thinking to a both/and conceptual stance that recognizes people have varying degrees of penalty and privilege. This approach allows for more complex situations where a person can be both an oppressor and oppressed at the same time (Collins, 2009). By making this point Collins is not saying that some groups experience oppression more harshly than others, because clearly some groups do. Collins reminds us that although oppressions may differ, the source of *all* oppression comes from the overarching structure of domination driven by White supremacy (Collins, 2009).

## Postcolonial Feminism

Given the above, third-wave feminism has been a huge leap forward for humankind in understanding the way oppression operates at multiple levels. Postcolonial feminists have also added to this understanding by challenging the essentialization of "Third World women." The word **postcolonial** sounds like it implies that colonialism is over, but it does not. Instead, it means that although traditional colonization is over, it continues by other means. **Third World women** are defined geographically:

> . . . the nation-states of Latin America, the Caribbean, sub-Saharan Africa, South and South-east Asia, China, South Africa, and Oceania constitute the parameters of the non-European Third World. In addition, black, Latino, Asian, and indigenous peoples in the United States, Europe, and Australia, some of whom have historic links with the geographically defined Third World, also refer to themselves as Third World peoples. (Mohanty, 2003, p. 47)

Mohanty (1984) also suggests that because of ongoing colonization around the world, Third World women are construed as a singular monolithic subject in (Western) feminist texts, and thus the heterogeneity of these groups of women is erased. Layered in these understandings of women in the Third World are racist assumptions with Western feminists portraying women in the Third World as ". . . sexually constrained . . . ignorant, poor, uneducated, tradition-bound, domestic, family-oriented, victimized" (Mohanty, 1984, p. 337) in contrast to Western women who are ". . . educated, modern . . . having control over their own bodies and sexualities, and the freedom to make their own decisions" (Mohanty, 1984, p. 337). Spivak (1989; 1996) describes this Othering process as the alterity of Third World women. You likely recognize these ideas as similar to those that inform the Orientalism of Edward Said (1979, 1994) that we spoke of in earlier chapters; this is because Said is also a postcolonial scholar, so this thinking overlaps at a conceptual level.

## Fourth-Wave Feminism

Figuring out the start of fourth-wave feminism is difficult since the fourth wave is a melding and overlapping of criticisms that still continue today about aspects of second- and third-wave feminism. It is also defined in many different ways by different authors.

In the United States, Baumgardner (2011) places the time of the fourth wave around the year 2008: the time when Barack Obama and Hillary Rodham Clinton were in the Democratic primaries and when tech-savvy women (who grew up with technology) were the youth who participated in the Take Your Daughter to Work Day initiatives. These women continued the work of feminism through social online sites such as "Exhale and Backline," an after-abortion talk-line, where both men and women receive the support they need after the procedure and in a context of no politicization or judgment about abortions (Baumgardner, 2011). Fourth-wave feminists also take up various issues in blogs, Twitter campaigns, and other social media sites. Hence, some would argue that the Internet is what marks the shift from third-wave feminism to fourth-wave feminism (Cochrane, 2013). Others contend that the Internet is not enough to mark a shift because the issues discussed online do not reflect all the voices of all women who need to be heard on these issues (Munro, 2013). Indeed, not everyone has access to the Internet and social media sites. As a result, only those women with this access are given a voice, and they are the ones who decide which issues to focus on.

Others argue that fourth-wave feminism is about social justice combined with spiritual or psychological consciousness-raising of the individual in relation to the community and broader social change, rather than being only defined by technology (Diamond, 2009; Peay, 2005; Wrye, 2009). Fourth-wave feminism has witnessed the influence of psychoanalysis by exploring how individual issues should not be conflated with conflicts rooted in social inequalities. Instead, women's stories are the contradictory personal narratives of one's life that include the unfinished or unresolved gender issues that were talked about in the past by other women (Diamond, 2009).

Regardless of the debates and disagreements about what fourth-wave feminism is, the Internet has provided a global forum for many feminists for discussion and activism. For some, the Internet has also created a "call-out" culture where sexism and misogyny in the media, television, literature, and film can be challenged through various social media sites. Overall, this social media–based feminism is a created space that is not only intolerant of all isms, but is also inclusive of diverse sexualities and cultures (Phillips & Cree, 2014). Of course, as mentioned above, this "diversity" extends only to those who have Internet access and the freedom to use it.

Outside the USA, Cochrane (2013) believes that fourth-wave feminism is active in the UK and around the world because of its focus on prevailing inequalities that currently exist and the activism that shows up in the "tens of thousands of women worldwide writing about the street harassment, sexual harassment, workplace discrimination and body-shaming [that] they encounter." Common to this group of feminists is the role that intersecting forms of isms play in their lives, whether the forms are the result of race, class, gender, age, ability, or sexuality. Also common to this group are the ways they can use spaces in the public sphere to express and share their experiences of exclusion, marginalization, and discrimination (Cochrane, 2013).

As the fourth wave of feminism has only just begun, and the third wave is far from over, it is difficult to be more definitive about their natures. Also, as pointed out at the beginning of this section, there are problems with the idea of waves because they overlap and sometimes their histories are not fully told, as is shown with the role of Black women in the first wave. The waves, however, provide a sense about how feminist thinking has developed and they certainly give a representation of how some scholars characterize this development.

## Indigenous Feminism

We considered listing Indigenous feminism under third-wave feminism, where we could categorize it as a form of postcolonial feminism. But seeing Indigenous feminism as a part of postcolonial feminism falls into the trap Mohanty (2003) cautions against, of homogenizing women impacted by colonialism. As well, conceptualizing Indigenous feminism as a part of any wave does not seem right. We spoke earlier about the problem of conceptualizing feminism in waves, and Indigenous feminism heightens these problems. In our opinion, Indigenous feminism cannot be categorized within any wave.

Indigenous women argue that "feminism is actually an indigenous concept that has been co-opted by white women" (Smith, 2011). Consequently, to place Indigenous feminism within a set of waves conceptualized by mostly White women is inherently problematic. Perhaps this is why some Indigenous women have been reluctant to call themselves feminists (Smith, 2011).

Of course, as noted above, Black women are speaking up about the Whiteness of feminism, and they are correcting the whitewashed history of the movement to claim their place within its history. There is a connection between Black feminists and Indigenous feminism. When Black feminists trended the hashtag #SolidarityIsForWhiteWomen on Twitter, this term resonated with Indigenous feminists, who like many Black feminists contend that feminism is not addressing their issues (Briggs, 2013). At the same time, however, the issues that Indigenous women face are not the same as the issues Black women or other women of colour face. Celeste Liddle, an Indigenous woman from Australia, points out that the struggles of Indigenous women are unique, because although these fights "are related to ongoing feminist struggles within other racially marginalized groups, they are not the same. By virtue of the fact that we are first peoples who have suffered under the process of colonisation within our own homelands" (Liddle, 2014).

Indigenous scholar Jodi Byrd, of the Chickasaw Nation of Oklahoma, points out that efforts to address social inequality and injustice through feminism, anti-racism, or activism that focus on issues of oppression along lines of class or sexuality all fail to tackle underlying issues of colonization that Indigenous women face (Byrd, 2011). We will show later, in Chapter 7, how anti-racism and even efforts to "decolonize" fail to address the issues Indigenous peoples face in a settler colonial context. For these reasons we feel uncomfortable categorizing Indigenous feminism under any wave, because although connected to other forms of feminism, it also stands apart—it has to stand apart if it is to address sexism in a settler colonial context.

Because Indigenous feminism addresses not just a male politics of oppression, but the oppression of a multi-gender, multi-racial, and multicultural settlement and domination of Indigenous land, it focuses on more than the status of women. Indeed, "a Native feminist politics seeks to do more than simply elevate Native women's status—it seeks to transform the world through indigenous forms of governance that can be beneficial to everyone" (Smith, 2011). We will address this and related issues in more depth in Chapter 7 when we speak of colonization and decolonization—particularly in an Indigenous context.

## Chapter Summary

In this chapter we have discussed various forms of racism, including anti-Black racism, anti-Jewish racism, anti-Muslim racism. We also clarified that White people can face racism, but the concept of "reverse racism" is a myth. Grasping this point is crucial, because to understand racism one has to understand the mechanisms, and especially the White supremacy, that underpins all forms of racism. We went on to examine how anti-racism is the primary form or work that addresses racism.

We also examined sexism, women's rights, and feminism. We explored what is commonly known as the "waves" of feminism and the ways these have opposed the oppression of women. We also looked at the limitations of waves as a conceptual framework. Lastly, we looked at intersectionality and how oppression cannot be understood as singular isms, but has to be seen as the way these overlap.

We started the chapter talking about Gary's Nan and the way she joined others to block Cable Street and stop a march of fascists from intimidating and physically harming the Jewish people who lived in that area. Gary's Nan was not Jewish, so why did she decide to take a stand? We will return to that question after we consider several more isms in the next chapter. In the meantime, however, we want to consider why not only Gary's Nan, but thousands of others took a stand that day. As mentioned at the start of this chapter, the East End of London was a place of poverty, crime, violence, and internal strife, so what made so many people come together and take a united stand? We do not know for sure, but we suggest that although East Enders may have been separated from each other by each facing different isms, they were joined together by an understanding that they were all collectively being trod down in similar way. We suspect that this understanding led to a solidarity that played a role in people taking a united stand against fascism.

Consequently, when in this text we explore specific isms, keep in mind that a key to anti-oppression is not in just understanding how each ism is different, it is also in understanding how they connect. Before moving on to explore additional isms, consolidate your learning about the specific isms addressed in this chapter by considering the discussion questions below.

## Discussion Questions

In the previous chapter we said that "race" is not "real," because it is a social construction. But in this chapter we spoke about the realities of racism.

It is easy to get confused about the way race is not real while racism is real, but understanding this point is essential. Discuss the following:

1. How can race not be real if racism is real?
2. How does one make the point that race is not real without undermining very real and important statements like "Black Is Beautiful" and "Black Lives Matter"?

## Activity

Explain to a friend why race is not real but racism is real, and ask your friend if your explanations are clear. Keep in mind that we are not asking you to get your friend to agree with your explanation; we are only asking you to find out from them if your argument is clear.

## Suggested Resources

The Battle of Cable Street: A short documentary. Retrieved from https://youtu.be/CXhxT0s1aRo

The Anti-Racism Experiment That Transformed an Oprah Show Audience | Where Are They Now | OWN. Retrieved from https://youtu.be/5NHeFgaVWs8

Collins, P.H., & Bilge, S. (2016). *Intersectionality*. Malden, MA: Polity Press.

Delgado, R., & Stefancic, J. (2017). *Critical race theory: An introduction* (3rd edn). New York, NY: New York University Press.

Green, J. (Ed.). (2017). *Making space for Indigenous feminism* (2nd edn). Halifax, Canada: Fernwood.

Maynard, R. (2017). *Policing black lives: State violence in Canada from slavery to the present*. Halifax, Canada: Fernwood.

Satzewich, V., & Liodakis, N. (2017). *"Race" and ethnicity in Canada: A critical introduction* (4th edn). Toronto, Canada: Oxford University Press.

# References

Alkan, S. (2016, April 1). Islamophobia skyrockets in Europe since Charlie Hebdo attack, report says. *Daily Sabah*. Retrieved from http://www.dailysabah.com/politics/2016/04/02/islamophobia-skyrockets-in-europe-since-charlie-hebdo-attack-report-says

Allen, T.N., & Lewis, A. (2016). Looking through a glass darkly: Reflections on power, leadership and the black female professional. *The Journal of Values-Based Leadership, 9*(2), 1–16.

Aylward, C.A. (1999). *Canadian critical race theory: Racism and the law*. Halifax, Canada: Fernwood.

B'Nai Birth Canada. (2015). *2014 annual audit of antisemitic incidents*. Retrieved from https://d3n8a8pro7vhmx.cloudfront.net/bnaibrithcanada/pages/174/attachments/original/1433967668/2014_report_English.pdf?1433967668

Baker, J.N. (1901). The segregation of white and colored passengers on interstate trains *The Yale Law Journal, 19*(6), 445–52.

Barnoff, L., & Moffatt, K. (2007). Contradictory tensions in anti-oppression practice in feminist social services. *Affilia: Journal of Women and Social Work, 22*(1), 56–70. doi:10.1177/0886109906295772

Baumgardner, J. (2011). *F'em!: Goo Goo, Gaga and Some Thoughts on Balls*. Berkeley, CA: Seal Press.

BBC. (2015, November 18). Paris attacks: Mosques attacked in US and Canada. *BBC News*. Retrieved from http://www.bbc.com/news/world-us-canada-34860882

Bell, D. (2004). *Silent covenants: Brown v. board of education and the unfulfilled hopes for racial reform*. New York, NY: Oxford University Press.

Bell, D. (2008). *Race, Racism, and American Law* (6th edn). New York, N.Y: Aspen Publishers.

Bell, D.A. (1980). Brown v. Board of Education and the interest-convergence dilemma. *Harvard Law Review, 93*(3), 518–33. doi:10.2307/1340546

Bishop, A. (2015). *Becoming an ally: Breaking the cycle of oppression in people* (3rd edn). Halifax, Canada: Fernwood.

Bleich, E. (2011). What is Islamophobia and how much is there? Theorizing and measuring an emerging comparative concept. *American Behavioral Scientist, 55*(12), 1581–1600. doi:10.1177/0002764211409387

Bracey II, G.E. (2015). Toward a critical race theory of state. *Critical Sociology, 41*(3), 553–72. doi:10.1177/0896920513504600

Briggs, K. (2013, October 10). Australian feminists need to talk about race. *The Guardian*. Retrieved from http://www.theguardian.com/commentisfree/2013/oct/11/australian-feminists-need-to-talk-about-race

Brodkin, K. (1998). *How Jews became white folks: and what that says about race in America*. Piscataway, NJ: Rutgers University Press.

Bullock, A., & Trombley, S. (Eds). (2000). *The new Fontana dictionary of modern thought* (3rd edn). London, UK: HarperCollins.

Butler, J. (2015). *Gender trouble: Feminism and the subversion of identity (reprint edition)*. New York, NY: Routledge Classics.

Byrd, J.A. (2011). *The transit of empire: Indigenous critiques of colonialism*. Minneapolis, MN: University of Minnesota Press.

Catterall, P. (1994). The battle of Cable Street. *Contemporary British History, 8*(1), 105–32. doi:10.1080/13619469408581284

Chamberlain, P. (2016). Affective temporality: Towards a fourth wave. *Gender and Education, 28*(3), 458–64. doi:10.1080/09540253.2016.1169249

Cochrane, K. (2013). *All the rebel women: The rise of the fourth wave of feminism*. London, UK: Guardian Books.

Collins, P.H. (1990). *Black feminist thought: Knowledge, consciousness, and the politics of empowerment*. Boston, MA: Unwin Hyman.

Collins, P.H. (2009). *Black feminist thought: Knowledge, consciousness, and the politics of empowerment*. New York, NY: Routledge.

Collins, P.H. (2013). *On intellectual activism*. Philadelphia, PA: Temple University Press.

Combahee River Collective. (1978). The Combahee River Collective Statement. Retrieved from http://circuitous.org/scraps/combahee.html

Constance-Huggins, M. (2012). Critical race theory in social work education: A framework for addressing racial disparities. *Critical Social Work, 13*(2), 1–16.

Crenshaw, K.W. (1989). Demarginalizing the intersection of race and sex: A Black feminist critique of antidiscrimination doctrine, feminist theory and anti-racist politics. *The University of Chicago Legal Forum, 140*, 139–67. doi:10.2307/1229039

Crenshaw, K.W. (1991). Mapping the margins: Intersectionality, identity politics, and violence against women of color. *Stanford Law Review, 43*(6), 1241–99.

Crowson, B. (2016). A hundred years of women having the vote—well, some women. *Alberta History, 64*(2), 2–7.

Cui, D., & Kelly, J. (2013). "Too asian?" or the invisible citizen on the other side of the nation? *Journal of International Migration and Integration, 14*(1), 157–74. doi:10.1007/s12134-012-0235-7

Dei, G. (1996). *Anti-racism education: Theory and practice*. Halifax, Canada: Fernwood.

Delgado, R., Stefancic, J., & Harris, A. (2012). *Critical race theory: An introduction* (2nd edn). New York, NY: New York University Press.

Diamond, D. (2009). The fourth wave of feminism: Psychoanalytic perspectives. *Studies in Gender and Sexuality, 10*(4), 213–23. doi:10.1080/1524065090322818

Evans, E., & Chamberlain, P. (2015). Critical waves: Exploring feminist identity, discourse and praxis in western feminism. *Social Movement Studies, 14*(4), 396–409. doi:10.1080/14742837.2014.964199

Fekete, L. (2014). The growth of xeno-racism and Islamophobia in Britain. In M. Lavalette & L. Penketh (Eds), Race, racism and social work: Contemporary issues and debates (pp. 33–51). Bristol, United Kingdom: Policy Press.

Fitzgerald, I., & Smoczyński , R. (2015). Anti-polish migrant moral panic in the UK: Rethinking employment insecurities and moral regulation. *Sociologický Časopis / Czech Sociological Review, 51*(3), 339–61. doi:10.13060/00380288.2015.51.3.180

Garner, S., & Selod, S. (2015). The racialization of Muslims: Empirical studies of Islamophobia. *Critical Sociology, 41*(1), 9–19. doi:10.1177/0896920514531606

Garrison, E.K. (2005). Are we on a wavelength yet? On feminist oceanography, radios and third wave feminism. In J. Reger (Ed.), *Different wavelengths: Studies of the contemporary women's movement* (pp. 237–56). New York, NY: Routledge.

Geddes, J. (2013, October 3). Canadian anti-Muslim sentiment is rising, disturbing new poll reveals: Angus Reid survey reveals a land of intolerance. *Macleans*. Retrieved from http://www.macleans.ca/politics/land-of-intolerance/

*Globe and Mail, The.* (2017, January 30). The Quebec City mosque attack: What we know so far. *The Globe and Mail*. Retrieved from http://www.theglobeandmail.com/news/national/quebec-city-mosque-shooting-what-we-know-so-far/article33826078/

Gray, M., & Boddy, J. (2010). Making sense of the waves: Wipe-out or still riding high? *Affilia, 25*(4), 368–89. doi:0.1177/0886109910384069

Green, E. (2016a, Dec 5). Are Jews white? *The Atlantic*. Retrieved from http://www.theatlantic.com/politics/archive/2016/12/are-jews-white/509453/?utm_source=twb

Green, E. (2016b, November 2015). The objectification of Muslims in America. *The Atlantic*. Retrieved from http://www.theatlantic.com/politics/archive/2015/11/paris-attacks-muslims-america-trump/417069/

Guglielmo, J., & Salerno, S. (2003). *Are Italians white? How race is made in America*. New York, NY: Routledge.

Henry, F., & Tator, C. (2010). *The colour of democracy: Racism in Canadian society* (4th edn). Toronto, Canada: Nelson Education.

hooks, b. (2015). *Feminism is for everybody: Passionate politics* (2nd edn). New York, NY: Routledge.

Huber, L.P., & Solozano, D.G. (2015). Racial microaggressions as a tool for critical race research. *Race, Ethnicity and Education, 18*(3), 297–320. doi:10.1080/13613324.2014.994173

Ignatiev, N. (1995). *How the Irish became white*. New York, NY: Roultledge.

Iugu, N., & Batin, L. (2013). The new "anti-semitism" according to Andre Glucksmann as a political problem. *Knowledge Horizons, 5*(2), 65–73.

James, C.E. (2007). "Reverse racism"? Students' responses to equity programs. In T. Das Gupta, C.E. James, R.C.A. Maaka, G.E. Galabuzi, & C. Andersen (Eds), *Race and racialization: Essential readings* (pp. 356–62). Toronto, Canada: Canadian Scholars' Press.

James, J. (1999). *Shadowboxing: Representations of black feminist politics*. New York, NY: St. Martin's Press.

Kalmar, I.D. (2009). Anti-semitism and Islamophobia: The formation of a secret. *Human Architecture: Journal of the Sociology of Self Knowledge, 7*(2), 135–43.

Katz, J.H. (2003). *White awareness: Handbook for anti-racism training* (2nd edn). Norman, OK: University of Oklahoma Press, Norman Publishing Division.

Keung, N. (2016, July 4). Ontario facing "epidemic of Islamophobia" survey finds. *Toronto Star*. Retrieved from http://www.thestar.com/news/immigration/2016/07/04/ontario-facing-epidemic-of-islamophobia-survey-finds.html

Laughlin, K.A., Gallagher, J., Cobble, D.S., Boris, E., Nadasen, P., Gilmore, S., & Zarnow, L. (2010). Is it time to jump ship? Historians rethink the waves metaphor. *Feminist Formations, 22*(1), 76–135. doi:10.1353/nwsa.0.0118

Leonardo, Z. (2004). The color of supremacy: Beyond the discourse of "white privilege." *Educational Philosophy and Theory, 36*(2), 137–52. doi:10.1111/j.1469-5812.2004.00057.x

Leonardo, Z. (2013). The story of schooling: Critical race theory and the educational racial contract. *Discourse: Studies in the Cultural Politics of Education, 34*(4), 599–610. doi:10.1177/1077800414557825

Leonardo, Z. (2015). Contracting race: Writing, racism, and education. *Critical Studies in Education, 56*(1), 86–98. doi:10.1080/17508487.2015.981197

Liddle, C. (2014, June 25). Intersectionality and Indigenous feminism: An Aboriginal woman's perspective. *The Postcolonist*. Retrieved from http://postcolonialist.com/civil-discourse/intersectionality-indigenous-feminism-aboriginal-womans-perspective/

Lipsitz, G. (2006). *The possessive investment in whiteness: How white people profit from identity politics (revised and expand edition)*. Philadelphia, PA: Temple University Press.

Lorde, A. (1984/2007). *Essays and speeches: By Audre Lourde: New foreward by Cheryl Clarke. (Reprint Edition)*. Trumansburg, NY: Crossing Press.

Lorde, A. (1997). Age, race, class, and sex: Women redefining difference. In A. McClintock, A.R. Mufti, & A.E. Shohat (Eds), *Dangerous liaisons: Gender, nation, and postcolonial perspectives* (pp. 374–80). Minneapolis, MN: University of Minnesota Press.

Mann, S.A., & Huffman, D.J. (2005). The decentering of second wave feminism and the rise of the third wave. *Science & Society, 69*(1), 56–91. doi:10.1521/siso.69.1.56.56799

Marendy, P.M. (2005). Anti-semitism, christianity, and the catholic church: Origins, consequences, and responses. *Journal of Church and State, 47*(2), 289–307.

McCaskell, T. (2005). *Race to equity: Disrupting educational inequality*. Toronto, Canada: Between the Lines.

Mohanty, C.T. (1984). Under Western eyes: Feminist scholarship and colonial discourses. *boundary 2, 12/13*(1–3), 333–58. doi:10.2307/302821

Mohanty, C.T. (2003). *Feminism without borders: Decolonizing theory, practicing solidarity*. Durham, NC: Duke University Press.

Morgan, A. (2016, July 25). Why Canada needs Black Lives Matter. *Toronto Star*. Retrieved from http://www.thestar.com/opinion/commentary/2016/07/25/why-canada-needs-black-lives-matter.html

Mullaly, B. (2010). *Challenging oppression and confronting privilege: A critical social work approach.* (2nd edn). Toronto, Canada: Oxford University Press.

Mullaly, B., & West, J. (2018). *Challenging oppression and confronting privilege: A critical approach to anti-oppressive and anti-privilege theory and practice.* (3rd edn). Toronto, Canada: Oxford University Press.

Mulligan, P. (2017, June 29). Trump travel ban will impact Canadians, immigration lawyer warns. *CBC News.* Retrieved from http://www.cbc.ca/news/canada/nova-scotia/trump-travel-ban-will-impact-canadians-immigration-lawyer-warns-1.4185143

Munro, E. (2013). Feminism: A fourth wave? *Political Insight, 4*(2), 22–5. doi:10.1111/2041-9066.12021

Nerenberg, D. (2002). The Rhineland massacres of Jews in the first crusade: Memories medieval and modern. In G. Althoff, J. Fried, & P.J. Geary (Eds), *Medieval concepts of the past: Ritual, memory, histography* (pp. 297–310). Cambridge, UK: Cambridge University Press.

OACAS. (2016). *One vision one voice: Changing the Ontario child welfare system to better serve African Canadians. Practice framework part 1: Research report.* Retrieved from http://www.oacas.org/wp-content/uploads/2016/09/One-Vision-One-Voice-Part-1_digital_english.pdf

Omi, M., & Winant, H. (1994). *Racial formation in the United States: From the 1960s to the 1990s* (2nd edn). New York, NY: Routledge.

Owusu-Bempah, A., & Wortley, S. (2014). Race, crime, and criminal justice in Canada. In S. Bucerius & M. Tonry (Eds), Oxford handbook of ethnicity, crime, and immigration (pp. 281–320). New York, NY: Oxford University Press. doi:10.1093/oxfordhb/9780199859016.001.0001

Panetta, A. (2016, March 16). 'I am a feminist,' Trudeau tells UN crowd: Support for gender equality should not be unusual in 2016, PM tells adoring women's conference in New York. *Toronto Star.* Retrieved from http://www.thestar.com/news/canada/2016/03/16/i-am-a-feminist-trudeau-tells-un-crowd.html

Parker, L., Ledesma, M.C., & Calderón, D. (2015). Critical race theory in education: A review of past literature and a look to the future. *Qualitative Inquiry, 21*(3), 206–22. doi:10.1177/1077800414557825

Parker, L. (2015). Critical race theory in education and qualitative inquiry: What each has to offer each other now? Qualitative inquiry. *Qualitative Inquiry, 21*(3), 199–205. doi:10.1177/1077800414557828

Pease, B. (2015). Doing profeminist research with men in social work: Reflections on epistemology, methodology and politics. In S. Wahab, B. Anderson-Nathe, & C. Gringeri (Eds), *Feminisms in social work research: Promise and possibilities for justice-based knowledge* (pp. 52–66). London, UK: Routledge Taylor & Francis Group.

Peay, P. (2005). Feminism's fourth wave. *Utne Reader, 128,* 59–60.

Perry, B. (2015). "All of a sudden, there are Muslims": Visibilities and islamophobic violence in Canada. *International Journal for Crime, Justice and Social Democracy, 4*(3), 4–15. doi:10.5204/ijcjsd.v4i3.235

Phillips, R., & Cree, V.E. (2014). What does the "fourth wave" mean for teaching feminism in twenty-first century social

work? *Social Work Education, 33*(7), 930–43. doi:10.1080/02615479.2014.885007

Pon, G., Giwa, S., & Razack, N. (2016). Foundations of anti-racism and anti-oppression in social work practice. In A. Al-Krenawi, J.R. Graham, & N. Habibov (Eds), *Diversity and Social Work in Canada* (2nd edn, pp. 38–58). Don Mills, Canada: Oxford University Press.

Rankin, J., Winsa, P., Bailey, A., & Ng, H. (2013, September 28). "Devastating. Unacceptable": Toronto police board chair appalled by Star findings that show a stubborn rise in the number of citizens stopped and documented by our police officers - with black males heavily overrepresented. *Toronto Star,* p. A1.

Riley-Smith, J. (2014). *The crusades: A history* (3rd edn). London, UK: Bloomsbury Academic.

Rossiter, A. (2001). Discourse analysis in critical social work: From apology to question. *Critical Social Work, 2*(1). Retrieved from http://www1.uwindsor.ca/criticalsocialwork/discourse-analysis-in-critical-social-work-from-apology-to-question

Said, E.W. (1979). *Orientalism.* New York, NY: Vintage Books.

Said, E.W. (1994). *Culture and imperialism.* New York, NY: Vintage Books.

Shapiro, F.R. (1985). Historical Notes on the Vocabulary of the Women's Movement. *American Speech, 60*(1), 3–16. doi:10.2307/454643

Sharfstein, D.J. (2003). The secret history of race in the United States. *The Yale Law Journal, 112*(6), 1473-1509. doi:10.2307/3657450

Shyrock, A. (2010). Introduction: Islam as an object of fear and affection. In A. Shyrock (Ed.), *Islamophobia/islamophilia: Beyond the politics of enemy and friend* (pp. 1–25). Bloomington, IN: Indiana University Press.

Sisneros, J., Stakeman, C., Joyner, M.C., & Schmitz, C.L. (2008). *Critical multicultural social work.* Chicago, IL: Lyceum Books.

Smith, A. (2011, September 8). Indigenous feminism without apology. *Unsettling America: Decolonization in theory and practice.* Retrieved from https://unsettlingamerica.wordpress.com/2011/09/08/indigenous-feminism-without-apology/

Snyder, G.F. (2015). "Marking whiteness" for cross-racial solidarity. *Du Bois Review, 12*(2), 297–319. doi:10.1017/S1742058X15000144

Spigelman, A. (2013). The depiction of Polish migrants in the United Kingdom by the British press after Poland's accession to the European Union. *International Journal of Sociology and Social Policy, 33*(1/2), 98–113. doi:10.1108/01443331311295208

Spivak, G.C. (1989). Who claims alterity. In B. Kruger & P.M. Mariani (Eds), *Remaking History, Dia Art Foundation, Discussions in Contemporary Culture* (pp. 269–92). Seattle, WA: Seattle Bay Press.

Spivak, G.C. (1996). *The Spivak Reader: Selected works of Gayati Chakravorty Spivak* New York, NY: Routledge.

Srivastava, S. (2009). "You're calling me a racist". In L. Back & B. Solomos (Eds), *Theories of race and racism: A reader* (2nd ed., pp. 534–57). London, UK: Routledge.

Stikkers, K.W. (2014). ". . .But I'm not racist": Toward a pragmatic conception of "racism". *The Pluralist, 9*(3), 1–17.

Tamdgidi, M. (2012). Beyond Islamophobia and Islamophilia as western epistemic racisms: Revisiting Runnymede Trust's definition in a world-history context. *Islamophobia Studies Journal, 1*(1), 54–81. doi:10.13169/islastudj.1.1.0054

Taras, R. (2013). "Islamophobia never stands still": Race, religion, and culture. *Ethnic and Racial Studies, 36*(3), 417–33. doi.org/10.1080/01419870.2013.734388

The Canadian Press. (2012, August 17). Asian-looking woman scientist image rejected for $100 bills. *CBC News*. Retrieved from http://www.cbc.ca/news/politics/asian-looking-woman-scientist-image-rejected-for-100-bills-1.1183360

Tilles, D. (2015). *British facist antisemeitism and Jewish responses, 1932–1940*. London, UK: Bloomsbury Academic.

Vogel, L. (1991). Telling tales: Historians of our own lives. *Journal of Women's History, 2*(3), 89–101. doi:10.1353/jowh.2010.0097

Walker, A. (1983/2004). *In search of our mothers' gardens: Womanist prose (Reprint Edition)*. New York, NY: Mariner Books.

Walker, R. (1992). Becoming the third wave. *Ms. Magazine, 11*(2), 39–41.

Wayne, T.K. (Ed.). (2011). *Feminist writings from ancient times to the modern world [2 volumes]: A global sourcebook and history*. Santa Barbara, CA: Greenwood.

Wikipedia. (2017). Semitic people. *Wikipedia, The Free Encyclopedia*. Retrieved from https://en.wikipedia.org/wiki/Semitic_people

Wrye, H.K. (2009). The fourth wave of feminism: Psychoanalytic perspectives introductory remarks. *Studies in Gender and Sexuality, 10*(4), 185–89. doi:10.1080/15240650903227999

Yee, J.Y., & Dumbrill, G.C. (2016). Whiteout: Still looking for race in Canadian social work practice. In A. Al-Krenawi, J.R. Graham, & N. Habibov (Eds), *Diversity and social work in Canada* (2nd edn, pp. 13–37). Toronto, Canada: Oxford University Press.

# Isms and Intersectionality Part Two: Heterosexism and Cissexism, Ableism, and Sanism

## In this chapter you will learn:

- What heterosexism and cissexism, ableism, and sanism are and what drives them
- What performativity is and how it relates to isms
- More about the way isms are addressed and resisted through anti-oppression

## Introduction

In the last chapter we began to explore a series of isms, and in this chapter we continue that process. By the end of this chapter we will have addressed several isms, but we will not have covered all isms or all forms of oppression: there is simply not the space to do this. Also keep in mind that we are only providing an introduction to the isms we have chosen to address. Indeed, any single ism we address in these chapters can become a subject of study in its own right.

At the end of this chapter you will have a good overview of isms and you will have the ability to recognize and name them. At that point we will return to the story we told of Gary's Nan (grandmother) in the previous chapter—about her taking a stand against fascism in 1930s London in the Battle of Cable Street. It is unlikely that Gary's Nan read a book like this one, which explains isms and speaks about how to oppose them. So why did Gary's Nan choose to defy the police and fight oppression, especially a form of oppression that was not directly impacting her? Was it for the reasons that we speculated at the end of the last chapter, or did she have some other motivation? At the end of this chapter we will ask you to speculate about answers to this question, and we will ask you to apply any lessons you learn from this story and her resistance to the way you take up anti-oppressive social work.

# Heterosexism and Cissexism

Society has a number of rules about sex, gender, and sexual attraction. Break these rules and one is likely to face various forms of oppression. We refer to these rules as **normative**, which does not mean "norm" as an average or what is most common, but as the way dominant society thinks *all* people *ought* to be. Being outside this norm does not simply mean becoming a numeric minority; it means being regarded as inferior, morally wrong, and "defective" in some way.

The normative rules and assumptions about sex and gender are:

- Only two sexes exist: male and female.
- One must act in accordance with the gender norms of one's assigned sex.
- One must only be attracted to and have sex with persons of the opposite sex.

These rules form the basis of what we refer to as the **iron cage of sex and gender normativity**. We show this iron cage in Table 6.1 below. Reading this table from left to right, the term "sex" refers to one's biological sex. We prefer to call this **assigned sex**, because it is usually assigned at birth based on the appearance of one's genitalia; those who appear to have a penis are designated male, those who appear to have a vagina are designated female.

One's gender is expected to align with the sex one has been assigned. The term **gender** is a social construction. It refers to the various expectations society has for the way men and women behave, dress, and even feel about themselves and their own identity. If one has been assigned a male sex one is expected to grow up doing stereotypical boy things and eventually "act like a man," and if one is assigned a female sex one is expected to do girlish things and eventually "behave like a lady."

Lastly, we are expected to only have romantic feelings and sex with people whose bodies have been assigned a sex opposite to our own.

Break any of these rules and one crosses the line from "normality" to "abnormality," which results in all manner of social sanction. Non-compliance with these iron rules places one outside the circle of dominance we showed in Chapter 4 (Figure 4.1, The

**Table 6.1** The Iron Cage of Sex and Gender Normativity

| Assigned Sex | Gender | Attraction |
|---|---|---|
| "Biologically" male (has a penis) | Acts the way society expects men to act, and largely feels comfortable with a male identity | Opposite sex (attracted to women) |
| "Biologically" female (has a vagina) | Acts the way society expects women to act, and largely feels comfortable with a female identity | Opposite sex (attracted to men) |

topography of oppression) and, as a result, one is likely to face various forms of discipline and punishment.

There is an increasing awareness that sex, gender, and human attraction are much more complex and fluid than the iron cage of sex and gender normativity implies. Great strides have been made to break the iron cage in sex education (Do, 2015) and in broader society. Especially helpful are info graphics like "The gender unicorn" that explain in simple terms the difference between sexual identity, gender expression, sex assigned at birth, physical attraction, and emotional attraction (Figure 6.1). This graphic also helps us understand that these concepts are continuums rather than binaries.

Even though progress has been made, violating the rules of the iron cage of sex and gender normativity still evokes oppression. Indeed, use of the gender unicorn and similar tools in schools has evoked considerable backlash from parents and religious groups who do not want children to be taught about sex and gender (Csanady, 2016). It is, of course, important for everyone to learn these lessons, especially in anti-oppression, because truth sets us free from all manner of iron cages and the related oppressions these hold in place. We review below the lessons needed to disrupt the iron cage of sex and gender normativity.

**Figure 6.1** The gender unicorn

Source: Graphic by TSER (Trans Student Educational Resources). Design by Landyn Pan and Anna Moore. http://www.transstudent.org/gender

## Key Concept

Learning the truth about ourselves and about the world we live in is important because truth sets us free from buying into and reproducing ideas and beliefs that oppress.

## Assigned Sex

Sex is usually assigned at birth based on the physical appearance of one's genitalia. But sex is not a binary. Not every baby's body conforms to usual male or female anatomy; in these cases the child is regarded as **intersex**. This can distress parents, particularly those who do not understand that intersex is a naturally occurring phenomenon. Given the pressure to conform to sex binaries, at birth doctors often assign the sex that the baby's anatomy resembles the most (Fisher et al., 2016). Sometimes doctors will test the child's chromosomes, but this does not settle the matter of sex, because some men have XX chromosomes that are usually associated with a female body, and some women have XY chromosomes that are usually associated with a male body (BBC, 2011; Harrison, 2010; Steinmetz, 2016). Consequently, at a biological level, assigning sex is far more complex than the iron cage portrays. Given the predominance of the iron cage, a common practice has been to "normalize" those born intersex with surgical intervention to alter their reproductive organs to match the sex they were assigned at birth (Fisher et al., 2016).

## Gender

Gender does not necessarily match sex (Joel et al., 2015). The idea that assigned sex and gender align is called **cisnormativity**, and oppression of those where these do not align is called cissexism. The word **cis** has Latin roots which means "on the same side," so in relation to sex and gender, cisnormativity is the idea that it is "normal" for one's sex and gender to align, and "abnormal" if these do not. A person who is **cisgender** (sometimes called **cis**) has their sex match their gender identity and gender expression.

**Gender identity** is the way one perceives one's own gender (either as male or female, as a mix of these, or as no gender at all), and **gender expression** "refers to appearance and behaviours that convey something about one's gender identity, or that others interpret as conveying something about one's gender, including clothing, mannerisms, communication patterns, etc." (Shlasko, 2014, p. 28). Consequently, a *cis male* is someone with an assigned male sex, who regards themself as male, and who acts mostly in ways that society expects men to act. A *cis female* is someone with an assigned female sex, who regards themself as female, and who acts mostly in the way society expects women to act.

**Transgender** refers to those who have or express a gender different from their assigned sex. The prefix **trans** means "across" or "the other side" and so literally transsexual means that one's gender is different from one's assigned sex. It is important not to confuse the term *transgender* with *transsexual*. To an extent, the term **transsexual** is interchange-able with transgender, but it is probably best to use the term transgender, because some authors claim that transsexual is a derogatory term, which results from it being associated with a medical diagnosis that pathologizes transgender as some form of identity disorder (Pyne, 2011). However, some people prefer to use the term transsexual, especially those who are **transitioning** through medical and surgical intervention to change their body to have their sex reassigned to better match their gender identity. Given the fluidity of language related to these concepts, we recommend doing what everyone ought to do in civil society; if one has to refer to a person's sex or gender, find out and use the term that a person themself prefers to be used.

Gender, just like sex, is not a binary, so it does not have to be expressed in a binary way. The term **agender** represents a genderless identity of expression, and **bigender** represents the merging of male and femaleness in one's gender identity or expression. Sometimes the term **gender non-conforming** is used to refer to sexual identities and expressions that are not aligned with society's gender expectations. Another term used to describe such non-conformity is **genderqueer**, which is also used as an umbrella term for sexual minor-ities as a whole (Holmes, 2016; Richards et al., 2016).

In a sense, the term "queer" does not only refer to a collection of sexual identities or ways of being, but to a process of challenging dominant norms and ideas. Indeed, at a theor-etical level the concept of **queer** emphasizes that sex and gender cannot be categorized or framed. Said differently, queer, and the process of queering, break the power of what we have called the iron cage of sex and gender normativity. Keep this in mind when using any of the terms and phrases we have introduced above. Do not replace one iron cage with another, and remember that people are more complex and fluid than the language we use to describe them.

## Sexual Attraction

The iron cage is also built on the notion of heterosexism. The prefix **hetero** has Greek ori-gins that mean different, so that "hetero" and "sex" means different sex, so **heterosexual** is attraction to the opposite sex. The suffix "ism" turns the concept into a form of oppression called **heterosexism**, which is the assumption that the human norm is opposite-sex attrac-tion, which is an assumption and practice referred to as **heteronormativity.** Like with any form of oppression, the ism is enforced through personal attitudes that discriminate in favour of opposite-sex relationships, and also by a range of laws and practices that operate at systemic and cultural levels in favour of opposite-sex and against same-sex relation-ships (Woodford, Kulick, Sinco, & Hong, 2014).

The sex one is attracted to is often referred to as **sexual orientation**. We adopt this usage, but we do not use it in a definitive way, because people's orientations are far too complex and fluid to be defined by who they may or may not be attracted to at any par-ticular point in time. Moreover, hidden in this understanding about sexual identity is the assumption that everyone must be sexually attracted to another person. This is not so, because one out of every 100 people is **asexual** ("ace"), with a low level or no sexual attraction to persons of any sex (Bogaert, 2004).

Those who are attracted to people of the same sex are sometimes referred to as lesbian, gay, or bisexual (**LGB**). In simple terms, **lesbian** refers to women who are romantically attracted to women, **gay** refers to men who are romantically attracted to men, and **bisexual** refers to someone who is romantically attracted to both men and women. Sometimes the term *queer* is used to refer to any of these combinations, though keep in mind that this is a reclaimed word, so use with the cautions for reclaimed words that we described in Chapter 3.

Also keep in mind when considering LGB relationships that, besides human attraction being too fluid to follow rules of opposites, sex and gender are fluid too. Consequently, do not assume that a person who is expressing or living a gender different from their assigned sex will be attracted to someone of the opposite sex. Trans people can be straight, gay, or bisexual, and to assume otherwise falls into the trap of heteronormativity—sex, gender, and attraction are far more fluid than this.

Another term used for same-sex attraction is *homosexual,* and the corresponding word *homophobia* refers to the oppression of those in homosexual relationships. The word has Greek roots. *Homos* means the same, which when combined with "sexual" refers to same-sex attraction. The corresponding term, heterosexual, uses the Greek word *heteros* meaning "different" or "other" to signal opposite-sex attraction.

Some consider the term "homosexual" derogatory because of its psychiatric and criminal connotations. Until 1973 the term referred to a psychiatric diagnosis under the *Diagnostic and Statistical Manual of Mental Disorders.* Until 1979, homosexuality was a criminal offence in Canada and remains so in many nations, including some where even now having a same-sex relationships is punishable by death (McPhail, McNulty, & Hutchings, 2016). As a result, we personally try to avoid the term "homosexual," and we do not like the term "homophobia" because of the connotations connected with "phobia" that we discussed in Chapter 5. Note, however, that not everyone avoids these terms; many progressive anti-oppressive journal articles and books have these words in their titles. Be careful, therefore, because although language is important, our analysis needs to go deeper than words (more about that later).

## Breaking Out of the Iron Cage of Sex and Gender Normativity

In many respects, **LGBTTIQQ2S** people and communities are breaking out of the iron cage of sex and gender normativity (on behalf of us all), as have third-wave feminists mentioned in the previous chapter. We have already addressed the terms "LGBTTIQ" above, which refer to lesbian, gay, bisexual, transgender, transsexual, intersex, and queer. In addition to these, the additional **Q** refers to those who are questioning their identity since they are in process, or do not want to apply a label at this point in time. The final letter 2S is an abbreviation for **Two-Spirit (2-Spirit)**, which is a term reclaimed by Indigenous peoples to describe those in their communities who are considered to have both male and female spirits, including the social roles they hold in the community. Two-Spirit is also an umbrella term used by Indigenous peoples to describe gender-diverse and sexually diverse people. A key distinction from the Euro-colonial framework of sex and gender is that "the term [Two Spirit] embodies an inseparable harmony between sexuality, spirituality, race, gender, and cultural identity" (Alaers, 2010, p. 71).

Despite advances in LGBTTIQQ2S rights, recent large-scale studies have found that "homophobia" is prevalent throughout school districts in all parts of Canada (Peter, Taylor, & Chamberland, 2015), that LGBT people are overrepresented in the criminal justice system (Center for American Progress & Movement Advancement Project, 2016), and that acts of oppression and violence toward LGBTTIQQ2S people are still common-place (Lee & Brotman, 2013; Toomey, McGuire, & Russell, 2012).

The oppression above is held in place by the iron cage of sex and gender normativity. One way to break the cage is to disrupt essentializing ideas about sex and gender—in other words, to disrupt the belief that one can infer some "essential" nature about people by a characteristic such as race, sex, or gender. One of the ways to create this disruption is to interrupt performativity.

**Performativity** is enacting societal expectations in a way that reinforces the iron cage. Consider the child in Figure 6.2. We are engaging with performativity if we con-sider this child as pretty rather than handsome, and if we assume that the child will continue to wear dresses, will grow up to be romantically attracted to boys, and will continue to enjoy wearing long hair, fancy hats, and frills. Quite possibly this will be so—and there is absolutely nothing wrong with that—but fulfilling such expectations is not the result of an essential nature programmed by sex. It is largely a behaviour shaped by the societal expectations we have and actions we take in relation to sex, gender, and other aspects of life—in other words, it is caused by performativity.

Butler (2015) explains that performativ-ity is the way patterns, such as the patterns we refer to as *gender* (i.e., being socially recognized as male, female, or non-binary), occur *through the way we act*. In other words, it is not some inherent aspect of gender that causes the behav-iours of boys wearing pants and girls wearing dresses. It is boys wearing pants and girls wear-ing dresses that create and reinforce these gen-dered behaviours. We are of course using "pants" and "dresses" here as a analogy for all the things that go into the performativity of stereotyp-ical male and female roles and ways of being. If you are not sure whether this is so, take another look at Figure 6.2. The child in the image is late American President Franklin D. Roosevelt, who is dressed as boys typically were in his era and

Bettman/Getty Images

**Figure 6.2** Child in a pretty dress

context (this photograph was taken in 1884). Given that what is regarded as typical male and female characteristics shift over time, one cannot fix and essentialize maleness and femaleness at any given moment in time. Butler suggests we disrupt traditional thinking on gender by being open to the possibility of non-essentializing fluid understandings of gender and other human categories or ways of being (Butler, 2015). We concur, but suggest that for this to be so, disruption of the cage is needed at the individual level (the way each of us think and act) and also at the structural and cultural levels in which the iron cage is operationalized. To break the iron cage requires direct action. The exact type of action changes in each setting and circumstance, we will talk more about this in later chapters. Change, however, can be difficult because the iron cage of sex and gender normativity is not only embedded in the ways we have been taught to think, but is embedded in the ways we have been taught to speak and write too. Consider the following sentence:

Roger does not like to play tennis because *he* is not very good at this sport.

The sentence is clearly gendered, but how could this sentence be made gender neutral? We suggest that depending on the way Roger identifies, the word "he" could be replaced with non-binary pronouns, such as "ze/hirs/hir, per/pers, zie/zirs/zir, etc" (Shlasko, 2014, p. 3), but in current English usage this seems awkward and does not flow. Indeed, English teachers and editors might be concerned about the readability of such revisions. Consequently, our approach would be to restructure the sentence to eradicate the need to refer to Roger's sex or gender, especially as these are superfluous to the topic. We would revise the sentence as follows:

Roger is not good at tennis, and as a result does not like or play it.

In this instance, we are quite happy with our edits, but we struggle in other instances. You have probably noticed that throughout this book where most authors will use "him or her," we use "their." We do this to avoid a gender binary. We know it sounds awkward, but so did the use of "he or she" when authors moved away from using the pronoun "he" to refer to everyone. Such change is important because we believe authors (especially of academic texts) are supposed to use language to expand the ways we think, not restrict it.

Given the way gendered ideas are embedded in our language and thought,  heterosexism, cissexism, and other oppressions of sexual minorities can be difficult to weed out and resist. We suggest that the beginning point of this work is understanding the iron cage of sex and gender normativity and looking for moments and contexts in which this can be disrupted and broken. Such work can come through our use of language. It can also come through other processes and conversations that jam and block cisnormative and heteronormative processes and assumptions. In addition, it involves ally work and direct action that is created in context-specific moments. The concept of an ally is addressing an oppression that does not impact you directly (Bishop, 2015).

# Ableism

**Ableism** is a form of oppression directed toward disabled people. Like all oppression, the concept of "difference" or deviation from a societal "norm" is at its heart. Ableism pushes down and holds back people who have a form of difference referred to as disability. The concept of **disability** cannot be understood apart from its corollary "able." To draw attention to the relationship between "disability" and "ability," some authors split the parenthesis "dis" from the word "ability" and render the term "**dis-ability**" or "**dis/ability**." Goodley (2014) explains:

> This is a split term that I believe acknowledges the ways in which disablism and ableism (and disability and ability) can only ever be understood simultaneously in relation to one another. The slashed and split term denotes the complex ways in which opposites bleed into one another. People find it difficult to define "normal" and "ability" but are far more ready to have a go at categorising "abnormal" and "disability". Dis/ability studies keep disablism and ableism, disability and ability in play with one another, to explore their co-construction and reliance upon one another. (Goodley, 2014, p. xiii)

Like Goodley, many activists and authors split "dis" from "ability," but many do not. We fall in the latter category, but trust that you will see from the way we render our arguments that we agree with Goodley that ability and disability are co-constructed.

Another semantic sometimes adopted in relation to disability is the term **people with disability**. This **people-first language** is thought to be more respectful, because it emphasizes the person before their disability (Dunn & Andrews, 2015). Others contend that the term **disabled person**, which places the person second, is more appropriate, because it reflects the reality that people are *disabled* by social and political processes (Sinclair, 2013; Titchkosky, 2001; Wolbring, 2012). Such disabling results from society being structured around a **corporeal standard** (the ideal physical body) as well as predominant mental, neuronal, cognitive, and behavioural norms. Recognizing this reality, the term "disabled person" makes clear that "disability" results from disablement.

**Disablement** is the process of making someone disabled (Goodley, 2014; Goodley & Runswick-Cole, 2011; Oliver, 1990). Every time an architect designs a home with steps and non-accessible washrooms, every time a teacher designs assignments to measure comprehension that emphasize correct standard spelling, and every time the rest of us accept these acts as the norm, disablement occurs. These acts tread down and hold back those with mobility or dyslectic characteristics. Similar forms of disablement operate at a society-wide level to form a central element in the oppression we call ableism.

Ableism does not stop at disablement; it also affects the ways we view the humanness of disabled people. Campbell (2001) defines ableism as "a network of beliefs, processes and practices that produce a particular kind of self and body (the corporeal standard) that is projected as the perfect, species-typical and therefore essential and fully human. Disability, then, is cast as a diminished state of being human" (Campbell, 2001, p. 44).

The practical effects of this assumed diminished humanity plays out in many ways ranging from patronizing attitudes toward disabled people (Mauerberg-deCastro, Campbell, & Tavares, 2016), believing disabled people cannot experience true love and should not marry or have sex (Turner & Crane, 2016), and sometimes even questioning whether disabled people have a right to life (Steinbach, Allyse, Michie, Liu, & Cho, 2016). This questioning of the right to life can play out in the type of hatred that drove Nazi attempts to exterminate disabled people (Hudson, 2011; Steinbach et al., 2016), or in the "kindness" that drives social workers and other helping professionals to assume that expectant mothers discovering that the fetus they carry has Down's syndrome or some other "defect" will automatically choose abortion (Steinbach et al., 2016). Of course, a mother may choose to terminate pregnancy—that choice is her legal right—but to assume that she will or should make this choice rather than have a disabled child devalues the life of all disabled people.

## Ableism Devalues All Human Life

Devaluing disabled life devalues all life, because physical and mental change due to aging is a natural part of the life cycle, and everyone's body and mind will eventually function differently from the predominant ableist norm. Indeed, accidents, illness, and injury are a part of ordinary life too, which means that from birth to old age, what we consider "disability" is a *normal* part of the life cycle. Ableism, therefore, by creating a world based on an "ideal" human mind and body that few can attain and none can maintain, denies the human condition itself. Such denial, aside from its impact on people defined as disabled, "causes pain to nondisabled people who are unprepared to deal with their own vulnerability and mortality when accidents and aging require that they do so" (Weeber, 1999, p. 21).

Given that ableism denies everyone's humanness, some authors call for an expansion of the definition of ableism to include acts and attitudes toward those "deemed normal" (Wolbring, 2012, p. 79). It is argued that the quest for the ablest ideal has led to **transhumanization,** which is an attempt to enhance and modify the species-typical body through technologies that seek to eliminate the aging process and/or find ways to increase the intellectual, physical, and psychological capacities of humans (Wolbring, 2012). These efforts are designed to produce **posthuman** beings (Allen, 2013)—if you have seen *The Bourne Identity* movie, you get the idea. The effects of such technologies potentially change not only our ability expectations, but also what we might potentially perceive to be "normal" healthy bodies (Wolbring, 2012). Although these are important points to consider, we need to be careful with the idea of "non-disabled" people being oppressed through transhumanism, or even by the regular aging process, because it can trivialize the fundamental issues of exclusion that disabled people face.

## The Medical Model of Disability

Posthumans aside, the key issue of ableism is the line between "normal" and "abnormal." Medicine plays a role in determining this line. Medicine has mapped the normal operating parameters of the human body and mind, which can be a good thing when one finds oneself not functioning as one expects, because a medical doctor can usually tell whether something is wrong, and can often treat and sometimes cure the problem. The **medical model** tends to conceptualize disability in a similar manner: "biological, genetic, hormonal, neurological and physiological language" Goodley (2014, p. 14) is used to frame disability as an illness or abnormality in need of a cure. The problem with the medical model is that it can fuel the **individual model of disability** (Donahue, 2016), in which disabling conditions are conceptualized as an "illness" that exists entirely within the disabled person's body or mind, rather than existing as a result of our structuring society around certain types of bodies and minds.

## The Social Model of Disability

In contrast to the medical and individual models of disability, the **social model of disability** locates disabling conditions in broader society. Indeed, given that everyone eventually differs from the ableist predominant norms, disability ought not to be regarded as **impairment** (a weakened or diminished human), but as being a part of the human condition itself. As such, the social model contends that the cause of disability is not located in the bodies or minds of people, but in the tendency for the world to be structured to be navigable only for those with bodies and minds that meet ableist ideals. The social model does not reject the idea of impairment and medical intervention altogether, but it firmly locates disability in the social and political processes of disablement.

The social model of disability emerged in the 1960s from what is often called the **disabled peoples' movement** (Barnes, 2013; Beresford, 2016a). Many groups formed and drove this movement: for example, the British Union of the Physically Impaired Against Segregation (UPIAS), a disability rights organization that challenged the medical model during the 1970s (Union of the Physically Impaired Against Segregation, 1976). The ideas of the UPIAS quickly gained academic support. Shakespeare and Watson (2001) cite significant contributions by Vic Finkelstein (1980; 1981), Colin Barnes (1991), and particularly Mike Oliver (1990, 1996).

The social model of disability looks at the relationship between impairment and disability. The original 1976 UPIAS and The Disability Alliance statement on the Fundamental Principles of Disability defined impairment and disability as follows:

- Impairment is "lacking part of or all of a limb, or having a defective limb or mechanism of the body" (cited in Barnes, 2012, p. 14).
- Disability is defined as "the disadvantage of restriction of activity caused by a contemporary social organisation which takes no or little account of people who have physical impairments and thus excludes them from participation in the mainstream of social activities" (cited in Barnes, 2012, p. 14).

The social model is ecological (Simplican, Leader, Kosciulek, & Leahy, 2015), because it considers the bodily person in the social environment, with disability being caused by the interaction of a person's impairment with their environment. The problem of disability, however, is not the body or the environment, but rather a lack of political will to create an environment that is inclusive of all people. As such, society excludes those who do not meet the ableist ideals and fall outside ableist norms. As a result, the social model of disability identifies ableism as oppression in a similar way to racism and other isms. Indeed, the social model of disability firmly identifies disabled people as an oppressed group (Shakespeare & Watson, 2001), with oppression rather than impairment causing disability.

## Key Concept

The social model of disability is particularly relevant in anti-oppressive social work, because it identifies ableism, in a similar way to racism and other isms, as oppression. As well, the activism of those involved with the social model of disability, along with their insistence that it is the voice of disabled people themselves that needs to lead advocacy and develop policy, points the way forward for anti-oppressive social work.

A key feature of the disabled peoples' movement is that it is directed by disabled people themselves, with the slogan **nothing about us without us** being taken up to reflect this (Charlton, 1998; Derby, 2013; Martin, 2012). This principle is crucial because not only does it tap the lived knowledge disabled people have about social practices that disable them, it also undoes the way disablement impedes the voice and participation of disabled people within decision making, debate, and political processes. Indeed, a part of ableism is to consider disabled people incapable of making their own decisions (Mladenov, 2015; Wang, Silverman, Gwinn, & Dovidio, 2015). Consequently, the disabled peoples' movement is involved in activism not only to change structural conditions that impact disabled people, but to change the personal prejudices and ableist culture that produce these structures.

The social model of disability has met with some success. It has been "adopted and adapted by national and international organizations [that are] controlled and run by disabled people" (Barnes, 2012, p. 14). The model, however, is not without its critics. Disputes exist about how to conceptualize "disability" and how to address ableism. Some of these disputes have become endlessly debated (Goodley, 2014). Exploring these arguments and counter arguments is beyond the scope of our text, but we consider below two important critiques of the social model.

## Critiques of the Social Model

First, the social model is criticized as "inadequate as a social theory of disablement" (Oliver, 2009, p. 49). Oliver points out, however, that the social model was never intended to be an all-encompassing theory to explain disablement because it is a *model*, not a *theory*. We concur with Oliver; in fact, we are not aware of any ecological model that provides any grand theory about anything. The fact that something is a model does not preclude taking up the model within a broader explanatory theory, but it ought to preclude critiquing a *model* for not being a *theory*.

Second, the social model has been critiqued for accepting the notion of "impairment" and for working in conjunction with the medical model to seek remedies (Oliver, 2009). The argument is that because different levels of human functioning are a normal part of human diversity, accepting the notion of "impairment" buys into ableist ideals. Indeed, consider people who identify as Deaf, who do not see themselves as having an impairment or a disability, but instead identify as belonging to a linguistic minority or culture (Reaume, 2014; Scully, 2012). Clearly, the notion of impairment is fraught with tension. Yet at the same time, not addressing some forms of "impairment" through physiotherapy, rehabilitative services, and medical intervention is fraught with tension too. These conceptual issues and the political and practical implications of them have led to lengthy debates within disability studies (Beaudry, 2016; Oliver, 2009; Watson, 2012).

Some of the tensions around disability result from a struggle between activists, scholars, and clinicians with efforts to appropriate concepts related to disability for partisan purposes that may not serve or reflect the views and interests of disabled people (Block, Kasnitz, Nishida, & Pollard, 2016). As a result, it can be difficult for the anti-oppressive social worker to navigate this terrain. Key principles to keep in mind, however, are first, ableism thrives when we construct the world in a way that excludes those with disabilities, and second, the exclusion driven by ableism silences and marginalizes the voice of disabled people themselves. Consequently, anti-oppression has to do the opposite; it has to include and centre the voice of disabled people. For that reason, we leave you with Stella Young's TED Talk where she explains disability. Of course, do not assume that Stella Young speaks for all disabled people. To do that denies diversity amoung disabled people, but Stella Young does raise key points that one needs to grasp to understand what the disabled people's movement is, and understand the social model of disability.

## Exercise 6.1

### I'm Not Your Inspiration

Watch the TED Talk by Stella Young "I'm not your inspiration, thank you very much" at https://www.ted.com/talks/stella_young_i_m_not_your_inspiration_thank_you_very_much, or alternatively locate the video on Stella Young's speaker page at https://www.ted.com/speakers/stella_young.

*continued*

After watching the video, discuss as a group and/or reflect alone and note in your journal:

1.   What things in the video changed the way you understand disability?
2.   What things in the video confirm the way you understand disability?
3.   What implications can you see of the social model for the way we address disability?

# Sanism

Sanism is a belief system that drives the oppression of people who have, or are thought to have, a "mental illness." Like all oppressions, "difference" is at the heart of the way sanism oppresses; the "difference" that sanism is directed toward is those who are "mentally ill."

As noted by Jennifer Poole, "you don't even have to have a diagnosis to experience sanism . . . you just have to look, or sound, or feel, or smell a little bit different than the everyday" (Poole, 2014). In other words, if you cope with life, or act or think in a manner that most people think of as different or a little odd, it does not take much for someone to explain this "oddness" as a "mental illness." The "mentally ill" label can be imposed informally by neighbours and community members (e.g., "the neighbour at the end of the street is 'crazy,'") or formally by a psychiatrist through a diagnostic process, or by both of these acts. Whether one gets the label "mentally ill" through a formal diagnosis by a psychiatrist, or the label "crazy" from the reactions of neighbours, the oppression is similar, although not entirely the same.

Stigma is an oppression shared by those formally diagnosed with a mental illness and those thought by the community to be "crazy." We will speak about stigma more fully in Chapter 10 when we address service users' perspectives. But for now, a simple explanation of **stigma** is marking someone as different in a way that "set[s] them apart" (Large & Ryan, 2012, p. 1099).

Once marked as mentally ill or "crazy," sanism singles someone out for being treated with "distrust, fear or avoidance" (Bartlett, 2014, p. 19), and for being referred to by derogatory epithets such as "loony" (which is short for "lunatic") and "psycho" (which is short for psychotic or "psychopath"), which (in their long form) are actually medical terms that are, or have previously been, used as diagnostic categories by psychiatrists. The fact that these medical terms are embedded in popular culture as insults reveals the prevalence and power of prejudice toward people considered to have a mental illness. Indeed, such terms and the attitudes associated with them drive "an irrational prejudice of the same quality and character as other irrational prejudices that cause and are reflected in prevailing social attitudes of racism, sexism, homophobia, and ethnic bigotry" (Perlin, 2013, p. 462).

## Oppression through Psychiatry

As Poole (2014) notes, anyone can face sanism, but for those formally diagnosed with a mental illness, oppression is sometimes compounded by the system that claims to help them—the psychiatric system itself (Moth & McKeown, 2016). Several factors allow oppression to operate through psychiatry and mental health systems. The first results from **mental illness** being inherently difficult to define and identify. Unlike physical illness where a diagnosis is usually based on objective tests that identify bacteria, viruses, or physiological changes that cause the body to literally become "ill," mental illness is mostly diagnosed through the symptoms one reports or the behaviours one exhibits. Science can be used to associate some brain and chemical changes with certain types of mental illness, and can also establish a genetic component in some conditions, but once a person's symptoms have a physiological base, they are no longer considered "mentally ill"; instead, they are considered to have a neurological or physiological disorder. There is no physiological test to determine whether one is mentally ill; mental illness is diagnosed entirely by a person's thoughts, feelings, and behaviour.

The thoughts, feelings, and behaviour that constitute mental illness are somewhat subjective (Frances, 2013). This subjectivity does not occur so much at an individual level, because the North American *Diagnostic Statistical Manual of Mental Disorders* (DSM), the *International Classification of Diseases* (ICD), or other diagnostic systems like the *Chinese Classification of Mental Disorders* (CCMD) ensure reliability by having very precise criteria for classifying symptoms and diagnosing mental illness. These DSM, ICD, and CCMD diagnostic criteria, however, are decided by committees, and as such they represent a type of collective subjectivity that those with the power to sit on these committees consider to be "ill" thoughts, feelings, and behaviour.

## Key Concept

Deciding what constitutes ill thoughts, feelings, and behaviour is fraught with oppressive potential. Prejudices are endemic in society, so we have to be very careful that mental health diagnostic systems, especially if based on widely accepted ideas about what is "normal," do not pick up and reproduce the prejudices and dominant norms that exist in society.

Having committees decide what constitutes ill thoughts, feelings, and behaviour is fraught with oppressive potential. We learned previously that personal prejudices are endemic in society. Consequently any diagnostic system based on a collective subjectivity about the "normal" can easily pick up and embody these prejudices. Indeed, as mentioned before, Black slaves trying to gain freedom were once diagnosed as suffering from a mental illness called drapetomania (Cohen, 2016). As a result, anyone challenging power relations can be considered "ill." For instance, when Elizabeth Packard from Jackson, Illinois questioned her husband, Reverend Theophilus Packard, on his religious views on child rearing and his support for slavery, she was declared "insane" and confined to the state asylum (Reaume, 2002). Even now, people who express a gender different from their assigned sex can be diagnosed as suffering from gender dysphoria or gender identity disorder, often referred to as "GID" (Pyne, 2011). In this respect, psychiatry and mental health services regulate society and exert a form of social control in a manner that fits the panopticon analogy made in Chapter 4.

## Vested Interests in Mental Illness

Oppression also infiltrates mental health and psychiatric systems through vested interests. Every profession is an industry that benefits from the ability to control and govern its own work on behalf of its members (Ackroyd, 2016). The best way to gain this control is to create a monopoly over a given area of work. For instance, in most jurisdictions one cannot use the title "social worker," or practise as a social worker, unless one pays fees to, and has the approval of, a licensing body. It is the same with law, nursing, medicine, real estate, and even plumbing. This "closed shop" approach is said to protect the public from poor service, but it also creates a monopoly of service that benefits professions (Ackroyd, 2016). Given this fact, the history of psychiatry is not just a story about the way medicine has come to understand mental illness. It is also the history of the way psychiatry, as a profession, has been able to drive "out its competitors—the women healers, the astrologers, ultimately even the psychoanalysts" (Burstow & LeFrancois, 2014, p. 3). In this manner, "medicalized individual models of mental illness . . . have increasingly been exported to colonize, subvert, and overshadow other cultural and societal understandings and interpretations of these fundamental experiences" (Beresford, 2013, p. ix). Indeed, even though the DSM and ICD consider cultural and societal contexts in diagnosis, these systems offer no cultural remedies. There is only mainstream psychiatry and big pharma. As such, the entire helping process related to mental health has been "deferred to the doctors and pharmaceutical industry" (Kinney & Wilson, 2016, p. 393).

We are not suggesting that psychiatry and mental health services do nothing to help. Indeed, we train social workers to operate in these systems, because people can and do face troubles and distress that can be helped by therapeutic and even medical intervention. We personally would not hesitate using these services if we felt the need. We both have family and friends who have benefited greatly from psychiatric and mental health systems, but we also have family and friends who count themselves lucky to have survived such systems. Psychiatry and mental health systems are like almost any institution anti-oppression deals with—rarely all bad or all good. A simple good guy vs. bad guy dichotomy works in movies but not in real life. Consequently, in addition to understanding the potential of psychiatry and mental health services to oppress, we also have to understand their potential to liberate, and to bring health and well-being to those experiencing some form of mental distress.

## Key Concept

The anti-oppressive social worker needs to understand the potential of psychiatry and mental health services to oppress, and also needs to understand the potential of such services to liberate and bring health and well-being to those experiencing mental distress. If a social worker sees psychiatry and mental health services as all good, or all bad, they are likely to fail those they serve.

### Mental Health and Anti-Oppression

Helping someone achieve "mental health" is certainly compatible with social work and anti-oppression. The World Health Organization (WHO) defines **mental health** as "a state of well-being in which every individual realizes his or her own potential, can cope with the normal stresses of life, can work productively and fruitfully, and is able to make a contribution to her or his community" (World Health Organization, 2014). But what about a person who is unable to gain "well-being" or "realize their own potential" because they are pressed down and held back by racism, sexism, heterosexism, or some other form of oppression? What if their lack of "mental health" is not an individual "illness," but an indication that society itself is "sick?" For instance, consider the soldier back from a war experiencing post-traumatic stress and no longer able to cope with ordinary life. Is this solder ill, or has society asked this soldier to see and do things that no human should have to see or do? In other words, is the soldier's reaction a normal reaction to abnormal events? Of course, perhaps therapy or medication will alleviate the soldier's condition, but even if that works, it does not mean that the soldier was ever ill.

Labelling the soldier home from war with PTSD as "mentally ill," or labelling as "mentally ill" a homeless person suffering distress from trying to survive on the streets, or the parent trying to feed and clothe children when there simply is not enough money, is doing what Laing and others refer to as "labelling madness in an insane world" (cited in Kinney & Wilson, 2016, p. 393). In such circumstances, rather than labelling the person "ill," the anti-oppressive social worker should label the world "ill." In other words, call out the human absurdities, social inequalities, and political inequalities that cause or contribute to personal "disorder," rather than perpetuating the myth that this is caused simply by the "ill" person suffering from a biomedical condition that has a biochemical cure.

## Key Concept

Anti-oppressive social workers often point out that the people who use mental health services are not ill. Rather, the world is ill.

## Exercise 6.2

### PTSD and Other Issues

If possible, undertake this exercise in groups.

Watch poet and spoken word artist Kate Tempest perform "Ballad of a Hero" at https://youtu.be/Xqd86is7y54.

Imagine that the family in this story is seeking social work help for the problems that the mother describes. As Kate Tempest recites the spoken word, take notes and list the issues and problems that you see that might become the focus of social work or medical intervention in a situation like this, and write a short summary statement of "the problem" from your social work perspective.

Once undertaken, compare your notes with others in your group. To what extent are the following ways of framing "the problem" reflected in your notes.

- A man potentially experiencing PTSD, combined with issues of alcoholism, which is causing him to be emotionally abusive to his partner, and has the potential to cause emotional/psychological harm to the children in the family
- A man experiencing the impact of an "ill" society, who is exhibiting an understandable reaction to being deployed in war, and suffering from a lack of social and institutional supports for soldiers who are experiencing these reactions

Consider the reasons for the way you have framed "the problem" in this case, and whose agendas and which ideological views this framing supports.

## Challenging Sanism

Psychologists are pushing back at the individualizing and medicalization of social ills. For instance, in the UK, the term **austerity ailments** is being used to refer to the impact government cuts (austerity measures) have on people. Psychologists even trace the clinical **aetiology** (cause) of these ailments to the impact of humiliation caused by dependency on food bank usage and the other consequences of poverty and marginalization (McGrath, Walker, & Jones, 2016). Such "ailments" having a social cause does not mean that psychologists (or social workers) ignore immediate personal distress. Instead, they review options the person might be interested in that can help with their personal distress. In addressing this particular type of distress, however, they would avoid calling it an "illness." Instead they would contextualize the distress in an analysis and understanding of a wider set of ruling relations (Cresswell & Spandler, 2016). They might also consider whether the person experiencing the distress wants only immediate personal help or wants assistance to address the political causes of these "ills." The anti-oppressive social worker will do exactly the same.

Given the above, should we even use the term "mental illness," or should we use some other language to describe these troubles? We use the term "mental illness" in our text, but by doing so are we buying into and perpetuating a biomedical model? What language should we use to describe these phenomena? Some authors use the term *mental distress*, but this term defines something everyone experiences at one time or another. For this reason, the DSM and ICD use the term "mentally ill" to refer specifically to distress over extended periods and reaching such proportions that a person's ability to function on a daily basis is seriously compromised. Classifying such distress through the DSM, ICD, or some other measure does have benefits, because if the person experiencing distress wants to know what others experiencing their symptoms have found helpful, the person helping them will be able to give an answer. The problem is, of course, that the answer is likely to be confined to a very narrow band of medical interventions. Although these interventions can help the person in distress (Fabris, 2011), we should be concerned that the primary beneficiary of this system is big pharma, and concerned that alternative non-medical means of help are increasingly rare.

## Anti-Psychiatry

Some critics address the propensity of psychiatry to oppress by rejecting the idea of "mental illness" altogether. Similar to some approaches to disability, where the idea of impairment is rejected, **anti-psychiatry** rejects the idea of "mental illness." In the 1960s, Thomas Szasz, although not fully aligned with anti-psychiatry, popularized the idea that "mental illness" is a "myth" (Szasz, 1961). Others had the same idea, including R.D. Laing, David Cooper, and Franco Basaglia (Menzies, LeFrancois, & Reaume, 2013). Laing, for instance, contended that psychiatrists could not diagnose "mental illness" because only those who live an experience can define its meaning (Laing, 1967). It was in this era that Michel Foucault (Foucault & Khalfa, 2006) examined "the history of madness" and the way the concept was being used to control and police those who did not fit societal norms as a way of constructing and controlling the Other. Peter Beresford (2013) summarizes the core concern of anti-psychiatry as the way medicine objectifies the "mentally ill" and negates the possibility of people living another form of human consciousness that society does not accept.

The problem with the anti-psychiatry movement is that it shifts the control of the discourse about mental illness and health from one group of powerful professionals to another. Instead of psychiatrists defining the reality and needs of the "mentally ill," academics and radical theorists are now doing this. As Peter Beresford reflects, all these commentators are "engaged with the subject as professional experts, rather than being involved or caught up in it on the receiving end" (Beresford, 2016b, p. 343). Such anti-psychiatry theorizing pays little attention to the real daily mental distress of people diagnosed as mentally ill nor the "concrete dilemmas facing people living in the world, which was how it actually was and not how many radical critics wanted it to be" (Pilgrim, 2016, p. 328).

Although anti-psychiatry provides few solutions to people's troubles or social ills, it does help to reconceptualize issues in a way that sets the stage for anti-oppressive approaches to mental illness. In our opinion, the most promising of these approaches is found in the voice of mental health system service users and survivors.

## Service User Solutions

So important is the voice of service users in anti-oppression, not only in mental health but also in all areas of social work, that we have a full chapter on this topic later in this book (see Chapter 10). Citing a number of studies and sources, Beresford points out that, in relation to mental health, service users have developed:

> . . . non-medicalised services like crisis houses, telephone helplines, direct payment schemes and personal support schemes, housing and employment support, advice and advocacy schemes, and specific support for black and minority ethnic service users. . . . They have developed groundbreaking ideas like "recovery" and "peer support," even though these have been subverted by policymakers and the service system. (Beresford, 2016b, p. 350)

With developing practical services and initiating political resistance, service users have been on the leading edge of challenging the way psychiatry and other systems perpetuate sanism. This is particularly so in Canada, where the first "Psychiatric Survivor Pride Day" was held in Toronto on September 18, 1993. The event, led by psychiatric survivors, protested the prejudice held against psychiatric survivors, consumers, and former patients living in the Parkdale area of Toronto (Reaume, 2008). The event, and the movement related to it, uses the name **Mad Pride**, which is a reclaiming by mental health service users of the word "Mad" to resist the negative meanings connected with it (Fabris, 2013; Poole & Ward, 2013). As such, "the term 'Mad' (upper case) instead of 'mad' (lower case) signifies the politicisation of madness as an oppressed identity" (Cresswell & Spandler, 2016, p. 359), though like many reclaimed words the reclaiming can be contested (Burstow, 2013). But one thing is clear: if the power of sanism is to be broken, it has to be done through the voice of service users (more about that in Chapter 10).

# Chapter Summary

In this chapter and Chapter 5 we reviewed several isms related to oppression along the lines of race, religion, gender, sexual identity and orientation, and various forms of "disability." We have not covered every ism, nor have we dealt with the ones we have addressed in great depth, because every ism we have addressed represents an entire field of study in its own right.

At the start of the chapter we reminded you of the story of Gary's Nan in the Battle of Cable Street (told fully at the start of Chapter 5). Although Gary's Nan told him about how she took part in the battle, she did not say why. The fascists were oppressing mostly Jewish people, Gary's Nan was not Jewish, and the fact that Jewish people were being pushed down and held back may have provided more room for her to get ahead. So why risk her life to fight in this battle? Do you have any ideas?

Unfortunately, we will never know why Gary's Nan decided to fight, because she is no longer here to tell us. Gary never thought to ask his Nan, because to him the answer seemed so obvious: his Nan thought it was simply the right thing to do. But why did she think it was the right thing to do? We suspect that the answer comes from the heart, not the head—she knew that it is simply right to help others, especially when they are being trod down and held back. A number of the philosophies about love and putting others first that we discussed in Chapter 3 may have given Gary's Nan the heart for joining the Battle of Cable Street. But we suspect that one of the things that enabled Gary's Nan to take action was her own experience of oppression. As a daughter of Irish immigrants and living in poverty, her entire family spent periods in the Workhouse (institutions for the poor). Also, when she was 4 years old, Gary's Nan was taken from her family by the state and placed in a British church-run residential school where they tried to train her to go into service (i.e become a servant) for wealthy families. This "training" did not work out so well for the state, because as soon as she was old enough she went home to the East End, married a sailor, and picked up a stick, and started fighting fascists.

We suspect the experience of oppression gave Gary's Nan a tendency to get involved in anti-oppression, but you do not need to experience oppression to oppose it. Indeed, the oppression Gary's Nan fought in the Battle of Cable Street did not impact her directly. The key lesson here, and the key lesson of the Battle of Cable Street, is that Gary's Nan reached out to support those who were "different" from her. It was not only Gary's Nan who did this. On that day in 1936 tens of thousands of others did exactly the same. Helping someone "different" from yourself who is trod down is the key to anti-oppression. Indeed, the way oppression works is for the dominant group to fight for their own rights and interests. Audrey Lorde notes, "The master's tools will never dismantle the master's house" (Lorde, 1984). In other words, oppression cannot be overcome by doing what the master does, by pursuing singular self-interest, even if that self-interest is pushing back at oppression. There can be no liberation for just one oppressed group unless there is liberation for all. As a result, anti-oppression can only come about from a community working across the difference of multiple isms.

## Discussion Questions

In this and the previous chapter, we have not addressed every ism or form of oppression known to exist. We anticipate, however, that you can take the lessons learned from the isms we have addressed in these chapters and apply them to ones we have not. All isms result from the dominant group building society around its own needs first, and the needs of "different" groups next, and in many instances actually exploiting the "different" groups to meet its own needs. Recognizing this process in action and understanding how it operates is essential in anti-oppression. Conclude this chapter by discussing or reflecting on the following:

1. Pick an ism we have not addressed in this or the previous chapter. When picking an ism, ensure that it is *not* an ism that impacts you personally.
2. Discuss how the ways in which the group impacted by the ism is marked within society as "different" in some way.
3. Discuss how the dominant group privileges its own needs or position in relation to this group in a way that causes the ism to operate.
4. Discuss what can be done to "battle" this ism and the processes that drive it.

## Activity

Explain to a friend what an ism is and how to recognize it. Give an example, but do not pick an ism that impacts you or your friend. Identify with your friend the way this ism benefits you, and invite your friend to explore how it benefits them too. Discuss with your friend how the ism operates, and what ought to be done to stop it.

## Suggested Resources

*Pop Queer-ies*. A Canadian "bi weekly podcast that explores the place of queer identities and feminism in pop culture media." Retrieved from https://player.fm/series/pop-queer-ies

*Disability*. CBC Special Edition of *The Current*. Retrieved from http://www.cbc.ca/1.3814141

*Ouch: Disability Talk*. BBC podcast from the UK. Retrieved from http://www.bbc.co.uk/programmes/p02r6yqw

Innes, R.A., & Anderson, K. (Eds). (2015). *Indigenous men and masculinities*. Winnipeg, Canada: University of Manitoba Press.

LeFrancois, B., Menzies, R., & Reaume, G. (Eds). (2013). *Mad matters: A critical reader in Canadian mad studies*. Toronto, Canada: Canadian Scholars' Press.

Neigh, S. (2012). *Talking radical: Gender & sexuality, Canadian history through the stories of activists*. Halifax, Canada: Fernwood Publishing.

O'Neill, B., Swan, T.A., Mule, N.J. (Eds). (2015). *LGBTQ people and social work: International perspectives*. Toronto, Canada: Canadian Scholars' Press.

## References

Ackroyd, S. (2016). Sociological and organisational theories of professions and professionalism. In M. Dent, I.L. Bourgeault, J.L. Denis, & E. Kuhlmann (Eds), *The Routledge companion to the professions and professionalism* (pp. 15–30). New York, NY: Routledge.

Alaers, J. (2010). Two-spirited people and social work practice: Exploring the history of Aboriginal gender and sexual diversity. *Critical Social Work, 11*(1), 63–79.

Allan, K. (2013). *Disability in science fiction: Representations of technology as cure*. Basingstoke, UK: Palgrave Macmillan.

Barnes, C. (1991). *Disabled people in Britain and discrimination: A case for anti-discrimination legislation*. London, UK: Hurst and Co. in association with the British Council of Organisations of Disabled People.

Barnes, C. (2012). Understanding the social model of disability: Past, present and future. In N. Watson, A. Roulstone, & C. Thomas (Eds), *Routledge handbook of disability studies* (pp. 12–29). London, UK: Routledge.

Barnes, C. (2013). The disabled peoples' movement and its future. *Ars Vivendi Journal, 5*, 2–7.

Bartlett, V. (2014). *A roadmap for federal action on student mental health*. Ottawa, Canada: Canadian Alliance of Student Associations. Retrieved from ttps://d3n8a8pro7vhmx.cloudfront.net/casaacae/pages/811/attachments/original/1463347855/CASA-

A-Roadmap-for-Federal-Action-on-Student-Mental-Health.pdf?1463347855

BBC. (2011, October 11). Male or female? Babies born on the sliding sex scale. *BBC Health*. Retrieved from http://www.bbc.com/news/health-14459843

Beaudry, J. (2016). Beyond (models of) disability? *Journal of Medicine and Philosophy, 41*(2), 210–28. doi:10.1093/jmp/jhv063

Beresford, P. (2013). Foreward. In B.B LeFrancois, R. Menzies, & G. Reaume (Eds), *Mad matters: A critical reader in Canadian mad studies* (pp. iv–viii). Toronto, Canada: Canadian Scholars' Press.

Beresford, P. (2016a). *All our welfare: Towards participatory social policy*. Bristol, UK: Policy Press.

Beresford, P. (2016b). From psycho-politics to mad studies: learning from the legacy of Peter Sedgwick. *Critical and Radical Social Work, 4*(3), 343–55. doi:10.1332/2049860 16x14651166264237

Bishop, A. (2015). *Becoming an ally: Breaking the cycle of oppression in people* (3rd edn). Halifax, Canada: Fernwood.

Block, P., Kasnitz, D., Nishida, A., & Pollard, N. (2016). Occupying disability: An introduction. In P. Block, D. Kasnitz, A. Nishida, & N. Pollard (Eds), *Occupying disability: Critical approaches to community, justice, and decolonizing disability* (pp. 3–14). New York, NY: Springer.

Bogaert, A.F. (2004). Asexuality: Prevalence and associated factors in a national probability sample. *Journal of Sex Research, 41*(3), 279–87. doi:10.1080/00224490409552235

Burstow, B. (2013). A rose by any other name: Naming and the battle against psychiatry. In B. LeFrancois, R. Menzies, & G. Reaume (Eds), *Mad matters: A critical reader in Canadian mad studies* (pp. 79–93). Toronto, Canada: Canadian Scholars Press.

Burstow, B., & LeFrancois, B.A. (2014). Impassioned praxis: An introduction to theorizing resistance to psychiatry. In B. Burstow, B.A. LeFrançois, & S. Diamond (Eds), *Psychiatry disrupted: Theorizing resistance and crafting the (r) evolution* (pp. 3–15). London, Canada: McGill-Queen's University Press.

Butler, J. (2015). *Gender trouble: Feminism and the subversion of identity (reprint edition)*. New York, NY: Routledge Classics.

Campbell, F.A.K. (2001). Inciting legal fictions: 'Disability's date with ontology and the ableist body of law. *Griffith Law Review, 10*(1), 42–62.

Center for American Progress, & Movement Advancement Project. (2016). *Unjust: How the broken criminal justice system fails LGBT people*. Retrieved from http://www.lgbtmap.org/file/lgbt-criminal-justice.pdf

Charlton, J.I. (1998). *Nothing about us without us: Disability oppression and empowerment*. Berkeley, CA: University of California Press.

Cohen, Z.M. (2016). *Psychiatric hegemony: A Marxist theory of mental illness*. London, UK: Palgrave Macmillan.

Cresswell, M., & Spandler, H. (2016). Solidarities and tensions in mental health politics: Mad studies and psychopolitics.

*Critical and Radical Social Work, 4*(3), 357–73. doi:10.1332 /204986016x14739257401605

Csanady, A. (2016, June 3). One in six Ontario parents considered pulling kids from school over new sex-ed curriculum: Poll. *The National Post*. Retrieved from http://news.nationalpost.com/news/canada/canadian-politics/one-in-six-ontario-parents-considered-pulling-kids-from-school-over-new-sex-ed-curriculum-poll

Derby, J. (2013). Nothing about us without us: Art education's disservice to disabled people. *Studies in Art Education, 54*(4), 376–80.

Do, T.T. (2015, February 26). Ontario's new sex ed curriculum 'the most up-to-date' in the country. *CBC News*. Retrieved from http://www.cbc.ca/news/canada/ontario-s-new-sex-ed-curriculum-the-most-up-to-date-in-the-country-1.2969654

Donahue, J.J. (2016). Frank Miller's daredevil: Blindness, the urban environment, and the social model of disability. In M.J.C. Cella (Ed.), *Disability and the environment in American literature: Toward an ecosomatic paradigm (ecocritical theory and practice)* (pp. 79–96). New York, NY: Lexington Books.

Dunn, D.S., & Andrews, E.E. (2015). Person-first and identity-first language: Developing psychologists' cultural competence using disability language. *American Psychologist, 70*(3), 255–64. doi:10.1037/a0038636

Fabris, E. (2011). *Tranquil prisons: Chemical incarceration under community treatment orders*. Toronto, Canada: University of Toronto Press.

Fabris, E. (2013). Mad success: What could go wrong when psychiatry employs us as "Peers"? In B. LeFrancois, R. Menzies, & G. Reaume (Eds), *Mad matters: A critical reader in Canadian mad studies* (pp. 130–40). Toronto, Canada: Canadian Scholars' Press.

Finkelstein, V. (1980). *Attitudes and disabled people: Issues for discussion*. New York, NY: World Rehabilitation Fund.

Finklestein, V. (1981). To deny or not to deny disability. In A. Brechin, P. Liddiard, & J. Swain (Eds), *Handicap in a social world*. Sevenoaks, UK: Hodder and Stoughton.

Fisher, A.D., Ristori, J., Fanni, E., Castellini, G., Forti, G., & Maggi, M. (2016). Gender identity, gender assignment and reassignment in individuals with disorders of sex development: A major of dilemma. *Journal of Endocrinological Investigation, 39*(11), 1207–24. doi:10.1007/s40618-016-0482-0

Foucault, M. (2006). *History of madness*. J. Khalfa (Ed.). London, UK: Routledge.

Frances, A. (2013). The new crisis of confidence in psychiatric diagnosis. *Annals of Internal Medicine, 159*(3), 221–2. doi:10.7326/0003-4819-159-3-201308060-00655

Goodley, D. (2014). *Dis/ability Studies: Theorising disablism and ableism*. London, UK: Routledge.

Goodley, D., & Runswick-Cole, K. (2011). The violence of disablism. *Sociology of Health and Illness, 33*(4), 602–17. doi:10.1111/j.1467-9566.2010.01302.x

Harrison, G. (2010). Me, my sex and I [Documentary Film]. UK: BBC.

Holmes, C. (2016). Exploring the intersections between violence, place, and mental health in the lives of trans and gender nonconforming people in Canada. In M. Giesbrecht & V. Crooks (Eds), *Place, health, and diversity learning from the Canadian experience* (pp. 53–75). New York, NY: Routledge.

Hudson, L. (2011). From small beginnings: The euthanasia of children with disabilities in Nazi Germany. *Journal of Paediatrics and Child Health, 47*(8), 508–11. doi:0.1111/j.1440-1754.2010.01977.x

Joel, D., Berman, Z., Tavor, I., Wexler, N., Gaber, O., Stein, Y., . . . Assa, Y. (2015). Sex beyond the genitalia: The human brain mosaic. *Proceedings of the National Academy of Sciences, 112*(50), 15468–73. doi:10.1073/pnas.1509654112

Kinney, M., & Wilson, T. (2016). Putting the politics back into 'psycho': Grass-roots consciousness raising in Liverpool. *Critical and Radical Social Work, 4*(3), 391–6. doi:10.1332/204986016x14736888146404

Laing, R.D. (1967). *The politics of experience and the bird of paradise*. Harmondsworth, UK: Penguin.

Large, M., & Ryan, C. J. (2012). Sanism, stigma and the belief in dangerousness. *Australian & New Zealand Journal of Psychiatry, 46*(11), 1099–1100.

Lee, E.O.J., & Brotman, S. (2013). SPEAK OUT!: Structural intersectionality and anti-oppressive practice with LGBTQ refugees in Canada. *Canadian Social Work Review/Revue Canadienne De Service Social, 30*(2), 157–83.

Lorde, A. (1984). The master's tools will never dismantle the master's house. In Sister Outsider (Ed.), *Essays and Speeches* (pp. 110–14). Berkeley, CA: The Crossing Press.

Martin, N. (2012). Disability identity–disability pride. *Perspectives: Policy and Practice in Higher Education, 16*(1), 14–18. doi:10.1080/13603108.2011.611832

Mauerberg-deCastro, E., Campbell, D.F., & Tavares, C.P. (2016). The global reality of the paralympic movement: Challenges and opportunities in disability sports. *Motriz, Revista De Educação Física, 22*(3), 111–23. doi:10.1590/S1980-6574201600030001

McGrath, L., Walker, C., & Jones, C. (2016). Psychologists against austerity: Mobilising psychology for social change. *Critical and Radical Social Work, 4*(3), 409–13. doi:10.1332/204986016x14721364317537

McPhail, R., McNulty, Y., & Hutchings, K. (2016). Lesbian and gay expatriation: Opportunities, barriers and challenges for global mobility. *The International Journal of Human Resource Management, 27*(3), 382–406. doi:10.1080/09585192.2014.941903

Menzies, R., LeFrancois, B., & Reaume, G. (2013). Introducing mad studies. In R. Menzies, B. LeFrancois, & G. Reaume (Eds), *Mad matters: A critical reader in Canadian mad studies* (pp. 1–22). Toronto, Canada: Canadian Scholars' Press.

Mladenov, T. (2015). Neoliberalism, postsocialism, disability. *Disability and Society, 30*(3), 445–59. doi:10.1080/09687599.2015.1021758

Moth, R., & McKeown, M. (2016). Realising Sedgwick's vision: Theorising strategies of resistance to neoliberal mental health and welfare policy. *Critical and Radical Social Work, 4*(3), 379–90. doi:10.1332/204986016x14721364317690

Oliver, M. (1990). *The politics of disablement*. Basingstoke, UK: Macmillan.

Oliver, M. (1996). *Understanding disability: From theory to practice*. London, UK: Macmillan.

Oliver, M. (2009). *Understanding disability: From theory to practice* (2nd edn). Basingstoke, UK: Palgrave Macmillan.

Perlin, M. (2013). "There must be some way out here": Why the convention on the rights of persons with disabilities is potentially the best weapon in the fight against sanism. *Psychiatry, Psychology and Law, 20*(3), 462–76.

Peter, T., Taylor, C., & Chamberland, L. (2015). A queer day in Canada: Examining Canadian high school students' experiences with school-based homophobia in two large-scale studies. *Journal Of Homosexuality, 62*(2), 186–206. doi: 10.1080/00918369.2014.969057

Pilgrim, D. (2016). Peter Sedgwick, proto-critical realist? *Critical and Radical Social Work, 4*(3), 327–41. doi:10.1332/204986016x14651166264390

Poole, J. (2014). Sanism. Retrieved from https://www.youtube.com/watch?v=hZvEUbtTBes

Poole, J., & Ward, J. (2013). "Breaking open the bone": Storying, sanism and mad grief. In B. LeFrancois, R. Menzies, & G. Reaume (Eds), *Mad matters: A critical reader in Canadian mad studies* (pp. 94–104). Toronto, Canada: Canadian Scholars' Press.

Pyne, J. (2011). Unsuitable bodies: Trans people and cisnormativity in shelter services. *Canadian Social Work Review, 28*(1), 129–37.

Reaume, G. (2002). Lunatic to patient to person: Nomenclature in psychiatric history and the influence of patients' activism in North America. *International Journal of Law and Psychiatry, 25*(4), 405–26. doi:10.1016/S0160-2527(02)00130-9

Reaume, G. (2008, July 14). A History of psychiatric survivor pride day during the 1990s. *Mad Pride Issue.* Retrieved from http://csinfo.ca/bulletin/Bulletin_374.pdf

Reaume, G. (2014). Understanding critical disability studies. *Canadian Medical Association Journal/Journal De l'Association Medicale Canadienne, 186*(16), 1248–9. doi:10.1503/cmaj.141236

Richards, C., Bouman, P., Seal, L., Barker, M.J., Nieder, T.O., & T'Sjoen, G. (2016). Non-binary or genderqueer genders. *International Review of Psychiatry, 28*(1), 95–102. doi: 10.3109/09540261.2015.1106446

Scully, J.L. (2012). Deaf identities in disability studies: With us or without us? In N. Watson, A. Roulstone, & C. Thomas (Eds), *Routledge handbook of disability studies* (pp. 109–121). London, UK: Routledge.

Shakespeare, T., & Watson, N. (2001). The social model of disability: An outdated ideology? *Research in Social Science and Disability, 2*, 9–28.

Shlasko, D. (2014). *Trans ally workbook: Getting pronouns right & what it teaches us about gender*. Oakland, CA: Think Again Training and Consultation.

Simplican, S.C., Leader, G., Kosciulek, J., & Leahy, M. (2015). Defining social inclusion of people with intellectual and developmental disabilities: An ecological model of social networks and community participation. *Research in Developmental Disabilities, 38*, 18–29. doi: 10.1016/j.ridd.2014.10.008

Sinclair, J. (2013). Why I dislike "person first" language. *Autism Network International, 1*(2), 1–2.

Steinbach, R.J., Allyse, M., Michie, M., Liu, E.Y., & Cho, M.K. (2016). "This lifetime commitment": Public conceptions of disability and noninvasive prenatal genetic screening. *American Journal of Medical Genetics Part A, 170*(2), 363–74. doi:10.1002/ajmg.a.37459

Steinmetz, K. (2016, February 23). Gender is not just chromosomes and genitals. *Time Magazine*. Retrieved from http://time.com/4231379/gender-south-dakota-bathroom-bill/

Szasz, T.S. (1961). *The myth of mental illness: Foundations of a theory of personal conduct*. New York, NY: Harper & Row.

Titchkosky, T. (2001). Disability: A rose by any other name? "People-first" language in Canadian society. *Canadian Review of Sociology/Revue Canadienne De Sociologie, 38*(2), 125–40. doi:10.1111/j.1755-618X.2001.tb00967.x

Toomey, R.B., McGuire, J.K., & Russell, S.T. (2012). Heteronormativity, school climates, and perceived safety for gender nonconforming peers. *Journal of Adolescence, 35*(1), 187–96. doi:0.1016/j.adolescence.2011.03.001

Turner, G.W., & Crane, B. (2016). Sexually silenced no more, adults with learning disabilities speak up: A call to action for social work to frame sexual voice as a social justice issue. *British Journal of Social Work, 46*(8), 2300–17. doi:10.1093/bjsw/bcw133

Union of the Physically Impaired Against Segregation & Disability Alliance. (1976). *Fundamental principles of disability*. London, UK: UPIAS & Disability Alliance.

Wang, K., Silverman, A., Gwinn, J.D., & Dovidio, J.F. (2015). Independent or ungrateful? Consequences of confronting patronizing help for people with disabilities. *Group Processes & Intergroup Relations, 18*(4), 489–503. doi:10.1177/1368430214550345

Watson, N. (2012). Resarching disablement. In N. Watson, A. Roulstone, & C. Thomas (Eds), *Routledge Handbook of Disability Studies* (pp. 93–105). London, UK: Routledge.

Weeber, J.E. (1999). What could I know of racism? *Journal of Counseling & Development, 77*(1), 20–3. doi:10.1002/j.1556-6676.1999.tb02407.x

Wolbring, G. (2012). Expanding ableism: Taking down the ghettoization of impact of disability studies scholars. *Societies, 2*(3), 75–83. doi:10.3390/soc2030075

Woodford, M.R., Kulick, A., Sinco, B.R., & Hong, J.S. (2014). Contemporary heterosexism on campus and psychological distress among LGBQ students: The mediating role of self-acceptance. *American Journal of Orthopsychiatry, 84*(5), 519–29. doi:10.1037/ort0000015

World Health Organization. (2014). *Mental health: A state of well-being*. Retrieved from http://www.who.int/features/factfiles/mental_health/en/

# 7 From Colonization to Decolonization

## In this chapter you will learn:

- Key concepts that can be used in decolonization
- What Indigenous sovereignty and resurgence are, and why they are important in anti-oppression
- Why truth and reconciliation is important, but why it may not go far enough in decolonizing

## Introduction

Dr Jacquie Green, director and associate professor at the University of Victoria School of Social Work, and Gary told a story about a White professor in Canada who was trying to engage in decolonization by bringing Indigenous knowledge into the academy. **Indigenous knowledge** is knowing developed by Indigenous peoples and is often built on traditional teachings and ways of knowing. We retell the story here.

> After hearing that Indigenous ways of knowing were a good thing, a White professor wanted to bring this knowledge into the academy, but did not know how. He read book after book but found no answers.
>
> "Maybe," he thought, "if I get in touch with nature, the answers will come to me." So, donning a backpack, he set out for the bush. After walking for several hours he sat beneath a large tree and began to think, but although bitten by mosquitoes and blackflies he was bitten by no ideas. Feeling sorry for himself, he sighed, "Will I ever learn how to include Indigenous knowledge in social work?"
>
> High in a tree Raven watched and began to worry. Experience had taught Raven that every time a White person included Indigenous peoples in something, the White people took something away from Indigenous peoples; there was no telling what this professor might come up with if left to his own devices. Raven decided to help.

"Hey," shouted Raven, "I can tell you how to do that."

The professor nearly jumped out of his skin! This was just a little too close to nature for him. But he quickly calmed his fears, realizing that perhaps this was the break he was looking for, and besides, there was sure to be at least one journal article in it! He grabbed his notebook and pen and asked Raven to explain.

"What you gotta do," Raven said, "is give the traditions and ways of knowing of the Qallunaat a part of your academic space. Once you've done that, you've got your problem beat!"

Excited, the professor said, "Tell me about the Qallunaat."

"The Qallunaat are a strange and ancient people," Raven replied. "They have three types of sage. The first type of sage keeps learning until their people call them a 'man without a marriage partner.' Now these sages don't have to be men and it's okay if they are married."

"So why call them a 'man without a marriage partner?'" the professor asked.

"Tradition," Raven answered. "Now if they keep on learning some of them will eventually reach the next level and people will call them 'a man with dog or a servant.' But again they may not all be men and they probably won't have dogs or servants."

"More tradition?" the professor asked.

"Yes, more tradition," Raven acknowledged. "Now, getting to the final level of knowing takes a lot more learning than the first two stages put together and not many of them can handle that much knowledge in their heads—but those who make it get to be called 'healers of thinking.' These are the real big shots in the tribe because they do all kinds of magic with words and numbers to determine which things are true."

As Raven spoke the professor took hurried notes, but when he looked up to ask where the Qallunaat might be found, Raven had gone. "Never mind," thought the professor, "I now know what I have to do. I will find the Qallunaat and invite them to the campus. There should be no problem giving them a small place in the academy where they can enjoy their ways of learning and strange traditions—as long as they promise not to interfere with anyone else at the school."

So the professor set out looking for the Qallunaat. First he travelled east and asked the Mi'kmaq if they knew the Qallunaat, but they said they'd never heard of them. Moving south he met the Mohawk and Lakota Nations who had not heard of the Qallunaat either. He journeyed west to the Salish who could not help him. He then turned north. Farther and farther he walked and when the Inuit saw him they came to greet him and said, "It is not often we see a White guy up here—what brings a Qallunaat like you this far north?"

Source: Dumbrill & Green, 2008, pp. 491–2, with minor modifications

By the end of this chapter you will understand enough about colonization to appreciate why Raven was worried about what the professor might do. You will also know enough about decolonization to understand the mistakes the professor was making, and you will know how to avoid those mistakes in your own social work practice. As well, you will have ideas about how to connect your anti-oppressive work to decolonization. At the end of this chapter, however, you will not know how to decolonize. We cannot tell you how to do that, because those answers come from relationship and dialogue, not from books. But by the end of this chapter you will know enough about truth and the possibilities of reconciliation for you to build relationships and engage in dialogue about how to decolonize.

# Undoing Colonization

Although empires have been built through colonization for thousands of years, White Europeans seem to have "perfected" and globalized this process. Certainly, the type of colonization that predominates in the world today is mostly White and European.

In this chapter, we focus mostly on settler colonization, which is the type of colonization that predominates in the Americas and Oceania. The biggest difference between **settler colonialism** and other forms of colonization is that in settler colonization the colonizers come to stay forever. In contrast, when Europe colonized Africa, India, Asia, and elsewhere, the majority of Europeans did not intend to stay. They came to exploit the land and people and take the wealth of that place back home to Europe. Indeed, the colonization of India was not initially undertaken by the British Crown, but by a corporation called the East India Company, which sent its employees and armies to rob and exploit the wealth of India for its own corporate aims (Oak & Swamy, 2012). In previous chapters we spoke of the way businessman Cecil Rhodes and others like him played a similar role in colonizing African nations. This is exactly what colonization is: a corporate enterprise.

## The Decolonization of Former Colonies

Decolonizing where Europeans went to exploit but not settle can seem relatively straightforward; the colonizers can be told to pack up and go home and the nation can declare independence. Colonizers are often reluctant to go, but with persistence they can eventually be sent on their way. Of course, colonization is not ended that easily, because after hundreds of years of colonizers building their own nations by treading others down, newly decolonized nations hardly find themselves on an even playing field when they emerge into independence. In addition, the trauma and upheaval to people, relationships, traditional borders, and social systems that colonization causes can damage and fracture nations so profoundly that they cannot simply pick up where they left off before colonization began. As well, colonization does not end when the colonizers pack up their military and go home. In a world dependent on trade and characterized by the dominance of global corporations, when the colonizers go home, **neocolonialism**, a new type of colonization but with the same ruling relations, becomes possible (Nkrumah, 1965/2009; Sartre, 2006).

The new colonialism takes over where the old colonialism leaves off. The old colonization extracts wealth and resources from colonized nations by direct rule, while the new colonialism allows the extraction of wealth without direct rule. For example, consider Guyana, a nation that has many current economic and immigration links to Canada. Guyana is on the northeast corner of South America between Brazil and Venezuela, and is politically and culturally aligned with the Caribbean.

European colonization of the region began in the seventeenth century with the Dutch, French, and British each capturing territory. The Indigenous population retreated, or were pushed, inland into the interior. Britain imported labour to the colony, first through slavery, then by indentured labour mostly from India (Rodney, 1981; St Pierre, 1999). These workers produced wealth for Britain mostly from sugar, lumber, gold, diamonds, and other commodities. Later, bauxite (the raw material of aluminum) became a major export, which in the years after colonization Guyana tried to leverage so that it could obtain the capabilities to produce its own aluminum (Sackey, 1981). But to this day these attempts have never been fully successful, so countries like Canada continue to import bauxite from countries like Guyana at low cost, which they turn into aluminum and export back to Guyana and elsewhere at a tidy profit.

## Key Concept

Colonization does not end when the colonizers pack up and go home. The deep global inequalities instigated by colonization mean that when the colonizers go home, the former colonial power can continue to exploit former colonies without the bother of direct rule.

## Decolonization on the Colonizer's Terms

Decolonization usually occurs on the colonizer's terms. Again we use Guyana as an example. "Decolonization" came to Guyana, as it did to many British colonies, after World War II (Gibbons, 2011). Britain giving up direct rule of Guyana was not decolonization from an Indigenous perspective, because once the British left, Indigenous land was ruled by the African, South Asian, and other people Britain had shipped there to work. Britain stood little to gain by exploring Indigenous rule in a Guyanese context because, for the most part, Indigenous peoples were not involved in the mass extraction of wealth from the land—something Britain needed to continue. It was clear that Britain planned to gain from decolonization because, just like critical race theory we discussed in Chapter 5 predicts, the freedom of the oppressed is contingent on it benefiting the oppressor.

Decolonization was not true independence for Guyanese of African, South Asian, or other non-Indigenous heritage either. Decolonization was imagined and enacted in a way that suited the British Crown. If the new "independent" nation stepped out of line in any direction, its "independence" was over. Indeed, when Guyana began a move toward "independence" in the 1950s, the democratically elected Prime Minister Cheddy Jagen stepped to the left and sought aid from Britain's rival the Soviet block. This resulted in Britain (backed by America) quickly sending in armed troops to suspend the constitution. "Independence" was taken away and only allowed when it was clear that the Guyanese government was going to serve British and American interests (Gibbons, 2011).

## Colonization and Decolonization—Both Are a Game of Domination

The same decolonization formula has been used around the globe to maintain the domination of former colonial powers and their allies. The world's superpowers prop up governments that suit their needs and topple ones that do not, such as the US involvement in the war in Vietnam starting in the 1950s, the US and British toppling of the democratically elected government of Iran in 1953, the US-sponsored attempted invasion of Cuba at the Bay of Pigs in 1961, the US invasion of Grenada in 1983, the US invasion of Panama in 1989, and the invasion of Iraq in 2003, to name a few. There is even more US activity in South America—so much that the US military has a special training camp at Fort Benning called the "Western Hemisphere Institute for Security Cooperation," formerly known as the "US Army School of the Americas." The US uses this facility to train dictators and insurgents to maintain or overthrow South American governments as suits the US interests (Monbiot, 2001).

We do not mean to single out the USA for criticism. Most nations engage in these activities to establish domination and maintain their own interests. We use the examples above because the West and particularly the USA have the power to fund foreign interference more effectively and on a larger scale than most. Nations do this to ensure their own security and trade. The former colonial powers and their allies tend to win this game, so just as in the days of direct rule, wealth is extracted and realized by former colonial masters. In many cases, rather than improve conditions for the newly independent nations, such neocolonialism allows the former colonial masters to take more and give less, and when the former colonies fall into deeper poverty as a result, the myths of White superiority (discussed in Chapter 4) and Western civilization (discussed in Chapter 2) are perpetuated.

Although the neocolonial system remains firmly in place today, it is constantly shifting and adapting, especially with the emerging economic dominance of India and China. These nations may in time unsettle the dominance of the West, but rather than replacing Western imperialism, these nations may replicate it. Indeed, China's trade involvement in Africa has been likened to Western colonialism (Junbo, 2007;

Taylor, 2006). Whether this is the case remains to be seen, but it is possible. Indeed, Dr Gerald Taiaiake Alfred, who is from Kahnawà:ke in the Mohawk Nation, and professor of Indigenous Governance and Political Science at the University of Victoria, contends that Western attitudes toward colonization are derived from "white society's understanding of its own power and relationship with nature" (Alfred, 1999, p. 21). In other words, the leaders of the Western world and White society see the oceans, the land, and nature as something to plunder and exploit, rather than something to care for. We suspect that the same could be said of China, India, and other industrial nations. Consequently, decolonization is not simply about stopping White colonial or neocolonial masters. It is about stopping an ideology that has become globalized, and stopping the end game that is focused on power over nature and domination over people, land, and water.

Any social worker operating in an international context needs to be aware of the history referred to above, along with the ways neocolonialism operates. It is also especially important to recognize that social work is a Western commodity sometimes linked to the colonization process, and is not always linked to anti-oppression (Gray, Coates, Yellow Bird, & Hetherington, 2013). As mentioned above, our text focuses more on the North America and Oceania contexts of settler colonialism, but even here an understanding of the way global colonialism and neocolonialism operate is an important backdrop to understanding the settler colonial context.

# Settler Colonization

Settler colonization, where the colonizers come, conquer, and plan to stay forever, uses exactly the same power dynamics and ruling relationships as other forms of colonization, but in a slightly different settler colonial way. Taiaiake Alfred explains that under settler colonialism, "Real control remains in the hands of white society because it is still that society's rules that define our life—not through obviously racist laws, but through endless references to the 'market,' 'fiscal reality,' Aboriginal rights, and 'public will.' And it is the white society's needs that are met" (Alfred, 1999, p. xii). In other words, just as colonialism and neocolonialism ensure the interests of mostly White nations are met on a global stage, settler colonialism ensures that the needs of White society are met on a national stage.

## Undoing Settler Colonialism

Although we separate settler colonialism from other forms of colonization, arguably the solution to both is the same. Settlers should pack up, go home, and return the land to the rightful Indigenous nations. Of course we recognize that in a settler colonial context, settlers "going back home" is unlikely to occur, and if it did this does not preclude neocolonialism occurring. In fact we are not suggesting that settlers "go back home," nor are Indigenous peoples suggesting this (more about that later), but we are suggesting that recognizing the legitimacy of this proposition is the starting point for solving issues.

Settlers need to walk into problem-solving conversations about decolonization accepting that they are guests on Indigenous land and not landlords. Only from the position and attitude of such acceptance can we move forward into respectful and honest conversations about what decolonization means in a settler-colonial context. These conversations must begin with a recognition that "the settler state has no right to determine indigenous futures" (Alfred, 1999, p. 47).

"Respectful conversations" means learning and being honest about the impact settler colonialism has had on Indigenous peoples and the land. By definition, settler colonialism is a form of genocide, because it is not only built on the principle of extracting wealth from land, it is also built on the principle of ensuring that "Indigenous peoples ultimately disappear as peoples, so that settler nations can seamlessly take their place" (Lawrence & Dua, 2005, p. 123). Dr Cyndy Baskin from Ryerson University School of Social Work, who is also known as On-koo-khag-kno kwe (the woman who makes links or who links things), tells us that Canadians are often not aware of the impact this genocide principle has had on Indigenous peoples. Cyndy helps us make links between settler colonialism and its effects:

> The near destruction of a land-based way of living, economic and social deprivation, substance misuse, the intergenerational cycle of violence, the breakdown of healthy family life, and the loss of traditional values for many Indigenous people today are the direct result of colonization and ongoing systemic oppression. (Baskin, 2016, p. 7)

In addition to the near destruction of Indigenous peoples, colonization has also brought near destruction of the land. No longer understood by Western society as a mother and sustainer of all life now and yet to come, the earth is seen as a commodity, as an inanimate object to be plundered and bled until it has nothing left to give. In this manner colonization takes not only territory, but destroys the land, the spirit of the land, and the people who have a physical, mental, and spiritual connection to the land.

## Key Concept

In Canada colonizers have not seen the land as a mother and sustainer of life. Instead they see the land as a commodity, as an inanimate object to be plundered and bled until it is empty and has nothing left to give. In this manner, colonization destroys the land, the spirit of the land, and the people who have a physical, mental, and spiritual connection to the land.

## Is Anti-Oppression with a Focus on Equity Enough?

It is not enough for anti-oppressive social workers to be aware of the impact of settler colonialism; we also have to do something about it, because social work does not simply address harms; it tries to change the things that brought the harm. But in a settler-colonial context, what does this change look like? What does decolonization set out to achieve and what can anti-oppressive social workers hope to achieve in this work?

In Chapter 1 we spoke of the search for equity being central in anti-oppression. In a settler-colonial context this is a little different and we have to ask whether equity goes far enough. Taiaiake Alfred explains that in these contexts, "there is more to justice than equity" (Alfred, 1999, p. vi). Indeed, ensuring equity and making sure that Indigenous peoples are no longer marginalized or impacted by racism will not right the past or the present, because it will not restore Indigenous nationhood or sovereignty, and Indigenous nationhood and sovereignty are the key to decolonizing in a settler-colonial context.

Indigenous sovereignty may not be the same as settlers imagine. It may not reproduce the way Western sovereign nation states govern their own people, land, and waters (Alfred, 1999). Exactly what nation and sovereignty look like from an Indigenous perspective is for Indigenous people to decide. Settlers do not decide this for Indigenous peoples; settlers just need to ensure that Indigenous peoples have the right to decide this for themselves.

Fortunately Indigenous communities have been very clear about what needs to change for their sovereignty to occur. To understand these things, however, we need to explore the context from which they emerge. Indeed, the groundwork for what needs to happen today was set out yesterday, in treaties that have rarely been honoured by settlers.

## Key Concept

Anti-oppression is based on the idea of achieving equity. But equity is not enough when it comes to settler colonialism. Stealing someone's land, robbing their sovereignty, taking their children, and then offering them an equitable share of what you have taken hardly seems fair.

## The Importance of Two Row Wampum and Other Treaties

In 1613, **Kaswentha**, also known as the **Two Row Wampum Treaty**, set out the relationship and sharing of space by the Haudenosaunee and the Dutch Crown, and this is also said to be the basis of sovereign relations between later settlers and European governments (Keefer, 2014). The Treaty states:

> We will not be like Father and Son, but like Brothers. [Our treaties] symbolize two paths or two vessels, travelling down the same river together. One, a

birchbark canoe, will be for the Indian People, their laws, their customs, and their ways. The other, a ship, will be for the white people and their laws, their customs, and their ways. We shall each travel the river together, side by side, but in our own boat. Neither of us will make compulsory laws nor interfere in the internal affairs of the other. Neither of us will try to steer the other's vessel. (Cited in Keefer, 2014, p. 14)

The treaty belt is made of wampum beads, with two rows of purple on a white background. The white beads represent "peace, friendship, and respect"; the purple beads represent two vessels travelling the same river, one European, the other Indigenous (Keefer, 2014). Some also say that the purple rows represent power: one is the power of settlers, the other the power of Indigenous peoples. They are side by side on a white backdrop of peace (Alfred, 1999).

At first sight the Treaty wording may seem gendered, but we suspect it is not, because Haudenosaunee government structure is female led (Porter, 2008). Maybe the phrase, "we will not be like Father and Son" is a response to European attempts to impose paternalistic male control over Indigenous peoples, or perhaps the Haudenosaunee were adopting the language of diplomacy of that day so White people would better understand it. We would have to ask traditional teachers to know for sure.

The Treaty does not mention people of colour, so where are they placed? Certainly Indigenous peoples and people of colour are both racialized and face racism, but their histories and their relation to Turtle Island are different. These differing histories mean that people of colour are not in the Indigenous canoe, because by definition, "Indigenous peoples are those who have creation stories not colonization stories, about how we/they came to be in a particular place" (Tuck & Yang, 2012, p. 6). Central to the concept of indigeneity is a historical continuity with a pre-conquest or settled territory (Keal, 2016). People of colour came to Turtle Island on the European ship, even though this was often not by choice, and although they may not be implicated in colonization stories in the same way as White people, their connection to pre-conquest territory is not the same as

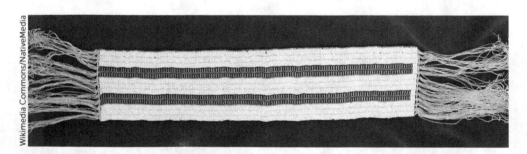

Wikimedia Commons/NativeMedia

**Figure 7.1** The Two Row Wampum

Indigenous peoples. (We will speak more later about the relationship between people of colour and Indigenous peoples).

The Two Row Wampum Treaty certainly does not speak to Indigenous–settler relations in Oceania or elsewhere, and it may not represent all First Peoples of Turtle Island, especially in some parts of the Canadian Maritimes, Quebec, British Columbia, or other places where formal treaties do not exist. There is, however, a broad recognition that the Two Row Wampum Treaty sets out an important principle in Indigenous–settler relations (Alfred, 2017, 1999; Mercredi & Turpel, 1993). Even in Australia the idea of separate Indigenous–settler sovereignties in one geographic space exists (Prokhovnik, 2015). Consequently, a good beginning point of decolonization in Canada would be for settlers to honour agreements that are in place, to immediately cease and desist ongoing activities that attempt to steer First Peoples into non-existence (i.e., non-existence as distinct peoples), and to have honest and respectful conversations about Indigenous sovereignty and resurgence. The concept of Indigenous **resurgence** is a reestablishment of Indigenous peoplehood, a reconnection to the land and traditions, and a reestablishment and renewal of what colonizers tried to take away.

## Key Concept

A good beginning point for decolonization in Canada would be for settlers to honour agreements that are in place, to immediately cease and desist ongoing activities that attempt to steer First Peoples into non-existence, and to have honest and respectful conversations about how to promote Indigenous sovereignty and resurgence.

There are other treaties and wampums that may help revise what sovereignty means and how nations coexist. One example is "The Dish with One Spoon" (Nahwegahbow, 2014), which speaks to sharing, to not taking everything, to leaving something for someone else, and to respecting each other and Mother Earth. Again, like the Two Row Wampum Treaty, this treaty is region-specific, but it carries relationship principles that have broader significance, and this teaching also seems to make it clear that the Two Row Wampum Treaty is not about isolation, but is about two separate peoples sharing space and co-operating with each other. Indeed, Taiaiake Alfred (1999) speaks of settlers and Indigenous peoples being allies.

Sharing involves a responsibility, not only to each other, but also to the land. Indeed, there is little point having two rows of sovereignty on the river if the people of one row destroy the river (environment) for everyone. Especially now in a context of global warming and environmental destruction, settlers co-operating with Indigenous peoples is even more important to ensure sustainability for everyone.

Some suggest that we are in so much trouble environmentally, politically, and economically that more than simple communication between the ship and canoe is needed.

Giibwanisi, an environmental activist and founder of the Oshkimaadziig Unity Camp, suggests that the Indigenous "canoes have been hijacked and are actually aboard the settler ship" (Kinch, 2014). Worse still, Giibwanisi contends that the settler ship has been hijacked too, because "the people that run it, the captains, they are not listening to the workers or to whomever, the deckhands and what not" (Kinch, 2014).

## What Do Treaties Mean Today?

Given that the settler ship is hijacked and out of control, what do treaties mean today? The first suggestion we have is that settlers need to put their ship in order. Settlers need to stop destroying the environment and harming people. Anti-oppression can help in that process, which is why we have spent time in previous chapters looking at power imbalances, politics, and the root causes of inequality and inequity. Beyond this, however, it is not for non-Indigenous authors like us to say what treaties mean in today's context, especially when most of our people have not taken time to learn them, and even when they did learn, they did not keep the treaties.

When settlers made treaties with Indigenous peoples, the settlers operated under several principles and teachings that undermined the treaties they made. The first was the principle of **terra nullius**, which is a Latin term that means "nobody's land." The settlers wrote this concept into law declaring that the land belongs to "nobody" if there was no pre-existing sovereign state or if the people living on the land were not Christian (Truth and Reconciliation Commission of Canada, 2015b). As the original Indigenous inhabitants were non-Christian, and they did not define sovereignty the same way Europeans did, settlers used the principle of terra nullius to take over Indigenous territories.

Another principle used by the settlers was the **doctrine of discovery**, which is the idea that if Europeans came and were able to occupy the land, the land belonged to the Europeans (Truth and Reconciliation Commission of Canada, 2015b). Of course Indigenous nations already occupied the land, but this was mostly disregarded and swept aside by the settlers.

Europeans, therefore, created and used terra nullius and the doctrine of discovery to occupy and make themselves the landlords of Indigenous territories, and to this day they have not repudiated these laws or recognized them as unjust (Truth and Reconciliation Commission of Canada, 2015b). We find it ironic that settler governments have no problem remembering and continuing to enforce ancient unjust European doctrines like terra nullius, but cannot do the same with just treaties like Two Row Wampum.

We contend that anti-oppression must engage with decolonization processes, and the starting point for that is to honour treaties. The issue is, however, what do these treaties mean today? We cannot say, because for settlers to now start interpreting what treaties mean in today's context when settlers never honoured them in the historical context in which they were first made seems offensive to us. Instead, we need to turn to those who remember these treaties and understand them in the bigger context of Indigenous teachings, and ask how settlers might honour these treaties today. Although we cannot say what the treaties mean in today's context, we have been taught that to make sense of the Two Row Wampum and similar treaties requires relationship. Indeed, by definition treaty emerges from relationship, and is enacted by all parties not only in relation to each other, but also in relation to Mother Earth on which the agreement is made.

## The Importance of Dialogue, Listening, and Undoing Domination

Relationship requires dialogue. Taiaiake Alfred (1999) and we suggest that non-Indigenous people enter this dialogue through listening. This is not to say that settlers do not bring good teachings and knowledge to the dialogue. As mentioned in Chapter 3, settlers bring wisdom from all over the world that includes golden rules, Ubuntu, Tikkun olam, and more. These teachings can bring much to decolonization, but in a settler-colonial context, the beginning point for settlers has to be listening.

Listening is important, because Indigenous peoples have been harmed by "well-meaning" settlers, especially White settlers whose power often comes from the Whiteness we described in Chapter 4. Harm comes when "help" is provided on the basis of what people with power want to give and not what the people without power want to receive. **Indian agents** (or **commissioners**) gave this type of "help." An Indian Agent was a Canadian bureaucrat, who was usually White, or was Whitened by years of working within the civil service, who managed Indigenous peoples on behalf of the Canadian government (Titley, 2009). Such agents enforced the **Indian Act**, which is legislation that continues to define who an "Indian" is in Canada, and sets out the principles by which the Crown manages their lives. The Indian Act is regarded by many as racist, paternalistic, and built on the idea that Indigenous peoples are not capable of knowing or managing their own affairs (Shewell & Finkel, 2005). As a result, the Indian Act operates in direct opposition to treaties like Two Row Wampum, and violates principles of natural justice and respect for human dignity.

Given the above, in any anti-oppressive or social justice setting, if someone accuses you of being an "Indian Agent," they are making a very damning accusation. This, however, is the accusation Kaikaikon makes of some would-be decolonizers. Kaikaikon, a member of the Loon Clan of the Anishinabek Nation, suggests that settler allies trying to decolonize can become:

> . . . Indian agents running around trying to do what's best for Indians. Because they're the ones who think they know it all, so they're helping us. Even by answering these questions [about decolonization], we use the English language and their ideology—we're using everything that's theirs. Even their Marxism. Somewhere there's our own war chiefs and our own ideas that we should be using to answer these questions. (Kinch, 2014, p. 20)

We suggest that social workers are particularly vulnerable to becoming "Indian Agents." Social workers want to help. This desire comes from a good place in our hearts, but we have to be careful how we do this. If you are a settler and are reading this chapter, and our words make you feel ready to boldly go and seek social justice for Indigenous peoples, you are in danger of becoming an "Indian Agent." Do not become that person. Put energy into entering discussions with Indigenous communities as a listener. Of course also dialogue and exchange ideas, but do so in a spirit of listening. In this context your role is to follow, not lead. Your job as an ally is to steer your own ship; do not even try to steer the birchbark canoe, because that would make you an Indian Agent.

> ## Key Concept
>
> If you are a settler and you feel ready to boldly go and seek social justice for Indigenous peoples, you are in danger of becoming an "Indian Agent." Do not become that person. Put energy into entering discussions with Indigenous communities as a listener. Of course also dialogue and exchange ideas, but do so in a spirit of listening. Your role is to follow, not lead. Your job as an ally is to steer your own ship; do not even try to steer the birchbark canoe, because that would make you an Indian Agent.

Even if you are Indigenous you can become an "Indian Agent," especially if you are learning to be a social worker. Social work schools teach primarily White ways and White knowing. As Kaikaikon points out, even decolonization talk is colonized with Western ideology. When you come to social work, books like this one written by settlers like us may be able to disrupt Western knowledge, but we cannot teach you Indigenous ways or the Indigenous path to take. If your social work program does not have Indigenous faculty members who teach these ways, if your course outlines do not include articles by Indigenous authors written from an Indigenous perspective, and if there are no Elders in residence at your school supporting your learning and your spirit, be very cautious about what you take into your head, your heart, and your spirit.

It was, of course, the recognition that Indigenous knowledge is important in social work and social work education that led the White professor in the story at the start of the chapter to go looking for it in the bush. The professor's intent was decolonization. One can already see from our discussion above that bringing Indigenous knowledge into the academy is not the same as decolonization, but it is a start. Let us consider this plan in more detail.

## The Professor and Raven

Clearly the White professor was well intended, but decolonization requires dialogue, so going off into the bush alone may have not been the best place to start. We discussed above how White people unilaterally doing what they think is best for Indigenous peoples is a problem. Fortunately Raven knew this, so Raven set a riddle to teach the professor what he needed to learn. Raven told the professor to find the Qallunaat and give them and their knowledge "a part" of academic space.

The professor set out on the quest to find and include the Qallunaat not realizing that he was a Qallunaat himself. (*Qallunaat* is an Inuit word often translated as non-Inuit or White people.) Raven knew, and the professor learned, that the answer to the riddle was for the White professor and his people to take up less space in the academy. Said differently, the problem the professor faced was not how to bring Indigenous knowledge into the academy, but how to get White people and White knowledge to move over, to stop dominating, and to make space for something else.

The implication of this lesson is that the professor did not have to be in charge of understanding or figuring out the right way to bring Indigenous knowledge into the academy. He could leave that to Indigenous people. The professor's role was making his own White people and knowledge systems stop dominating. Said differently, the professor's role was not to steer the birchbark canoe, but to steer his ship out of the way of the birchbark canoe.

Raven also provided the professor with a bonus lesson of seeing through the exnomination and invisibleness of his own Whiteness (concepts we discussed in Chapter 4). The professor was given the opportunity to see himself as the strange Other. The professor was puzzled by the exotic three levels of Qallunaat "sage" (someone who has attained wisdom) that Raven referred to as a "man without a wife," a "man with dog or a servant," and a "healer of thinking." The professor thought that this was some form of "backward" thinking that would be hard to incorporate and take seriously in a forward-moving modern learning institution. But when he realized that these strange sages referred to those with bachelor's, master's, and doctoral degrees, he had the opportunity to see himself as Other and grasp the way Othering works. Indeed, knowing oneself in relation to others is the beginning of decolonization; this is why Rasmussen (2001) advocates for "Qallunology," which is "to get white folks to examine and change their own destructive behavior" (p. 113).

## Key Concepts in Decolonization

As mentioned above, we as non-Indigenous scholars are not going to say how to decolonize from our one-sided perspective. At the beginning of this book we said that anti-oppression must be created in the moment. It also has to be created in dialogue. Nowhere is this more important than in decolonization. We cannot give a "recipe" for decolonization, but we can highlight mistakes to avoid, and some key concepts and attitudes that may be helpful in building decolonizing alliances and turning these into action.

### Do Not Confine Decolonization to a Metaphor

Tuck and Yang (2012) caution against using the term "decolonization" as a metaphor. A **metaphor** is a phrase or word used in a non-literal way. So when decolonization is used as a metaphor, the word is not being used to refer to a literal decolonization of land and territory, instead it is being used as an analogy. It is used to refer to decolonizing classrooms, decolonizing minds, or decolonizing something else, but never to mean establishing Indigenous sovereignty and decolonizing land.

Decolonization requires what the Anishinabek refer to as **Biskaabiiyang,** which means a return to one's self and a reinterpretation of teachings in today's context (Simpson, 2011) and a physical and spiritual return to the land (Gardner & Peters, 2014). In other words, "decolonization" is not a metaphor; it is a physical and practical return of Indigenous sovereignty and a relationship to the land (Tuck & Yang, 2012). Indeed, "when metaphor invades decolonization, it kills the very possibility of decolonization; it recenters Whiteness, it resettles theory, it extends innocence to the settler, it entertains a settler future" (Tuck & Yang, 2012, p. 3). In other words, confining the term *decolonization* to a metaphor is a form of colonization in itself, because we take over (colonize) the term and use it for all manner of social justice issues that serve our progressive purposes, but refuse to allow the term to be used as a place to conceptualize and support Indigenous sovereignty and resurgence.

We confess we are guilty of using the term decolonization as a metaphor. For instance, Gary talks of decolonizing child welfare, June talks of decolonizing social service agencies, and we both speak of decolonizing social work education. We use the term "decolonize" in these contexts because colonization has infiltrated all these areas and all aspects of life. Indeed, in previous chapters we have talked about how child welfare was used (and continues to be used) as a tool of colonization. Given the pervasive nature of colonization in almost everything social workers deal with, we cannot talk about or do the right thing without weeding out colonization from everywhere (Freire, 2001; Gray et al., 2013). As a result, we continue to use the term, but we are careful to not limit it to a metaphor. We do not "swap out prior civil and human rights based terms" (Tuck & Yang, 2012, p. 2) and replace them with "decolonization" to give the appearance of addressing settler colonialism.

## Do Not Opt Out of Responsibility Based on One's Own Marginality

It is not only White settlers who have to examine their complicity in setter colonialism. People of colour need to do so too (Lawrence & Dua, 2005). When it comes to who is a settler, we adopt Lawrence and Dua's (2005) definition that if you are not Indigenous, you are a settler. Some authors disagree with this argument. They contend that people of colour are a different class of settler than White people; for instance Sharma and Wright (2008) question whether Black slaves, un-free indentured Asians, or Indigenous people from elsewhere who settle can be considered settlers in the same way as White people.

We recognize that slaves had no choice but to "settle" here, but to characterize people of colour in Canada (or the USA and Oceania) as predominantly the descendants of slaves misrepresents modern demographics. Most people of colour immigrated here by choice for a better life. Even indentured labourers or servants had choice; they joined a colonizing project for a stake on Indigenous land (Lai, 1993). We are not suggesting that those who chose indenture had viable alternative options. Their own nations had been colonized and they undoubtedly faced poverty and appalling conditions. Indeed, unless desperate why else would they leave family and friends and sell themselves into what amounted to a form of slavery for a free passage and the future promise of Indigenous land?

One cannot claim that all Whites had much of a choice either. Thousands of Whites sold themselves into indentured servitude for the chance to escape the poverty and disease of Europe (Galenson, 1981). Also, 150,000 White children were deported from Britain to Canada, Australia, and Zimbabwe as forced unpaid labour (Humphreys, 2011; Letnell, 1998). As well, 162,000 White British convicts were bound in chains and transported to Australia (Abjorensen & Docherty, 2015) and 50,000 to the USA (Vaver, 2011). Neither White convict labour nor White indentured servitude is to be confused with the enslavement and transportation of Black Africans, but neither should indentured labourers from South Asia and elsewhere. Consequently, one cannot draw a simple binary line between people of colour and Whites in relation to settlement.

Of course we recognize that it hardly seems fair to consider those who "settled" because of being forcibly relocated in the same way as those who elected to immigrate and settle Indigenous land. The term "settler" implies some intent, so we concur that slaves cannot be considered settlers, and in Australia the term "White settler" was not used for White convicts transported to the colony against their will (Prokhovnik, 2015). We respect these historical differences, but in today's modern context, most Canadians, whether they are White or people of colour, exhibit and enact the intent to stay settled. Given this fact, it makes little sense to argue that Canada's Whites and people of colour populations are a fundamentally different class of settler based on the ways their ancestors got here.

Of course, most people of colour do not gain as much from settlement as most Whites do, because they are racialized into positions or marginality. We made that abundantly clear when examining racism and outlining the need for anti-racism and the establishment of equity. Indigenous people also face racism and so, in relation to the dynamics of race, people of colour and Indigenous peoples are different from Whites. But one must not conflate being on the receiving end of racism (which Indigenous people and people of colour face) with being on the receiving end of settler colonialism (which Indigenous people in Canada face but people of colour do not). If we resolve racism so it no longer exists, people of colour and Whites will still be settlers occupying Indigenous land, but the problem of settler colonialism will not have changed.

## Key Concept

Anti-oppressive social workers need to be involved in anti-racism and also decolonization. But do not conflate the two, because anti-racism and decolonization are not the same. If we resolve racism so it no longer exists, people of colour and Whites will still be settlers occupying Indigenous land, and the problem of settler colonialism will not have changed.

Not conflating anti-racism and decolonization in a settler-colonial context is crucial. Lawrence and Dua (2005) contend that "Canadian anti-racism is furthering contemporary colonial agendas" (p. 123). They explain that:

> . . . within antiracism theory and practice, the question of land as contested space is seldom taken up. From an Indigenous perspective, it speaks to a reluctance on the part of non-Natives of any background, to acknowledge that there is more to this land than being settlers on it, that there are deeper, older stories and knowledge connected to the landscapes around us. (Lawrence & Dua, 2005, p. 126)

Anti-racism failing to address colonization is an example of what Crenshaw (2016) refers to as intersectional failure (as discussed in Chapter 5). Crenshaw focuses primarily on such failure at the intersection of anti-racism and gender, but the formula also applies to the intersection of racism and settler colonialism. Anti-racism does not have to be this way. We have both been involved in anti-racism activism for a long time: Gary since the early 1980s in the UK and later in Canada, and June since the late 1990s in Canada and also in the UK. Neither of us conceive of anti-racism in such a narrow way. We concur with Lawrence and Dua (2005) that anti-racism has been narrowed so that the issue of settler colonialism is hardly addressed at all. We believe that a narrow anti-racism can only create more intersectional failures, and it also prevents us from addressing the real problem that anti-racism and settler colonialism address, which is Whiteness and White supremacy. Anti-racism and decolonization must be allied movements if they are to address the underlying cause of oppression. We will be talking more about how to do this without one movement marginalizing the other later in Chapter 9.

## Do Not Opt Out of Responsibility by Trying to Become Indigenous

When settlers hear about colonization, it can evoke a flight for innocence. This is the same when learning about any form of oppression one might be implicated in, because it is not nice being implicated in something bad, so the natural desire is to try and un-implicate oneself.

Wanting to be un-implicated is a good thing; it means you do not want to be a part of injustice. The answer, however, is not to become un-implicated by taking flight, but by changing what it is you are implicated within. Don't jump off the ship and take flight to the birchbark canoe. Take charge of the ship and get it to stop oppressing!

One of the ways of taking flight to the canoe is what Tuck and Yang (2012) call "settler nativism" (p. 10). This is where a settler discovers a native ancestor and suddenly becomes "Native." In one instance, we came across a settler who, within a few weeks of discovering an Indigenous ancestor on an ancestry website, was speaking authoritatively on behalf of all Indigenous Nations. The person was not yet sure which Nation their ancestor was a part of, but this did not stop the "former settler" from feeling confident in speaking for all of them!

The discovery of an Indigenous ancestor can be an important life event and can open up a wonderful opportunity to discover one's past and to redefine one's future. We have seen many people use this opportunity to connect with and become a part of ancestral communities. Some go on to learn that community's language, ways, and teachings, and they become leaders in decolonization and even teachers of Indigenous knowledge. But such processes take time and much learning; these processes are not to be confused with the quick flights to innocence driven by settler guilt. Ultimately what an Indigenous ancestor means is determined by the Indigenous community, not by the person claiming title.

> Ancestry is different from tribal membership; Indigenous identity and tribal membership are questions that Indigenous communities alone have the right to struggle over and define, not DNA tests, heritage websites, and certainly not the settler state. Settler nativism is about imagining an Indian past and a settler future. In contrast, tribal sovereignty has provided for an Indigenous present and various Indigenous intellectuals theorize decolonization as Native futures without a settler state. (Tuck and Yang, 2012, p. 13)

## Get Over Guilt and Get into Action

When we refer to guilt, we mean **White guilt**, which is "feelings of guilt among Whites that may develop in response to systemic inequality" (Garriott, Reiter, & Brownfield, 2016, p. 160). In other words, feelings of guilt, shame, and related emotions come from recognizing that one is benefiting from colonization, racism, or some other forms of oppression.

In relation to settler colonization, people of colour can also experience White guilt, because even though they do not gain from setter colonialism in the same way most Whites do, people of colour benefit from the occupation of Indigenous land. When settlers of colour feel this guilt we still refer to it as "White guilt" because the benefits come from the machinery of Whiteness and White supremacy. As discussed in Chapter 4, one does not have to be White to gain benefits from Whiteness.

If you are feeling White guilt, do not feel guilty about feeling it, because in a sense feeling it is a good thing. Feeling White guilt is linked to recognizing one's unearned privilege and to developing an awareness of inequality (Garriott et al., 2016; Spanierman, Poteat, Wang, & Oh, 2008). But White guilt is also associated with immobilization and an inability to address issues of oppression (Spanierman et al., 2008). It is self-indulgent because it focuses one's energy on the self and trying to feel better rather than trying to do something about oppression (Katz, 2003). Because White guilt is so immobilizing and self-centred, the position we take is that one needs to "get over it" and "get into action." We do not imply that one forget it or not feel it; instead we suggest turning the personal energy one pours into guilt toward social justice and action.

In turning energy into action, we need to be clear that the White guilt we are talking about is not guilt about the past. You did not commit the crimes of the past, so you are not responsible for them. Indeed, as mentioned in Chapter 4, W.E.B. Du Bois (1903) said that the generation of Whites after slavery were not responsible for slavery. That generation, however, was responsible for what they did to perpetuate oppression against Black people after slavery, and they were responsible for not undoing the legacy of slavery. The same principle applies to our generation: we are not personally responsible for what our ancestors did, but we are responsible for not making what they did right, and we are responsible for continuing to live off the avails of their crimes.

Settlers, particularly White settlers, have to move beyond guilt. Some years ago we went to a national social work conference and signed up for a workshop where Indigenous Elders were going to speak about what settlers could do to decolonize. There were about 20 people in the workshop—like us, they were mostly settlers. We sat in a circle and the Elders asked us to each introduce ourselves and say what we hoped for in the workshop.

One by one the settlers gave their name and declared something about their social locations (i.e., race, gender, and so on). They also "confessed" that they were "settlers" and "colonizers" on Indigenous land. Some did so with tears, and then assured the Elders that despite being a part of the occupation, they had come as allies to help.

The Elders responded to this distress with compassion, with warm reassuring nods and sometimes words of comfort. We noticed how this made each person who confessed a little happier; many wiped away tears and became settled. By the time the entire circle of settlers had finished speaking and had gained some comfort the allotted time for the workshop had ended. There was no time for the Elders to speak. The workshop was over.

We have seen the type of process described above occur many times. What occurs in these moments is that Whiteness centres itself. We spoke in Chapter 4 about the fluidity of Whiteness, how it adjusts to each new challenge to its power by re-centring itself as the centre of attention. This had occurred right before our eyes in the workshop.

We wondered for a long time why the Elders let this re-centring of Whiteness occur—why did they not speak up to disrupt it—because the point of the workshop was for the Elders to speak and for settlers to go away having learned something about how to decolonize. It took us a long time to realize that the Elders had actually taught a powerful lesson about colonizing and decolonizing while hardly saying a word.

## Exercise 7.1

### What Was the Lesson?

If possible, undertake this exercise in groups:

1. Reflect on the story of the workshop and say what lesson the Elders taught.
2. Reflect on the meaning of that lesson for you and your work.
3. If you find it difficult figuring out the lesson, it may help to use the Internet, or knowledge you may already have, about Indigenous pedagogies.
4. If you need an additional clue to help you, consider the story of the professor and Raven, and try to find out about the Trickster and how the Trickster

teaches (because there is a distinct possibility that Raven may have been the Trickster, and perhaps the Trickster was having an influence on the lessons of this workshop too).

Settlers need to get over (or a least set aside) the focus they often have on their own guilt and "get into action." When we say "action," as mentioned above, we do not mean interfere with the birchbark canoe, but instead start taking responsibility for the settler ship. Settlers need to start to honour treaties, stop removing Indigenous children from their homes in disproportionate numbers, agree to provide adequate funding to First Nations (including honouring the funding commitments already promised to First Nations), stop moving First Nations communities to land so starved of resources that it can hardly sustain life, stop treading First Nations people down so far that Indigenous youth give up on life and commit suicide in epidemic numbers. Our list could go on even further, but we suspect you get the point.

## Has Anti-Oppression Been Effective in Decolonization?

We believe that anti-oppression has huge decolonization potential, especially if the key concepts in decolonization we shared above are applied. As yet, however, the potential for anti-oppression to decolonize has not been realized. Indeed, when Taiaiake Alfred spoke to Kwa'kwala'wakw, an Indigenous political organizer in Victoria, British Columbia, he asked her, "Do you feel that some of the efforts that are underway now, with the social work or social-services approach, are helping?" Kwa'kwala'wakw replied, "I think it is a pile of crap" (Alfred, 1999, p. 13).

Kwa'kwala'wakw has a point; sometimes even anti-oppression cannot be relied on to be anything other than "crap." Indeed, Cindy Blackstock, a member of the Gitksan First Nation, professor of social work at McGill University, and executive director of the First Nations Child and Family Caring Society of Canada, contends:

> There is little evidence to suggest [that anti oppression] is effective when applied to First Nations child welfare. . . . There is no historical evidence that the anti-oppressive social work movement engaged in any widespread or sustained action in the area. For example, the historical record shows no evidence that AOP social workers protested against residential schools throughout their 100 years of operations ending in 1996, nor have they mobilized to address the vast over-representation of First Nations children in care today. (Blackstock, 2009, p. 32)

One could debate Blackstock's points. For instance, one could argue that the term "AOP" (anti-oppression) did not exist in the early days of residential schools so how could there have been AOP protests? Even so, social work has always had a commitment to social justice; yet despite this "commitment" there were no sustained social work protests against these schools. We could also dispute Blackstock by pointing out that we know of several workers who have protested and addressed the overrepresentation of First Nations children in care. But these workers aside, we have to concede that Blackstock is entirely right; social work as a whole has not taken a firm stand on this issue, and there has been no widespread opposition or action in Canada to stop this type of disproportionality. Blackstock cements her argument with the point that "there are more First Nations children in state care today than at any point in history, including during residential school operations" (Blackstock, 2009, p. 2). In Chapter 1, we spoke of oppression being identified by patterns, and the pattern is clear: anti-oppressive social work has not stopped the way Indigenous sovereignty and Nations are being pressed down by the child welfare system. Kwa'kwala'wakw describes the problem she has with social work. She says that social work is taking "what is already fragmented and fragmenting it even more" (Alfred, 1999, p. 14). She likens social workers to people who want to make a wheel by making lots of spokes and putting them in all the wrong places, and never including spokes from the Indigenous side of the wheel. Clearly, anti-oppressive social work needs to do a better job at decolonizing.

## So What Is the Anti-Oppressive Social Worker to Do about Colonization?

Anti-oppressive social work needs to be allied with the principle of decolonization and Indigenous sovereignty. At the very least, this principle has to mean that Indigenous communities determine if and how social work operates in their communities. Do the social work agencies you work within deliver services in a manner that are relevant to Indigenous communities? Do Indigenous communities have the right to regulate who calls themselves a "social worker" and do social work in their communities and Nations? Does your social work school have Indigenous faculty and Indigenous texts, and does it teach Indigenous social work? If the answer to any of these questions is "no," your anti-oppressive task is to help make these things so.

### Key Concept

Does your social work school have Indigenous faculty members? Do you have Indigenous content in your curriculum? Does the social work agency or system you work within deliver services in a manner relevant to Indigenous communities? Do Indigenous peoples have the right to regulate who calls themselves a "social worker" and does social work in their Nations and communities? If the answer to any of these questions is "no," your anti-oppressive task is to help make these things happen.

In addition to the above, at a broader societal level, Indigenous peoples have been clear about what needs to change. Indigenous scholars and leaders have clearly articulated the issues (for instance Alfred, 1999; Mercredi & Turpel, 1993). These leaders may not always agree with each other on the best ways Indigenous peoples should address the issues, but they consistently put the same issues on the table, particularly sovereignty and nationhood. Social workers need to not only hear and respond to these leaders, but also need to find ways to engage in and support this change process themselves. There are a number of initiatives through which anyone can join in this change process—we will address two: Truth and Reconciliation, and Idle No More.

## Truth and Reconciliation

Canada's Truth and Reconciliation Commission (TRC) was formed in 2008 and delivered its final report in 2015. The Commission was an attempt to inform and educate about injustices toward Indigenous peoples, particularly the injustice of residential schools, which in combination with the Sixties Scoop has been regarded as a form of genocide (Downey, 1999). The idea of the Commission was for truths to be told to pave the way for reconciliation to begin. In our opinion, the Truth and Reconciliation Commission report (2015a, 2015b) should be read by all Canadians and especially by social workers, given the occupation's involvement in some of these injustices.

The Commission acknowledges that settler and government apology is important, but also recognizes that one cannot stop at an apology. Action is needed to undo the ongoing legacies of colonization. In particular, action is needed to address issues of sovereignty. The Commission states that Indigenous peoples (First Nations, Inuit, and Métis) have treaty rights that must be honoured. Specific recommendations include:

> i. Repudiate concepts used to justify European sovereignty over Indigenous lands and peoples such as the Doctrine of Discovery and *terra nullius*.
> ii. Adopt and implement the *United Nations Declaration on the Rights of Indigenous Peoples* as the framework for reconciliation.
> iii. Renew or establish Treaty relationships based on principles of mutual recognition, mutual respect, and shared responsibility for maintaining those relationships into the future.
> iv. Reconcile Aboriginal and Crown constitutional and legal orders to ensure that Aboriginal peoples are full partners in Confederation, including the recognition and integration of Indigenous laws and legal traditions in negotiation and implementation processes involving Treaties, land claims, and other constructive agreements. (Truth and Reconciliation Commission of Canada, 2015a, p. 5)

The Truth and Reconciliation Commission (2015b) says that to achieve the above, and to "restore what must be restored, repair what must be repaired, and return what must be returned" (p. 1), we need to establish a "new and respectful relationship between Aboriginal and non-Aboriginal Canadians" (p. 1), along with "sustained public education and dialogue . . ." (p. 4). There are several practical ways you can get involved in this work. You can explore these in the following exercise.

## Exercise 7.2

### Truth and Reconciliation

If possible, undertake this exercise in groups.

1. Visit the Canadian National Centre for Truth and Reconciliation website at http://www.trc.ca.
2. Explore the documents containing history, testimony, and calls to action or other content that you chose at the site. There is a considerable amount of information at this website. So, for this exercise, choose a specific issue from the site that interests you, and bookmark the remainder of the site for exploring later on.
3. Reflect on what you learn from the site and the implications for your work.
4. Look at the "toolkits" on the site and consider using one of these to take part in the Truth and Reconciliation process yourself. Consider working with others in a social work setting (agency, placement, classroom) to take up one of these toolkits as a group.

What stands out for us on the TRC website as particularly important for social workers is the Commission highlighting the need to address disproportionality and disparity between settler and Indigenous social, health, and economic services and outcomes. Also important for social workers is the Commission's call for "Supporting Aboriginal peoples' cultural revitalization and integrating Indigenous knowledge systems, oral histories, laws, protocols, and connections to the land" (Truth and Reconciliation Commission of Canada, 2015b, p. 126). We interpret this, in a social work context, as ensuring that Indigenous knowledge systems (and the keepers of this knowledge) play a central role in teaching social workers and shaping social work systems.

The question, however, is whether truth and reconciliation will lead to decolonization. We are concerned that it may not, and that the call for action that involves sovereignty may be ignored. Indeed, in the very moment the Commission was calling for truth, the Canadian government denied the truth that disproportionality and disparity were occurring in relation to First Nations' children, and they only reluctantly conceded truth after Cindy Blackstock obtained a ruling against the government in the Canadian Human Rights Tribunal (The Canadian Press, 2016). During this period the government also refused to initiate an inquiry into the truth about Missing and Murdered Indigenous Women (Boutilier, 2014). Even though the new Liberal government has now approved that inquiry, we are not optimistic about change. The Canadian government has consistently refused to honour legally binding treaties about sovereignty, so why would they honour non-legally binding Commission calls to action on sovereignty in the future?

## Key Concept

We are concerned that Canada may be looking for reconciliation without truth. In the very moment that the Canadian government was making commitments to reconciliation, they were also denying the truth that First Nations' communities were receiving disproportionately poor children's services and outcomes. The government was also refusing to initiate an inquiry into the truth about Missing and Murdered Indigenous Women.

We are not alone in our concern. Simpson reflects, "I wonder how we can reconcile when the majority of Canadians do not understand the historic or contemporary injustice of dispossession and occupation, particularly when the state has expressed its unwillingness to make any adjustments to the unjust relationship" (Simpson, 2011, p. 21). We suspect that some of the easier calls to action, mostly the ones that call for the truth about the past, will be taken up, but not those that call for truth about the present nor those that call for Indigenous sovereignty in the future. Test for yourself whether our prediction is true. Look out for the words "truth and reconciliation" along with "decolonization" showing up in course curricula. If you see lots about truth and reconciliation but nothing about sovereignty, then be concerned that little is changing. Indeed, we are concerned that settlers will engage with the past and realize Canada's terrible history in relation to First Peoples; they will become stuck looking back, and will be unable to connect this to the present or the future. Simpson goes further in expressing this concern:

> If reconciliation is focused only on residential schools rather than the broader set of relationships that generated policies, legislation, and practices aimed at assimilation and political genocide, then there is a risk that reconciliation will "level the playing field" in the eyes of Canadians. In the eyes of liberalism, the historical "wrong" has now been "righted" and further transformation is not needed, since the historic situation has been remedied. (Simpson, 2011, p. 22)

We suggest that Canadians need to be on guard against such misinterpretations. Again we suggest that social workers and others trained in anti-oppression have a key role in such debates, for they should not only understand that the playing field is uneven, but be able to articulate this so that the broader public understands (more about this in later chapters).

In this context, the anti-oppressive social worker must support calls for change. One of the ways this can be done is engaging with Idle No More.

## Idle No More

Idle No More formed in 2012 in Saskatoon as a grassroots movement of Indigenous women and allies. The impetus for the movement was proposed government legislation that further undermined Indigenous sovereignty and also threatened the environment. This movement quickly spread to become what some argue is one of the largest Indigenous movements ever known in Canada (Graveline, 2012; Idle No More, nd; Lightfoot, 2016).

The Idle No More website has a wealth of information about past and current issues the movement has engaged with. A core concept of the movement is Indigenous sovereignty rights, and these rights are not simply a "right" to the land, but a responsibility for and connection with the land. This is reflected in the following statement by the movement:

> Idle No More seeks to assert Indigenous inherent rights to sovereignty and re-institute traditional laws and Nation to Nation treaties by protecting the lands and waters from corporate destruction. Each day that Indigenous rights are not honored or fulfilled, inequality between Indigenous peoples and the settler society grows. (Idle No More, nd)

The Idle No More website provides direct links to get involved. It is also full of educational resources and information. For instance, during the last Canadian general election, the website provided info graphics on where each political party stood in relation to a number of Indigenous rights and environmental issues.

We consider it an imperative that the anti-oppressive social worker engage with sites such as this, and become involved with issues like some of those raised on that site. We contend that it is important for the practitioner to grasp the importance of this type of work. From a White European "scientific" evidence-informed practice perspective, these connections may not be clear, because many people take up such practice in a way that separates things. As a result, the social worker can easily sit in an office face to face with a service user and imagine that whatever troubles are being addressed in those walls has little to do with the politics that goes on outside them. But all of these things are connected. Making connections to things that once were connected but no longer seem to be is a part of challenging oppression. In particular, there is a connection between the land and bodies that has to be understood.

Erin Marie Konsmo, a Métis/Cree artist from Alberta, connects the colonization of land with the colonization of bodies. Konsmo juxtaposes the way land is conceptualized and exploited under *terra nullius* with the way people's bodies are too. This juxtaposition draws attention to the way that violence toward the environment transfers to bodies and suggests,

From an Indigenous Feminist perspective, resistance to violent legal frameworks (such as *terra nullius*) can be taken up when we fight for the self-determination of our bodies as Indigenous Peoples. (Erin Marie Konsmo as cited in Lilley, 2013, p. 93)

We see connections between what Konsmo says above and what Idle No More is concerned about, and issues the Occupy Movement raises, particularly in the ways corporations see the environment (and to an extent people) as something to exploit. Indeed, the Occupy Movement in Canada, UK, USA, and elsewhere around the world was not just about financial inequality, but about a broader context of exploitation and systemic inequalities (Bapuji, Riaz, Shrivastava, & Ivanova, 2015). Clearly there is a connection between the concerns of Occupy and Idle No More, but just as important as making connection between ideas is the ability to distinguish between ideas and understand their differences.

## Making Alliances while Being Mindful of Differences

We have to be careful about conflating things that seem similar. Although there seems to be an overlap between the concerns of Indigenous movements like Idle No More and Occupy, important distinctions must be made. Occupy is a movement of mostly middle-class White people irritated that they are losing a foothold on the "American dream" (and Canadian dream) as a result of increasing disparities in wealth. It troubles us, however, that the American and Canadian dream is built on occupied land. As a result, the very concept of "occupy" as a call for freedom is problematic. Indeed, Indigenous activists point out that the concept of "occupy" is a problem because from their perspective the problem is occupation (Gray et al., 2013). Imagine what it looks like from an Indigenous perspective, thousands of mostly White middle-class settlers taking to the streets built on Indigenous land shouting, "occupy." This is a poor choice of a rallying cry for a movement when from an Indigenous perspective it was large crowds of White people occupying land that started the problem in the first place (Gray et al., 2013).

We are not suggesting that there are no overlaps between the Occupy Movement and Indigenous movements. Indeed, when Gary attended Occupy in Toronto, a number of Mohawk warriors came to support. A Mohawk presence at Occupy was not unique; we often notice when settlers struggle with social justice issues and try to make things right, Indigenous peoples come to help. We wonder if the reason Indigenous peoples do this is another treaty long forgotten by most settlers about a Covenant Chain, which is the agreement that settlers and Indigenous peoples hold hands and join in love and friendship, so that when one is in trouble the other will come to help. What non-Indigenous people need to do, however, is ensure that we take up our own human rights and equity issues in ways that avoid further undermining the rights of Indigenous peoples. Of course the other lesson is for settlers to go help Indigenous peoples address the social justice issues that impact them. But remember the professor at the start of this chapter—settlers need to help in ways that avoid the mistakes the professor was making.

## Chapter Summary

In this chapter we have looked at various forms of colonization with particular attention to settler colonialism in Canada, which in many ways also applies to the USA, Australia, New Zealand, and similar locations. We have critiqued ideas of decolonization that stop at the metaphorical level and do not address issues of land and Indigenous sovereignty. We have considered the important work of the Truth and Reconciliation Commission in Canada, but have raised concerns that these may be taken up in a manner that fails to bring real change.

We do not mean to be negative about the prospect for truth, reconciliation, or the other issues that must be addressed to decolonize in a settler colonial context. We do have to face the fact, though, that at a government or at a broader societal level there may not be an impetus for change. Indeed, in relation to Indigenous rights, even social work has only produced what Kwa'kwala'wakw calls "a pile of crap" (Alfred, 1999, p. 13). Indeed, even anti-oppression has failed to make a difference (Blackstock, 2009).

We do have hope, however, and that hope is YOU! You and a new generation of social workers and citizens are the wildcard in this situation. A **wildcard** is someone who is unpredictable, who refuses to operate within the status quo, who thinks and acts outside the box. The professor in the story at the start of this chapter was a little bit of a wildcard—maybe not to begin with because he started out on his own trying to do things in the same old White ways—but if he learned the lessons Raven set for him, he might become a wildcard. He might do something unpredictable, and instead of seeing it as his job to figure out how to decolonize the academy, he might learn that the process begins by him getting out of the way. Of course his work does not end there, but his work certainly needs to begin with helping to move the colonizing structures out of the way. The next things that need to occur will then emerge from the conversations and relationships that follow.

## Discussion Questions

Consider the following questions:

1. What implications does the professor's story at the start of this chapter, and the lessons the professor needed to learn, have for you, your workplace, and the ways you will take up social work?
2. What will you do in response to the Truth and Reconciliation calls for action?
3. What role will you play in decolonization?

## Activity

Research and discover the history of the land your school or workplace is on. Who are the original people of this land? What is the history of this land and these people? Is there a treaty in place governing this land, and if so what are the terms of that treaty?

# Suggested Resources

"Canadian Aboriginal History: Did You Know?" by APTN, at https://youtu.be/i8QmxU6IZHw (Part 1), https://youtu.be/9gVCSIHq6cc (Part 2),

Cannon, M. J., & Lina, S. (Eds). (2018). *Racism, colonialism, and Indigeneity in Canada.* Toronto, Canada: Oxford University Press.

Baskin, C. (2016). *Strong helpers' teachings: The value of Indigenous knowledges in the helping professions* (2nd edn). Toronto, Canada: Canadian Scholars' Press.

# References

Abjorensen, N., & Docherty, J.C. (2015). *Historical dictionary of Australia* (Fourth edition). Lanham, Maryland: Rowman & Littlefield.

Alfred, T. (1999). *Peace, power, righteousness: An Indigenous manifesto.* Toronto, Canada: Oxford University Press.

Alfred, T. (2017, February 28). The great unlearning. Retrieved from https://taiaiake.net/2017/02/28/the-great-unlearning/

Bapuji, H., Riaz, S., Shrivastava, P., & Ivanova, O. (2015). Inequality, corporate legitimacy and the Occupy Wall Street movement. *Human Relations, 68*(7), 1209–31.

Baskin, C. (2016). *Strong helpers' teachings: The value of Indigenous knowledges in the helping professions* (2nd edn). Toronto, Canada: Canadian Scholars' Press.

Blackstock, C. (2009). Why addressing the over-representation of First Nations children in care requires new theoretical approaches based on First Nations ontology. *Journal of Social Work Values and Ethics, 6*(3).

Boutilier, A. (2014, March 7). Conservatives reject inquiry for murdered, missing Aboriginal women. *Toronto Star.* Retrieved from http://www.thestar.com/news/canada/2014/03/07/conservatives_reject_inquiry_for_murdered_missing_aboriginal_women.html

Crenshaw, K. (2016, March 14). Kimberlé Crenshaw - On Intersectionality - keynote - WOW 2016. Retrieved from https://youtu.be/-DW4HLgYPlA

Downey, M. (1999, April 26). Canada's "genocide." *Maclean's, 112*(17), 56–9.

Du Bois, W.E.B. (1903). *The souls of black folk.* Chicago, IL: A.C. McClung and Co.

Dumbrill, G.C., & Green, J. (2008). Indigenous knowledge in the social work academy. *Social Work Education: The International Journal, 27*(5), 489–503.

Freire, P. (2001). *Pedagogy of the oppressed* (M. B. Ramos, Trans. 30th annivesary edn). New York, NY: Continuum.

Galenson, D.W. (1981). *White servitude in colonial America: An economic analysis.* New York, NY: Cambridge University Press.

Gardner, K., & Peters, R. (2014). Toward the 8th fire: The view from Oshkimaadzing Unity Camp. *Decolonization: Indigeneity, Education & Society, 3*(3), 167–73.

Garriott, P.O., Reiter, S., & Brownfield, J. (2016). Testing the efficacy of brief multicultural education interventions in white college students. *Journal of Diversity in Higher Education, 9*(2), 158–69. doi:10.1037/a0039547

Gibbons, A. (2011). *The legacy of Walter Rodney in Guyana and the Caribbean.* Lanham, MA: University Press of America.

Graveline, F.J. (2012). IDLE NO MORE: Enough is enough! *Canadian Social Work Review, 29*(2), 293–300.

Gray, M., Coates, J., Yellow Bird, M., & Hetherington, T. (Eds). (2013). *Decolonizing social work.* Farnham, UK: Ashgate.

Humphreys, M. (2011). *Empty cradles (oranges and sunshine).* London, UK: Corgi Books.

Idle No More. (nd). Idle No More. Retrieved from http://www.idlenomore.ca

Junbo, J. (2007, February 8). China's role in Africa: China is not now and is not likely to become a colonziing power in Africa. *Beijing Review, 50*(6), 14–5.

Katz, J.H. (2003). *White awareness: Handbook for anti-racism training* (2nd edn). Norman, OK: University of Oklahoma Press, Norman Publishing Division.

Keal, P. (2016). Indigenous sovereignty. In T. Jacobsen, C. Sampford, & R. Thakur (Eds), *Re-envisioning sovereignty: The end of westphalia?* (pp. 315–30). New York, NY: Routledge.

Keefer, T. (2014, March/April). A short introduction to the Two Row Wampum. *Briarpatch, 43*(2), pp. 14–16. Retrieved from https://briarpatchmagazine.com/articles/view/a-short-introduction-to-the-two-row-wampum

Kinch, M. (2014, March/April). Hijacked canoes and settler ships: Indigenous activists discuss environmentalism and settler allies. *Briarpatch, 43*(2), pp. 16–20. Retrieved from http://briarpatchmagazine.com/articles/view/hijacked-canoes-and-settler-ships

Lai, W.L. (1993). *Indentured labor, Caribbean sugar: Chinese and Indian migrants to the British West Indies, 1838–1918.* Baltimore, MD: The Johns Hopkins University Press.

Lawrence, B., & Dua, E. (2005). Decolonizing antiracism. *Social Justice, 32*(4), 120–43.

Lentell, H. (1998). Families of meaning: Contemporary discourses of the family. In G. Lewis (Ed.), *Forming nation, framing welfare* (pp. 253–94). New York, NY: Routledge.

Lightfoot, S. (2016). *Global Indigenous politics: A subtle revolution*. New York, NY: Routledge.

Lilley, P. (2013). 'Art through a birch bark heart: An illustrated interview with Erin Marie Konsmo. *Radical Criminology: An Insurgent Journal,* (2), 69–96.

Mercredi, O., & Turpel, M.E. (1993). *In the rapids: Navigating the future of the First Nations*. Toronto, Canada: Viking.

Monbiot, G. (2001, October 30). Backyard terrorism: The US has been training terrorists at a camp in Georgia for years— and it's still at it. *The Guardian*. Retrieved from http://www.theguardian.com/world/2001/oct/30/afghanistan.terrorism19

Nahwegahbow, B. (2014). Wampum holds power of earliest agreements. *Windspeaker, 32*(1), 20.

Nkrumah, K. (1965/2009). *Neo-colonialism: The last stage of imperialism*. Bedford, UK: Panaf Books.

Oak, M., & Swamy, A.V. (2012). Myopia or strategic behavior? Indian regimes and the East India Company in late eighteenth century India. *Explorations in Economic History, 49*(3), 352–66. doi:10.1016/j.eeh.2012.03.002

Porter (Sakokwenionkwas), T. (2008). *And grandma said . . . Iroquois teachings as passed down through the oral tradition*. Bloomington, IN: Xlibris.

Prokhovnik, R. (2015). From sovereignty in Australia to Australian sovereignty. *Political Studies, 63*(2), 412–30. doi:10.1111/1467-9248.12069

Rasmussen, D. (2002). Qallunology: A pedagogy of the oppressor. *Canadian Journal of Native Education, 25*(2), 105–116.

Rodney, W. (1981). *A History of the Guyanese working people, 1881–1905*. Baltimore, MD: Johns Hopkins University Press.

Sackey, J.A. (1981). Elasticity of substitution and employment generating capacity of a bauxite firm in Guyana. *Social and Economic Studies, 30*(2), 45–70.

Sartre, J.-P. (2006). *Colonialism and neocolonialism*. Abingdon, UK: Routledge Classics.

Sharma, N., & Wright, C. (2008). Decolonizing resistance, challanging colonial states. *Social Justice, 35*(3), 120–38.

Shewell, H. (2005). *"Enough to keep them alive": Indian welfare in Canada, 1873–1965*. University of Toronto: Toronto, Canada

Simpson, L. (2011). *Dancing on our turtle's back: Stories of Nishnaabeg re-creation, resurgence, and a new emergence*. Winnipeg, Canada: Arbeiter Ring Publishing.

Spanierman, L.B., Poteat, V.P., Wang, Y.-F., & Oh, E. (2008). Psychosocial costs of racism to white counselors: Predicting various dimensions of multicultural counseling competence. *Journal of Counseling Psychology, 55*(1), 75–88. doi:10.1037/0022-0167.55.1.75

St Pierre, M. (1999). *Anatomy of resistance: Anti-colonialism in Guyana 1823–1966*. London, UK: MacMillan Education.

Taylor, I. (2006). *China and Africa: Engagement and compramise*. Abingdon, UK: Routledge.

The Canadian Press. (2016, January 26). Ottawa discriminated against kids on reserves, human rights panel says. *Toronto Star*. Retrieved from http://www.thestar.com/news/canada/2016/01/26/ottawa-discriminated-against-kids-on-reserves-human-rights-panel-says.html

Titley, B. (2009). *The Indian commissioners: Agents of the state and the Indian policy in Canada's prairie west, 1873–1932*. Edmonton, Alberta: University of Alberta.

Truth and Reconciliation Commission of Canada. (2015a). *Truth and Reconciliation Commission of Canada: Calls to action*. Retrieved from Winnipeg, Canada: http://www.trc.ca/websites/trcinstitution/File/2015/Findings/Calls_to_Action_English2.pdf

Truth and Reconciliation Commission of Canada. (2015b). *What we have learned: Principles of truth and reconciliation*. Retrieved from Winnipeg, Canada: http://www.trc.ca/websites/trcinstitution/File/2015/Findings/Principles_2015_05_31_web_o.pdf

Tuck, E., & Yang, K.W. (2012). Decolonization is not a metaphor. *Decolonization: Indigeneity, Education & Society, 1*(1), 1–40.

Vaver, A. (2011). *Bound with an iron chain: The untold story of how the British transported 50,000 convicts to colonial America*. Westborough, MA: Pickpocket Publishing.

# 8 The Problem of Poverty, Class, Capital, and the Social Order

## In this chapter you will learn:

- What the social order is and how it shapes our everyday lives
- How the social order produces poverty and inequality
- The way we each internalize and reproduce the social order
- The implications of the above for anti-oppression

## Introduction

December 26, 2004, seemed like any other Sunday, but when June heard the news she called friends; she needed to talk. Gary went to church unaware, he expected to find people happy in the holiday spirit, but instead people were crying. In the quiet of the night an earthquake in Sumatra caused a **tsunami**; a giant tidal wave, that killed over 227,000 people (Telford & Cosgrave, 2007) in nations as far apart as Indonesia, Sri Lanka, India, Thailand, Somalia, Myanmar, the Maldives, Malaysia, Tanzania, the Seychelles, Bangladesh, South Africa, Yemen, Kenya, and Madagascar. The earthquake and tsunami were so powerful that it made the entire planet vibrate and the earth shift on its axis (Hopkin, 2004).

People and nations were so shocked that they made unprecedented efforts to help (Telford & Cosgrave, 2007). Armies from around the world put down weapons to provide relief and rescue, supermarkets asked shoppers for donations at checkout points, and people gathered in synagogues, mosques, temples, and town halls to figure out how to help. Gary met in a back room of a church in Hamilton with millwrights, engineers, doctors, and nurses who all wanted to go and help immediately. This group never went, because after liaising with friends already in the disaster zones, they realized that they would get in the way of relief rather than add to it. Many groups with better logistics went, but many like the group Gary met with decided that the best way to help was to provide funds to support relief efforts. Worldwide, close to US$14 billion was donated by people determined to help (Telford & Cosgrave, 2007).

Meanwhile, as tsunami relief efforts were underway, a greater disaster was quietly unfolding; millions of people were dying from poverty and hunger every day. The exact figures are difficult to determine and can be calculated in differing ways, but the claim that poverty kills a child every 10 seconds is probably accurate (Alexander, 2013), which gives an annualized figure of some 3 million child deaths per year. If one includes adults, some anti-poverty websites claim 21,000 deaths a day (poverty.com, accessed 1 January 2017, gave an annual rate of 7.6 million), while others claim as many as 18 million hunger-related deaths per year (Chen & Ravallion, 2004).

We do not like counting mortality rates in the manner above, because counting "death by the second" sensationalizes the issue, and focusing on hunger oversimplifies the impact of both hunger and poverty. Nevertheless, at least 7.6 million deaths per year are caused through poverty and hunger, which is an annual death rate equivalent to 33 tsunamis every year. Said differently, this death rate is more than two tsunamis every month, and this continues year in and year out, forever.

Why does this alternative ongoing disaster not get the same attention and response as a one-off tsunami? By the end of this chapter, you will have answers to this question. You will grasp how we contract with the social order to respond to some types of disasters and to largely ignore others, and you will have gained insights into what this means for anti-oppression.

## Inequality and the Social Order

The social order is poverty. This statement might sound a little strange, because the **social order** is usually thought of as the way we organize ourselves as a society, the rules and constitutions we live by, and the mutual understanding we all have about the way we live and relate to each other. If the social order is how we choose to organize ourselves as a society (Hechter & Horne, 2009), how does it make sense for us to call "poverty" the "social order"?

We believe it makes sense to say poverty *is* the social order, because society seems to have always organized itself in a way that created wealth for a few and poverty for many. Society also seems to have settled into the belief that the poor will always be with us and that poverty is simply a natural part of life. We contend that there is nothing natural about poverty at all. It is not a part of natural life. It is a part of the way we choose to organize life.

## Key Concept

The only reason poverty is still with us is because we as a society are not prepared to end it. The problem is not poverty—the problem is us!

## Exploring the Social Order

The social order refers to a set of conditions and processes that we all tacitly agree to. There are two parts of this agreement, and two interrelated concepts, that make up the social order.

First, the social order is an **operating system** that society uses to organize itself. There are many types of society and many types of social operating systems, and they all operate a bit like different computers. For instance, Macs use an operating system called OS and PCs use a system called Windows. You can use applications on a Mac and programs on a PC to produce the exact same work, but in each the underlying operating system that enables this work to happen is different. It is the same with society. There are many different ways of organizing a society, but in all these systems similar things happen; one way or another, every society will produce goods and services, will raise and educate children, will govern and police itself, etc.

Marx and Engels identify several systems that have operated through the ages. These include feudalism, capitalism, socialism, and communism (Marx & Engels, 2002). There are many other ways of periodizing history, but Marx is so influential in social science that we focus on his periodization. Of course Marx's original rendering of history has been taken up by critical scholars in many different ways over the years, but rather than explore these many variations, we take up Marx's ideas in a somewhat simple introductory representation of classic Marxist theory.

According to Marx, **feudalism** is a system in which most people live and work on land owned by lords or barons appointed by a monarch. In capitalism, most people work producing things in factories, businesses, or some other setting owned by a proprietor or corporation. In **socialism,** most of the wealth-creating mechanisms are democratically owned and controlled by the people. **Communism** is a form of socialism that produces a classless society with no private property and in which common interests and collaboration rather than competition drive the economy and relationships (Marx & Engels, 2002).

In all these various systems, not everyone works producing crops or commodities. Some people work directly for the government to make sure that the system is preserved and continues to function; such workers include tax inspectors, police officers, jail guards, soldiers, policymakers, schoolteachers, and even social workers. In a communist system, however, it is thought that the state will eventually fade away and become obsolete, with leadership occurring naturally among the people. So far this type of social order has not emerged in any communist nation that we are aware of; instead various types of centralized bureaucratic collectivism have emerged instead. This does not mean that a vanishing state cannot occur in communism; it just means that it has not, and it also means that a state can call itself one thing (rule by the people) while being another (rule by an elite).

The term "social order" also refers to the way people tend to co-operate with the operating system. People buy into a social contract with the system by giving up some of their individual liberty in exchange for the system bringing some degree of safety, security, and stability (Friend, 2017; Simpson, 2006). People do not physically sign such social contracts because they are usually tacit rather than written, although a nation's written constitution could certainly be regarded as part of these agreements.

All of us, inasmuch as we live in a nation state, are parties to such contracts. We are automatically opted in and we cannot opt out, and most of us do not even think of this arrangement as a contract but instead regard it as a natural part of life. If one migrates, however, and becomes a citizen of another country, one may be asked to think about this issue and may have to take an oath that buys into some form of contractual understanding with one's new nation. For instance, when Gary came to Canada and became a citizen, he had to agree to the following contract:

> I swear (or affirm) that I will be faithful and bear true allegiance to Her Majesty Queen Elizabeth II, Queen of Canada, Her Heirs and Successors, and that I will faithfully observe the laws of Canada and fulfil my duties as a Canadian citizen.
>
> (Canadian Oath of Citizenship)

June has never sworn or affirmed the above. She does not have to, because she was born in Canada and has always been a Canadian citizen, but even so there is an understanding that the above applies to June too.

Not everyone gets the same benefits from the social order, but even so, enough people co-operate with the system to keep it in place. Sometimes people rise up and object, but the power mechanisms we discussed in Chapter 3 urge people to conform and discipline them when they do not. Sometimes these power mechanisms are not enough to stop revolt, so people overthrow the entire operating system and replace it with something new, but in most nations this level of revolutionary change is rare.

## How the Social Order Produces Poverty

In previous chapters, we examined how colonization, Whiteness, White supremacy, and multiple isms operate at personal, systemic, and cultural levels to lift some up and tread others down. These processes produce wealth for some and poverty for others, and they certainly explain much of the inequality within the world today. But inequality existed long before civilization emerged in Europe; poverty pre-dates the inventions of race, Whiteness, White supremacy, and many of the isms we have examined. Although these factors play a key role in poverty and inequality today, they have not always done so, so what is the root cause of poverty and inequality?

There are many theories about the cause of poverty, some of which blame poor people or communities for their own plight. These include **individual theories of poverty** that claim the poor are lazy and do not want to work, or theories that a **culture of poverty** exists amoung the poor that creates defeatist attitudes that prevent people from getting ahead (Lewis, 1969; Small, Harding, & Lamont, 2010). Other scholars have developed

**systemic theories of poverty** that explain poverty as the result of systemic inequalities (Rist, 2016). We have demonstrated the impact of systemic factors in previous chapters.

Systemic factors certainly explain much of the inequality in the existing social order, and we suggest that this has been the same throughout history. Indeed, hundreds of years ago, Rousseau contended that the root cause of poverty was the invention of a system that allowed private property (Simpson, 2006). Some modern scholars agree, claiming that private property is the systemic cause of all oppression and almost every evil from rape to racism (Bishop, 2015). Although we agree that poverty is systemic, we do not agree that it can be explained by private property alone. Indeed, June grew up hearing stories from her mother about poverty and oppression in China where private property was banned, so how can private property be the cause when poverty and oppression also exists in places where private property is prohibited?

We contend that the systemic cause of poverty is not banning or allowing private property, but instead is the result of a social contract that allows, ". . . different privileges, which some men [sic] enjoy to the prejudice of others; such as that of being more rich, more honoured, more powerful or even in a position to exact obedience" (Rousseau, 1762/2016, p. 98). In other words, poverty, ". . . is a logical outcome of our social order. . . . our social order is premised on inequality, discrimination, and the preservation of privileges" (Copp, 1970, p. 737). Before we consider how this social order holds together, it is important to map its impact and to understand how poverty plays out around the world.

## Poverty in the Global South

The term **Global South** is used to refer to poorer nations that are mostly in the earth's southern hemisphere; alternative terms include **developing** or **underdeveloped nations,** or the **Third World.** The term is the flipside of the **Global North**, which refers to nations sometimes called the **First World**. These include Canada, the USA, Australia, New Zealand, the nations of Western Europe, parts of Asia, and a number of other nations with similar more developed economies. All of the terms used to describe the North–South divide are problematic, but whatever term one uses, the thing to remember is that this division is neither geographic nor accidental; it is the product of the colonization we discussed in Chapter 7.

The United Nations has focused considerable effort on ending poverty at a global level, particularly in the Global South. Efforts in the Global South focus primarily on **absolute poverty**, which is defined as:

> . . . a condition characterised by severe deprivation of basic human needs, including food, safe drinking water, sanitation facilities, health, shelter, education and information. It depends not only on income but also on access to services. (United Nations, 1995)

Absolute poverty cannot be measured by money alone. For instance, if one lives in a region where there is no access to safe drinking water or medical care, money is not much help. Similarly, if one lives in a region where wealth is shared by a community, and where goods and services are exchanged in kind through mutual support, then money matters less and does not reflect the resources one has access to. Although definitive figures cannot be given, in an effort to quantify financial subsistence levels, the figure of US$1.90 a day is currently used. In its poverty reduction efforts, the United Nations Development Programme initially set a Millennium Developmental Goal of reducing by 50 per cent the number of people surviving on less than US$1 a day. In 2015, the World Bank revised the subsistence level for inflation to US$1.90 a day (United Nations, 2015).

The Millennium goal has met with some success: in 1990, 44 per cent of the world's population lived below the subsistence level and this was reduced to 10 per cent by 2015. Although this is progress, it is nowhere near what is needed. We need to react to global poverty like the never-ending tsunami that it is.

## The Problem of How We Conceptualize the Global South

One of the reasons we do not address poverty in the Global South effectively is the way aid rather than trade is seen as the answer. We are not suggesting that trade alone will solve the problem, and we do not have anything against aid. Our issue is with the way the Global South and aid are conceptualized by the North. Consider the efforts of the charity supergroup "Band Aid" founded in 1984 by Bob Geldof and Midge Ure. Comprising many leading recording artists, beginning with a focus on famine relief in Ethiopia in 1984 and more recently on an Ebola crisis in 2014, the band has released songs that have raised millions in aid for Africa.

We do not like criticizing Geldof, Midge Ure, or Band Aid because they have certainly done a great deal to address poverty and inequality, but the fact remains that the Band Aid representation of Africa is problematic. The original 1984 Band Aid song, "Do They Know It's Christmas?" can be viewed on a number of websites and YouTube channels. We find the tune quite catchy, and it is sung by pop stars whose work we usually enjoy. Band Aid, however, misrepresents Africa and the issues the continent faces. The original 1984 lyrics portray Africa as a place where it never snows (but it does snow in Africa—especially in the Atlas Mountains of the north and the ski resorts of the south); where food does not grow (but food does grow and Africa has some of the most fertile farmland on the planet); where it never rains (but it does rain in Africa and some regions have monsoons), where there are no rivers (but Africa has an abundance of rivers including the second-longest river in the world); and where people may not know when Christmas comes (but of course people in Africa know when it is Christmas—it's that time of year when people in the Global North sing songs that make them think they are the saviours of the world rather than the cause of its problems).

The more recent Band Aid 30 version of the song from 2014 (also accessible on many Internet sites) has changed a number of the lyrics but still falls into the misrepresentation trap. Those working in Africa have drawn attention to this misrepresentation

(Beamont-Thomas & O'Carroll, 1984) and the ways such lyrics create stereotypes that become a part of the problem rather than the solution (Adebajo, 2015). Indeed, these pop star efforts and the discourses they buy into and reproduce prevent people recognizing and addressing the real problem. The problem is not Africa or the Global South—it is the Global North.

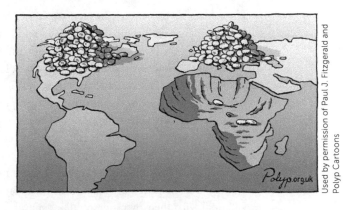

**Figure 8.1** The exploitation of Africa

## The Problem of Poverty in the South Lies in the North

Poverty in Africa has little to do with the nature of Africa and everything to do with the nature of Europe and North America. Today's poverty in Africa was instigated about 500 years ago when slavery and colonization took African labour and natural resources to make the Global North rich, and continues today through neocolonial processes. Consequently, the problem that causes poverty in Africa is not located in Africa, but in the Global North. If one wants to end poverty in Africa or in the rest of the Global South, one has to address the problem of the Global North exploiting the South.

## Aid May Help the South, But It Often Helps the North More

There is no doubt that aid can help recipients in the South, but it helps the donors in the North too. Indeed, a by-product of the 2004 tsunami was the reconstruction of disaster zones in a way that transferred land and resources away from local people and into the hands of international developers and corporations (Rice & Haynes, 2005). Under the cover of disaster, human rights and usual due processes were suspended to facilitate relief, during which predatory developers were able to take over coastlands, build tourist resorts, and block the ability of the fisher people who previously lived there to earn their traditional living on the coast (Klein, 2007).

Through these and similar processes, rather than help, such corporations actually extract an estimated US$100 billion every year from the Global South (Oxfam America, 2016, p. 1). There is a proverb about it being better to remove the need for charity than give charity. The proverb says, "Teach someone to fish rather than give them a fish," but the proverb makes no sense when the people in the South already know how to fish but cannot do so because the people from the North have cut off their access to the ocean.

It is not only corporate aid that benefits the North at the expense of the South. Consider the American government relief program that gave rice to Haiti. This program produced wealth for American farmers who sold rice at a profit to the American government relief program, but produced poverty in Haiti by flooding the market with free rice and destroying the livelihood of local rice farmers who could no longer sell their produce. This destruction had a ripple effect throughout Haiti where the loss of jobs and income in the farming sector caused losses in others (O'Grady, 2016).

In addition to aid to the South benefiting the North at a systemic level, the process of giving aid can also meet the *personal needs* of givers in the North at the expense of the South. The group Gary met with at a Hamilton church following the tsunami worked hard to ensure that they did not fall into this trap. Everyone in the group felt a personal need to go and help, but they ensured that the personal needs of the tsunami survivors came first. Too many well-intended aid trips turn into something that gives those providing help a way to deal with their own personal angst and sadness about poverty and disaster, rather than providing the help the intended recipients need. Sometimes such missions result in the locals caring for the visiting helpers rather than the other way around (Sinervo, 2015). Such "aid" efforts easily become exotic self-indulgent "adventure tourism." The group Gary was a part of realized that they could do more good by sending money and supplies to those already helping in the disaster zone than by going themselves. At least in this instance, the personal needs of the helped were placed before the needs of the helpers. We are not dismissing the emotional need to help, because these feelings come from the heart, but we have to connect these feelings to the head and to an understanding about what is really needed. We are also not dismissing those who do go South to help. Many social workers, doctors, nurses, engineers, and others have given up the financial security of successful careers in Canada to live and help permanently in the Global South. Do not think that, by critiquing the global social order, we are critiquing people who have not waited for systemic change but have headed South to give whatever help they can.

Notwithstanding the efforts of those who go to help, because of the way systems work, aid to the South helps the North at a cultural level too. Aid reinforces, in the minds of many, the perception of the North as a place of answers and solutions, and the South as a place where people have an inability to help themselves. It reinforces ideas of the superiority of White people and White systems. Of course, the North is not superior, and it has its own problems with poverty too.

## Key Concept

It is important to be involved in aid, but get involved in a way that really helps. Also, if you talk to people about the aid you give, avoid doing so in a way that reinforces the myth that the North is a place of people with answers and solutions, and the South is a place of people with the inability to help themselves. Instead, talk about how colonization started the problem that causes the need for aid, and how neocolonialism continues it.

# Poverty in the Global North

Anyone strolling through a downtown Canadian city will know that absolute poverty exists in the Global North too. Not only is homelessness evident, but a lack of caring for the poor is evident too. Throughout the Northern world public benches are designed to prevent the homeless from sleeping on them (Cheung, 2016), shop doorways contain spikes to prevent the homeless from finding shelter (Petty, 2016), and the police constantly move the homeless along (Cooper, 2017). There are exceptions to these rules. For instance, Vancouver has public benches that convert into sheltered sleeping places for the homeless (Lus, 2014). But Vancouver's benches go against the trend, and for the most part the Global North invests a great deal ensuring that the basic needs of those who have absolutely nothing are hardly met, or if they are met this is done at the minimal level needed to survive.

Although absolute poverty exists in the North, poverty in developed nations tends to be measured in relative terms. **Relative poverty** is the income and resources one has in relation to others. Poverty can also be measured by being able to afford food, shelter, and other basic necessities; Canada uses this type of measure. Canada has no "poverty line" but has developed a **low income cut-off** (LIC), which is a calculation based on the percentage of net income a person or family spends on shelter, food, and basic necessities compared to others in their community.

Canada also uses a **market basket measure** (MBM) as a measure of poverty, which calculates the funds needed to afford basic food, shelter, and living supplies. Once one falls below these levels it is a struggle to survive without turning to some form of charity. Such poverty and reliance on services causes what we referred to in the previous chapter as "austerity ailments" (McGrath, Walker, & Jones, 2016). This is where the stress and humiliation of relying on benefits and charity detract from one's mental health and well-being, and exacerbate any other issues or problems one may be facing too. In this manner, poverty evolves into something that goes beyond finance in ways that can erode personal relationships, psychological and spiritual well-being, physical health, family connections and community cohesion, etc. (Moskowitz, Vittinghoff, & Schmidt, 2013). One can never really understand this type of poverty unless one lives within it (Jeppesen, 2009), but one way to consider the impact is to examine the effect of income disparity (see Exercise 8.1 on income disparity).

Income disparity not only affects what we can afford, it affects our bodies too. Income inequality kills about 40,000 people a year in Canada (Raphael & Bryant, 2014; Tjepkema, Wilkins, & Long, 2013) and 874,000 in the USA (Galea, Tracy, Hoggatt, DiMaggio, & Karpati, 2011). A direct comparison between these US and Canadian data is difficult because we are not able to establish whether the same measures were used, but international comparisons can be made in relation to child poverty.

We do not like child-poverty measures because if children live in poverty, it is because their parents live in poverty, so why not count adults and children together?

## Exercise 8.1

### Income Disparity

If possible, undertake this exercise in groups.

If you are already familiar with living in poverty, feel free to draw on that experience in this exercise. If you have not had this experience, use this exercise to imagine and think through the impact of income disparity.

At the time of writing, Canadian child welfare social work entry-level positions offer a salary range of about $60,000 to $75,000 per year. Not all social work positions in Canada and elsewhere offer these types of salary, but many do. Consider, for a moment, that you work in such a position at a $75,000 salary level, and also imagine that you have a partner in the same line of work with an identical salary; this gives you a combined gross household income of $150,000 per year. Imagine that you have two children under the age of 16, which means that you would also likely qualify for a small amount of Canadian Child Benefit of about $230 a month, which annualized brings your income to about $152,760. If either of you move into a social work management position you can look forward to a household income of over $200,000 per year.

Now consider the families you serve. Not all service users live in poverty, but as this chapter is about poverty, imagine a family that does. Using Ontario as an example, let us imagine a family of two parents with two children surviving on Ontario Works benefits at 2017 levels.

| | |
|---|---:|
| **Couple with two children under 17 basic needs** | $476 |
| **Couple with two children shelter allowance** | $727 |
| **Canadian Child Benefit** | $900 |
| **Ontario Child Benefit** | $226 |
| **Total income per month** | $2,329 |
| **Annual gross income** | $27,948 |

In the calculations above we have not considered the impact of different tax brackets on net incomes, nor have we calculated the relative gains from social work employee group pension plans, drug plans, dental plans, and so on. Even so, it is fair to estimate based on the figures above that a social work couple has an income of about five times that of the couple on benefits, and the social work couple can look forward to this differential increasing even more as they progress in their careers. This differential allows us to begin to measure the impact of income disparity.

Imagine that you are a member of the social work couple we described above with two children between the ages of 6 and 16 years. Now imagine a comparable family on benefits, which has (as shown above) a household income approximately five times less than yours. The relative cost of goods and services for this family are five times more than you pay. Of course, the price they pay is the same price you pay, but in relative terms, this is five times more of their income than yours. We have made a list below of the estimated costs (including taxes) that you would pay for a can of pop from a dispensing machine, a school photograph, a family trip to the movies, a pair of ice skates, and a child's bicycle (the cheapest one we could find at a well-known Canadian store) and the cheapest Mac laptop we could find. Next to this is the relative cost to the family on benefits.

| Item | Actual cost for social work family | Relative cost for family on benefits |
|---|---|---|
| Can of pop | $2 | $10 |
| 8x10 school photo | $15 | $75 |
| Family movie pass | $50 | $250 |
| Youth hockey skates | $45 | $225 |
| Child's bicycle | $124 | $620 |
| MacBook Air | $1355 | $6775 |

Add your own items to the list above. Now imagine you are a parent in the family on benefits paying the relative prices on the right, and answer the following questions:

1. How do you feel paying these prices?
2. How would you feel if a social worker helping you arrived at your home driving a new car, and in small talk told you how their children just came back from summer camp, and that they had just bought a MacBook to help their children complete school assignments?
3. How would you feel about your children's chances for success in the future?
4. What would be the ongoing impact on your family in future generations if your children had no school photos?
5. Given that social workers have limited access to funds for providing financial relief, how would you like social workers to help?

Although answering the above questions from the perspective of a parent living on benefits or low income may give you a glimpse into the impact of poverty, do not assume that this exercise will really let you know what it is like living in this situation. Especially, do not assume that people living in poverty lack resilience, ingenuity, and agency, or that they need your charity or want you feeling sorry for them.

Finalize the exercise by watching and reflecting on Richard Wilkinson's work on harm caused by inequality at https://www.ted.com/speakers/richard_wilkinson.

We suspect it is a leftover from attitudes that blame adults for their own poverty (more about that in Chapter 10). Children certainly cannot be blamed for being poor, so counting child poverty rather than family poverty is more likely to gain public sympathy.

Although we object to measuring poverty by counting children and not adults, the best forms of comparative data are for children. The Canadian Centre for Policy Alternatives has calculated the child poverty rates in Canada compared to other Organisation for Economic Co-operation and Development (OECD) nations. We reproduce these data in Figure 8.2. As can be seen, the poverty rate in Canada at 18% is among the worst in the OECD nations and not much better than the USA. New Zealand and Australia come close behind Canada; the UK fares much better at just below 10 per cent, but this places the UK among the worst OECD nations in Western Europe. Nordic nations rank among the best, with scores below 5 per cent, which show that determined nations can reduce poverty if they choose.

## Poverty Is Not Random—It Has a Footprint We Recognize

Poverty is not random. Its footprint treads those down who fall outside the circle of first-class citizenship that we showed in Chapter 4 (Figure 4.1). This is especially apparent when

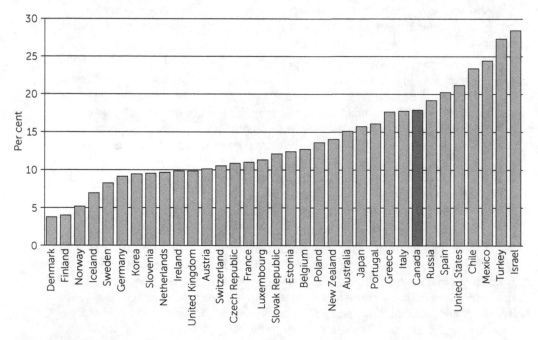

**Figure 8.2** Child poverty rates in OECD nations

it comes to race and gender. Figure 8.3 shows how Canada's 18 per cent poverty rate shifts by geography, race, gender, Indigenous status, and other variables.

The pattern in Figure 8.3 shows that poverty impacts White people the least at 13 per cent, and Indigenous people on reserve the most at 60 per cent. This does not mean that White people are not oppressed by poverty—the Canadian rate of 13 per cent is an entirely unacceptable figure, and the 60 per cent among Indigenous people is a national shame. Canada is often ranked as one of the best nations in the world to live,

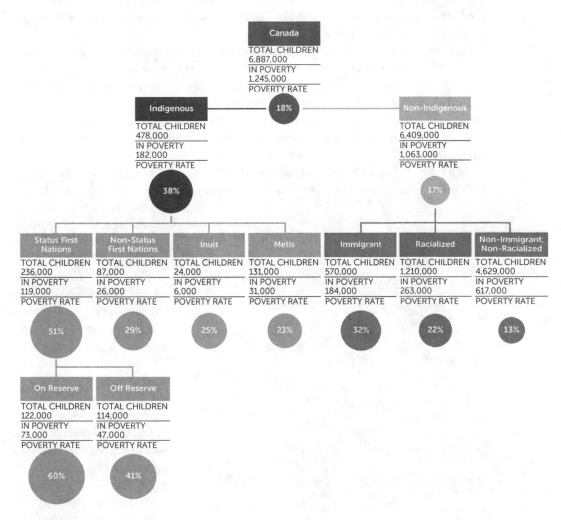

**Figure 8.3** The Poverty Footprint

but not if you are Indigenous. That is evident from the footprint of poverty shown in Figure 8.3.

## Poverty Is Stratified by Class

A person's economic and social position within society is called **socioeconomic status** (SES). A similar concept that refers to one's position in society is **social class**. One's SES and class tend to be categorized in a hierarchy. SES is usually divided into upper, middle, and lower levels, or upper, middle, and working class, with sometimes an "under class" being added. These designations are shown in Figure 8.4 along with the types of work people usually undertake at each level.

As Figure 8.4 shows, SES or class is usually related to the type of work one does. More specifically, class is usually produced by one's relationship to wealth-making mechanisms. Marx explains this as class being a function of one's relationship to the mode of production (McLellan, 2000). A **mode of production** is the way society produces what it needs to sustain itself and to produce wealth. Modes of production are inextricably linked to the social order because society is ordered around the work of sustaining and maintaining itself.

Marx divides human history into stages defined by five different modes of production; the primitive community, slave state, feudal state, capitalism, and the socialist society (Marx & Engels, 2002). Each of these represents a different social order based on a different way of producing wealth with differing rules about who belongs where on the hierarchy (i.e., who rules whom, who works for whom, and who wins or loses).

History, according to Marx, has seen the progression of one system to another, with each change shifting the social order and hierarchy. For instance, within feudalism, a monarch (usually a king but sometimes a queen) sat on a throne at the head of the hierarchy, beneath which were the nobility, clergy,

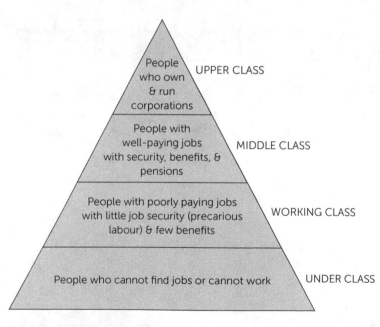

**Figure 8.4** Social class

Source: Adapted from a video by Tim McCaskell, retrieved from https://vimeo.com/6803752

merchants, guild artisans, and finally serfs. Each of these strata, or classes, had a differing relationship with wealth-making mechanisms, and a corresponding different SES.

Within feudalism, the monarch on the apex of the hierarchy allocated or dismissed dukes, barons, earls, and other nobility who managed land, and one way or another everyone else relied on that land and the favour of the monarch and nobility to survive. Within this system the monarch and nobility had a very high SES, and serfs were close to the bottom and were in an exploitable position because of their dependency on the upper levels. Of course, because the serfs provided most of the labour to make the system work, their work was the root of everyone's wealth. Serfs provided the means of everyone's survival, but those on the top had the power to discipline and punish. This enabled a social order in which, no matter how much everyone relied on the work of the serfs, the serfs remained poor and the rich remained rich.

Feudalism lost its dominance with the emergence of the industrial revolution. Land and farming retained wealth-producing value, but industry and manufacturing set the stage for a revolution in the social order. The middle class, or what Marx called the bourgeoisie, developed and gained ownership of industry and manufacturing, which became the dominant means of production in what is known as capitalism. The serfs became the working class or proletariat, and now sold their labour power to the bourgeoisie in return for wages. In this system the bourgeoisie pay the proletariat less than the value their labour produces. Marx refers to this difference as surplus labour. In this manner, the bourgeoisie exploit the proletariat, because they never pay workers the true value of their labour. They keep the surplus for themselves.

Marx contends that the binary within any social order between those who have power and wealth and those who do not creates a **class struggle**, and a **dialectic** (tension and interaction) between these opposing classes, that invariably result in a revolutionary change. Sometimes revolution is violent, like the French or Russian revolutions, or sometimes it is a type of gradual morphing from one system to another, like the British shift from feudalism to capitalism.

Social order and social change are much more complex than the above suggests. In Canada and other nations with a monarch, capitalism and feudalism blur, because the idea of an alliance to a sovereign still exists, especially in the UK where landed aristocracy still hold considerable wealth, and in Canada where new citizens have to swear allegiance to the Queen. Moreover, identifying those who own and control the means of production within capitalism is not straightforward, especially when ownership is dispersed among shareholders. In addition, professional classes like medicine and law do not fit into the bourgeoisie vs. proletariat binary. Who "owns" industries like medicine, law, education, and even social work? What is their product? Who benefits most from them at the expense of whom?

Marx understood these complexities, as does modern Marxism, and modern scholars unpack these complexities at multiple levels, which we do not have the space to explore here. But even if one disagrees with the Marxist basic analysis and the complex ways it is taken up today, there seems little doubt that the social order produces classes that are stratified in relation to one's ability to either own or benefit from the way wealth is produced within society. Indeed, if one follows the money, there is no doubt that the system is producing wealth for some and poverty for others.

# A Tale of Multiple Capitals, Doxa, and Domination

The work of Pierre Bourdieu adds several dimensions to the understanding of class and its relationship to SES (Bourdieu, 1985, 1996). We discussed in Chapter 3 the way Bourdieu understands power. Likely you remember that Bourdieu connects power to capitals, so here in this chapter where we explore how capitals are connected to wealth, poverty, and the social order, we need to return to Bourdieu. Likely you also remember from Chapter 3 that Bourdieu sees capital as multidimensional and not just economic (Bourdieu, 1986). The recognition by Bourdieu that there are many capitals is useful to us in understanding the social order and how it is related to wealth and poverty.

As mentioned in Chapter 3, Bourdieu's ideas are complex and can be hard to grasp, but social work scholars are increasingly taking up the explanatory power of Bourdieu's ideas. As a result, it is important for you to have an understanding of these ideas to be able to keep up with this literature, and to also make better sense of the way that class and capital operate.

## Multiple Capitals

A key contribution Bourdieu makes is recognizing that capital can be economic, cultural, or social, and these combine to become symbolic (Bourdieu, 1986, 1987, 1989). As explained in Chapter 3, *economic capital* is understood by Bourdieu in a similar way to Marx: it is owning the means of production, or having some other way of being able to benefit from the surplus labour of workers (Wacquant, 1987). *Cultural capital* is, in part, having formal education and qualifications common among the middle and upper classes. It is also **embodying** (internalizing and demonstrating) the posture, tastes, and mannerisms of the middle and upper classes, and having the clothing, living accommodation, cars, jewellery, and other trappings of the social elite (Bourdieu, 1986). *Social capital* is who you know, how well you know them, and the extent you can draw on relationships with them to open doors and get ahead (Bourdieu, 1986). To an extent, the old school tie discussed in Chapter 1 is a visual marker or symbol of social capital. We pointed out in Chapter 3 that all of these capitals are sources of power. We now point out that all of these capitals are also sources of wealth.

Despite the ability of Bourdieu's ideas to explain power and wealth, there are problems with Bourdieu's analysis. Garrett (2007) points out that Bourdieu does not understand race, racism, or the way oppression operates in a multicultural context, and that Bourdieu considers attention to such issues a distraction from the central issues of "capitalism, class, exploitation, domination and inequality" (Garrett, 2007, p. 364). Given what we have said in Chapter 4 about Whiteness and Chapter 5 about racism, it ought to be obvious that, like Garrett (2007), we have a problem with Bourdieu not grasping Whiteness and not taking racism seriously. This does not mean, however, that we reject all of Bourdieu's ideas, because if we keep the insights Bourdieu offers into capitals, and combine it with what we know about racism and other isms, we gain a deeper understanding into the way oppression works. Bourdieu's idea of multiple capitals helps us understand that the social order, along with wealth, power, and influence, are not just driven by economic capital, but by many capitals.

## Many Fields and Their Relationship to Habitus

Other concepts Bourdieu has developed that help us understand the social order are habitus and field. Again, we briefly mentioned these in Chapter 3. The sum of all one's capitals is called habitus (Bourdieu, 2005). Habitus is a reflection of a person's unique way of being, and it is also the way a person embodies the broader social world they live within. Although the social world we are raised within makes our habitus, do not think of this as deterministic, because we make our social world too. Consequently, habitus is a dynamic reflection of a balance, or perhaps compromise, between ourselves and our environment (Bourdieu, 1989).

Our capitals, expressed through habitus, play out in what Bourdieu calls fields. As mentioned in Chapter 3, a field is a social space; it can be geographic like a nation or province, or conceptual like academia, medicine, politics, the military, social work, and so on (Thomson, 2014). We are all simultaneously members of many fields. Each field has its own **doxa**, which is a set of rules or protocols (written and unwritten) for the way to behave and take up such spaces (Bourdieu & Eagleton, 1994). Bourdieu likens a *field* to the space where a game is played (Wacquant, 1989), somewhat like a hockey rink, with *doxa* being the rules of the game, somewhat like the NHL Rule Book (though unlike the NHL regulations, doxa is not always written).

When we enter a field our habitus is converted into symbolic capital, which means that our economic, cultural, and social capitals take on symbolism that creates specific meanings by reflecting (or not reflecting) the doxa of a field (Bourdieu, 1986). As a result, people within a field will immediately evaluate us in relation to the doxa of that field, and assign us a ranking or position within that field's social structure. In other words, they evaluate our position in that part of society by what we wear, how we act, and so on. This ranking is not only based on our following unwritten rules about dress, conduct, and so on; it is also based on our **disposition**, which is the way that we and our habitus embody that space (Swartz, 1997, 2007).

In Chapter 3 we explained symbolic capital with an example of hiring a lawyer. The concepts of doxa and disposition enable us to take that example one step further.

The lawyer in that example who exhibited the symbols of power and success was following a doxa and exhibiting a disposition that many successful lawyers exhibit (at least in TV shows like *Suits*). But doxa and embodiment are also deeper than the trappings of success; they are also a sense of comfort, confidence, and belonging (usually that others can sense) in a given field. For instance, in Chapter 2, Russell Brand explained how those who grew up in wealth, attended private schools, went to an elite university, and then entered the British Houses of Parliament feel quite at home in these places. This is because the Houses of Parliament in the UK, just like the Parliament buildings in Canada, follow the exact same grand architectural patterns, and follow the same rules of etiquette and human relations as the universities, schools, and in some cases the family homes of the elite. In this manner, whether in Canada or the UK, the social elite quite literally feel "at home" in government corridors of power.

## Gaining a Deeper Understanding—Extending Bourdieu to Race

Even a beginning understanding of Bourdieu's ideas open up the possibility of a much deeper and dynamic analysis of the social order and the way various forms of capital relate to wealth and poverty. Indeed, the capital Bourdieu refers to as symbolic has profound material implications. The issue of wealth and poverty, the power to push down and lift up, does not only rely on material things, but instead depends on having access to many forms of capital that become symbolic and are converted into material gain.

## Extending Bourdieu's Ideas

We mentioned above that Bourdieu does not consider the issue of race, which means that for us his ideas fall short of explaining the social order. But one can extend Bourdieu's ideas to consider the body as a form of capital. What the "capital" of one's body symbolizes is shaped by racism, sexism, and other isms. Dr Winnie Lo, who introduced us to Bourdieu in Chapter 3, alerted us to the possibility of thinking about the body through a Bourdieuian lens and considering race, gender, and other social locations as a form of capital. Using this analysis, race, gender, and even a body type that matches the "ideal standard" is a form of capital that gives one a head start; add the right accent, education, clothing (cultural capital), and a few elite friends (social capital), and all this shapes the way one is read and responded to by others.

If at a conceptual level you grasp how one's social locations are a form of capital, this means you have a sound understanding about theories of racism and other isms, and also have a good understanding of Bourdieu. None of these ideas are easy to grasp, but if you have grasped or are even just beginning to grasp them, you are well on your way to having deep insights into what is occurring within the social order.

## Key Concept

There is nothing wrong with combining theories to deepen what we know. We can take a theory about race, and another theory about capitals, and combine them. This way you gain a deeper understanding of society than you can with each theory on its own. Some scholars might disagree with us and will argue that you cannot mix and match ideas like this. But if nobody mixed ideas there would never be any new theory. Remember what we said in Chapter 2 about thinking for yourself. Do not let any one single theorist dictate the way you make sense of the world.

## Reconceptualizing Internalization as Habitus

Besides providing a more multidimensional understanding of the social order, Bourdieu's ideas open up another benefit for anti-oppressive analysis; they help us gain a more nuanced understanding of internalized oppression. The concept of **internalized oppression** refers to the way members of oppressed groups internalize dominant ideas about their own group and oppress themselves (Mullaly, 2010). Alternative words sometimes used for internalized oppression are self-hate, learned helplessness, internalized racism, and so on. We object to these descriptions because, although not intended in this way, the idea of internalized oppression can be taken up as suggesting that the oppressed are somehow responsible for internalizing dominant ideas and for oppressing themselves. The idea of internalized oppression can also be misinterpreted to mean that the oppressed have not resisted domination enough.

Of course internalized oppression is a real phenomenon. Benjamin Zephaniah made this clear in the "rong radio station" poem we referred to in Chapter 4; this is why Zephaniah said that he wanted to "arrest" himself. We also suspect the reason Zephaniah deliberately spelt the word "wrong" as "rong" was to disrupt the social order at the language level. We have to acknowledge the reality that oppression from the outside can impact the way we think, feel, or even act on the inside, but rather than using the term "internalized oppression," we prefer Bourdieu's concept of habitus.

Habitus does not single out the oppressed as those who internalize the social order; instead habitus is about how we all internalize and shape the rules (doxa) of the game (field). These rules not only include internalized oppression, but also include internalized domination, which is a sense of entitlement and privilege that those in a position of domination take up and reproduce. Internalized oppression is not separate from these larger rules of the game. Bourdieu is anti-dualistic, which means he sees all actions as the result of interaction between habitus and field rather than from just one or the other (Bourdieu, 2005; Postone, LiPuma, & Calhoun, 1993). As a result we cannot conceptualize internalized oppression as something oppressed people simply do to themselves in isolation from others who follow the rules of the game. We prefer to use the term *habitus* over *internalized oppression* because it acknowledges that to some extent every one of us internalizes the rules of the game.

Although Bourdieu contends that there are many games, and we concur, we contend that in the current social order there is one central game that rules and binds them all: a game called neo-liberalism.

## Neo-Liberalism: The Game That Rules

Neo-liberalism is the current means through which wealth is maintained for a few and poverty for many. How neo-liberalism does this can be difficult to discern, because unless one looks closely at the social order, one hardly sees the role neo-liberalism plays. Indeed, the success of neo-liberalism results from it appearing to be nothing at all:

> So pervasive has neoliberalism become that we seldom even recognise it as an ideology. We appear to accept the proposition that this utopian, millenarian faith describes a neutral force; a kind of biological law, like Darwin's theory of evolution. But the philosophy arose as a conscious attempt to reshape human life and shift the locus of power. (Monbiot, 2016)

Because it is difficult to see and name neo-liberalism, it is sometimes conflated with Whiteness, which has similar characteristics. Although Whiteness and neo-liberalism are similar, they are not the same; neo-liberalism is the game, Whiteness is a set of rules that give certain players an advantage in the game. This distinction is important, because some scholars claim that neo-liberalism is the root of *all* problems (Monbiot, 2016). We disagree. It is certainly the root of most of our problems, but not all of them; if we ended neo-liberalism we would still have Whiteness, which means another game would simply replace the old one with the same rules of exclusion and inclusion that shape who wins. Certainly, however, neo-liberalism is interwoven with Whiteness. It is the current social order, and it provides the machinery that divides the rich from the poor. Because neo-liberalism is largely invisible, it is often not seen as an ideology that shapes the game of life.

Another reason it is difficult to grasp the nature of neo-liberalism is that the name can be confusing. The word is based on **liberalism**, which is a word derived from "liberty." Liberalism carries connotations of freedom from oppression and freedom from the domination of the state or some other ruling mechanism (Hanesworth, 2017). We contend that such freedom never existed, at least not for everyone, but the ideas of liberty and freedom certainly did. We need to be clear that neo-liberalism has nothing to do with the liberal idea of freedom for the people. Quite the opposite—it is the freedom of big business and international corporations at the expense of the people (Harvey, 2007). Neo-liberalism may create the illusion of freedom for the individual, but in reality it is the exact opposite; the disappearance of the middle class and the growing gap between rich and poor is evidence (Baines & McBride, 2014).

Neo-liberalism represents a shift in sovereignty from the state to bankers and corporations. With global corporations owning more wealth than many nations, they have enough power to control governments, even the governments of superpowers (Orr, 2013; Younge, 2014). This became quite evident in the 2008 banking crisis with "the transfer of banking debts onto government balance sheets" (Davies, 2016, p. 130). In a world of globalization and a global market, international banks and corporations have so much power that they can dictate terms to governments. If banks fail the global economy fails, and if large global corporations decide to pull out of a nation that nation fails, or so the bankers and corporations tell us.

Neo-liberalism, therefore, has retooled the social order so that market relations govern all "political, economic, and social arrangements within society" (Springer, Birch, & MacLeavy, 2016, p. 2). The basic principle of this system is the freedom of corporations: freedom from regulation, from taxation, from control by the state, from national boundaries, from worker demands or unions, and from environmental or social responsibility.

The origins of neo-liberalism can be traced back to classical economics and the **laissez-faire** (a lack of regulation) idea that a free market will balance society in a way that is efficient and fair to all (Smith, 1982). Of course, history has taught us that a classical free market does not make everything work perfectly for everyone, and as a result governments have taken various degrees of responsibility to ensure the well-being of citizens. In the nineteenth and even more so in the twentieth centuries, governments ensured the health and well-being of people through health-care systems that are free at the point of delivery and through a range of employment insurance and similar schemes (Chappell, 2014; Qwul'sih'yah'maht & Kundoqk, 2009). Neo-liberalism is in the process of changing all of this.

How neo-liberalism affected this shift is difficult to track; it is said to have started its dominance in the 1980s with the economic policies of British Prime Minister Margaret Thatcher and American President Ronald Reagan (Schultz, 2017). It has changed over the years so that today's neo-liberalism looks nothing like it did in the 1980s (Davies, 2016)—so much so that today's scholars can no longer even agree on what neo-liberalism is (Venugopal, 2015). This obviously causes a problem because neo-liberalism:

> . . . lives on as a problematic rhetorical device that bundles together a proliferation of eclectic and contradictory concepts; a tableau of critical explorations of the material world by non-economists, clustered together by a shared signifier that thematically links them to a broader set of morally devolved referents about markets, economics, subjectivities, state authority, globalization or neo-colonialism. (Venugopal, 2015, p. 183)

Today we hear the term *neo-liberalism* used by social work scholars as a catch phrase for everything that is bad. We resist such rhetoric, and instead urge a more precise use of the term to refer to the current shift away from the state looking out for the welfare of its citizens, and toward the state looking out for the welfare of corporations. As such neo-liberalism is an:

> . . . economic and political system that benefits the rich and powerful at expense of the rest, causing the gains of economic growth over the last several decades to go disproportionately to the already wealthy. (Oxfam America, 2016, p. 1)

For those who look, evidence for the neo-liberal system being supported by the state at the expense of citizens can be found everywhere. For example, Oxfam America has set out the way the US government uses public funds to support private corporate interests in a form of reverse socialism that takes money from the poor and gives it to the rich.

- From 2008 to 2014 the 50 largest US companies collectively received $27 in federal loans, loan guarantees, and bailouts for every $1 they paid in federal taxes.
- From 2008 to 2014 these 50 companies spent approximately $2.6 billion on lobbying while receiving nearly $11.2 trillion in federal loans, loan guarantees, and bailouts.
- Even as these 50 companies earned nearly $4 trillion in profits globally from 2008 to 2014, they used offshore tax havens to lower their effective overall tax rate to just 26.5 per cent, well below the statutory rate of 35 per cent and even below average levels paid in other developed countries. Only 5 of 50 companies paid the full 35 per cent corporate tax rate.
- These companies relied on an opaque network of more than 1600 disclosed subsidiaries in tax havens to stash about $1.4 trillion offshore. In addition to the 1600 known subsidiaries, the companies may have failed to disclose thousands of additional subsidiaries to the Securities and Exchange Commission because of weak reporting requirements.
- Their lobbying appears to have offered an incredible return on investment. For every $1 spent on lobbying, these 50 companies collectively received $130 in tax breaks and more than $4000 in federal loans, loan guarantees, and bailouts (Oxfam America, 2016, p. 2).

The workings of neo-liberalism can be seen in Exercise 8.2. The video in this exercise is somewhat oversimplistic, but it is a good introduction to the notion of neo-liberalism, and it also addresses the way class and other variables intersect.

## Exercise 8.2

### Neo-Liberalism as a Water Balloon

If possible, undertake this exercise in groups.

Watch the Tim McCaskell video "Neoliberalism as Water Balloon" at https://vimeo.com/6686131.

Describe in your own words the way race and similar variables fit onto the stratification shown in Figure 8.4.

# The Problem of the Existing Social Order

The current social order transfers money and resources from the poor to the rich. How else could only 62 people manage to accumulate more wealth than half of the people on the entire planet put together (Oxfam America, 2016)? It cannot be because these wealthy people work harder or are smarter than anyone else, because how can 62 people work harder or be smarter than 7.6 billion?

Wealth for a few and poverty for the many comes so consistently from the social order that we say that poverty *is* the social order. Indeed, almost every major social order in history that we are aware of has created wealth for a few at the expense of the many. Long before neo-liberalism, Robin Hood tried to reverse this process by "robbing from the rich and giving to the poor." This process made him an "outlaw," which by definition means he operated outside the existing social order. In other words, he was breaking the rules of the game.

Robin Hood is most probably a legend that started about 600 years ago. We suspect that the story has resonated down the centuries because people intuitively know that "Robin got it right." We are not condoning armed robbery, but something needs to stop the robbery by neo-liberalism and the robbery by any other social order that allows the rich to consistently take from the poor. We suspect that every nation and culture has an intuitive understanding of social justice in this regard, which is why not only tales of Robin Hood, but legends and true stories of people who fought unjust systems such as Sparticus, Viriatus, Geronimo, Chief Big Foot, and others continue to be told.

## Key Concept

The stories of Robin Hood and others like him have been told around the world for centuries. We suspect the reason such stories continue to be consistently told is because deep down we intuitively know that "Robin got it right." We do not suggest that social workers use Robin's anti-poverty methods, but we do suggest that we use his analysis.

We contend that the public reactions to the tsunami of 2004 show that people are not prepared to stand by and let others suffer. The public reaction to the tsunami shows that when people see and understand a need, they are willing to take collective action to help others. We say the same is so with poverty. If people can understand the nature of the problem of poverty and inequality, and if they understand that we have the means to solve it, action will follow. Of course, for action to be effective, it also requires an understanding that inequality and poverty "is a political and not a charity problem" (Procacci, 2007, p. 27). This is crucial because the charity of tsunami relief funded a second disaster where, as mentioned earlier, corporate interests utilized tsunami relief to destroy the livelihoods of many in the disaster zones (Klein, 2007; Rice & Haynes, 2005). Change has to happen not through charity that attempts to alleviate poverty, but by changing the social order.

## Chapter Summary

We began this chapter recounting the tsunami of 2014 and the ways it stimulated an un-precedented global aid response. We suggested that the relief response to the tsunami shows that when disaster strikes, people have the compassion and the ability to mobilize and do something to help. Given that people help in disasters, we asked why the more deadly never-ending ongoing disaster of global poverty does not get the same attention and response as a one-off tsunami. We suggested that by the end of this chapter you would have answers to this question. Having an answer to this question is crucial for the anti-oppressive social worker, because poverty is oppression. If something is stopping people from mobilizing to stop oppression, social workers need to know what this something is.

We have suggested throughout this chapter that poverty comes from the social order—the way we organize ourselves as society based on rules and processes designed to make a few wealthy at the expense of the many. We have contended that this way of organizing ourselves as a society along with the wealth and poverty it creates have become accepted as a natural part of life. By accepting this social order as natural, it has become invisible to many, so unlike a tsunami it is often not seen and responded to as the deadly disaster that it truly represents. Even when people do recognize the disaster of global poverty and inequality, it can seem too great to resolve. Without understanding the social order that drives it, people do not know where or how to bring change. We have provided you with many ways of recognizing the way that the social order and poverty are connected so that you have the conceptual tools to recognize what is occurring and to join with others to develop plans for change.

Change is possible. We have made it clear that we have the means to end poverty immediately. The only thing that is stopping us from doing so is that we choose not to (Kent, 2011, 2016). Indeed, about 25 per cent of the annual income of the 100 richest people in the world would immediately end global poverty (Oxfam International, 2013), as would a small proportion of the $700 billion bailout given to Wall Street bankers (Kent, 2011), or 10 per cent of the money the world spends on its military (Goldsmith, 2016). We can end poverty. We simply need to change government spending priorities, and to give people the same state support currently given to corporations.

Of course it is easy for us to point out that the resources needed to solve the problem of world poverty already exist, but how are we going to achieve the shift in the social order and in spending priorities to make this so? Also, what are we to replace the existing social order with? We do not have the answer to these questions, and we suggest that social work does not have the answer either. Instead of "changing the world," we suggest that social work offers those it serves the insights and assistance in doing this themselves.

## Discussion Questions

Discuss or reflect on the following:

1. Recount a time or an incident when you tried to help address poverty.
2. Recall how you understood the nature and cause of poverty in that moment.
3. Outline the ways this chapter has changed, or confirmed, your previous understanding of poverty and the ways you will address it.

## Activity

There are a number of anti-poverty organizations in Canada. Search the Internet for these organizations and:

1. Try to determine how these organizations conceptualize poverty and its causes.
2. Try to find and compare organizations that conceptualize the causes of poverty differently.
3. Name those differences, reflect on why they might arise, and notice if they cause any differences in the ways these organizations attempt to address poverty.
4. Which of these organizations most reflect the way you understand poverty? Explain your answer.

## Suggested Resources

Canada Without Poverty. Retrieved from http://www.cwp-csp.ca/

Make Poverty History Canada videos. Retrieved from https://www.youtube.com/user/mphvideos

Oxfam Canada. Retrieved from https://www.oxfam.ca/

Jefferson, P.N. (2018). *Poverty: A very short introduction*. Toronto, Canada: Oxford University Press.

# References

Adebajo, A. (2015, July 13). Celebrity efforts to "save Africa" have often only reinforced stereotypes. *The Guardian*. Retrieved from https://www.theguardian.com/global-development/commentisfree/2015/jul/13/celebrity-save-africa-stereotypes-bob-geldof-live-aid

Alexander, R. (2013, June 18). Does a child die of hunger every 10 seconds? *BBC News*. Retrieved from http://www.bbc.com/news/magazine-22935692

Baines, D., & McBride, S. (2014). Introduction: Context and fight-back. In D. Baines & S. McBride (Eds), *Orchestrating austerity: Impacts and resistance* (pp. 1–8). Black Point, Canada: Fernwood Publishing.

Beamont-Thomas, B., & O'Carroll, L. (2014, December 9). Ebola survivor Will Pooley calls Band Aid "cringe-worthy cultural ignorance." *The Guardian*. Retrieved from https://www.theguardian.com/music/2014/dec/09/will-pooley-band-aid-30-ebola

Bishop, A. (2015). *Becoming an ally: Breaking the cycle of oppression in people* (3rd edn). Halifax, Canada: Fernwood.

Bourdieu, P. (1985). The social space and the genesis of groups. *Theory and Society, 14*(6), 723–44.

Bourdieu, P. (1986). The forms of capital. In J. G. Richardson (Ed.), *Handbook of theory and research for the sociology of education* (pp. 241–256). Westport, CT: Greenwood Press.

Bourdieu, P. (1987). What makes a social class?: On the theoretical and practical existence of groups. *Berkeley Journal of Sociology, 32*, 1–17.

Bourdieu, P. (1989). Social space and symbolic power. *Sociological Theory, 7*(1), 14–25.

Bourdieu, P. (1996). *The state nobility: Elite schools in the field of power* (L. C. Clough, Trans.). Stanford, CA: Stanford University Press.

Bourdieu, P. (2005). Habitus. In J. Hillier & E. Rooksby (Eds), *Habitus: A sense of place* (2nd ed., pp. 43–52). London, UK: Routledge.

Bourdieu, P., & Eagleton, T. (1994). Doxa and common life: An interview. In S. Zizek (Ed.), *Mapping ideology* (pp. 265–77). London, UK: Verso.

Chappell, R. (2014). *Social Welfare in Canadian Society* (5th edn). Toronto, Canada: Nelson Educational.

Chen, S., & Ravallion, M. (2004). How have the world's poorest fared since the early 1980s? *The World Bank Research Observer, 19*(2), 141–69. doi:10.1093/wbro/lkh020

Cheung, R. (2016, September 17). How Hong Kong's hostile architecture hurts city's homeless and poor. *South China Morning Post (online)*. Retrieved from http://www.scmp.com/lifestyle/article/2019619/how-hong-kongs-hostile-architecture-hurts-citys-homeless-and-poor

Cooper, V. (2016). No fixed abode: The continuum of policing and incarcerating the homeless. *Policing: A journal of policy and practice, 11*(1), 1–10. doi:10.1093/police/paw015

Copp, J.H. (1970). Poverty and our social order: Implications and reservations. *American Journal of Agricultural Economics, 52*(5), 736–44.

Davies, W. (2016). The new neoliberalism. *New Left Review 101*(September/October), 121–34.

Friend, C. (2017). Social Contract Theory. In J. Fieser & B. Dowden (Eds), *The internet encyclopedia of philosophy: A peer-reviewed academic resource*. Retrieved from http://www.iep.utm.edu/soc-cont/

Galea, S., Tracy, M., Hoggatt, K.J., DiMaggio, C., & Karpati, A. (2011). Estimated deaths attributable to social factors in the United States. *American Journal of Public Health, 101*(8), 1456–65. doi:10.2105/AJPH.2010.300086

Garrett, P.M. (2007). The relevance of Bourdieu for social work: A reflection on obstacles and omissions. *Journal of Social Work, 7*(3), 355–79. doi:10.1177/1468017307084076

Goldsmith, B. (2016, April 4). Just 10 percent of world military spending could knock off poverty: Think tank. *Reuters*.Retrievedfromhttp://www.reuters.com/article/us-global-military-goals-idUSKCN0X12EQ

Hanesworth, C. (2017). Neoliberal influences on American higher education and the consequences for social work programmes. *Critical and Radical Social Work, 5*(1), 41–57. doi:10.1332/204986017X14835298292776

Harvey, D. (2007). *A brief history of neoliberalism*. Oxford, UK: Oxford University Press.

Hechter, M., & Horne, C. (Eds). (2009). *Theories of social order: A reader* (2nd edn). Stanford, CA: Stanford University Press.

Hopkin, M. (2004). Sumatran quake sped up Earth's rotation. *Nature: International Weekly Journal of Science*. Retrieved from http://www.nature.com/news/2004/041229/full/news041229-6.html

Jeppesen, S. (2009). From the "war on poverty" to the "war on the poor": Knowledge, power and subject positions in anti-poverty discourses. *Canadian Journal of Communication, 34*(3), 487–508.

Kent, G. (2011). *Ending hunger worldwide*. New York, NY: Routledge.

Kent, G. (2016). *Caring about hunger*. Sparsnäs, Sweeden: George Kent and Irene Publishing.

Klein, N. (2007). *The shock doctrine: The rise of disaster capitalism*. New York, NY: Metropolitan Books, Henry Holt and Company.

Lewis, O. (1969). Culture of Poverty. In D. P. Moynihan (Ed.), *On understanding poverty: Perspectives from the social sciences* (pp. 187–220). New York, NY: Basic Books.

Lus, S. (2014, July 2). Homeless benches in Vancouver draw international attention. *CBC News*. Retrieved from http://www.cbc.ca/news/canada/british-columbia/homeless-benches-in-vancouver-draw-international-attention-1.2692269

Marx, K., & Engels, F. (2002). *The communist manifesto*. London, UK: Penguin Classics.

McGrath, L., Walker, C., & Jones, C. (2016). Psychologists against austerity: Mobilising psychology for social change. *Critical and Radical Social Work, 4*(3), 409–13. doi:10.1332/204986016x14721364317537

McLellan, D. (Ed.). (2000). *Karl Marx: Selected writings* (2nd edn). New York, NY: Oxford University Press.

Monbiot, G. (2016, April 15). Neoliberalism – The ideology at the root of all our problems. *The Guardian*. Retrieved from http://www.theguardian.com/books/2016/apr/15/neoliberalism-ideology-problem-george-monbiot

Moskowitz, D., Vittinghoff, E., & Schmidt, L. (2013). Reconsidering the effects of poverty and social support on health: A 5-year longitudinal test of the stress-buffering hypothesis. *Journal of Urban Health, 90*(1), 175–84. doi:10.1007/s11524-012-9757-8

Mullaly, B. (2010). *Challenging oppression and confronting privilege: A critical social work approach*. (2nd edn). Toronto, Canada: Oxford University Press.

O'Grady, M.A. (2016, October 16). The curse of charity in Haiti: Sustained foreign aid, such as rice, drives many local producers out of business. *The Wall Street Journal*. Retrieved from http://www.wsj.com/articles/the-curse-of-charity-in-haiti-1476653140

Orr, D. (2013, June 8). Neoliberalism has spawned a financial elite who hold governments to ransom. *The Guardian*. Retrieved from http://www.theguardian.com/commentisfree/2013/jun/08/neoliberalism-financial-elite-governments-ransom

Oxfam America. (2016, April 16). *Broken at the top: How America's dysfunctional tax system costs billions in corporate tax dodging*. Retrieved from https://www.oxfamamerica.org/static/media/files/Broken_at_the_Top_4.14.2016.pdf

Oxfam International. (2013, January 19). Annual income of richest 100 people enough to end global poverty four times over. Retrieved from http://www.oxfam.org/en/pressroom/pressreleases/2013-01-19/annual-income-richest-100-people-enough-end-global-poverty-four

Petty, J. (2016). The London spikes controversy: Homelessness, urban securitisation and the question of "hostile architecture." *International Journal for Crime, Justice and Social Democracy 5*(1), 67–81. doi:10.5204/ijcjsd.v5i1.286

Calhoun, C., Li Puma, E., & Postone, M. (1993). Introduction: Bourdieu and social theory. In M. Postone, E. LiPuma, & C. Calhoun (Eds), *Bourdieu: Critical perspectives* (pp. 1–13). Chicago, IL: University of Chicago Press.

Procacci, G. (2007). Genealogies of poverty: From inclusion towards exclusion. *Development and Psychopathology, 50*(2), 26–30. doi:10.1057/palgrave.development.1100383

Qwul'sih'yah'maht [Robina Thomas], & Kundouqk [Jacquie Green]. (2009). Children in the centre: Indigenous perspectives on anti-oppressive child welfare practice. In S. Strega & S.A. Esquao [Jeannine Carriere] (Eds), *Walking this path together: Anti-racist and anti-oppressive child welfare practice* (2nd ed., pp. 24–44). Halifax, Canada: Fernwood.

Raphael, D., & Bryant, T. (2014, November 23). Income inequality is killing thousands of Canadians every year. *Toronto Star*. Retrieved from http://www.thestar.com/opinion/commentary/2014/11/23/income_inequality_is_killing_thousands_of_canadians_every_year.html

Rice, A., & Haynes, K. (2005). *Post-tsunami reconstruction and tourism: A second disaster?* Retrieved from http://www.tourismconcern.org.uk/wp-content/uploads/2014/12/Post-tsunami-reconstruction-and-tourism-a-second-disaster.pdf

Rist, R. (2016). Introduction. In R. C. Rist, F. P. Martin, & A. M. Fernandez (Eds), *Poverty, inequality and evaluation: Changing perspectives* (pp. 1–5). Washington, DC: International Bank for Reconstruction and Development/The World Bank.

Rousseau, J.J. (1762/2016). *The social contract and discourses* (G. D. H. Cole, Trans.). Woodstock, Canada: Devoted Publishing.

Schultz, D. (2017). Public administration in the age of Trump. *Journal of Public Affairs Education, 23*(1), 557–62.

Simpson, M. (2006). *Rousseau's theory of freedom*. London, UK: Continuum.

Sinervo, A. (2015). Brokering aid through tourism: The contradictory roles of volunteer coordinators in Cusco, Peru. *Tourist Studies, 15*(2), 156–74. doi:10.1177/1468797614563434

Small, M.L., Harding, D.J., & Lamont, M. (2010). Reconsidering culture and poverty. *ANNALS of the American Academy of Political and Social Science, 629*(1), 6–27. doi:10.1177/0002716210362077

Smith, A. (1982). *The wealth of nations: Books I–III edited with an introduction and notes by Andrew Skinner*. London, UK: Penguin Books.

Springer, S., Birch, K., & MacLeavy, J. (2016). An introduction to neoliberalism. In S. Springer, K. Birch, & J. MacLeavy (Eds), *The handbook of neoliberalism* (pp. 1–14). New York, NY: Routledge.

Swartz, D. (1997). *Culture & power: The sociology of Pierre Bourdieu*. Chicago, IL: The University of Chicago Press.

Swartz, D.L. (2007). Recasting power in its third dimension: Review of Steven Lukes' Power: A radical view. *Theory and Society, 36*(1), 103–9. doi:10.1007/s11186-006-9018-5

Telford, J., & Cosgrave, J. (2007). The international humanitarian system and the 2004 Indian Ocean earthquake and tsunamis. *Disasters, 31*(1), 1–28. doi:10.1111/j.1467-7717.2007.00337.x

Thomson, P. (2014). Field. In M. Grenfell (Ed.), *Pierre Bourdieu: Key concepts* (2nd ed., pp. 65-81). New York, NY: Routledge.

Tjepkema, M., Wilkins, R., & Long, A. (2013). *Cause-specific mortality by income adequacy in Canada: A 16-year follow-up study*. Retrieved from http://www.statcan.gc.ca/pub/82-003-x/2013007/article/11852-eng.htm

United Nations. (1995). World summit for social development, Copenhagen, 6–12 March 1995: president Francois Mitterrand of France addresses the summit meeting.

Retrieved from https://www.un.org/development/desa/dspd/world-summit-for-social-development-1995.html

United Nations. (2015). We can end poverty: Millennium development goals and beyond 2015. Retrieved from http://www.un.org/millenniumgoals/

Venugopal, R. (2015). Neoliberalism as concept. *Economy and Society, 44*(2), 165–87. doi:10.1080/03085147.2015.1013356

Wacquant, L.J.D. (1987). Symbolic violence and the making of the French agriculturalist: An enquiry into Pierre Bourdieu's sociology. *Journal of Sociology, 23*(1), 65–88. doi:10.1177/144078338702300105

Wacquant, L.J.D. (1989). Towards a reflexive sociology: A workshop with Pierre Bourdieu. *Sociological Theory, 7*(1), 26–63. doi:10.2307/202061

Younge, G. (2014, June 2). Who's in control—Nation states or global corporations? *The Guardian.* Retrieved from http://www.theguardian.com/commentisfree/2014/jun/02/control-nation-states-corporations-autonomy-neoliberalism

# 9 Doing Anti-Oppression: The Social Work Dream

## In this chapter you will learn:

- What anti-oppression is and where it came from
- The differences and similarities between anti-racism and anti-oppression
- The limitations and possibilities of anti-racism and anti-oppression
- How there has always been oppression and anti-oppression
- Why social work cannot achieve anti-oppression

## Introduction

When June first met Gary in 1995, he was delivering a series of anti-racist training workshops to an Ontario Children's Aid Society. June decided to sit in. She was curious to see what the training entailed and how it related to her own emerging work on anti-oppression.

After the training, June thought Gary's workshop was relatively good. Indeed, she noted that Gary even understood that anti-racism was not just concerned with race, but other sites of difference and related isms too. At the same time June also recognized that Gary was out of date, and she told him so. "The trend," she said, "is to talk about anti-oppression, not anti-racism." June told Gary that he needed to "get with the times."

Back then Gary had never heard of anti-oppression. He began to panic, thinking that he had lost touch with what was important. June told Gary not to worry, because she would teach him the key anti-oppression concepts and ideas, and she did.

The next time Gary delivered training, June sat in again to see how he had integrated the lessons. June was pleased to see that Gary had revised his work, but also surprised to see that all he had done was replace the "anti-racism" title on some of his overhead slides with the term "anti-oppression." Gary still talked about anti-racism, he taught the participants to do the exact same anti-racism work, but now placed it within an overarching framework of anti-oppression.

June smiled; this worked perfectly. By the end of this chapter you will understand why this change worked, what the benefits of making this change were, what the limitations were, and ways to avoid common pitfalls and mistakes in taking up both anti-racism and anti-oppression.

## What Is Anti-Oppression?

For many, doing anti-oppression is the social work dream, because it is far better to address the root causes of problems than simply try to alleviate the symptoms. Social work, however, did not invent anti-oppression. Anti-oppression is as old as oppression itself. Of course it was not always called anti-oppression; it was just called doing what was right, and entire societies tried to do it. Indeed, Indigenous traditions that go back hundreds and perhaps thousands of years speak of teachers and peacemakers who developed ways for people to live in harmony together with a fair social system (Alfred, 1999; Porter, 2008).

### Key Concept

Social work did not invent anti-oppression. Anti-oppression is as old as oppression itself. Of course it was not always called anti-oppression; it was just called doing what was right, and entire societies tried to do it.

A number of ancient societies also attempted to prevent the social order from promoting some at the expense of others. For instance, almost four thousand years ago in what is now Iraq, laws existed to protect widows, children, and women in cases of divorce (Hammurabi, 1750 BCE/1971). In ancient Israel, laws forbade landowners from harvesting everything that their fields produced; they had to leave some harvest for the poor to gather

**Figure 9.1** Ancient anti-oppression

(Simkins, 2017). As well, there were laws that prevented monopolies or other systems of exploitation from being developed. For instance in some ancient societies, in the year of jubilee, which occurred every 50 years, all debts were forgiven and all lands were returned to their original communities (Simkins, 2017).

The law of jubilee and similar practices were based on an understanding of the way oppression operates; if a community lost access to its land through bad luck, bad judgment, bad politics, or some other calamity, whoever gained ownership of that land could exploit the community by owning the means of production. The jubilee recognized that once inequality takes hold, it produces more inequality, and those who gain from this process can quickly own everything while everyone else has next to nothing. The jubilee stopped how far this type of inequity could go. Of course, similarly to today, there were also laws that were used to oppress, but the existence of laws to achieve equity shows that the work of seeking social justice is not new.

## Exercise 9.1

### Your Own Traditions

If possible, undertake this exercise in groups. Think about and name a religious, spiritual, cultural, or philosophical tradition that influences you and undertake the following.

1.  Say how old that tradition is. (If you do not know, try to find out the answer).
2.  Look at the history of that tradition, and try to find statements or principles that align with anti-oppression.
3.  Say what that tradition means to you, and how it shapes your approach to social justice and anti-oppression.
4.  If you have no tradition that informs your interest in social justice, think about where your interest in social justice comes from and share this.

## Anti-Oppression—Social Work's Way of Seeking Social Justice

What we now call anti-oppression is one of the ways social work seeks to promote social justice. As stated in Chapter 1, anti-oppression is an umbrella term that brings together a number of social justice theories and approaches that oppose oppression (Baines, 2017). Because anti-oppression is not a theory but simply an umbrella for theories and perspectives, anti-oppression in itself does not help workers understand oppression or know what to do about it. To understand oppression and to do something about it one has to look at the theories and perspectives under the umbrella, not the umbrella itself.

The theories that inform anti-oppression are not prescriptive—none of them tell workers what to do. Workers have to figure this out themselves through a deep understanding of the theories under the umbrella. Workers also have to be aware of context because, as mentioned in Chapter 1, the influence of an array of shifting interwoven social variables can cause what is anti-oppressive one moment to be oppressive the next.

Even if one is familiar with the full range of theories and perspectives under the anti-oppression umbrella, this can never be sufficient to carry out any form of social work. Service users do not usually come to social workers asking for help resolving oppression, nor do social workers arrive at service users' doors to resolve oppression. The primary focus of social work is always something else.

Although anti-oppression is never our primary focus, it needs to always be a focus that shapes the primary thing we do. Social workers engage with service users for primary reasons such as a child being hurt or neglected, someone being in a violent relationship, a parent feeling unable to manage their children, someone trying to overcome an addiction, someone needing to be discharged from hospital but having no supports to go home, someone having relationship challenges, and so on. We have no mandate from the state, from agencies, or the service users themselves to do anything other than address the issues that brought us to the service user's door. If we go in with an agenda to use service users' troubles to lever the social change we desire, we would be exploiting their struggles to further our own social or political agenda. Of course we might argue that the change we have in mind would be "good for them," but isn't this exactly what social workers said to Indigenous communities when we were taking their children away to residential schools or into state care in the Sixties Scoop? Social workers need to be careful not to impose on service users their own ideas of what is good or just.

## Key Concept

Do not use service users' troubles to lever the social change you desire, because this exploits service user troubles to further your own political agenda. Social workers need to be careful not to impose their own ideas of what is good or just on those they serve.

## All Social Work, Including Anti-Oppression, Starts with Immediate Need

Social work needs to begin by addressing the immediate troubles people ask for help with. Social work does this by drawing on theories and approaches like task-centred practice, brief solution-focused therapy, family group conferencing, community development, and so on. Ideally, we discuss a proposed approach with the service users or communities involved and jointly decide the way to proceed. In this process our expertise is helping to facilitate dialogue and identifying and competently implementing the agreed-on approach (Payne, 2015). If the help needed is not in the scope of our practice or is outside our capabilities, we refer the service user to someone else who can help.

In this book we do not cover any of the approaches or helping theories mentioned above. You will learn these in other social work texts. Such practical helping theory and practice, along with service user's and community's own ideas about what helps, will be the foundation of your work. Anti-oppression comes in by adding another dimension to the conversations you have with service users and communities about the troubles and issues they are asking for help with.

## Key Concept

As an anti-oppressive social worker, you can use almost any form of practice. What makes your work anti-oppressive is having conversations with service users about the way various forms of oppression may be causing or compounding their troubles, and considering with service users what can be done about this.

## Integrating an Anti-Oppressive Perspective into Social Work

Anti-oppression causes us to ask critical questions about the way various forms of oppression may be shaping the trouble that is causing the need for social work help. For instance, if a parent is hurting their child or failing to meet their child's needs to the extent that it has become a child protection issue, there are all types of theories that can be used to analyze what is occurring and provide help for the parent to turn this situation around. But what if the problem is caused or compounded by the frustration and stress of living in poverty, or perhaps at times having no money to meet the child's physical needs? Some form of crisis intervention, perhaps anger management and child management, and maybe even some budgeting and financial assistance, may give the parent exactly what they need to manage over the next few days and coming weeks. But these coping interventions do not address the long-term problem and might even cause the parent to blame themselves for not being good enough as a parent. This does not mean we do not deliver these coping interventions. The parent may need these interventions to manage today and tomorrow, but it is here that anti-oppression comes in. We refuse to label this parent as the problem, but instead identify the inequalities that are treading the parent down as the problem. Our focus shifts to not only helping the parent cope, but partnering with the parent (and perhaps other parents in the same position) to look for remedies to these oppressive underlying causes.

Anti-oppression is not only initiated by the circumstances in individual cases, but can also be initiated as a result of the patterns we see in our work and the outcomes it produces.

In several chapters we have spoken of discerning oppression through patterns, or through the "footprint" oppression leaves behind. For instance, if you notice that it is primarily the children of parents living in poverty that you and your agency are bringing into care, or if you notice disproportionate numbers of Black and Indigenous children in care, this ought to alert you to the fact that there is something awfully wrong with the service you are delivering. Of course this "awfully wrong" service is exactly what has occurred across Canada with Indigenous children (Blackstock, 2009; Trocme, Knoke, & Blackstock, 2004) and in Ontario with Black children (Contenta, Monsebraaten, & Rankin, 2014a, 2014b; Rankin, 2014).

## Sometimes Getting Social Work to Do Anti-Oppression Requires a Struggle

Data about disproportionate numbers of Indigenous children in care should have triggered an immediate anti-oppressive social work response. Sadly no effective anti-oppressive response occurred. Blackstock points out that anti-oppressive social work did nothing to prevent the overrepresentation of First Nations children in care (Blackstock, 2009). As well, Children's Aid Societies did not release data about Black children being over-represented in care. Our attempts to ascertain whether such data existed and to gain access to it consistently failed. It took a freedom of information request by the *Toronto Star* to discover that the data existed. Once published, the footprint of oppression that child welfare left on Black families and communities was seen, and it became obvious to everyone that something was awfully wrong. Of course Black families and communities knew something was wrong all along but, denied the data to prove it, they could do little to address the issue.

Once oppression is recognized, anti-oppression does not tell us what to do about it. Some readers may find this frustrating. We have spent considerable time in previous chapters exploring the theories under the anti-oppression umbrella, but none of these "tell" social workers what to do. Instead, these theories provide the basis from which social workers can unravel and make sense of what is occurring, and then in partnership with the communities involved formulate an anti-oppressive response for that particular moment (or interrelated moments). Consequently, when Ontario data about Black children being over-represented in care came to light, there was no formula that told anyone what to do about it. As a result, agencies and workers had to invent a plan. Of course they drew on other jurisdictions that had recognized and addressed this problem before, but they had to customize a response to fit Canada, and more specifically Ontario. This work is an ongoing project, but the initial work and plan they devised are reproduced in the "One Vision One Voice" documents (OACAS, 2016a, 2016b). Though late in coming, we personally believe that the One Vision One Voice documents are a good example of the way anti-oppression translates into practice.

## Exercise 9.2

### Anti-Oppression in Child Welfare

If possible, undertake this exercise in groups.

Examine Ontario Association of Children's Aid Societies (OACAS) "One Vision One Voice" Website at http://www.oacas.org/what-we-do/government-and-stakeholder-relations/one-vision-one-voice/.

Review the One Vision One Voice Reports (available for download at the above site). Consider the following questions:

1. What problems does the report identify?
2. What strategy has been developed to address the problems?
3. Who developed the strategy?
4. What part has research played in defining the problem and developing the strategy?
5. Which theories and ideas expressed previously in this book resonate for you when you read the reports?
6. What strengths and limitations do you see in these reports and plan?
7. Do you see One Vision One Voice as an anti-oppressive initiative, an anti-racism initiative, an initiative against anti-Black racism (i.e., an initiative that opposes racism against Black people), or all of these?
8. Explore the reasons for your answers.

## Naming Anti-Oppression, Anti-Racism, and Initiatives against Anti-Black Racism

In the exercise above, did you view the One Vision One Voice initiative as opposing oppression, racism, or anti-Black racism? If you saw it as all of these, then you are conceptualizing anti-oppression, anti-racism, and initiatives against anti-Black racism in a similar way to us. Anti-oppression is an umbrella term, anti-racism falls under that umbrella and addresses a wide range of racisms, and initiatives that focus on opposing anti-Black racism also fall under that umbrella. We would, however, lean toward referring to One Vision One Voice as an initiative against anti-Black racism because anti-Black racism is the primary form of oppression being addressed by One Vision One Voice.

As well as using anti-oppression as an umbrella term, the term "anti-racism" can be used as an umbrella term too. The anti-racism approach June and Gary had been using focused on the same objectives as today's anti-oppression. Anti-racism not only addressed anti-Black racism, it also addressed sexism and other forms of oppression (Dei, 1996;

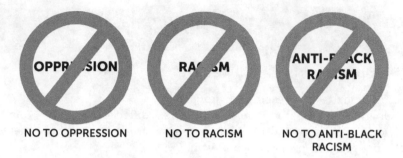

NO TO OPPRESSION    NO TO RACISM    NO TO ANTI-BLACK RACISM

**Figure 9.2** Opposing oppression, racism, and anti-Black racism

Hall, 1992; Yee & Dumbrill, 2016). Anti-racism, at least the way we understand it, has never simply been about race. For instance, the well-known race scholar Paul Gilroy centred his work on racism, but he saw racism as inextricably linked to other forms of oppression such as class and colonization (Gilroy, 1987, 1990).

Gilroy's anti-racism scholarship emerged from his work with another well-known race scholar, Stuart Hall, in their work in the Centre for Contemporary Cultural Studies (CCCS) at the University of Birmingham (1982). The CCCS brought together an analysis of race, class, gender, and other variables that went on to inform British and Canadian anti-racism.

## The Influence of the CCCS on Anti-Racism

Hall, Gilroy, and other scholars at the Birmingham CCCS also gave birth to what has become the global discipline of Cultural Studies (University of Birmingham, 2017), which works to understand today's society by merging sociology, politics, anthropology, history, and literary criticism, etc. Given the broad scholarship of CCCS, although their scholarship on race provided a foundation for anti-racism, this anti-racism was contextualized in a broad critical understanding of how society operates, and as such the anti-racism work it generated considered much more than race. In fact, the CCCS was not only a place of critical thought, but was also a place that embodied a new way of doing scholarship and conceptualizing the social order. Within CCCS, "conventional boundaries between teachers and students were intentionally broken down at the Centre, creating a democratic approach to learning that was a training ground for several noted public intellectuals who produced numerous foundational texts" (University of Birmingham, 2017). We contend that the way the CCCS connected scholarship, thinking, and addressing oppression (inside and outside its own institution) provides a model that Canadian social workers and social work schools may want to consider.

## The Genealogy of Our Anti-Racism and Anti-Oppression Work

When Gary came to Canada from the UK, he engaged in anti-racism using what he learned in the British context. June also tapped into this same **intellectual genealogy** (the scholarly tradition and ideas that inform one's work) by tracing the influence of Canadian anti-racism back to the CCCS, and studying at the University of Birmingham, Department of Cultural Studies and Sociology as a part of her PhD during the 1990s. (At that time the CCCS was merged with this department.)

Once June returned to Canada, as told in the story at the start of this chapter, she realized that Gary's use of anti-racism as an umbrella term for multiple oppressions was running into trouble. People were not grasping how the entry point of race leads to an understanding of how Whiteness and White supremacy underwrite multiple forms of oppression in society (as explained in Chapter 4). In other words, in a workshop context, it was hard to make the concept of "anti-racism" work as an umbrella concept, because people found it difficult to move past the entry point of race to grasp the interconnected-ness of other forms of oppression. As a result, a form of intersectional failure (described in Chapters 5 and 8) was occurring, with people failing to grasp multiple oppressions and the way they often combine.

One cannot blame workshop participants for this failure; they already had a series of complex social work practice theories that they had to know and use to undertake their work. Asking them to learn an array of additional theories that explained why "racism" also means sexism, sanism, ageism, and an array of other oppressions during a workshop was expecting a bit much. At a theoretical level, anti-racism may be the perfect entry point to understand multiple forms of oppression, but we acknowledge that this involves tricky theoretical and intellectual work. Is it realistic in the context of a short workshop in the field to expect participants to make these theoretical connections, especially in organiza-tions where conceptual energy needs to focus on action rather than theoretical analysis? Of course theory and practice are inseparable, but it was clear that in the field a much more direct route from theory to practice was needed. That route was provided by the term "anti-oppression," which right from the start makes it clear that the practice opposes all oppression, not just racism.

Although Gary changed the title of his work to "anti-oppression," as described in the story at the start of this chapter, the exact same "anti-racism" content was used as before. The anti-racism theoretical underpinnings and explanations of the work remained the same, but the small linguistic shift to "anti-oppression" was a constant reminder to participants that talk of race and racism was an entry point to understand multiple oppressions.

## A Shift in the Field from Anti-Racism to Anti-Oppression

Aside from our pragmatic adoption of anti-oppression as an umbrella term, there was a shift in the field away from anti-racism and toward anti-oppression for other reasons. This shift also influenced our decision to adopt anti-oppression. To understand these shifts, and how they influenced social justice work in Canada, we need to look at the UK, where they began.

During the 1970s and 1980s, anti-racism made significant gains in the UK with many jurisdictions adopting anti-racism policies and equal opportunity hiring processes. In 1984 the Greater London Council (GLC) declared an anti-racism year (McLaughlin, 2005). In this period the controlling body of social work education in the UK, the Central Council for Education and Training in Social Work (CCETSW), required all social workers to be trained in anti-racism (CCETSW, 1991; Pierson, 2011). Despite this progress, by the 1990s anti-racism was all but dead—killed by a political backlash. Anti-racism was declared a failure and written out of the social work curriculum (Macey & Moxon, 1996).

We are not sure that anti-racism was a failure. Perhaps it was too much of a success—it threatened White supremacy so much that it was shut down by a racist backlash. We are not the first to believe that racism drove the shift away from anti-racism to anti-oppression. The backlash occurred at the very time Margaret Thatcher's government adopted neo-liberal principles with attempts to dismantle the welfare state and equity initiatives. Indeed, the backlash was exactly what Gilroy and others expected and referred to as the "Empire Striking Back" (Centre for Contemporary Cultural Studies, 1982). In other words, because racism is rooted in imperialism (as noted in Chapter 2), as soon as anti-racism or any other social justice approach starts to become effective, one can expect those who benefit from imperialism to create a backlash that either stops or waters down anti-racist or social justice initiatives.

## Key Concept

Once your anti-racism or anti-oppressive work starts to be successful, expect a backlash. Many of those who benefit from Whiteness and White supremacy, or any other form of dominance, will try to shut down anything that threatens their dominance. Consequently, make sure you get as much public buy-in for your work as possible because that makes it harder for it to be shut down.

The adoption of anti-oppression in Canada may have watered down anti-racism here too. Sakamoto & Pitner (2005) cite a number of arguments that suggest that in Canadian social work the language of anti-oppression "waters down the nature of oppression and privilege" (p. 444). Pon, Giwa, and Razack (2016) suggest that anti-oppression emerged in Canada in part to offer "White social work professors and practitioners relief from difficult conversations about racism" (p. 45). We are not entirely convinced that this is the case—we do not see how one can teach anti-oppression effectively without having difficult conversations about racism—but we concede that the term "anti-oppression" might give an instructor an excuse to ignore racism if they wanted to. So we concede that, for some, the shift from anti-racism to anti-oppression might represent a watering down of anti-racism.

## Why We Remain Committed to Anti-Oppression

We had mixed feelings about taking up anti-oppression given the way that it may have emerged as a reaction to anti-racism. We wondered, should we revert back to anti-racism and resist anti-oppression? Or should we use the emergence of anti-oppression as an opportunity to engage a much larger proportion of the population in social justice work? In other words, could we use anti-oppression to even more clearly explain anti-racism and also how it intersects with other oppressions? We chose to take up anti-oppression and gained the benefit of the broader umbrella nature of the term "anti-oppression," but we stubbornly carried on doing the exact same anti-racist work under this new umbrella. This is seen in the story of the training that Gary was doing in the 1990s, and in the chapters of this book, where we ground our anti-oppression work in a thorough detailed analysis of racism and colonization, through which we uncompromisingly uncover imperialist and White supremacist foundations of what we, along with Gilroy and others, call "the empire."

Although we sought to defeat the empire by taking up anti-racism work under a new name (anti-oppression), we also needed to critically reflect on what was going wrong with anti-racism, lest a similar backlash attempt to eliminate or water down anti-oppression too. Indeed, Williams (1999) cautioned that any failings of anti-racist theory would ultimately remain with anti-oppression—anti-oppression might fail in the same way anti-racism did. We have to stop these failings because, as any Star Wars movie fan knows, the way to defeat an empire is not to just survive their attack, but to learn an empire's strategy and outwit them the next time around. So what went wrong with anti-racism and how can one make sure this does not go wrong with anti-oppression?

# What Was Wrong with Anti-Racism, and What Is Wrong with Anti-Oppression

What caused the downfall of anti-racism in British social work in the 1980s and 1990s continues to be discussed (Humphries, 1997; Pierson, 2011; Singh, 2013). To guard against a similar downfall in anti-oppression, we detail a number of mistakes that were said to have been made by anti-racism, and we consider how to avoid these mistakes when doing anti-oppression. These mistakes include:

- Theoretical inadequacy
- All talk, no change
- Ideological dogma and the banishment of dialogue
- Anti-racism as a party political divide
- An agenda of total transformation
- The reduction of everything into binaries
- Cherry-picking oppressions
- Failure to understand that we are the system

## Theoretical Inadequacy

Anti-racist social work was said to be ". . . theoretically inadequate, being informed by neither sociological, political nor economic theory or research on racism" (Macey & Moxon, 1996, p. 297). This claim is a little puzzling, because as shown in previous chapters, anti-racism is supported by robust theory and research. The criticism of theoretical inadequacy may have arisen because CCETSW never provided a definition of anti-racism in the education it set out for social workers (Humphries, 1997). The criticism may also have arisen by social work education failing to adequately explain and connect theory to practice.

Social work is primarily a doing discipline, not a theorizing discipline. Of course, as we demonstrated in Chapter 2, all doing rests on theory and thinking, so theory is crucial. But sometimes the focus on doing is lost in social work education. We have noticed, particularly in Canada, that the social work academy has become increasingly preoccupied with the theoretical and ideological at the expense of the practical. Indeed, our academic careers hinge on the extent to which our work is disseminated and cited in high-end academic journals read by other academics. The impact our work has on the people actually doing social work in the field or on the way service is delivered counts for little in evaluating our performance. Our progress in our careers requires multiple references from professors about the way our work makes academics think, but nothing from those who do social work, or those who receive it, about the way our work shapes how people think and act in the field.

It is hard to say why British anti-racism was considered theoretically inadequate. We sometimes wonder if it was perfectly adequate, but those in power simply refused to acknowledge the truths it conveyed. What is clear, however, is that there was a problem, because many social workers did not know how to turn the ideas of anti-racism into practice (Humphries, 1997). With workers unclear how to operationalize anti-racism, and powerful forces in society resisting it, no wonder it failed once workers were outside the classroom.

We see the same danger in anti-oppression, with students and workers complaining that they do not know how to operationalize anti-oppression (Ross, 2017). It is not just academic work on anti-oppression that fails to translate to the world of practice, but much of what occurs in the academy fails to make the grade in the field (Staniforth, Fouché, & O'Brien, 2011). There appears to be an academic/practice divide where what is learned in social work schools is experienced by the field "at best, as an intellectual curiosity and, at worst, as authoritarian and esoteric" (Healy, 2001). The esoteric nature of work in the academy is being set straight by a number of authors who are increasingly emphasizing the "doing" part of anti-oppression (see for instance Al-Krenawi, Graham, & Habibov, 2016; Baines, 2017; Cocker & Hafford-Letchfield, 2014; Morgaine & Capous-Desyllas, 2015; Mullaly & West, 2018; Esquao & Strega, 2015; Wehbi & Parada, 2017). We suggest that more work of this nature is needed.

In addition to academics focusing on the "doing" of social work, we suggest that, to fully bridge the academic-practice divide, more research and writing partnerships are needed between academics, practitioners, and service users. Indeed, practitioners say that they do not trust social work scholarship that is purely academic; they want to see more service user-led and practitioner-led research that is relevant to the work they are doing (Staniforth et al., 2011). We agree and we will address this issue in the next chapter, where we will argue that unless what social work does emerges from a dialogue among academics, practitioners, and service users, it will never be anti-oppressive.

## All Talk, No Change

Although anti-oppression education is not very good at translating theory into practice, it is very good at getting people to say the right things. As language and thought are inextricably linked, getting language right is a precursor to getting action right. This is also why theory is crucial. Action has to be built on sound theory, so anti-oppression has to be built on sound ideas. The problem arises when anti-oppression fails to move past ideas and talk.

Gary noticed this pattern of talk in the British anti-racism of the 1980s. Gary's first social work job was working for a large borough (municipality) in London's inner city that proudly proclaimed on its literature and letterheads that it was an "anti-racist organization." Gary noticed that most of the staff and almost all the senior management were White, and he also heard from racialized communities that they felt many of the agency practices were racist. Gary sent a memo to the Director suggesting that the claim of being anti-racist was "false advertising" and that the agency ought to hold off declaring itself "anti-racist" until it actually was. The Director replied saying that the organization claiming to be anti-racist did not imply that the organization had achieved anti-racism, only that it was in the process of doing so. We have no reason to doubt that the director and that organization was committed to anti-racist change, but our point is that calling something "anti-racist" does not make it so.

The same is so with anti-oppression in Canada. June and Gary have helped several Ontario Children's Aid Societies implement anti-oppressive plans and policies. None of this anti-oppression talk caused these agencies to release their race-based data on disproportionality even though we emphasized this was essential for anti-oppression to occur. When the data was eventually uncovered and published by the *Toronto Star*, Children's Aid Societies were harshly criticized for Black children being over-represented in care. These and other criticisms of child protection agencies caused Ontario Premier Kathleen Wynne to say that she was considering "blowing up" our Children's Aid Society mess (Cohn, 2015). Wynne went on to accuse the child protection system of being "a throwback to Dickensian times" and "bogged down in bureaucracy" (Cohn, 2015). Of course it was right to critique the child welfare system, but Wynne neglected to mention that her government and previous Ontario governments were largely responsible for the mess Wynn wanted to blow up.

The problem with oppression is that when it is discovered, everyone responsible wants to point the finger away from themselves and toward someone else. This is a natural response, because nobody wants to be considered a racist or an oppressor. The problem is that we are all implicated in oppression—but in a climate of blame and shame, if we critically examine and declare the way we are implicated, we leave ourselves open to attack. This problem can be made worse by anti-oppression and anti-racism training, because people learn the right things to say so that on the surface organizations appear to be no longer oppressive, but underneath nothing has changed. In a climate where everyone is looking to blame someone else for oppression, it is very hard to move beyond talk. If we are to turn talk into walk, we need to make it possible for people and organizations to be honest about the ways they are implicated in oppression. Only then can real change begin. (We will explore this issue more in Chapter 12.)

## Ideological Dogma and the Banishment of Dialogue

A further complaint about British anti-racism was that professors taught it as an ideology and belief system that students had to follow if they wanted to be social workers (Humphries, 1997). This approach shut down students' ability to ask questions and critique anti-racism for fear that professors would think them ideologically unsuitable for the profession.

It was impossible for students to go from this type of education into the field with a robust operational understanding of anti-racism, because students never got to interrogate it. Instead of being equipped with an ability to do anti-racism, they were equipped with a belief and value system that could not be questioned. Indeed, questioning this belief system was interpreted as a sign that a person had a human failing. It meant that the person was a racist and supported oppression.

We see the same happening with anti-oppression. A number of students have complained to June that they are never allowed to question or criticize what professors say about anti-oppression. On one occasion a racialized undergraduate social work student told Gary that she asked a professor how she might integrate anti-oppression with her Christian faith. The professor told the student that she needed to leave the school of social work, walk across the university parking lot to the Divinity School, and enrol there instead. Fortunately, the student did not follow this advice; she went on to obtain a PhD, and she is now a professor whose research focuses on anti-oppression and anti-racism. This student had to learn on her own the ways faith and anti-oppression can co-exist. We have both had conversations with Muslim, Jewish, Hindu, and other students whose faith drives their commitment to social justice. All of them recounted similar experiences about the way anti-oppressive teaching shut down the conversations they wanted to have about how to take up social justice in the faith communities to which they belong.

Social workers, and especially social work students, have to be free to dialogue, and to interrogate ideas. Presumably the academy teaches social work students things they do not already know. How can one learn if not allowed to question? When you take up anti-oppression, make sure that you ask questions and that you open up space for others to dialogue and ask questions, rather than shut down questions and dialogue.

## Key Concept

When you learn and take up anti-oppression, be sure to ask lots of questions, because getting answers to your questions will make your anti-oppression stronger. Also make sure that you open up space for others to dialogue and ask questions, rather than shut down questions and debate.

Of course questions can be used as a form of micro-aggression, or can be used to shut down the teaching of anti-oppression and disrupt everyone's learning. Consequently, instructors may have to sometimes challenge questions that are actually a form of microagression, but the instructor must do so in a way that does not reproduce oppression. As well, there can come a point where some students get bogged down and perpetually repeat the same questions. An instructor may need to move the class beyond such moments and find other ways to help those students who are stuck to grasp the ideas. At the same time, everyone has to be careful not to shut down curiosity and a genuine desire to learn, because open and honest dialogue without judgment is essential in anti-oppression.

### Anti-Racism as a Party Political Divide

The banishment of dialogue about anti-racism, anti-oppression, and other forms of social justice work comes in part from a political divide. When Jeffrey Greenwood, chair of CCETSW, wiped anti-racism from the British social work curriculum, he justified it by saying that social work had become bogged down in "politically correct nonsense" (Greenwood, 1993, cited in Macey & Moxon, 1996, p. 297). The British right-wing Tory government congratulated social work for their decision to abandon anti-racism, they said that they applauded "the triumph of 'common sense' over 'left-wing, politically correct ideology'" (Macey & Moxon, 1996, p. 298). This statement reveals how anti-racism got caught in the middle of a left–right party political struggle.

Anti-racism was stuck in an entirely polarized political struggle with Margaret Thatcher's Conservative party with a neo-liberal agenda on the hard right, and the British Labour Party, which had been increasingly influenced by what was seen to be a Trotskyist radical agenda, on the hard left (Stewart, 2016). In this polarized environment, Labour councils (on the left) were keen to implement anti-racism, and central government (on the right) was keen to shut it down. Dialogue between opposing views about anti-racism was impossible. The right shut down debate by saying that anti-racism and other social justice measures were "political correctness" created by a "loony left." At the same time, the left dismissed criticisms of anti-racism and other social justice measures as the rhetoric of right-wing racists. Dialogue between these opposing views was impossible. Each side dismissed the other without the possibility of even a conversation (McLaughlin, 2005).

Those on the right won this battle of ideologies; as mentioned above, anti-racism was written out of the social work curriculum (Pierson, 2011).

The lesson for Canada that we draw from these events is that it is a mistake to link anti-racism with a political party perspective, and we see this mistake happening with anti-oppression. If you doubt that this is occurring in anti-oppression, try declaring in an anti-oppression class that you vote conservative, and see how this works out for you. If we link anti-racism, anti-oppression, or any other social justice agenda to only ideas on the left, what happens to Black people, women, LGBTTIQQ2S people, people with disabilities, or others who face oppression and yet lean to the political right? Is it fair for social work to only work toward their liberation on our left leaning political terms? Of course we are unsure how one can achieve social justice from the right of the political spectrum, but we are keen to dialogue with oppressed people who do think that this is possible and to question their ideas. We do this because, rather than shut down dialogue between political opposites, we believe that it is important for anti-oppression to encourage the dialogue of opposing ideas. Indeed, according to Marx (as explained in Chapter 8), it is the interaction of opposites that brings revolutionary change.

We suggest that if you are only engaging with people about anti-oppression who hold the same political views as yours, you are not doing the type of anti-oppression work that stands a chance to create real change outside a classroom full of like-minded people. To bring real change one usually needs a broad consensus. Indeed, in the classroom, when you say that you want to work for the liberation of the oppressed, who are you referring to? Macey and Moxon (1996) raise this issue in relation to anti-racism. They ask, when anti-racists say they support Black perspectives and want Black people to have a voice, "which Black perspective" and "*whose* Black voice" are they referring to (p. 306)? If the only Black perspective they listen to is from Black people who agree with their own politics, they need to ask whether they are really promoting Black rights, or whether they are co-opting Black liberation struggles to promote their own political views.

Given the above, we contend that a mistake anti-oppression is in danger of making is to lock its work and fortune into one political party's ideology. If anti-oppression is to work, it has to include not only the voices of the oppressed who agree with our politics, but people of other political persuasions who also want to see the end of oppression.

## Key Concept

If you are only engaging in anti-oppression with people who have the exact same political views as yours, you are not really doing anti-oppression. Real anti-oppressive change requires action and consensus by a broader range of people than your like-minded friends. Make sure, therefore, that you are discussing oppression and ways to address it with people whose views are different from your own.

## An Agenda of Total Transformation

Other problems emerge from anti-oppression being linked exclusively to the politics of the left. Indeed, the solution to oppression is often seen as a "fundamental social transformation" (Mullaly, 2001, p. 316) that is invariably conceptualized by anti-oppressive scholars in the politics of the left (Baines, 2007; Mullaly, 2010). In this vision, the end of oppression is inextricably linked to the overthrow of neo-liberalism and the development of a new social order (Featherstone, Strauss, & MacKinnon, 2015). We have no problem with this vision; in fact in Chapter 8 we implicate the social order and neo-liberalism as primary culprits behind oppression. The problem is that it is a little difficult for the social worker in direct practice to overthrow the existing social order.

Although the overthrow of neo-liberalism and capitalism would be very nice, we do not see it occurring any time soon. We have no desire to water down anyone's radical vision, but in the current neo-liberal context we see little prospect of the revolutionary ideas of the left gaining enough political traction to bring fundamental social change. We consider it irresponsible for social work to develop a model for social justice that makes those on the societal margins wait for the political climate to be right for the type of revolution we think is needed to fix the world order. In fact, this overt revolutionary agenda may actually prevent any form of anti-oppression occurring, because we fail to engage many less radical people who might otherwise be committed to social justice. In addition, an agenda of total social transformation being a part of anti-oppression makes it especially difficult for those social workers working in government departments and agencies run by community boards to take up anti-oppression, because in these settings there is often less openness to radical ideas and almost no openness to a fundamental transformation of society.

Our approach relies less on revolution and more on pragmatics. We contend that the anti-oppressive imagination needs to be unlocked from solutions rooted only in left-leaning revolution, and needs to be linked to a broader spectrum of political possibilities. This un-locking does not mean we neglect critical theory. It does not mean that we think that the right has viable solutions to oppression, but keep in mind that we do not think that the left has all the ideas needed to achieve social justice either. We also suggest that in the current political climate, anti-oppression may suffer the same fate as British anti-racism in the 1980s and 1990s: if always overtly radical it will make itself politically untenable and will be wiped off the social work agenda.

**Figure 9.3** Waiting for revolution

## The Reduction of Everything into Binaries

Reducing something into binary opposite means seeing things as "good" or "bad" and nothing in-between. This occurred in anti-racism, with the oppressor and oppressed created as binaries. If a person was Black they were oppressed, if they were White they were an oppressor (Williams, 1999). We have seen this occur in both anti-racism and anti-oppression, with White people being seen only by their privilege, and Black people being seen only by their oppression. This process dehumanizes both Black and Whites and sets up a type of performativity where Black and White people are forced into prescribed roles.

These prescribed roles place Whites in a position where they participate in a ritual of confessing their privilege, which, as noted by Smith (2013), does not do anything to "dismantle the structures of domination that enabled their privilege" (p. 263). In this manner anti-racism begins and ends with Whites adopting the attitudes and words of contrition, and learning to use the language of anti-racism to show that they have been converted from bad to good White people. Within this performance, Black people are expected to perform the role of either a victim or an expert who speaks for all Black people (Keating, 2000). In anti-oppression, a slightly different form of performativity occurs in which White people have the hope of another form of salvation. Whites can remain contrite until they identify a form of oppression that they experience themselves, and they can then use this to force the confession and contrition of others.

The above process dehumanizes everyone, robs people of authenticity and agency, and oversimplifies the way oppression works. The entire process is uncomfortable for "the oppressor" and "the oppressed." It creates division and is not conducive to anti-racist or anti-oppressive change. Within anti-oppression it can create a type of competitive musical chairs, with people taking on alternating oppressor and oppressed roles. This might be a good thing if we could see how it means we are all implicated in oppression and nobody is "innocent." But the danger is to focus on these dichotomous moments and to only see who is most oppressed rather than see how the system works to make this so. We are not suggesting that one should refrain from examining one's own social locations. Self-locating is essential to both anti-racism and anti-oppression, but the purpose of locating oneself is to move from the individual to the systemic. If we do not see the process of locating oneself as connected to the systemic, we may misunderstand anti-oppression as the process of bringing individual people down rather than bringing systems of inequality down. The lesson here is to engage in the examination of one's social location, but to not forget why we are doing this. It is to recognize and do something about the systems of inequality that tread those in some locations down and lift others up.

Of course sometimes in both anti-racism and anti-oppression some people cannot even get through the process of analyzing social location to grasp the way oppression situates us. In these circumstances it is difficult for that person to move on and consider systemic issues. Someone unable to grasp that the world's playing field is uneven or that the game played upon it advantages some at the expense of others has more learning to do before they are ready to undertake competent social work. In these circumstances, however, we need to be careful that someone's apparent inability to learn about oppression does not result from our teaching about it in overly simplistic dehumanizing binary ways. We also need to be certain that this person really fails to understand. It is possible the person does understand the issues, and simply understands it differently or has a different analysis. We have to be particularly cautious on this point because another way binaries operate in anti-oppression is to paint everybody who disagrees with us, or anyone who does not see things the exact way we do, as an "oppressor." Such reaction shuts dialogue down, alienates those committed to anti-oppression from each other, and prevents people joining together to overthrow oppression.

## Key Concept

Don't assume everyone who disagrees with you disagrees with anti-oppression.

## Cherry-Picking Oppressions

One of the strengths of British anti-racism is that it made it difficult to avoid talking about racism. Few people like talking about racism, and many institutions are invested in denying its existence, so to situate anti-racism as the entry point for social justice means that one cannot avoid talking about racism.

Replacing anti-racism with anti-oppression creates a way of avoiding the issue of racism (Williams, 1999). We mentioned above that we do not understand how oppression can be addressed without talking about racism, but we concede that anti-oppression is so broad that someone could claim to be doing anti-oppression while completely ignoring forms of oppression they feel uncomfortable with. Someone could reframe anti-oppression to suit their own interests. Anti-oppression makes it easier for any one of us to "reframe clients' stories through our own positioned and preferred narratives" (Brown, 2012, p. 46).

There is of course nothing wrong with becoming an expert on one narrative or one way of looking at things. We need people to do this so that they can drill down into the specifics of single forms of oppression. At the same time, however, we need to be mindful of all forms of oppression, especially how they intersect, and we have to be careful that in addressing the oppression that concerns us the most we are not ignoring or making other oppressions worse.

In anti-oppression, alliances across multiple forms of difference are essential. It is not always easy to achieve alliances with people "who may or may not be like us." It is far easier to slip back from thinking across multiple differences to thinking in binaries or focusing on the single narrative we are familiar with. But coalitions are essential in anti-oppression, and this is the exact point raised by Black Lives Matter (http://www.blacklivesmatter.ca) regarding Toronto Pride (http://www.pridetoronto.com). In 2016 Black Lives Matter members halted the Toronto Pride Parade because "not all communities who participate in Pride are actually able to be free in that celebration" (Alexandria Williams cited in Battersby, 2016). Of particular concern was the contradiction of Pride organizers accepting police floats and booths at the Pride Parade whereas the presence of police is not a sign of safety to LGBTTIQQ2S members of the Black community and other communities (Paling, 2016). Black Lives Matter has drawn attention to police killings of members of the Black community and oppressive practices such as carding (Paling, 2016). Members of Black Lives Matter questioned why the Pride Parade allowed participation by the police in a celebration of LGBTTIQQ2S rights when Black members of LGBTTIQQ2S communities continue to be oppressed by the police. This challenge to Toronto Pride reminds us that none of us can be free unless we are all free—our freedom is all interconnected.

Desmond Tutu draws attention to our interconnectedness through the teaching of Ubuntu we discussed in Chapter 3 (Rankin, 2012; Rankin, Winsa, Bailey, & Ng, 2013; Warren, Tomaskovic-Devey, Smith, Zingraff, & Mason, 2006). Although Ubuntu is an African philosophy, Tutu presents it as a universal human truth, so we have no hesitation to share it as such. This teaching claims that a person can only be a person in relation to other people; we are only human through relationships with others (Tutu, 2011). Desmond Tutu explains, "We belong in the bundle of life [together], and I want you to be all that you can be, because that is the only way I can be all I can be. I need you, I *need* you to be you so that I can be me. And that is why when you dehumanize another, whether you like it or not, inexorably, you are yourself dehumanized" (Tutu, 2017).

Many religions take up this principle in the golden rule (discussed in Chapter 3), which is the idea that we must do for the Other what we would want to have done for us. One rendering of this story in the Christian tradition, not that Christians have always grasped and applied this principle, is told in the story of the Good Samaritan. In this story a Samaritan helps a Jewish priest, even though they are theologically, nationally, and politically opposed to each other. The entire point of this story is that our sibling is not only the person who is the same as us, but is also the person who is different. This lesson translates into anti-oppression perfectly. If we are interested in addressing oppression, and if we are a member of an oppressed group ourselves, of course we must use our experience of oppression to speak out about our own group. At the same time, however, even if we are oppressed as an "Other" ourselves, we must also ask who is the Other to me. We must ask who else is being oppressed here. We need to reach out to that person and group, form an alliance, and invest in their freedom too. This is important because their freedom is connected to yours, and yours to theirs.

## Failure to Understand That We Are the System

We want to draw attention to a final mistake. Instead of recognizing that we (as social workers and social work educators) are implicated in the system that oppresses, we sometimes see ourselves as blameless or righteous. This mistake occurred in the UK where councils (government agencies and municipalities) undertaking anti-racism began to clash with communities they served over their anti-racist agenda. Rather than revisit their methods, or question whether they might be oppressing those resisting in other ways, agencies blamed these clashes on the communities they served being racist (Humphries, 1997). When social workers, who are a part of mainstream government organizations, start to blame the communities they serve for a lack of progress in anti-racism or anti-oppression, one knows that social work has come off the rails. This social work institutional attitude amounts to the oppressor blaming the oppressed for their own oppression.

This mistake can occur in more subtle ways too. It is hard for social workers, especially when they have a strong personal commitment to anti-oppression, to see that once they work within a system they are implicated in oppression in a different way. This requires a shift in the way they understand and undertake anti-oppression work. We were recently in an organization where middle managers were unhappy with the way their organization dealt with an incident of racism. The managers met to decide what to do. One manager, a strong proponent of anti-oppression, suggested standing outside the organization with placards and making a lot of noise. We suggested that instead, perhaps it might be more appropriate to call all the decision makers together, review what had happened, and then devise ways for it to not happen that way the next time. The manager who had suggested placards and noise responded saying that her radical nature and anti-oppressive training made her much more comfortable attacking the institution from outside with placards and noise. We pointed out to the manager that she actually was the institution, so there was no point standing outside and protesting against herself. Instead, she needed to take responsibility for what the organization was doing by taking a stand against oppression as a manager inside the organization.

A danger of anti-oppression and any social justice approach is that sometimes we feel uncomfortable being the institution. We are much more comfortable being on the outside, because being on the inside means that we have to face the possibility that we might in fact be the problem. In Chapter 12 we will look more closely at how to work inside organizations to bring anti-oppressive change.

# Anti-Oppression Is the Social Work Dream, Not an Optional Extra

We do not care whether you call it anti-oppression, anti-racism, or anti-Black racism, as long as you are doing it, and as long as you are not pushing people down because they are not calling it the same thing you are. As you do your anti-oppression (or whatever you are calling it), we suggest you try and avoid the mistakes made in British anti-racism that we described above, so that we can keep anti-oppression on the social work agenda. We also think it is important that anti-oppression is not framed as an optional extra in social work, but instead as something that is inseparable from every form of social work we do. At the start of this chapter we called anti-oppression the "social work dream." We call it this because the dream of any helping occupation is addressing causes rather than treating symptoms. Anti-oppression has to be seen as a part of all social work.

A factor that can lead to people believing anti-oppression is optional is that social work is often portrayed as a divided occupation, with some believing its work ought to focus on "fixing" the individual (which is said to have nothing to do with addressing oppression), and others thinking it ought to "fix" society (which is thought to have everything to do with addressing oppression because it focuses on underlying social causes of people's troubles). When the story of social work's history is taught, this division is often presented as a dichotomy between micro and macro perspectives, with the two founding organizations of social work, the Charity Organization Society and Settlement House Movement, representing opposite ends of this spectrum (Lundy, 2011).

This story of contrasting approaches is so fundamental to the way social work sees itself that it is worth retelling and deconstructing. We suggest that the story portrays a false dichotomy that hides the fact that anti-oppression has a place across the full spectrum of modern social work activities. The story also hides the fact that anti-oppression can and must be undertaken in both individual and macro community work, and that those doing both types of work can be equally oppressive if they are not thinking critically about their practice.

## The Charity Organization Society

The story about the binary opposite types of social work begins with the **Charity Organization Society** (COS) that was founded in Britain in 1869 and spread to Europe, Australia, and North America. The British COS was led by Helen Bosanquet and Octavia Hill, and the American COS by Mary Richmond. The COS tried to bring organization and scientific logic to help the poor with "friendly visitors" (who were mostly White middle-class women) going into the homes of the "deserving poor" to provide aid and to help them cope and adapt (Lundy, 2011; Pierson, 2011).

The COS emphasis was primarily on people who, because of loss of employment or ill health, needed help. According to the story, rather than looking at the structural factors that contributed to their situation, the COS wanted to ensure that those who were given help did not become dependent on others, and instead took responsibility for themselves. Indeed, the very idea of "friendly visitors" was that the poor would gain by the friendship and attention of their betters (Hick & Stokes, 2017).

The COS also rejected the idea of the state being involved in helping the poor and addressing related social issues. To the COS, a public collective solution would destroy people's ability to take responsibility for their own independence and well-being. Any relief provided should always be temporary, a last resort, and not encouraged (Pierson, 2011).

The COS model is said to have given rise to the casework model of social work. Indeed, friendly visitors became social workers. Many years later the British COS changed its name and became known as the Family Welfare Association (FWA). The FWA is where Gary undertook his field placement when he was a social work student. At that time the agency specialized in psychoanalytic casework. Most social worker agencies and social workers who specialize in individual casework and counselling trace their practice genealogies back to the COS.

## The Settlement House Movement

Meanwhile, also back in the dawn of social work, a very different kind of organization was also emerging, the **Settlement House Movement.** This organization started in Britain in 1884 shortly after the COS began, and like the COS became a global movement. The first Settlement House, known as Toynbee Hall, was built in one of the poorest neighbourhoods of Victorian London. Imagine the neighbourhood of Dickens's *Oliver Twist*, or more accurately the neighbourhood of Jack London's (1903) documentary text *The People of the Abyss*, and you will get a sense of the poverty and issues its inhabitants faced. This was the same neighbourhood that the COS served, but the difference was the Settlement House people did not simply visit, they moved in. According to the story, in contrast to the COS who wanted to fix people, these Settlement House people were radical and out to change society at a systemic level by providing education classes, Boys and Girls Clubs, and other social activities for the poor (Pierson, 2011).

## The COS versus Settlement Movement—A False Dichotomy

Today, the different approaches of the COS and Settlement Movement are said to reflect the two different orientations within social work (Lundy, 2011). One orientation (the COS) focuses on helping to change the individual (or the way they cope and so on), and the other (Settlement Movement) focuses on fixing society (structural and systemic change). The COS typifies social work that does not pay attention to oppression; the Settlement Movement typifies an approach that does.

We contest the idea that the COS and Settlement House Movement form an ideological and practice dichotomy. Even though the COS focused primarily on individual need, the COS co-founder Octavia Hill, similar to the Settlement Movement, provided education for the poor and women (Lundy, 2011), offered housing at low rent so the poor could escape the tyranny of landlords, and fought for green space and access to healthy environments for the poor. Though perhaps not compatible with modern ideas about structural change and anti-oppression, these measures, especially the possibility of escaping tyrannous landlords, undoubtedly pushed back against systems that trod down the poor. In other words the COS included in their scope of practice attention to the structural causes of people's troubles.

In contrast, the Settlement Movement, although seen as radical and progressive and addressing structural issues, comprised mainly the middle-class and upper classes, and especially students from elite universities (Pierson, 2011) who saw themselves as "better" than the poor they were living with. Indeed, these radicals thought that their own middle-class values and manners rubbing off on the poor might help solve poverty because it would help the poor become better people (Pierson, 2011). In addition, the solution these elites had in mind was not always revolution (Oakley, 2017), but instead was a return to an idyllic "village-like" pre-industrial environment that they thought would be much better for the poor (Pierson, 2011). These Settlement House ideas were totally out of touch with the structural issues the poor faced because they failed to understand that even before the Industrial Revolution, the life for the poor they were "helping" was far from idyllic.

In raising the above points we are not claiming that the COS and Settlement Movement cannot be contrasted, but we are saying that they do not form the distinct dichotomy that our social work stories tend to suggest. When we take a more nuanced look at this history, we see oppression and anti-oppression in the work of both. We also suggest that unless social workers can offer service users and communities both individual and systemic help, we are not doing anti-oppression, because we are not meeting the needs of the downtrodden.

## Social Work Has to Focus on the Individual and on Society

Although we contend that the difference between the COS and the Settlement Movement was not as great as some social workers imagine, these two organizations are taken up as representative of a very real division in the way social workers think about the work they do: "fixing" people, or "fixing" society (Morley, Macfarlane, & Ablett, 2014). Not everyone dichotomizes social work in this way, but there is considerable infighting within the occupation about which of these two philosophies should drive social work (Lundy, 2011). We contend (and will argue in Chapter 11) that both approaches are needed, and that if social workers cannot offer both, they fail those we claim to serve.

The COS and Settlement House story has a third dimension that is rarely noticed. Both the COS and Settlement Houses involved mostly wealthy, middle-upper-class, White people making decisions about what they thought was best for the poor. These wealthy helpers were all well-intended and they gave up much to live with the poor and provide help. We have to respect them for doing that, and for helping to found social work. But these middle-upper-class helpers understood and interpreted the troubles of the poor from their own perspective, and offered solutions based on their understanding the world. These solutions did not always make sense in the world of those they served. This model of helping, with social workers deciding what is best, continues today. In our opinion, as long as social work help is determined by the wealthy middle and upper classes who have not experienced the need for help themselves, rather than being determined by those who have the lived experience of needing help, no form of social work can claim to be anti-oppressive. You will learn more about this issue in the chapters to come.

## Chapter Summary

In this chapter we have examined anti-oppression and the ways it emerged, in part, from the "failure" of anti-racism. We describe how we never saw anti-racism as a "failure," but instead saw it being wiped from the social work curriculum as a racist backlash. We argued that although we do not see anti-racism as a failure, ultimately it did fail in social work, because it was wiped from the curriculum in the UK. What occurred in the UK has implications in Canada too. We have to learn from what happened in the UK so that anti-oppression, and the social justice approaches found under this umbrella, do not suffer a similar fate.

Anti-oppression replaced anti-racism. Although anti-oppression is now the primary means by which social work attempts to engage in social justice, it is not without its own weakness, much of which it inherited from anti-racism. We consider both anti-racism and anti-oppression viable entry points to address a range of social justice issues. This is why, in the story at the beginning of the chapter, June and Gary used both terms interchangeably.

In this chapter we have suggested that it does not matter whether you call your focus on social justice anti-oppression, anti-racism, initiatives against anti-Black racism, or some other name, as long as you are doing social justice work, and you are not putting others down for calling their social justice work something else.

Ultimately, however, social work answers to oppression will never be enough on their own. As we will discover in the next chapter, for anti-oppression to happen, social work knowledge and theory has to be combined with service users' knowledge and theory.

## Discussion Questions

Discuss the following questions:

1. What name do you give the social justice work you do and why do you use this name?
2. What things do you do to address oppression under this name?
3. How do you ensure that you pay attention to issues of intersectionality?
4. Think back to the isms we discussed in Chapters 5 and 6, and consider additional isms we have not mentioned there. Is there an ism you have not given much thought to, that you know little about, and that you have not resisted and challenged? If so, consider why, and discuss ways you can join your social justice work with those who do address this ism, so you can both become stronger.

## Activity

Explore the issues related to the murder of Vincent Chin. Start by reading about Vincent on the documentary website "Vincent Who," and also view the videos on the documentary webpage. Additional information can be found on YouTube. Consider what anti-oppression, anti-racism, initiatives against anti-Black racism, and other social justice work can learn from the alliances that formed as a result of the hate-crime murder of Vincent. https://www.vincentwhofilm.com/

## Suggested Resources

Wehbi, S., & Parada, H. (Eds). (2017). *Reimagining anti-oppression social work practice*. Toronto, Canada: Canadian Scholars' Press.

Canadian Race Foundation, an organization "dedicated to the elimination of racism and all forms of racial discrimination in Canadian society." Retrieved from http://www.crrf-fcrr.ca

Video on "what our movements can learn from penguins" by Janaya Khan, writer, educator, movement strategist, and co-founder of Black Lives Matter Canada. Retrieved from https://youtu.be/TQ707s2Xi7Q

## References

Al-Krenawi, A., & Graham, J.R., & N. Habibov (Eds). (2016). *Diversity and social work in Canada* (2nd edn). Toronto, Canada: Oxford University Press.

Alfred, T. (1999). *Peace, power, righteousness: An Indigenous manifesto*. Toronto, Canada: Oxford University Press.

Baines, D. (2017). Anti-oppressive practice: Roots, theory and tensions. In D. Baines (Ed.), *Doing anti-oppressive practice: Social justice social work* (3rd ed., pp. 2–29). Halifax, Canada: Fernwood Publishing.

Baines, D. (Ed.). (2007). *Doing anti-oppressive practice: Building transformative politicized social work*. Halifax, Canada: Fernwood Publishing.

Battersby, S.-J. (2016, July 3). Black Lives Matter protest scores victory after putting Pride parade on pause. *Toronto Star*. Retrieved from https://www.thestar.com/news/gta/2016/07/03/black-lives-matter-protest-scores-victory-after-putting-pride-parade-on-pause.html

Battle, M. (1997). *Reconciliation: The ubuntu theology of Desmond Tutu*. Cleveland, OH: The Pilgrim Press.

Blackstock, C. (2009). Why addressing the over-representation of First Nations children in care requires new theoretical approaches based on First Nations ontology. *Journal of Social Work Values and Ethics, 6*(3).

Brown, C.G. (2012). Anti-oppression through a postmodern lens: Dismantling the master's conceptual tools in discursive social work practice. *Critical Social Work, 13*(1), 34–65.

Buqa, W. (2015). Storying *Ubuntu* as a rainbow nation. *Verbum et Ecclesia, 36*(2), 1–8. doi:10.4102/ve.v36i2.1434

CCETSW. (1991). *Requirements and regulations for the diploma in social wor (Paper 30)* (2nd edn). London, UK: Central Council for Education and Training in Social Work.

Centre for Contemporary Cultural Studies. (1982). *The empire strikes back: Race and racism in 70s Britain*. London, UK: Hutchinson & Co. (Publishers Ltd.).

Cocker, C., & Hafford-Letchfield, T. (Eds). (2014). *Rethinking anti-discriminatory and anti-oppressive theories for social work practice*. Houndmills, UK: Palgrave Macmillan.

Cohn, M. R. (2015, December 22). Premier ponders blowing up our CAS mess. *Toronto Star*. Retrieved from https://www.thestar.com/news/canada/2015/12/22/premier-ponders-blowing-up-our-cas-mess-cohn.html

Contenta, S., Monsebraaten, L., & Rankin, J. (2014a, 11 December). Just 8% of Toronto kids are black but 41% of kids in care are black: The stunning disparity is being called "a modern-day residential schools system." Critics believe that poverty, cultural misunderstanding and racism are to blame. *Toronto Star*, p. A1.

Contenta, S., Monsebraaten, L., & Rankin, J. (2014b, December 11). Why are so many black children in foster and group homes? *Toronto Star*. Retrieved from https://www.thestar.com/news/canada/2014/12/11/why_are_so_many_black_children_in_foster_and_group_homes.html

Dei, G.J.S. (1996). Critical perspectives in anti-racism: An introduction. *Canadian Review of Sociology and Anthropology, 33*(3), 247–67. doi:10.1111/j.1755-618X.1996.tb02452.x

Esquao, S.A. [Jeannine Carriere] & Strega, S. (Eds). (2015). *Walking this path together: Anti-racist and anti-oppressive* child welfare practice (2nd edn). Halifax, Canada: Fernwood.

Featherstone, D., Strauss, K., & MacKinnon, D. (2015). In, against and beyond neo-liberalism: The "crisis" and alternative political futures. *Space and Polity, 19*(1), 1–11. doi:10.1080/13562576.2015.1007695

Gilroy, P. (1987). *There ain't no black in the Union Jack*. London, UK: Hutchinson.

Gilroy, P. (1990). The end of anti-racism. *New Community, 17*(1), 71–83.

Hall, S. (1992). New ethnicities. In J. Donald & A. Rattansi (Eds), *"Race," culture and difference* (pp. 252–9). London, UK: Sage Publications in Association with The Open University.

Hammurabi. (1750BCE/1971). *The Hammurabi code, and the Sinaitic legislation: with a complete translation of the great Babylonian inscription discovered at Susa, by Chilperic Edwards*. Port Washington, NY: Kennikat Press.

Healy, K. (2001). Reinventing critical social work: Challenges from practice, context and postmodernism. *Critical Social Work, 2*(1). Retrieved from http://www1.uwindsor.ca/criticalsocialwork/reinventing-critical-social-work-challenges-from-practice-context-and-postmodernism

Hick, S., & Stokes, J. (2017). *Social work in Canada: An introduction* (4th edn). Toronto, Canada: Thompson Educational Publishing, Inc.

Humphries, B. (1997). The dismantling of anti-discrimination in British social work: A view from social work education. *International Social Work, 40*(3), 289–301.

Keating, F. (2000). Anti-racist perspectives: What are the gains for social work? *Social Work Education, 19*(1), 77–87.

London, J. (1903). *The people of the abyss*. London, UK: Macmillan.

Lundy, C. (2011). *Social work, social justice, and human rights: A structural approach to practice* (2nd edn). Toronto, Canada: University of Toronto Press.

Macey, M., & Moxon, E. (1996). An examination of anti-racist and anti-oppressive theory and practice in social work education. *British Journal of Social Work, 26*(3), 297–314.

McLaughlin, K. (2005). From ridicule to institutionalization: Anti-oppression, the state and social work. *Critical Social Policy, 25*(3), 283–305. doi:10.1177/0261018305054072

Morgaine, K., & Capous-Desyllas, M. (2015). *Anti-oppressive social work practice: Putting theory into action*. Thousand Oaks, CA: Sage Publication.

Morley, C., Macfarlane, S., & Ablett, P. (2014). *Engaging with social work: a critical introduction*. Port Melbourne, Australia: Cambridge University Press.

Mullaly, B. (2001). Confronting the politics of despair: Toward the reconstruction of progressive social work in a global economy and postmodern age. *Social Work Education: The International Journal, 20*(3), 303–20. doi:10.1080/02615470120057406

Mullaly, B. (2010). *Challenging oppression and confronting privilege: A critical social work approach* (2nd edn). Toronto, Canada: Oxford University Press.

Mullaly, B., & West, J. (2018). *Challenging oppression and confronting privilege: A critical approach to anti-oppressive and anti-privilege theory and practice*. (3rd edn). Toronto, Canada: Oxford University Press.

Ngcoya, M. (2015). *Ubuntu*: Toward an emancipatory cosmopolitanism? *International Political Sociology, 9*(3), 248–62. doi:10.1111/ips.12095

OACAS. (2016a). *One vision one voice: Changing the Ontario child welfare system to better serve African Canadians. Practice framework part 1: Research report*. Retrieved from http://www.oacas.org/wp-content/uploads/2016/09/One-Vision-One-Voice-Part-1_digital_english.pdf

OACAS. (2016b). *One vision one voice: Changing the Ontario child welfare system to better serve African Canadians. Practice framework part 2: Race equity practices*. Retrieved from http://www.oacas.org/wp-content/uploads/2016/09/One-Vision-One-Voice-Part-1_digital_english.pdf

Oakley, A. (2017). The forgotten example of "settlement sociology": Gender, research, communities, universities and policymaking in Britain and the USA, 1880–1920. *Research for All, 1*(1), 20–34. doi:10.18546/RFA.01.1.03

Paling, E. (2016, July 3). Black Lives Matter parade protest brings sweeping changes to Toronto Pride. Huffpost. Retrieved from http://www.huffingtonpost.ca/2016/07/03/black-lives-matter-toronto-pride-parade-changes_n_10798402.html

Payne, M. (2015). *Modern social work theory* (4th edn). London, UK: Palgrave Macmillan.

Pierson, J. (2011). *Understanding social work: History and context*. Maidenhead, UK: Open University Press.

Pon, G., Giwa, S., & Razack, N. (2016). Foundations of anti-racism and anti-oppression in social work practice. In A. Al-Krenawi, J.R. Graham, & N. Habibov (Eds), *Diversity and Social Work in Canada* (2nd ed., pp. 38–58). Don Mills, Canada: Oxford University Press.

Porter, T. (2008). *And grandma said . . . Iroquois teachings as passed down through the oral tradition*. Bloomington, IN: Xlibris.

Rankin, J. and Winsa, P. (2012, March 9). Known to police: Toronto police stop and document black and brown people far more than whites. *Toronto Star*. Retrieved from http://www.thestar.com/news/insight/2012/03/09/known_to_police_toronto_police_stop_and_document_black_and_brown_people_far_more_than_whites.html

Rankin, J. (2014, December 11). When CAS comes knocking. *Toronto Star*, p. A33.

Rankin, J., Winsa, P., Bailey, A., & Ng, H. (2013, September 28). "Devastating. Unacceptable": Toronto police board chair appalled by Star findings that show a stubborn rise in the number of citizens stopped and documented by our police officers—with black males heavily overrepresented. *Toronto Star*, p. A1.

Ross, M. (2017). Social work activism within neoliberalism: A big tent approach. In D. Bains (Ed.), *Doing Anti-Oppressive Practice: Social justice social work* (3rd ed., pp. 304–20). Halifax, Canada: Fernwood Press.

Sakamoto, I., & Pitner, R.O. (2005). Use of critical consciousness in anti-oppressive social work practice: Disentangling power dynamics at personal and structural levels. *British Journal of Social Work, 35*(4), 435–52. doi:10.1093/bjsw/bch190

Simkins, R. (2017). Care for the poor and needy: The Bible's contribution to an economic and social safety net. *Journal of Religion and Society, Supplement Series 14*, 4–13.

Singh, S. (2013). Anti-racist social work education. In A. Bartoli (Ed.), *Anti-racism in social work practice: Critical approaches to social work* (pp. 25–47). St. Albans, UK: Critical Publishing Ltd.

Smith, A. (2013). Unsetttling the privilege of self-reflexivity. In F.W. Twine & B. Gardener (Eds), *Geographies of privilege* (pp. 263–79). London, UK: Routledge.

Staniforth, B., Fouché, C., & O'Brien, M. (2011). Still doing what we do: Defining social work in the 21st century. *Journal of Social Work, 11*(2), 191–208. doi:10.1177/1468017310386697

Stewart, H. (2016, August 10). Tom Watson sends Corbyn "proof of Trotskyist Labour infiltration." *The Guardian*. Retrieved from http://www.theguardian.com/politics/2016/aug/10/tom-watson-sends-corbyn-proof-of-trotskyist-labour-infiltration

Trocme, N., Knoke, D., & Blackstock, C. (2004). Pathways to the overrepresentation of Aboriginal children in Canada's child welfare system. *Social Service Review, 78*(4), 281–313. doi:10.1086/424545

Tutu, D.M. (2007). Ubuntu discussion with students during Semester at Sea 2007. Retrieved from http://www.youtube.com/watch?v=gWZHx9DJR-M

Tutu, D.M. (2011). *God is not a Christian: And other provocations*. J. Allen (Ed.). New York, NY: HarperOne.

University of Birmingham. (2017). About CCCS: history and project. Retrieved from http://www.birmingham.ac.uk/schools/historycultures/departments/history/research/projects/cccs/about.aspx

Warren, P., Tomaskovic-Devey, D., Smith, W., Zingraff, M., & Mason, M. (2006). Driving while black: Bias processes and racial disparity in police stops. *Criminology: An Interdisciplinary Journal, 44*(3), 709–38. doi:10.1111/j.1745-9125.2006.00061.x

Wehbi, S., & Parada, H. (Eds). (2017). *Reimagining anti-oppression social work practice*. Toronto, Canada: Canadian Scholars' Press.

Williams, C. (1999). Connecting anti-racist and anti-oppressive theory and practice: Retrenchment or reappraisal? *British Journal of Social Work, 29*(2), 211–30.

Yee, J.Y., & Dumbrill, G.C. (2016). Whiteout: Still looking for race in Canadian social work practice. In A. Al-Krenawi, J.R. Graham, & N. Habibov (Eds), *Diversity and social work in Canada* (2nd edn, pp. 13–37). Toronto, Canada: Oxford University Press.

# 10 Without Service Users' Theory There Is No Anti-Oppression

## In this chapter you will learn:

- What service users' knowledge and theory are and why they are crucial in anti-oppression

- Why service users need a union and what social workers can do to help make that happen

- How a service users' union may not only help service users, but may also help social workers

## Introduction

When Gary was a social work student, he was browsing random social work books at the library when he came across *The Client Speaks: Working Class Impressions of Casework* by Mayer and Timms (1970). This book reported a study into service users' perspectives at the agency where Gary was undertaking his placement. The book was on none of Gary's reading lists, but the more he read, the more he thought it ought to be. The study showed how some service users of working-class backgrounds found the in-depth counselling offered by the agency unhelpful.

Gary took the book to his professors who said that they did not consider the findings relevant. Not perturbed, Gary presented the book at a staff meeting at his placement agency. The presentation did not go well. Similar to Gary's professors, the agency workers said that they did not find the book useful. Gary politely persisted, arguing that some of the points made by service users about the mismatch between what the agency offered and some of the issues working-class clients faced might be worth considering. The agency staff did not change their position and Gary sensed a level of hostility emerging in the meeting. He had already been feeling uneasy as a working-class person in this very middle-class environment. Gary's sense of unease was now increasing.

After that meeting Gary was asked whether he understood social work and the mission of the agency, and questions were raised about whether he would pass his placement. Gary went on to do well in his placement, but he realized that he had caused offence by crossing an unwritten line by asking the wrong questions. By the end of this chapter you will know what that line is, why social workers tend to still hold it in place, and why doing anti-oppressive practice requires us to cross that line.

## Talking about a Revolution

Mayer and Timms (1970) ideas had the kernels of revolution: the idea that social work clients ought to have their opinions about the help they receive taken seriously. The idea of asking service users what they thought about the help they needed and the help they got was not entirely new, but Mayer and Timms are regarded by many as the pioneers of this type of study (Maluccio, 1979; Rees, 1978; Sainsbury, 1975).

Although somewhat revolutionary, Mayer and Timms's ideas were limited in scope. Their research transferred the power to define what was occurring in casework away from clinicians and toward academic researchers. There was no transfer of power to define or interpret events to the clients themselves. Indeed, Mayer and Timms suggested that working-class clients finding a mismatch between agency services and their troubles did not necessarily need a different kind of service, but needed help to better understand the benefits of the service they were offered. Others saw a different significance in Mayer and Timms's findings, and suggested that the clients rather than the researchers or social workers had it right, and perhaps the "modes of helping in current casework practice are unsuitable and irrelevant to most human problems presented to agencies by clients" (Silverman, 1972, p. 132).

The possibility that service users know more about the help they need than social workers or researchers overturns beliefs about the nature of social work and those the discipline helps. There is a long-held assumption that if someone needs social work, this must result from them not knowing what to do or from being unable to do it; otherwise why would they come to a social worker for help?

### Beliefs That the Needy Do Not Know Best

The idea that social workers know more, or are more able, than service users is built upon long-standing attitudes toward those who need some form of social assistance. One of the influences that bolstered such views was the British 1834 Poor Law Amendment Act, which established the principle of **less eligibility** in poor relief. This principle was driven by the idea that poverty was a choice—anyone who was poor only had themselves to blame, and consequently was undeserving of any help (Gregory, 2008). Different rules applied to those who could not work due to being too ill or frail; they were considered the **deserving poor**. Anyone else who needed help was labelled **undeserving poor**, and the only help they were offered was the workhouse. **Workhouses** were residential institutions with brutish conditions and hard labour regimes. This was the principle of less eligibility in action—the idea of making relief as uncomfortable as possible so that people would stop choosing poverty.

Stigmatization was also a part of the less-eligibility principle (Dumbrill & Lo, 2009; Gregory, 2008). The word "stigma" means to be marked, and in this context it meant being marked as less than those who did not need help. To go to the workhouse was considered a shame and inmates were looked down upon—at least that is what the policy attempted to achieve (Fraser, 1973; Gregory, 2008). We are not sure if the poor looked down on other poor people who were forced into the workhouse. In those days poverty was endemic. Anyone who was poor had to know that it was not their fault, so we suspect that some of the poor did not fully buy the rhetoric that poverty was a choice. Perhaps, therefore, the poor felt no shame in receiving the little relief they were offered, but there is certainly no doubt that they had to suffer shameful treatment to get it.

## The Idea That Social Workers Know Best

Modern social workers do not (or should not) view those they serve as undeserving nor blame them for their own plight. Instead social workers should recognize that service users' personal troubles are linked to oppressive structures. At the same time, however, deep cultural messages remain about those who need help, especially if they are poor. One only has to read the tabloid press to see talk of "lazy" and "undeserving" people on benefits to recognize that the old poor-law attitudes remain alive and well (Gregory, 2008). These tabloid press reports both reflect and reinforce judgmental attitudes toward those receiving social assistance, and this can sometimes trickle over into the way social workers see service users.

Of course social work is not just concerned with the poor, but social work did emerge from efforts to help the poor, and remains largely focused on helping those who are trying to get along with few resources. As well, the very nature of seeking social work situates social workers as competent knowers and service users as those who do not know and cannot do. Such helping involves social workers assessing service users and helping them to find better solutions to their problems. Mayer and Timms's (1970) research opened the possibility to flip this relationship around so that service users could assess social workers and help them find better ways of doing social work. To many, the potential of this flipped thinking was unsettling and sounded like revolution—and to an extent it was—because it identified what is now known as service users' knowledge and theory.

# Service Users' Knowledge and Theory

Service users' knowledge and theory emerges from the lived understanding that service users have of the troubles they face and the policies and practices designed to address them. The terms "service users' knowledge" and "service users' theory" are often used interchangeably, but Dumbrill and Lo (2015) give them distinct definitions. They see **service users' knowledge** as the understanding and insight service users have into the troubles they face and services they receive, and **service users' theory** as the refinement of such knowledge into the type of theory, as described in Chapter 2, that has the ability to *describe*, *explain, predict,* and *control.* As such, service users' theory provides an alternative to the ideas that policymakers and social workers develop about what leads to service users' troubles and what might alleviate them.

## There Has Always Been Service Users' Theory

Peter Beresford points out that there has always been service users' knowledge ". . . from the earliest days of secular and religious charity and the beginnings of state interventions and the old Poor Law" (Beresford, 2000, p. 492). There has always been service users' theory too, although it is often ignored because listening to service users' knowledge or theory threatens the social order. Indeed, if service users' troubles are compounded by structural issues—and if these are the result of oppression—then listening to service users' ideas about the origins of their troubles and the solutions needed is likely to challenge the social order itself. This is undoubtedly why poor laws, less eligibility, the workhouse, and stigma were used to remove the credibility of the downtrodden and to silence those who needed social supports. This way, even if those on the margins did speak, nobody would listen, because they were considered unable to manage their own affairs and certainly unable to have insights into problems within the social order.

## How Service Users' Knowledge and Theory Threaten Social Work Power

Service users' theory and knowledge threaten social work too. Social work has traditionally followed a medical model (Beresford, 2000), which means that in the same way that physicians gain power and prestige by understanding patient ills and remedies, social work has attempted to establish itself as a profession by understanding service users' ills and remedies. If one concedes that service users understand their own troubles and their remedies, this would undermine the power of social work as a profession. We personally reject the idea that social work ought to emulate medicine, but because many see social work in this way, service users' knowledge and theory can easily be seen as a threat to the existence of the occupation.

Service users' knowledge and theory also threaten the power social work gains from the state. Social work manages to exist, in part, because the state can rely on the profession to implement the social policies the state mandates. In other words, social workers are expected to interpret service users' troubles within policy frameworks set by the state, and are expected to deliver the remedies that these policies allow. If social work suddenly started interpreting service users' troubles through service users' theory, and started offering remedies that service users said were needed, the social work profession might quickly lose the funding and mandate of the state.

Although the threats above to social work as a profession may be real, we contend that this should not deter social work from pursuing service users' knowledge and theory. Indeed, social work's mission is neither to serve the state, nor its own interests as a profession. Its mission is to serve the communities and people who use its services.

# Why Service Users' Theory Is Essential in Anti-Oppression

If service users' personal troubles are caused or compounded by oppressive structures, then by definition their lack of agency and voice within society have to be seen as causing or contributing to the troubles that bring them to social work for help. As a result, if social work fails to give service users' agency and voice in shaping the way their troubles are understood and resolved, social work becomes a part of the oppressive system they face. Indeed, if social workers do not hear and utilize service users' knowledge and theory, they are treading down and silencing the collective voice and opinions of those who receive service.

It is quite remarkable, therefore, that little has been done to involve service users in shaping the way anti-oppression is understood and taken up. Wilson and Beresford (2000) refer to this as a paradox: ". . . that the people who are meant to be the beneficiaries of this development [anti-oppression] seem to have been so little involved and gained so little from it" (p. 554). Wilson and Beresford (2000) further contend that anti-oppressive scholars and practitioners may grasp how marginalized groups are oppressed within society, but do not grasp how these groups are also oppressed by social work. This oversight is why we, in Chapter 4, place recipients of social work services as an oppressed group that falls outside first-class citizenship.

Wilson and Beresford (2000) are careful to not suggest that social workers and service users are mutually exclusive groups, because they merge and overlap. We offer the same caution—we both know many social work students and professors who are also social work service users—but the point remains that the social work voice, not the service users' voice, dominates. This has to change. Indeed, Wilson and Beresford contend that anti-oppression is currently "a façade of 'anti-oppressive practice' which in reality appropriates and incorporates the knowledges and experiences of service users, *whilst still retaining the power to determine what it is that counts as 'anti-oppressive'* which is, for us, the most oppressive aspect of its 'anti-oppressive' stance" (Wilson & Beresford, 2000, p. 565). Unless service users' knowledge and theory are central in social work, and unless service users have control over that theory and how it is used, social work cannot claim to be anti-oppressive.

## Social Work Theory and Knowledge Are Important Too

By emphasizing the importance of service users' theory, we are not suggesting that social workers have no independent and distinct knowledge or theory to offer. Social workers bring crucial insights about how society works and also bring expert clinical or practical help that many service users may need. Indeed, even though service users' personal troubles are often caused or compounded by oppressive structures, not every service user problem has a structural cause. Rich privileged people and even billionaires who are not trod down by oppression sometimes have personal problems that take them to counselling;

surely poor people and the oppressed are just as able as rich people to have such troubles. Indeed, if we deny that the oppressed can have personal problems unconnected to their oppression, it means that we deny the agency and humanity of the marginalized, because we only see them in relation to their oppression.

A lesson Gary had to learn in his student placement was that despite Mayer and Timms questioning the utility of the work offered by his placement agency, working-class and otherwise marginalized people do have purely personal problems that they want to address through in-depth personal counselling. Consequently, many of the staff at Gary's placement agency had spent their entire careers developing and refining in-depth psycho-dynamic counselling skills that they offered free of charge to working-class service users. There was nothing inappropriate or oppressive about this. In fact it levelled the playing field—it ensured that working people with personal problems could access the same ther-apy that in most circumstances only the very rich could afford. If service users coming to this agency did not need this type of in-depth specialized service, they were referred else-where to a service that could meet their need more appropriately. Recognizing the value of this specialized service helped Gary understand why some of the workers at this agency got irritated with him for highlighting research that critiqued the agency's approach to intervention. If the agency stopped offering this service, who else would offer this service to those who needed it but could not afford to pay?

## Need, Not Ideology, Should Drive Service

Social work service has to be geared to addressing the trouble a service user is requesting help with. If a person seeks help with a trouble that has primarily a structural cause, and a social worker interested in being a therapist interprets this as an entirely personal problem and offers only therapy, then this would be oppressive. In fact this might also be exploitive, because interpreting the trouble this way meets the worker's need to deliver therapy and not the service user's need for something else. The reverse is also true. If a person seeks help with an entirely personal problem, but a social worker interested in social action in-terprets this as resulting from oppression and offers only social action, then this would be oppressive. This would also be exploitive, because the worker would have met their own need to engage in social action rather than the service user's need for something else.

## Key Concept

In the social work you do, are you able to recognize and address both personal and social issues? You need to, because service users' troubles can result from both, or a combination of the two. Anyone trying to narrow social work to just one or the other likely has their own interests in mind rather than those of the service users.

Service users' troubles are rarely entirely personal or entirely structural, which is why social work needs to focus on both. Anyone trying to narrow social work to one or the other likely has their own interests, rather than those of the service users, in mind. This is why service users' knowledge and theory is important. The direction social work takes is too important to be left to social workers alone. Service users need to have a say too.

The disabled peoples' movement (discussed in Chapter 6) has been central in having service users' knowledge and theory recognized. Their catch phrase, "nothing about us without us" (Beresford 2000), succinctly articulates their message and demands. This demand is not a replacement of social work knowledge and theory with service users' knowledge and theory, but recognition that both need to shape the way forward. We suggest this needs to occur with service users taking the lead.

# Drawing upon Service Users' Theory and Knowledge

Over the past two decades, service users' voice and knowledge have become a central part of social work in Europe (Cabiati, 2016; Levy et al., 2016). Particularly in the UK, the involvement of service users in the design and sometimes delivery of service has become "a cornerstone of social care and social work policy and philosophy" (Beresford & Croft, 2001, p. 295). Indeed, for some time, British social work programs have been required to have service user involvement (Franklin, Hossain, & Coren, 2016; Robinson & Webber, 2013; The College of Social Work, 2012).

Canada lags seriously behind in these efforts. There is no Canadian requirement that service users have any say in the way Canadian social work is delivered, or the way workers are educated and evaluated. This Canadian lack of attention to service users' voice, knowledge, and theory is unfortunate, because service users' voice has huge anti-oppressive potential.

Although there is no requirement for service users' in Canada to have a say in the way social workers are educated or trained, there have been some efforts to achieve this. For instance, Wilfrid Laurier University's Faculty of Social Work undertook focus groups with service users to help determine the characteristics of effective social workers, and have built these into their admission requirements and assessment of student suitability for the field (Watters, Cait, & Oba, 2016). This initiative does seem to not involve service users in direct contact with students and leaves social work academics with the power to translate these ideas into policy and practice, but it still represents a significant step in giving service users a say.

McMaster School of Social Work has also attempted to provide service users with a voice in social work education and worker training. These efforts have taken place through **community-based research**, in which community members (service users), organizations, and agencies become equal partners in designing, undertaking, and owning research that informs policy, practice, and social work education. An example is a partnership that was formed between McMaster university researchers, mothers living with HIV (who had received child welfare services), agencies providing services related to HIV and AIDS, and child welfare agencies. In this project, service users were involved in researching what social work students and practising child protection workers understood about providing services to those living with and affected with HIV. Drawing on their lived experience of their own needs and being on the receiving end of child welfare intervention, service users helped analyze the data, draw inferences, and design education and training to meet student and worker learning needs. Service users then helped deliver that education and training (Greene et al., 2016). Using pre-training and post-training measures of worker attitudes, skills, and knowledge, the service users were able to evaluate the effectiveness of the education and training by mapping progress students and workers had made. This project was centred on the power of service users to decide what was important and to train social workers themselves. In another community-based research project, refugee parents developed and delivered teaching materials for social work students and social workers in ways to work with their communities (Dumbrill & Lo, 2009).

Many more Canadian examples could be given of service users shaping the ways social work is delivered and taught. The issue, however, is that such efforts rely on the innovation of individual social workers, academics, or organizations to share their power and make space for service users' voice, knowledge, and theory. It is different in the UK: as mentioned above, the government and social work organizations have put their might into insisting that service users have a say. The problem is that although these efforts in the UK have huge anti-oppressive potential, it is unclear if this potential is being realized or if the power relations that underpin oppression are being changed. If Canada is to build the potential of service users' perspectives into its anti-oppression efforts (and we suggest it must), Canada needs to learn from the limitations of this approach that are becoming evident in the UK.

Before we critique the British system, we need to be clear that there is evidence that British service user involvement in social work delivery, design, and education is to an extent driven by the central idea that service users' have an absolute right to have a say in anything that impacts them (Matka, River, Littlechild, & Powell, 2010). This is the core anti-oppressive principle in these efforts; it is a step in the undoing of the silencing and the lack of agency by those on the margins. We do not want our critique of British efforts to diminish the importance of this work. At the same time, however, we want to draw attention to some of the problematic ways service users' perspectives can be used and even abused.

## Things to Avoid When Utilizing Service Users' Knowledge and Theory

There are a number of ways that involving service users in social work education and service delivery could exploit and perpetuate oppression. Previous chapters in this book have attempted to provide you with an in-depth understanding of how oppression operates and is sustained. We examined oppression in such depth so that you can recognize it and avoid replicating it in projects and initiatives that you are involved in. As a result, you should be able to involve service users in ways that promote anti-oppression rather than perpetuate it. In the following exercise consider oppressive mistakes an uninformed social worker might make when involving service users.

## Exercise 10.1

### How Not to Involve Service Users

If possible, undertake this exercise in groups. Imagine that you want to involve service users in helping develop social policy, social work services, or social work education.

1. Imagine and list the WRONG ways of doing this. In other words, if you were to involve service users in a way that was oppressive rather than anti-oppressive, or at the very least involve them in a way that gave them no real say in what was occurring, how would you do this? (Of course in real life you would not want to involve service users in an oppressive way. But the best way to avoid oppressing in real life is to think about how your project might oppress, and then make sure that you avoid doing that.)

2. Watch Peter Beresford speak about "How not to do service user involvement" at https://youtu.be/flD8jrfL3K8 and compare your ideas with his. (Note: This should be obvious but we state it just in case someone does not realize—Beresford is using satire. He (like us) is completely committed to getting service user involvement right.)

To build on your and Beresford's ideas about how not to do service user involvement, we list below warnings about some of the potential mistakes that it may be easier to fall into. Keep in mind that the mistakes we warn against overlap and compound each other, so that a number of these mistakes could happen at the same time.

## Do Not Promote Your Own Ideas at the Expense of Service Users

A primary mistake is to co-opt service users to work on your agenda and objectives, rather than you working on their agenda and objectives. For instance, the delivery of social work and social work education in Europe, and particularly in the UK, has been taking place in an era of cost cutting. As a result, service users have been recruited in projects aimed at "improving outcomes for service users and other key stakeholders without increasing overall cost" (Moullin, 2017, p. 442). Being co-opted by governments to help social service agencies to do more with less is hardly a form of service user liberation. In this context, service user involvement is seen simply as a means to boost what is sometimes called the "three Es" of efficiency, economy, and effectiveness (Beresford, 2000). In other words, service user involvement is all about government and social work management agendas, and not service users' agendas.

## Key Concept

Service user involvement is not about getting them to help you achieve your objectives; it is about you helping them to achieve their objectives. Social work needs to be about service users' needs, not your needs.

We have no doubt that service users will be able to help achieve these government and management objectives, but this is primarily a government rather than a service user agenda. We suspect that service users helping achieve these objectives will not be paid the fees that professional management consultants usually enjoy, which is something we consider unfair. Also, by drawing service users into projects that focus on doing more with less, rather than challenge the structures of oppression, these projects actually involve service users in helping to maintain their own oppression by promoting austerity measures (Levy et al., 2016). Indeed, it has been noted that service user:

> . . . involvement framed within neoliberalism has failed to achieve meaningful redistribution of power, as the scope for individual service users to achieve a voice and responsibility in decision-making has been within narrowly defined boundaries. Involvement has been understood as a bureaucratic requirement rather than a meaningful redistribution of power. (Levy et al., 2016, p. 867)

## Do Not Restrict Service Users to Superficial Roles

Caution also needs to be expressed at the ways service users are involved in the social work educational system. The British government requires that service users are involved in all aspects of student selection and the training of social workers (Department of Health, 2002), but because there is no stipulation about how this should occur, the practice varies between institutions (Matka et al., 2010). Examples of the way this requirement is taken up includes service users helping to select students for admission to social work programs (Matka et al., 2010), grading entrance exams and helping to develop questions for such tests (Robinson & Webber, 2013), evaluating students' interviewing skills (Dill, Montgomery, Davidson, & Duffy, 2016), and service user families "hosting" social work students to enable them to better understand service users' lives (Levy et al., 2016).

All of these educational projects have anti-oppressive potential, but they have dangers that need to be considered too. For instance, as a part of students spending time with host service users' families, students are asked by their school to explore questions such as:

> If your host family could give a message to policy makers in your local authority/ health board about the services and supports they require, what would that message be? (Levy et al., 2016, p. 870)

The alternative question we would ask such students to explore is, why service users are not taking those messages to policymakers themselves. From an anti-oppressive perspective, the voice of service users has to be heard in its own right and not fed to policymakers by social workers or simply reflected upon in papers by social work students. Keep in mind that, as explained in previous chapters, power is inherent in all forms of oppression. Consequently, in any exercise or process involving service users, one has to ask who holds the power to make meaning, to evaluate, and to speak. If a process does not change power relations, then one must question whether it is anti-oppressive. In the example above, one also has to ask whether the practice might actually be oppressive, because if it teaches social work students that they, rather than service users, are the ones to make meaning of service users' lives and give voice to the policies service users need, the entire exercise reinforces existing power relations rather than challenging them.

We also feel somewhat uneasy with the concept of social work students joining "host families." To us it seems a somewhat voyeuristic anthropological project—a trip into another world—with the mission to learn about the people who live there. It is reported that such hosting improves students' abilities to communicate with and appreciate the lives and struggles of service users, but for us, if students have to visit the marginalized to learn to communicate with them, it raises serious questions about who is being recruited into social work. Indeed, Gupta and Blewett (2008) identify an objective of service users' involvement in education as helping social work students learn to be "non-punitive and genuinely supportive" (p. 459). We would hope that someone entering a social work program would be further along in the development of their humanity than needing to spend time with service users in order to learn that they should be supportive rather than punitive toward them.

## Do Not Patronize or Underestimate Service Users' Expertise

We notice subtle forms of Othering and patronization in some of the literature on service user involvement. An example is Mayer and McKenzie (2017) who speak of mental health service users co-producing knowledge with practitioners. **Co-production** is "commonly conceptualised as a more equal sharing of power and decision-making between a dichotomy of service user and service provider, each bringing valuable and different assets to the process" (Mayer & McKenzie, 2017, p. 1181). Mayer and McKenzie study what they call "experts by experience" who are mental health service users who become paid peer helpers (i.e., they are paid to use their expertise to help other service users).

The problem with Mayer's and McKenzie's work is that one of the evaluative criteria for the paid expert-by-experience program is based on whether the program helps "experts by experience" feel empowered and have boosted self-esteem. In contrast, the evaluation of social workers is not usually based on whether social workers feel empowered and have boosted self-esteem; it is based on whether they provide effective help. So the evaluation criteria of "experts by experience" shows that they are not really seen as helpers or a part of the service provision system, but instead as people who need help themselves. If the work of "experts by experience" were truly on par with social workers, the evaluation criteria would be whether they help other service users.

We have no objections to the role of paid "experts by experience," nor do we object to them being empowered or gaining boosted self-esteem through this work. This role is very similar to peer helping, which has been taken up successfully in mental health services (Cook et al., 2012; Gates & Akabas, 2007; Ross, Hart, Jorm, Kelly, & Kitchener, 2012). We see these types of paid helper initiatives as central in anti-oppression (more about this potential later). Our objection is to framing the purpose of co-production and "experts by experience" as a process that meets the needs of the service users, rather than considering the work they do as bona fide helping on par with the help social workers offer. Indeed, Mayer and McKenzie's (2017) review of the literature on co-production contains several references that reveal how service users in helping roles are seen as less than social workers. Not only does the theme consistently emerge for the need of helper-by-experience programs to empower service users who are helping, there is also emphasis on how these programs increase the social capital of the "experts by experience" (Brandsen & Pestoff, 2006). We contend that the process operates the other way around. Having "experts by experience" on one's team might increase an agency's cultural capital in service users communities, and "experts by experience" actually empower the social workers they work alongside to do a better job.

Another clue that service users are not seen as full experts is the way that Mayer and McKenzie (2017) say that, as a result of being employed as "experts by experience," service users become transformed to "feel valued," develop a "new identity," and as a result report feeling "normal" (pp. 1184–5). This "normalization" of service users, along with claiming that they will be "empowered" by working alongside social workers, devalues both their humanity and their expertise. It seems similar to the ideology employed by the Settlement House Movement and COS (mentioned in Chapter 9), which contends that if the poor and marginalized mix with their betters they will be set on a path of self-improvement.

As mentioned above, we are not critiquing the idea of experts by experience or the concept of peer helpers. Indeed, we see these as central in any anti-oppressive strategy. Any agency undertaking these measures needs to be given credit for this valuable work. These agencies also need to recognize that what is anti-oppressive about this process is not that service users will be transformed for the better by working alongside social workers, but that social work will be transformed for the better by working alongside service users.

## Do Not Limit Recruitment of Service Users to Those Who Confirm Your Own Ideas

A tendency has been noticed for social workers to only select service user participants who reflect the values and beliefs held by social workers themselves (Gupta & Blewett, 2008). Such service users have, in Bourdieu's terms, the cultural capital to get along in social work and higher educational spaces, and become the "privileged voice of service users to the exclusion of silent, hard to reach groups" (Levy et al., 2016, p. 869).

We do not like the term "hard to reach" because it implies that the difficulty lies in the group that cannot be reached by social work. Quite the opposite, it is social work's inability to reach out in appropriate ways that is the issue, not the inability of the group to be reached. These semantics aside, the point Levy and colleagues make is well taken; there are those who will not be reached in the usual social work ways. In other words, service users selected for involvement are likely to be those who will not shake up the field or disturb social work's ways of thinking and doing, and as a result will reinforce existing social work systems rather than challenge them. Selecting such service users builds a form of confirmation bias (a term we defined in Chapter 2). Indeed, Terry (2017) suggests that selectively listening only to service users who say what social work educators want to hear perpetuates what Margolin (1997) refers to as social work's belief in its own goodness.

Excluding certain service users can be the result of unconscious convenience or bias because it is simply easier to engage with those one already knows, and it is more comfortable to discuss issues with those whose views are similar to one's own. Exclusion can also be deliberate. In Canada, John Dunn, a former Crown ward of the Ontario child welfare system, has been active and vocal in critiquing the system and the way it raised him. With inside information and lived experience about how that system works, he has been keen to share his knowledge and theory about how to bring improvements. John does not always say what the system wants to hear, but we contend that growth occurs by hearing and considering opinions contrary to one's own. As part of his efforts to bring change, John applied to attend a Canadian symposium on the outcomes of child and family services. John engaged in protracted advocacy in an attempt to attend, but reports receiving the following response:

> Admission to this symposium is by invitation only. This is not the time nor the place for survivors of the child welfare system to tell their story. (cited by Dunn, 2003)

When Gary spoke to John about the events above, John reflected on the irony that he, as a "child welfare outcome," was not allowed at a child welfare outcomes conference. We find many of John's ideas vibrant and insightful. We do not agree with all John says, but we do not always agree with all that our social work colleagues say either. When we disagree with our colleague' ideas, we do not refuse to dialogue with them or attempt to lock them out of symposiums or debate. When we disagree we embrace debate, because dialogue in moments of disagreement often produces entirely new ideas. Even if dialogue does not produce new ideas, we should never exclude service users from conversations or symposiums, because the principle of "nothing about us without us" needs to apply to every service user, not just the ones we agree with.

## Exercise 10.2

### The Potential of Service Users' Knowledge and Theory

If possible, undertake this exercise in groups.

Peter Beresford, who is both a service user and a leading academic in the UK, says that a new manifesto for social care is needed. Beresford suggests that service users should write it (Beresford, 2016).

1. Review Beresford's arguments and the user-led manifesto for change at https://www.theguardian.com/social-care-network/2016/dec/06/new-manifesto-for-social-care-is-essential-service-users-should-write-it.
2. Consider how the ideas in the manifesto might be taken up in a Canadian context.
3. Name some of the changes in social work and social policy that you think a project like this might bring.

## How Service Users' Knowledge and Theory Tap into the Word on the Street

To more fully appreciate service users' knowledge and how it becomes theory, one has to return to its original purpose, which is to give service users a way to manage and survive. In many respects, service users' knowledge and theory is the "word on the street," based on real-life experience of what might help them or harm them. We use the term **word on the street** to refer to knowledge and wisdom that circulates through communities by word of mouth.

The word on the street we are most familiar with relates to child welfare, because our work focuses on child welfare, and Gary's research examines child protection service users' knowledge and theory. As a result most of our examples will be from child welfare. Child welfare is a useful focus because it is arguably one of the most intrusive and powerful forms of social work. Consequently, if child welfare can find ways to incorporate service users' voice, knowledge, and theory, then all other sectors should be able to do so too.

## Examples of Service Users' Knowledge and Theory in Action

An example of service users' theory in action comes from a mother at a shelter Gary interviewed. This mother had received child protection intervention and had used this knowledge to develop theory that she was disseminating to other service users. The mother told Gary: "I can get any worker to co-operate with me."

Gary asked her to explain. The mother said that the first thing a service user should do is take an interest in the social worker by asking them how their week has been or what type of day they are having, or ask some other question that shows you care about them as a human being. The mother cautioned that one should not pry too much into the social worker's life with these questions, because workers like to keep their privacy, but it is important to ask enough to show the worker that you care about them as a person and do not simply see them as a worker.

The mother said that next one has to find out what the worker's problem is, and to then help them to solve it. The mother said that one has to remember that a child protection worker will not know you nor trust you, and will likely see you as the problem, so if you do not regard yourself as the problem, you have to help the worker see that fact. The mother explained:

> You gotta look at it from their perspective; they think this child is in danger and you have to prove them wrong. You gotta show them differently. . . . Unless you prove them wrong they're going to stick with their gut feeling. And I guess that's what a lot of people do you know in general, they stick to their gut feeling until they're proven wrong.

The mother said that throughout this process a service user should focus on trying to identify and disprove any negative views the worker might have about them and their parenting abilities. The mother found that this strategy not only helps alleviate a worker's child protection concerns, but also turns a worker into someone who is willing to engage and offer real help with the issues and problems a service user may be struggling with.

When the mother taught these strategies to other mothers at the shelter, she cautioned them that child protection intervention would likely make them feel threatened and defensive, and they might want to fight back and even become hostile. The mother advised against this and suggested that instead of becoming angry, service users should focus energy on the needs of their child, because anger and hostility toward a worker might make things worse rather than better for their child.

Gary came across other parents teaching the same lessons. For example, a father explained that parents do not usually want child protection intervention because it is a threat, but once a child protection worker shows up a parent cannot make them go away by resisting. The father explained that one needs to co-operate to make them go away, and that in this co-operation there can sometimes be ways to turn the worker from being someone who is a threat to one's family into being someone who is supportive. He said, "don't throw that opportunity [for support] away, because it can be valuable."

## Service Users' Knowledge about Dangers

Knowledge that social work, particularly child protection work, can be a threat is on the street everywhere. This is particularly so with those who face oppression such as Black communities (Contenta, Monsebraaten, & Rankin, 2014; OACAS, 2016; Rankin, 2014), Indigenous communities (Blackstock, 2009; Trocme, Knoke, & Blackstock, 2004), and those living in poverty (Pelton, 1989; Russell, Harris, & Gockel, 2008). Indeed, in British Columbia, Callahan, Field, Hubberstey, and Wharf (1998) found that mothers living in poverty understood that it was a part of their job as parents to protect their children against child protection workers. Those on the margins don't need to read research about dispro-portionality to know this, because they already know it by listening to the word on the street.

## Service Users' Knowledge of Workers and Systems That May Help

The word on the street not only informs communities about the overall risks and benefits of service, it also discerns and informs about the strengths and limitations of specific workers. Juliana Chooi, a Children's Aid Society manager, tells a story of when she was a child protection intake worker. The agency received a referral from the community that three young children were often seen at a play area unsupervised where they seemed to be unsafe. This was designated as a "12-hour referral," which requires immediate response, and Juliana attended the home where the children lived to investigate. The mother who opened the door to Juliana became highly distraught; the mother shouted at Juliana and refused to let Juliana enter her home to speak to her children, and slammed the door telling Juliana to never come back.

Juliana returned to her office to contemplate her next move. Given the nature of the referral, an investigation had to be done, but Juliana had no desire to involve the police and escalate the situation. Juliana's phone soon rang and it was the mother who had sent her on her way. The mother apologized for her outburst, and said that a neighbour who was one of Juliana's previous clients had heard about the noisy incident and dropped in to tell her that Juliana was a "good worker" who could be trusted to be honest and helpful. The mother asked if Juliana would mind returning to start the process again (personal communication Juliana Chooi, May 23, 2017).

Clearly the word on the street in that mother's community was strong, because it knew the type of worker Juliana was. At that time in Juliana's career she boasted of a zero apprehension record—she always found ways to work out problems with communities and extended families to keep children safe without bringing them into state care. But what about parents who do not have access to a strong word on the street or dependable service users' knowledge and theory to guide them? How does one find out the best way to understand and respond to social workers? In these circumstances social workers have all the power, or as some parents have described, they have "absolute power" (Dumbrill, 2003). Clearly this situation needs to be remedied.

## Exercise 10.3

### Developing Theory from the Word on the Street

If possible, undertake this exercise in groups.

1. List the word on the street about social workers in a community or communities you belong to.
2. If working in a group, compare and contrast this knowledge to those of other communities represented in your group, and consider the reasons for similarities and differences.
3. Develop this knowledge into theory; take all this information and theorize only on the basis of this information about what social work is and what it does.
4. How confident would you feel engaging with social workers on the basis of the knowledge you have developed in this exercise?

## Helping to Develop Service Users' Knowledge and Theory

Central to anti-oppression is balancing power and, as discussed in Chapter 3, knowledge is a form of power. Without knowledge, without a dependable word on the street refined into theory to inform service users' action, service users are in a position of perpetual disadvantage in relation to social workers. Even when social work is not authoritative and potentially threatening like child protection, the service user disadvantage remains.

Why are social workers educated about ways of working with service users, yet service users not educated about ways of working with social workers? Indeed, even the British efforts to give service users a voice focuses on equipping workers for the encounter with service users, not on equipping service users for the encounter with social workers. When child protection services users began to ask Gary about this imbalance, he decided to work with them to develop a service user's guide to child protection services. Gary was not the first to think of this idea (see, for instance, Family Inclusion Network of Western Australia, 2009; McCarthy et al., 2003). As reported elsewhere (Dumbrill, 2010) the idea of a service users' guide did not work out as well as Gary hoped (we will explain why later), but the process of attempting to develop a guide gave crucial insights into how anti-oppression needs to be taken up, and what needs to happen for a viable service users' guide to be developed.

# A Service Users' Guide: Why Knowledge Is Not Enough

Partnership and collaboration between workers and service users is crucial in any form of social work (Dumbrill, 2017; Young & Dumbrill, 2010). Without service users having dependable knowledge of what they are getting into and how the process works, the social work–service user partnership will always be one-sided. As a result, even though social work claims the relationship it has with service users is a two-way process (Damiani-Taraba et al., 2017; Gladstone et al., 2012), it is conceptualized and managed almost entirely from the social work end. To balance this relationship, it seemed to us that a service users' guide written by service users and for service users was a good idea.

It soon became evident that developing a guide was not going to work, because what service users said was contradictory. Some service users spoke of how to engage with workers positively, while others suggested that engagement is impossible and that it is best for parents to "take their children and run" at the first sight of a social worker. This mixed advice was not because service users' knowledge was faulty and that it could not be formed into viable theory, but because within the scope of this project it could not be formulated into something that could encompass every possible scenario that a parent might encounter with child protection services. Indeed, social workers study full time for approximately four years to obtain the qualification needed to work with service users, more if they have a master's degree, plus they have extensive post-qualifying training that focuses on the different types of situations they will encounter in any specific field they work within. How could a service users' guide compete with this training and knowledge?

In addition, and more importantly, social workers are supported by an entire system and infrastructure designed to maintain their advantage. Service users were able to identify the elements of these systems that gave workers so much more power than service users:

- Workers are familiar with intervention processes, while parents do not usually understand the process.
- Workers know the legal parameters of their work, while parents are often unaware of their legal rights.
- Workers are aware of an array of interventions from which to choose, while parents are usually only aware of the options their worker chooses to present.
- Workers are familiar with the consequences and likely outcomes of parents accepting or not accepting intervention, while parents have no independent means to anticipate the outcomes or consequences of their choices.
- Workers have supervisory and peer support to cope with the emotional stress of intervening, while parents often lack similar support.
- Workers are able to consult with supervisors and other experts about the way intervention is unfolding and about the best ways to manage parents, while parents usually have no advice about how to manage workers (Dumbrill, 2010, pp. 198–9).

Social work can never help liberate service users though a relationship in which social workers hold all the power. This power is particularly evident in child protection; parents on the receiving end of these services have clearly articulated what it is like being on the receiving end of that power.

> A father explained, "They've got power—'scary power.'" A mother reiterated, "They've got power and you either listen, or you don't listen, and you suffer the repercussions." (Dumbrill, 2010, p. 197)

Of course not all social work carries the power to intervene against a service user's wishes as it does in child protection, but that does not make the relationship on which social work rests any less one-sided. In any social work relationship, the social worker holds all the power; the worker decides the game to be played and the rules that it will be played by. The only option service users have is to play the game social work offers, or to walk away with no help at all. This is hardly an equal relationship, and as such mirrors the inequalities and lack of power that people on the margins face from multiple systems in everyday life. It also mimics the principles of the workhouse. Indeed, although social work today may be more benevolent than the workhouses of yesteryear, just as yesterday's workhouse guardians decided what was in the interests of the poor, today's social workers decide what is in the best interests of service users.

## A Service Users' Union: An Answer to Social Work Power

Service users have a solution to the problem of social work power: a service users' union (Dumbrill, 2010; Dumbrill & Lo, 2009). One of the tasks service users saw the union undertaking was peer support. A parent explained, "We need something that goes with CAS [intervention], a group of people [parents] that have been through it" (Dumbrill, 2010, p. 199). This peer support was not just to fight off the power of child protection. Service users were not seeing child protection as all bad and offering nothing of value. Many service users recognized the need for child protection services and for workers to have access to power. Indeed, if our analysis about the imbalance between social work and service users is read as a dichotomy between bad powerful social workers and good powerless service users, then the point we (and many of the service users we spoke to) are trying to make is missed. The problem is not social work nor social work power, but the fact that this power is so one-sided. One-sided power that has no checks or balances not only has the potential to become unjust, but one-sided power can often evoke resistance rather than change.

A father who was a child protection service user articulated the way social work power can stop change. The father explained that he was parenting inappropriately in a way that was harming his children. The father said that his child protection social worker had good ideas about what he needed to do to change—he needed counselling for some deep-seated problems—but the power imbalance prevented him from acknowledging that there was a problem. It ought to be obvious that it would be hard for a parent to hear what a social worker is saying in these circumstances because social work brings change through engagement and relationship, and engagement is about balance. The father had a solution for this power imbalance:

> You [need] a support system in place; as soon as something happens there should be somebody there for parents. I wouldn't have even gone to counselling unless I had somebody there to say, "You're obviously confused." (Dumbrill, 2010, p. 199)

The "somebody" the father referred to was a friend who took him aside and said that he had best listen to his social worker, because the worker was right; he did have some problems and the way he was parenting his children was not right. As a result of this advice from a peer, the father was able to hear his worker, and he got the help he needed. The father went on to explain how important his friend's advice had been in this process, and said that he wanted to be this type of friend to other fathers. We spoke of this type of peer-support role earlier and the danger of only seeing it as a means to empower peer helpers and make them feel valued. This is not what motivated the service users in the study referred to above; this father and other service user parents did not want to become peer helpers to meet their own needs. They wanted to help social workers meet the needs of other service users. They suggested that they do this through peer helping that would provide:

- Information about the intervention processes
- Advice about basic parental rights
- Emotional support
- Advice about ways to respond to intervention
- Advice about intervention options that workers may not have suggested
- Advice about the benefits or consequences other parents had faced when accepting or not accepting various intervention plans (Dumbrill, 2010, p. 200)

Service users understood, however, that peer support does not go far enough. Of course it provides knowledge, but contrary to the belief that knowledge is power, knowledge without power achieves little in an unequal relationship. To truly level the playing field between social workers and service users requires service users gaining access to political power. The way to achieve this is moving beyond peer support to take up the type of political power that unions wield.

Child protection agencies have already given this type of power to Foster Parent Associations (FPAs). These associations have considerable power. When Gary was a supervisor of foster care at a Children's Aid Society, the FPA president met regularly with him to discuss any issues or concerns that foster parents had in their working relationship with the agency. If Gary was unable to resolve the concerns, the FPA president would take them up with the agency's executive director or board of directors.

The type of issues that the FPA would regularly raise would be social workers who were unresponsive to the needs of foster parents or foster children. Gary would trouble-shoot these issues with the worker's supervisor and if these were not resolved they would eventually become a worker performance issue. As a result, just as workers have the power to evaluate the performance of foster parents, foster parents also have the power to evaluate workers (in both positive and negative ways), and this power is connected directly to the agency management structure. In a sense, the knowledge foster parents have of worker strengths and limitations is similar to the word on the street that we mentioned above about the work of Juliana Chooi. Unlike foster parents' knowledge that feeds directly into social work power structures in a way that recognizes successes or corrects problems, service users' knowledge on the street is entirely disconnected from these power structures, so service users have to simply live with these system problems (as well as deal with the issues that brought them into contact with services).

## Key Concept

Have you worked as a social worker or social services worker? Do you hope to one day work as a social worker or social services worker? If so, what was or will be the word on the street about you and your work? Currently in Canadian social work, there is no guarantee that you will ever find out.

Other rights granted to FPAs but denied to service users were regular consultation on agency policy and procedures, and on the training and supports that foster parents needed. The FPA had real power in these processes; if they felt the agency was too de-manding, they would threaten to go on strike and take no more placements. As well, if a foster parent was ever accused of abusing or neglecting a child, the foster parent had the right to be supported throughout the process by another foster parent who was trained to be present and support them through the entire investigation. It is known that foster parents being given these rights helps to create a better agency relationship with foster parents and this brings benefits to the children in their care (Carbino, 2006; Pasztor & McFadden, 2006).

In the process of Gary discussing the prospect of a service users' union with parents who were receiving child protection intervention, he outlined for the service users the rights foster parents had through their FPA. Service users were astounded. They asked, if it is known that these measures enable foster parents to work better with the agency and if this is proven to be in the best interests of the children in their care, why was this not being done for service users and their children? The only answer we know to that question is not one that we like—the principle of less eligibility remains unchanged.

# Plans for a Service Users' Union

It is not for us but for service users to decide how to build their union. Child protection service users have shared with us the idea of an organization that is similar to FPAs. FPAs have local branches with boards and presidents who deal with the local agency, and these local branches are linked through a provincial or territorial network, and also a national body (http://www.canadianfosterfamilyassociation.ca).

The ultimate objective of FPAs at a local and national level is to provide good foster care—achieved by providing support and advocacy for foster parents—because good support makes good foster parents. A child protection service users' union could use a similar formula. The union would be focused on the ultimate objective of ensuring that parents and children receiving child protection intervention get the services and resources they need. Similar to FPAs, the union branches would address local issues that arise with child protection services, and would link with its provincial or territorial and federal network to address broader child welfare policy issues.

The idea of service users' unions is not just for those receiving child welfare services. The exact same issues and needs play out in other areas of social work too. We envision other service user groups also forming unions, and the multiple service users' union groups liaising with each other to become an even stronger collective voice.

## A Service Users' Union Will Liberate Social Workers Too

Ultimately, a service users' union will not only help service users, it will help social work too. Social work cannot stand up to oppression, or build the occupation in an anti-oppressive way, unless done so with the help of a service users' union.

Without a service users' union, social work will remain locked into an inadequate form of practice, because it will addresses service users' personal troubles at the micro level. The "social work dream" of anti-oppression we spoke of in the previous chapter will never be realized. This is particularly so for child protection social work, which has shown a consistent inability to address these broader issues (Dumbrill, 2010; Swift, 1995). This is because:

> . . . the problem for child protection social work is that state funding and regulation ensure that practice is focused on protecting children from the failings of parents, and away from protecting children and families from the failings of the state. Social work mission statements may require workers to stand up for parents on socio-political issues, but their job descriptions rarely do. (Dumbrill, 2010, p. 202)

Social workers do not have the power to change this. It is ironic that social workers have enormous power over service users' lives but very little power over their own work. Hemmed in by regulations and funding formulas, the state restricts what social workers do and how they can do it. Service users, millions of them across the country, face no such constraints. Herein lies the true irony: it may be that service users have the power to liberate social work, rather than social work having the power to liberate service users.

**Figure 10.1** The results of non-union work

At the moment a service users' union of the type and scale proposed does not exist in Canada, and as far as we know nothing on this scale exists anywhere else. To develop such an organization will require funding, and we have suggestions for the way that may occur. We contend that anyone funding a social work agency be required to direct a percentage of that funding to the development of a service users' union. We suggest this start with child protection services, mental health services, and all services that provide benefits or aid to service users. We suggest this starting point because to us it seems unjust for the state or any other body to fund an organization to intervene in service users' lives (often against the service user's will), or to be able to provide or withhold the necessities of life, and have no mechanism to ensure that the voice of service users depending on these services be heard. We envision the service users' union also providing peer support, and we imagine in the foyer of every agency a union office staffed by service user representatives and peer helpers. This or some similar vision, we believe, is the means to make the social work dream of a practice that is anti-oppressive become reality.

## Chapter Summary

In this chapter we explained what service users' knowledge and theory is, and why social work cannot achieve anti-oppression without it. We have outlined some of the mistakes that can be made when developing service users' knowledge and theory, and involving service users in social work processes. We have argued that, ironically, service users rather than social workers have the power and potential to enable practice to become anti-oppressive.

At the start of this chapter we spoke of the way Gary raised in his placement whether service users might know more than social workers about the help they need. This suggestion should be seen neither as a criticism of the agency he was placed in, nor as a criticism of the specialized service that the agency offered. Quite the opposite, service users often depend on the type of expertise Gary was learning at that agency. Our critique is not about the skills, knowledge, and theory that social workers bring. It is not even a critique about social workers having power. Our critique is about the lack of something that social workers cannot bring—service users' knowledge, theory, and power. We said at the start of the chapter that when Gary suggested that we make space in our agencies and practice for service users' knowledge and theory (and by implication their power), he crossed an unwritten line, and we suggested that by the end of this chapter you will know what that line was, and why social workers still hold that line in place. By now, you ought to have ideas of what this line is.

## Discussion Questions

In this chapter we have not named the line that Gary crossed by suggesting that social work service users may have a good understanding of their own needs and the services they require to meet those needs. There are many ways this line could be described. As a group, discuss the following:

1. How would you describe that line?
2. Why do you think June and Gary say that it is important to cross that line?
3. Look back to previous chapters in this book where we have spoken of lines that separate the oppressor and the oppressed. What part of that analysis fits the line we have discussed in this chapter and why?
4. In answering question 3 above, do not fall into the trap of seeing or portraying social work as always oppressive, or always anti-oppressive. Instead develop a more nuanced analysis, and think through what ideas from this chapter might be used to ensure that social work dream of being anti-oppressive comes true.

## Activities

1. Watch Parts 1 and 2 of the Canadian documentary on CanGrands at https://youtu.be/IEyE9I2V-Fo. CanGrands is a service user organization that is focused on the needs of grandparents and other kin caregivers. This organization fulfills many of the functions we have suggested a service users' union can undertake. Consider the work CanGrands does and the benefits models like this can bring. Consider also the questions this raises for you and why.

2. Listen to John Dunn on CBC talk about his experience of being in foster care at https://vimeo.com/32406446. John is trying to make a contribution to improving the child welfare system. He was also prohibited from attending a child welfare outcomes conference. What are your thoughts on what John says in this radio show? What do you think he might offer to social workers?

## Suggested Resources

Beresford, P. (2016). *All our welfare: towards participatory social policy.* Bristol, UK: Policy Press. Mental Health service user involvement, a documentary by City University London (UK), which explores mental health service user movements in the UK and Uganda, at https://www.youtube.com/playlist?list=PL9DF4354EB30AC2BE

## References

Beresford, P. (2000). Service users' knowledges and social work theory: Conflict or collaboration? *British Journal of Social Work, 30*(4), 489–503. doi:10.1093/bjsw/30.4.489

Beresford, P. (2016, December 6). New manifesto for social care is essential—service users should write it. *The Guardian (online).* Retrieved from http://www.theguardian.com/social-care-network/2016/dec/06/new-manifesto-for-social-care-is-essential-service-users-should-write-it

Beresford, P., & Croft, S. (2001). Service users' knowledges and the social construction of social work. *Journal of Social Work, 1*(3), 295–316.

Blackstock, C. (2009). Why addressing the over-representation of First Nations children in care requires new theoretical approaches based on First Nations ontology. *Journal of Social Work Values and Ethics, 6*(3).

Brandsen, T., & Pestoff, V. (2006). Co-production, the third sector and the delivery of public services. *Public Management Review, 8*(4), 493–501. doi:10.1080/14719030601022874

Cabiati, E. (2016). Teaching and learning: An exchange of knowledge in the university among students, service users, and professors. *European Journal of Social Work, 19*(2), 247–62. doi:10.1080/13691457.2015.1024615

Callahan, M., Field, B., Hubberstey, C., & Wharf, B. (1998, June). *Best practice in child welfare: Perspectives from parents, social workers and community members.* Child, Family and Community Research Program, University of Victoria School of Social Work, Victoria, Canada.

Carbino, R. (2006). Family foster care: Voices from around the world. *Families in Society: The Journal of Contemporary Social Services, 87*(4), 467–8. doi:10.1606/1044-3894.3559

Contenta, S., Monsebraaten, L., & Rankin, J. (2014, 11 December). Just 8% of Toronto kids are black but 41% of kids in care are black: The stunning disparity is being called 'a modern-day residential schools system.' Critics believe that poverty, cultural misunderstanding and racism are to blame. *Toronto Star,* p. A1.

Cook, J.A., Copeland, M.E., Floyd, C.B., Jonikas, J.A., Hamilton, M.M., Razzano, L., . . . Boyd, S. (2012). A randomized controlled trial of effects of wellness recovery action planning on depression, anxiety, and recovery. *Psychiatric Services, 63*(6), 541–7. doi:10.1176/appi.ps.201100125

Damiani-Taraba, G., Dumbrill, G.C., Gladstone, J., Koster, A., Leslie, B., & Charles, M. (2017). The evolving relationship between casework skills, engagement, and positive case outcomes in child protection: A structural equation model. *Children and Youth Services Review, 79,* 456–62. doi:10.1016/j.childyouth.2017.05.033

Department of Health. (2002). *Requirements for social work training.* Retrieved from http://www.scie.org.uk/publications/guides/guide04/files/requirements-for-social-work-training.pdf?res=true

Dill, K., Montgomery, L., Davidson, G., & Duffy, J. (2016). Service user involvement in social work education: The road less travelled. *Field Educator, 6*(2), 1–9.

Dumbrill, G.C. (2003). Child welfare: AOP's nemesis? In W. Shera (Ed.), *Emerging perspectives on anti-oppressive practice* (pp. 101–19). Toronto, Canada: Canadian Scholars' Press.

Dumbrill, G.C. (2010). Power and child protection: The need for a child welfare service users' union or association. *Australian Social Work, 63*(2), 194–206. doi:10.1080/03124071003717655

Dumbrill, G.C. (2017). Emic and alliance: Anti-oppressive social work in child protection. In D. Baines (Ed.), *Doing anti-oppressive practice: Social justice social work* (3rd ed., pp. 57–69). Halifax, Canada: Fernwood Publishing.

Dumbrill, G.C., & Lo, W. (2009). What parents say: Service users' theory and anti-oppressive child welfare practice In S. Strega & S.A. Esquao [J. Carriere] (Eds), *Walking this path together: Anti-racist and anti-oppressive child welfare practice* (pp. 127–41). Halifax, Canada: Fernwood Publishing.

Dumbrill, G.C., & Lo, W. (2015). Adjusting a power imbalance: There is no anti-oppression without service users' voice. In Esquao, Sohki Aski [J. Carriere] & S. Strega (Eds), *Walking this* path together: Anti-oppressive child welfare practice (2nd ed., pp. 124–38). Halifax, Canada: Fernwood Publishing.

Dunn, J. (2003). John Dunn's advocacy blog Keep up to date on the advocacy work I have been involved in. Retrieved from https://afterfostercare.blogspot.com/2003/02/p-r-e-s-s-r-e-l-e-s-e-for-immediate.html

Family Inclusion Network of Western Australia. (2009). Finding your way with the department of child protection and family support: Information for parents dealing with the department of child protection & family support. North Perth, Australia: The Family Inclusion Network of Western Australia Inc.

Franklin, P., Hossain, R., & Coren, E. (2016). Social media and young people's involvement in social work education. Social Work Education: The International Journal, 35(3), 344–56. doi:10.1080/02615479.2016.1154710

Fraser, D. (1973). The evolution of the British welfare state: A history of social policy since the industrial revolution. London, UK: Macmillan.

Gates, L.B., & Akabas, S.H. (2007). Developing strategies to integrate peer providers into the staff of mental health agencies. Administration and Policy in Mental Health, 34(3), 293–306. doi:10.1007/s10488-006-0109-4

Gladstone, J., Dumbrill, G.C., Leslie, B., Koster, A., Young, M., & Ismaila, A. (2012). Looking at engagement and outcome from the perspectives of child protection workers and parents. Children and Youth Services Review, 34(1), 112–18. doi:10.1016/j.childyouth.2011.09.003

Greene, S., O'Brien-Teengs, D., Dumbrill, G.C., Ion, A., Beaver, K., Porter, M., & Desbiens, M. (2016). A community-based research approach to

developing an HIV education and training module for child and family service workers in Ontario. In H. Montgomery, D. Badry, D. Fuchs, & D. Kikulwe (Eds), Transforming child welfare: Interdisciplinary practices, field education, and research (163–85). Regina, Canada: University of Regina Press.

Gregory, J. (2008). Poverty from workhouse to the welfare state. History Today, 58(7), 44–52.

Gupta, A., & Blewett, J. (2008). Involving services users in social work training on the reality of family poverty: A case study of a collaborative project. Social Work Education: The International Journal, 27(5), 459–73. doi:10.1080/02615470701380261

Levy, S., Aiton, R., Doig, J., Dow, J. P. L., Brown, S., Hunter, L., & McNeil, R. (2016). Outcomes focused user involvement in social work education: Applying knowledge to practice. Social Work Education: The International Journal, 35(8), 866–77. doi:10.1080/02615479.2016.1240160

Maluccio, A. N. (1979). Learning from clients: Interpersonal helping as viewed by clients and social workers. New York, NY: Free Press.

Margolin, L. (1997). Under the cover of kindness: The invention of social work. Charlottesville: University Press of Virginia.

Matka, E., River, D., Littlechild, R., & Powell, T. (2010). Involving service users and carers in admissions for courses in social work and clinical psychology: Cross-disciplinary comparison of practices at the University of Birmingham.

British Journal of Social Work, 40(7), 2137–54. doi:10.1093/bjsw/bcp142

Mayer, C., & McKenzie, K. (2017). '. . . it shows that there's no limits': The psychological impact of co-production for experts by working in youth mental health. Health and Social Care in the Community, 25(3), 1181–9. doi:10.1111/hsc.12418

Mayer, J.E., & Timms, N. (1970). The client speaks: Working class impressions of casework. London, UK: Routledge and Kegan Paul.

McCarthy, J., Marshall, A., Collins, J., Arganza, G., Deserly, K., & Milon, J. (2003). A family's guide to the child welfare system. Washington, DC: Georgetown University Center for Child and Human Development.

Moullin, M. (2017). Improving and evaluating performance with the Public Sector Scorecard. International Journal of Productivity and Performance Management, 66(4), 442–58. doi:10.1108/IJPPM-06-2015-0092

OACAS. (2016). One vision one voice: Changing the Ontario child welfare system to better serve African Canadians. Practice framework part 2: Race equity practices. Retrieved from http://www.oacas.org/wp-content/uploads/2016/09/One-Vision-One-Voice-Part-1_digital_english.pdf

Pasztor, E.M., & McFadden, E.J. (2006). Foster parent associations: Advocacy, support, and empowerment. Families in Society, 87(4), 483–90.

Pelton, L.H. (1989). For reasons of poverty: A critical analysis of the public child welfare system in the United States. New York, NY: Praeger.

Rankin, J. (2014, December 11). When CAS comes knocking. Toronto Star, p. A33.

Rees, S. (1978). Social work face to face: Clients' and social workers' perceptions of the content and outcomes of their meetings. London, UK: Edward Arnold.

Robinson, K., & Webber, M. (2013). Models and effectiveness of service user and carer involvement in social work education: A literature review. The British Journal of Social Work, 43(5), 925–44. doi:10.1093/bjsw/bcs025

Ross, A.M., Hart, L.M., Jorm, A.F., Kelly, C.M., & Kitchener, B.A. (2012). Development of key messages for adolescents on providing basic mental health first aid to peers: A Delphi consensus study. Early Intervention in Psychiatry, 6(3), 229–38. doi:10.1111/j.1751-7893.2011.00331.x.

Russell, M., Harris, B., & Gockel, A. (2008). Parenting in poverty: Perspectives of high-risk parents. Journal of Children and Poverty, 14(1), 83–98. doi:10.1080/10796120701871322

Sainsbury, E.E. (1975). Social work with families: Perceptions of social casework among clients of a family service unit. London, UK: Routledge & Kegan Paul.

Silverman, R. (1972). John E. Mayer and Noel Timms, "The client speaks: Working class impressions of casework" (Book Review). Social Service Review, 46(1), 132–4. doi:10.1086/642816

Swift, K.J. (1995). Manufacturing "bad mothers": A critical perspective on child neglect. Toronto, Canada: University of Toronto Press.

Terry, S. (2017). *Re-imagining child welfare with service users: What children's social workers need to be taught in school*. (MSW), McMaster University, Hamilton, Canada.

The College of Social Work. (2012). *Reforming social work qualifying education: The social work degree*. Retrieved from: http://cdn.basw.co.uk/upload/basw_105219-6.pdf

Trocme, N., Knoke, D., & Blackstock, C. (2004). Pathways to the overrepresentation of Aboriginal children in Canada's child welfare system. *Social Service Review, 78*(4), 577–600. doi:10.1086/424545

Watters, E.C., Cait, C.-A., & Oba, F. (2016). Social work curriculum review case study: Service users tell us what makes effective social workers. *Canadian Social Work Review, 33*(1), 27–44. doi:10.7202/1037088ar

Wilson, A., & Beresford, P. (2000). 'Anti-oppressive practice': Emancipation or appropriation? *British Journal of Social Work, 30*(5), 553–73.

Young, M., & Dumbrill, G.C. (Eds). (2010). *Clinical counselling: A vital part of child welfare services – part 3*. Toronto, Canada: Clinical Counselling in Child Welfare Committee.

# 11

# How to Do Anti-Oppression with Individuals, Families, and Communities

## In this chapter you will learn:

- What limits your ability to do anti-oppressive practice
- What service users say anti-oppressive practice is
- Why a heart and the ability to love are important in anti-oppression

## Introduction

When June visited Hong Kong she was trying to get from Central District (中環) to Lantau Island (大嶼山) but she did not know the route to take. June decided to ask for directions and noticed a group of fellow Canadians enjoying beer outside a pub. June asked, "Can you give me directions to Lantau Island?"

The people said they would. Several pulled out smartphones, others compared maps, and for some time they debated differing ideas and pointed in various directions. Eventually the conversation came to an end and one of the people turned to June and said, "I am sorry, but we don't think you can get there from here."

Of course this was a joke; a similar joke is told in different places around the world. Even though an old joke that has been told many times, it is actually true in relation to some destinations, anti-oppression being one of them. By the end of this chapter you will understand why you cannot get to do anti-oppression from social work's current location, and you will know what needs to change to be able to do so.

## Why You Can't Do Anti-Oppression from Here

Anti-oppression in the current social work environment is impossible. Baines (2011) describes how anti-oppression requires a "fundamental reorganization of all levels of society" (p. 4) and to achieve this the anti-oppressive social worker must "integrate the search and struggle for social change directly into the social work experience" (p. 4). The problem is that the social work experience itself is a part of the power imbalance service users face within society. Without the collective service users' voice discussed in the previous chapter, service users have no say in shaping the services they receive nor the new social order that social workers are trying to bring about. Baines contends that service users need to have a voice. She says that service users:

> . . . need to be active in their own liberation and that of others. Their experience is also a key starting point in the development of new theory and knowledge, as well as political strategies and resistance. Their voices must be part of every program, policy, planning effort, and evaluation. (Baines, 2011, p. 7)

Service users' voice is not a part of every social work program, policy, planning effort, or evaluation, and for the most part service users' theory and knowledge does not inform what Canadian social workers do. As a result, one cannot get to anti-oppression from here. Without the type of service users' organizations we described in the previous chapter, anti-oppression will always remain out of reach. Any form of "liberation" conceived by social workers and not by service users themselves is not liberation. Service users cannot be liberated by a new social order imagined and delivered by social workers. They can only be liberated by gaining power and having their own voice in shaping social change, because without power any new social order is just going to eventually tread service users down all over again.

## Key Concept

If service users have no collective say in the social work you deliver, or the vision that you and other social workers develop to transform society, the social work you are doing may not be anti-oppressive at all.

If we cannot get to anti-oppression from social work's current position, what is a social worker to do? Workers can, of course, support the development of service users' unions or similar organizations through which service users can gain power. But in the meantime, where is the social worker to begin when service users or communities need immediate help? One place to begin is to simply ask service users themselves what they think social workers should do.

## Anti-Oppressive Starting Points That Work

We have been involved in a number of projects that have asked service users how we ought to do social work, and in particular how we ought to do anti-oppression. This starting point does not undo the power imbalance that has to be addressed if social work is to be anti-oppressive, and as such this is an imperfect starting place. This starting point, however, is a place that any practitioner, policymaker, or program evaluator can start from right now. We have been doing this type of asking for several years, and below we share some of the answers we have encountered.

## Have a Heart and Learn to Love

Service users have said that social workers need to be human, to have a heart, and to treat those they serve with respect (Dumbrill, 2017; Dumbrill & Lo, 2008, 2009). These ideas, especially the notion of having a heart and treating people as human, may sound uncritical and might be confused with a "Kumbaya" attitude that denies the existence of inequality. Such attitudes promote the notion that all we need to do is recognize we are all human and everything will work out fine. Anyone who knows anything about oppression knows that we are not all treated as human and that simply "having a heart" and caring about someone is never going to stop oppression. Nevertheless, the service users we have spoken to have consistently made the point that social workers need to have a heart, and we think this idea is much more radical than it seems.

The need for a social work heart was conveyed most succinctly by refugee parents in a photovoice study in which Gary was involved called "Your Policies, Our Children: Refugee Parents Speak about Canadian Social Service Systems" (Dumbrill & Lo, 2008).[1] **Photovoice** is a participatory, community-based research method in which participants convey messages in words and pictures (Wang & Burris, 1994; Wang, Ling, & Ling, 1996). Using this method, refugee parents conveyed what they believed social workers needed to know and do in order to better understand and serve their families and communities.

The study began in 2007 and lasted about a year. Eleven refugees (nine women and two men) took part; eight originated from West Africa and three from South-west to Central Asia; three participants arrived in Canada as landed immigrants rather than refugees, but the process they followed in leaving their former homelands caused them to regard themselves as refugees. Participants signed informed consents under a research ethics protocol approved by the McMaster University Ethics Review Board.

Participants had experienced a broad range of Canadian social work services and had ideas about how to improve them. Some of the participants said that social workers did not have hearts, and needed to find ways to have them. A participant gave an example. Speaking through an interpreter who was a part of the research team, the participant explained how her social assistance had been cut off and she was left without money, so she went to her social worker to resolve the issue:

> When I went to this social assistance agency, my social worker used my children to interpret because I did not understand English. She started scolding me, and my children translated, "You need to manage money better and if you cannot afford

---

[1] Some of the results of this study were subsequently published in the article "Your policies, our children: Messages from refugee parents to child welfare workers and policymakers" (Dumbrill, 2009).

food you have to go to the food bank!" I felt so ashamed, because I had been going to the food bank already for a long time, but I did this secretly so my children would not know. And now my children were finding out [about the food bank] and also they were hearing me being scolded by the worker. (Dumbrill, 2009)

Other participants in the study recounted similar stories of disrespectful and condescending treatment by social workers, and they began to develop theory that perhaps social workers do not care about the people they are helping.

Gary, who was involved in the project, said to participants that in his opinion most social workers did have hearts, but the service users remained skeptical and wondered why, if social workers do have hearts, they do not show it.

To emphasize the importance of social workers having a heart, participants took the picture below of the mother involved in the story. The study participants said that they wanted this photo shown to social work students to communicate the shame and humiliation that social work without a heart causes service users to feel.

Of course it is quite possible that this mother's social worker did have a heart, and perhaps this and the many similar stories that the other participants told might have other explanations. Maybe all of these workers had hearts, but simply lacked self-awareness about the impact their attitudes and actions have on others. Whatever the cause, it became clear in this study that service users want and need social workers to have a heart, and they suggested that if a social worker does not, or does not have the ability to show this, they ought to be thinking of a different career. Participants did not say that social workers needed to always get things right, and they understood that social workers had "off days" too, but there was a

Photo by Gary C. Dumbrill. Reprinted with permission of *Child Welfare Journal*

**Figure 11.1** The impact of heartless social work

very clear expectation that social workers needed to treat service users with respect and had to also take responsibility for their actions. The mother in the incident went on to explain:

> In the end I found out that my assistance was stopped because of an error of my caseworker. . . . When you care about people, you should understand the implications of your actions and make sure that you know what you are doing. I was in the hospital because of the stress of losing my assistance and not being able to care for my family. My caseworker didn't even say she was sorry. (Dumbrill, 2009)

We contend that all social work, not just anti-oppression, has to begin with caring. Of course anti-oppression has to move beyond caring to engage in action that pushes back at oppressive structures, but unless that action begins in caring and love for the person or communities we serve, much of what we do will be useless. Indeed, the way oppression operates is to treat those it treads down as less eligible, less deserving, less human, as not worthy of care and consideration. In other words, oppression involves a systemic process of dehumanization and a disregard (uncaring) for those trod down by the machinery of oppression. If you do not love, and cannot convey caring, you align yourself with this machinery.

Perhaps the power of love to prevent us being co-opted by the machinery of oppression is why Dr Martin Luther King Jr wrote from the Birmingham jail about the need to love even those who oppress us (King, 1967, 1994), and this is certainly why Desmond Tutu speaks of the importance of love and Ubuntu (Battle, 1997; Tutu, 2011).

Even if it is difficult to take up the love for the oppressor King and Tutu suggest, it ought to be obvious that we should love those we are trying to assist. Che Guevara contended that even though it sounds ridiculous, "the true revolutionary is guided by great feelings of love" (Guevara, 1965). In the same manner since the 1970s, Third World feminists have understood the importance of a "love-politics grounded in communal and interpersonal bonds" as central in revolutionary social change (Havlin, 2015). We suggest that if in anti-oppression we have lost the ability to love and the understanding of why love matters, we have lost touch with the reason revolution and anti-oppression are important.

## Exercise 11.1

### How Will You Make a Difference?

If possible, undertake this exercise in groups.

1. List your caring qualities.
2. List the ways that you believe that you communicate each of these caring qualities to others.

3. Once you have completed the above, ask a friend or someone who knows you well (and who will be honest with you) to also make a list of your caring qualities. (Do not prompt them or show them your list. Let them do this without any help from you.)

4. Compare your assessment of your own caring qualities with the list your friend made of your caring qualities, and reflect on any differences.

5. Ask your friend what it is you have done that communicated the caring qualities they noticed about you. (In other words, how did your friend know that you have the qualities that they put on the list?)

6. Next, dig a little deeper. Reflect on what you know about yourself, and also ask your friend and others who know you well about any circumstances or moments your caring might not shine through, and in what circumstances or toward which groups of people you sometimes show uncaring, judgmental, and even hostile attitudes. Reflect on how you will guard against these moments, and also how you will address whatever causes these reactions to arise within you.

## Be "Different" and Make a Difference

Service users who say that their social workers got anti-oppression right said that their social workers were "different" in some way. This idea has emerged in almost all of our research, but emerged most clearly in a small in-depth study Gary undertook called "Looking for Anti-Oppression."[2] This study took place in 2012 and involved 14 participants: 5 service users and 9 workers. Service user participants were parents who had received child welfare intervention and who were recruited because they said their workers got anti-oppression right. In two cases service users and their workers were interviewed together; in another two cases service users elected to be interviewed alone; seven workers who were identified as "getting anti-oppression right" were also interviewed alone. All data was gathered under a McMaster University ethics protocol.

Service users in this study were able to say how workers who got anti-oppression right were "different." A mother articulated this in the following manner:

> She [the worker] was a godsend like just a godsend, because I'll tell you when I first went in there I had my walls up, I had my boxing gloves on and I was ready. And when I sat down in front of her she . . . She just didn't talk about anything that I didn't want to talk about and her attitude was just completely different. . . . (Dumbrill, 2012)

[2] The results of this study were published in the article "Anti-oppressive child welfare: How we get there from here" (Dumbrill, 2012).

Another parent describes her worker as an "angel," and said that as soon as she met her she knew that this worker was going to be "different." When asked what it was about the worker that was "different," the mother said, "It was basically her aura. I felt the warmth there, the caring I could see it in her eyes, I knew that I could trust her. . . . [Now] if I have a problem I don't call anybody, I call my angel [CAS worker]. She's good." (Dumbrill, 2012)

It is possible that these workers were retrospectively attributed angelic and "sent by god" qualities because the case outcomes eventually turned in ways that the service users thought helpful. This is unlikely though, because in the examples above, the service users and workers were interviewed together, and both agreed that from the very start something "clicked" and worked well. We suspect, therefore, that the eventual case outcomes did not cause the service users to consider their workers "different" or a "godsend," but instead the final case outcomes simply confirmed a difference they sensed from the start. We also contend that if from the start a service user and worker think that something is going to be "different" in a good way, it is easier to make this so.

Of course a service user and worker "clicking" is not necessarily anti-oppressive, but what workers and service users went on to do after certainly was. For instance, the mother who described having "her boxing gloves on" had already lost two children who had been made permanent Crown Wards several years earlier, and she was now in the process of losing a third. The worker enabled the mother to get her third child back, and the worker then went on to fight her own agency to have the Crown Ward decision on the other two children reversed, so that they were also returned home. As well, against the advice of her own agency, the worker managed to facilitate visits and an ongoing positive relationship between the mother and the foster home where the children had been previously placed as Crown Wards, and today that foster parent remains a friend and support to the mother who has now moved past the addictions, violence, and other issues that had previously pushed her down.

The anti-oppression this worker engaged in did not start with fighting the system. It began with helping the mother fight painful issues she was struggling with at a personal level. The mother said that the worker helped her to come to terms with the role she played in her own difficulties. "I had to struggle with having an understanding of why they [the CAS] were so hard on me for my first 2 [children]" (Dumbrill, 2012). The mother went on to explain how the worker helped her do this:

She [the new worker] comes from a different [place]. . . . She worries about the person first and not the content; I believe when you worry about the person first you'll get further than worrying about the content. Like instead of her sitting across from me saying, "so you're a 'junkie' and this is your file well good luck but you're never getting your son [back]," it wasn't like that. We worked together. . . . Lucky that I ended up with a worker that understood. (Dumbrill, 2012)

When asked what it was that first made her realize that her worker was "different," the mother said that as soon as she met the worker she simply "knew that I could trust her; I knew that she was here to help me. I knew that it didn't matter what my past [was] because she didn't want to know my past, unless I wanted to [tell her about it]" (Dumbrill, 2012).

The worker had a similar view about that first meeting. The worker said that she refused to base her vision of the future on past events in the mother's file. The worker said that the mother's file "is not my client," and instead regarded the file as something that reflected other moments, interactions with other workers, and other realities from the past. This past did not have to be the future. This does not mean that the past was not considered at all. The mother described how she told her worker all about her past, including details that were not in the file, but together the mother and worker interrupted the past and changed the future.

## The Role of Good Casework and Common Sense

We contend that the attitude of the worker above, and whatever it was that the worker did to convey it, was not anti-oppression but instead was simply good casework. This good casework went on to help the mother address issues of violence and addictions that had pushed her down in the past. It was, however, this good casework that made anti-oppression possible; with addictions and violence addressed through casework, the worker and the mother could successfully fight systems, attitudes, and even other social workers to make a different future possible. The mother and worker contend that this working together to push back and defeat these systems and attitudes was "getting anti-oppression right," and we concur. It seems, therefore, that traditional good casework and anti-oppression are interwoven.

In the "Looking for Anti-Oppression" study there were other examples of workers achieving anti-oppression by doing something different from that which the system and sometimes service users expected. One child protection worker described attending a home that was so unhygienic that it was unsafe for the children to remain. Ordinarily, the children would be removed until the parent or parents could make the home safe, but the worker interrupted that system by trying a different approach. The worker said:

> I stopped to think about the amount of work when you apprehend a child. . . .
> I thought, "I [will] work alongside her showing her what needs to change." We literally set apart cleaning her home . . . cleaning out this fridge that was full of mold and cleaning floors that were full of food and piles of junk . . . we just started moving the mountains. I had another worker come and join me so there were 3 of us in the home. What I found amazing was that this client, who was quite private about her issues . . . started talking about these things. So while we were literally working side by side she opened up about the difficulties she had. (Dumbrill, 2012)

In recounting the story above we are not suggesting that social workers doing house-work is anti-oppression, but the social worker seeing that in this instance the routine systemic response was not going to help, and doing something different, was anti-oppressive. The worker recognized that it was not common sense to pour so many resources into removing a child against a parent's consent, when the issues could be resolved with far fewer resources, by simply rolling up one's sleeves and helping to clean up the problem.

The term **common sense** is often seen as problematic in anti-oppression (Baines, 2011), most likely because the term has been co-opted by some governments as a policy catch-phrase (such as the "Common Sense Revolution") in a backlash against equity and social justice programs and other efforts that challenge the existing social order (Crines, Heppell, & Dorey, 2016; *The Globe and Mail*, 2001). We understand the political and also deeper philosophical issues with the term "common sense," but we think that anti-oppression scholars problematizing the phrase is a mistake, because on the street the term refers to everyday wisdom. That wisdom tells us that paying social workers and lawyers vast amounts of money to remove children from dirty homes when a little help cleaning will solve the problem not only makes no sense, but is also a complete waste of taxpayer's money.

Given the above, we want to reclaim the idea of common sense, because if you as a worker recognize that something you are asked to do makes no sense and is not helping those you serve, you may need to interrupt that process and do something different. Of course you have to question your senses (more about that below when we consider critical self-reflection), but this does not mean that you give up using the everyday wisdom of common sense.

## Be Ready to Move Mountains

The worker we mentioned above, who decided to help clean a house rather than remove children, referred to the amount of cleaning that was needed as "moving mountains." This phrase became one of the many "en vivo" themes that emerged in the study. The term **en vivo** is a research term for a code, concept or theme that has emerged in research, that the researcher has labelled with the exact word or phrase a participant used to describe it. Because an en vivo code is a participant's own words, it gets as close as possible to the idea a participant is conveying. If several participants use that exact same word or phrase, the concept or code has to be taken very seriously. In this study, many participants used the term "moving mountains." As such, we have to see this concept as a part of anti-oppressive practice.

In another case where mountains were moved, a mother of a child without an Ontario Health Insurance Plan (OHIP) card became hostile with medical staff when she was unable to obtain medical treatment her child needed. An immediate referral was made to CAS and this became a "child protection issue" because of the mother's behaviour. The case should have been easy to resolve since the child was eligible for OHIP coverage. The mother simply had to go and get the card. The busy worker could have called the OHIP office to tell them this, and could have told the mother to go back and try again, but instead the worker decided to go to the OHIP office with the mother. The worker described what occurred:

When we got to the [OHIP] counter the person actually turned us away and said, "You have to come back with a picture ID." [But] she [the mother] didn't have a picture ID [and was not able to get one] and I'm thinking, "Oh, now this mountain is like this." (Dumbrill, 2012)

The mother became angry with the OHIP official, but with the worker's help, the mother and OHIP official eventually managed to dialogue, and the mother got the OHIP card without a photo ID. The mountain was moved.

What was anti-oppressive about this process? The worker contended that anti-oppression began with the somewhat unusual step (for a child protection worker) to physically travel with the mother to get the OHIP card. This allowed the worker to experience first hand the "mountains" this mother encountered in life. Mountains occur because health-care and similar bureaucracies tend to be designed for standardized people and situations, and navigating those systems when things go wrong requires a standardized negotiation response. If one's life experience is not "standard" or one's way of interacting and problem solving is somewhat "unusual," "mountains" will occur. If one shows frustration in response, service providers often call child protection, security, or even the police. Anti-oppression was the worker realizing that this was "one of the things in life that she [the mother] struggled with and that had closed down a lot of systems for her" (Dumbrill, 2012). In response, the worker continued to offer this mother support to navigate systems in ways that got better results. Of course, one could argue that a better anti-oppressive response would be to change the systems so mountains do not occur for people whose lives and ways of interacting are "different." But this mother had no time to wait for systemic change. Her child needed medical treatment immediately, and she needed a worker who was able to help her get it.

## A Few Words about "Angels"

Along with the theme of "moving mountains," workers being "angels" or "godsends" also emerged as another en vivo theme. "Angels" and "moving mountains" began to emerge as a core concept (an organizing idea) in the ways service users and workers envision

## Key Concept

Anyone outside the circle of first-class citizenship will face mountains that those in the centre do not. Your job as an anti-oppressive social worker is to address those mountains. Keep in mind that the service user may not have time to wait for systemic change, so the remedies you build with service users may have to be immediate. After that immediate help you can talk with service users about longer-term systemic change.

anti-oppression. We have some trouble with the term "angels"; it is not a word we would choose to convey anti-oppression. Gary has previously explained our concerns, and our decision to use the term, as follows:

> I would not have chosen the word "angels" to describe anything in research because, for me at least, it conjures up white religious images painted on the ceilings of Eurocentric churches. But "angel" was coded "en vivo" from the words of parents, and "moving mountains" was what workers said they did. As a researcher I can't simply change these words because I do not like them. As the research progresses other words that better describe these concepts and processes may emerge, but for now I have to work with this description and these terms. Also, the analogy of angel is not entirely inappropriate because the concept is familiar to people from a diverse range of cultures and faiths. Angels do not necessarily have a race or specific gender and they exist in Islam, Christianity, Judaism, Sikhism, Hinduism, Bahá'í, and many other faiths. Angels also appear in secular non-religious culture. Angels in both religious and popular imagination are thought of as kind and caring beings who are not constrained by our ordinary earthly ways of doing things. In many Hollywood movies, because angels are not human, they often think and act outside the box of human regulation to do "the right thing." Paradoxically, in most of these movies, these non-human angelic acts contain lessons for us about how to be more human toward each other. (Dumbrill, 2012, p. 3)

## Discerning How to Make a Difference

The examples we encountered of making a difference all involved some form of pushing back at systems or working outside the regular way social work is undertaken. Despite these examples, we are not suggesting that workers need to always fight the system or work outside the box to be anti-oppressive, nor do we suggest that the system is always oppressive. Indeed, people have spent an inordinate amount of time to make systems anti-oppressive (more about that in the next chapter) so that often the anti-oppressive thing to do is simply to follow what the system says you should do. Anti-oppressive workers need to discern when to follow the system and when to resist it. All of the information we have shared in this book so far ought to help you to discern these differing moments. Exercise 11.2 gives you the opportunity to refine these skills.

## Making a Difference by Fighting Racism (and Other Isms)

In the "Your Policies, Our Children" study, refugees saw a role for social work fighting racism and said, "The undercover racism in Canada is far beyond limit" (Dumbrill & Lo, 2008). By "undercover" they meant that although racism exists in Canada, it is illegal, so when it

## Exercise 11.2

### A Time to Challenge, a Time to Comply

If possible, undertake this exercise in groups.

1. Think of a moment when you were anti-oppressive in the past, or might need to be in the future, by challenging systems.
2. Think of a moment when you were anti-oppressive in the past, or might need to be in the future, by following systems.
3. Reflect on how you tell the above two moments apart. How do you know when to oppose systems, and how do you know when to do what the system says?

occurs it does so in mostly (but not always) deniable "undercover" ways. Participants gave examples of being on the receiving end of both overt and covert racism. One participant said:

> I wanted to wear a poppy for Remembrance Day but I was afraid to do so because a white lady came up to my friend from Pakistan and told her, "Take that poppy off, it is only for Canadians to wear." (Dumbrill & Lo, 2008)

Another participant added:

> My daughter won an iPod from [a well-known coffee shop], but they didn't give it to her. We went three times, my husband went too, but they say "sorry," and we are still waiting for the iPod. I wondered if they [the coffee shop workers] took advantage of the language barrier. They know you won't report or complain, "what happened to that iPod." (Dumbrill & Lo, 2008)

The accumulative impact of such oppression is enormous. A mother in the study took a photograph of a path that was so narrow that a person has to walk alone with nobody alongside to help (Figure 11.2). She explained how this represented her experience raising children in Canada.

> You don't see anyone, just a narrow road with no one to help—Canada can be like this. Back home you can leave your kid with your family or neighbour and go to work but here you can't. I'm not trying to blame it on racism but if you are black and you have white neighbours sometimes they won't let their kids play in

your house. They don't trust me so why should I trust them? Back home your kids can go over to your neighbour's house, but here you can't do it because they're so scared, they're just so scared. So I mean it's hard, it's very hard. (Dumbrill, 2009)

Racism was the predominant form of oppression that refugees spoke of, and it was embedded in numerous settlement barriers they described. Participants said that social workers need to be aware of these issues, and if social workers want to help, they need to address these issues. This means that if you do not see, recognize, and acknowledge everyday racism and other isms, you will not be much help to those being trod down by oppression. In fact, if you are not able to see undercover isms at play, you are a part of the problem, because it is difficult enough for a service user to deal with oppression without having to convince their social worker that it is happening.

Photo by Gary C. Dumbrill, Reprinted with permission of *Child Welfare Journal*

**Figure 11.2** A difficult path

## Be Critically Self-Reflective and Reflexive

In the "Looking for Anti-Oppression" study, two agency anti-oppression leaders were interviewed. These leaders were recognized by service user communities and the field for pushing back against racism and other forms of oppression. These leaders spoke of the need for anti-oppressive social workers to engage in critical self-reflection.

### An Overview of Critical Self-Reflection and Reflexivity

Critical self-reflection is related to the critical thinking we spoke of in Chapter 2. Broadly speaking, such reflection and reflexivity involve engaging in critical thinking in relation to oneself, to our relationship to those we serve, to the knowledge systems we are using to make sense of issues, and to our own feelings, thoughts, actions, and motivations.

The terms "reflection" and "reflexivity" are different but tend to be used interchangeably (D'Cruz, Gillingham, & Melendez, 2007; Thompson & Pascal, 2012). Critical reflective practice has its roots in the work of Schön (1983), who contends that practice is more than a technical endeavour with pre-packaged solutions, but instead involves artistry. A part of this art is to develop and test knowledge in the process of practice through reflection. Here, "taken literally, reflective refers to the process of thinking about the work we undertake—that is, we reflect on our actions either at the time (reflection-in-action) or at a suitable opportunity thereafter (reflection-on-action)" (Thompson & Pascal, 2012, p. 319). From an anti-oppressive perspective, the "critical" part of this process involves "analysis at a broader socio-political level that takes account of cultural and structural factors that are so important in shaping professional practice and the social and political circumstances in which such practice occurs" (Thompson & Pascal, 2012, p. 322). A central part of this analysis entails questioning power relations (D'Cruz et al., 2007).

Reflexivity is similar, but is sometimes said to be different, with "'reflectivity' [being seen] as referring more to a *process* of reflecting on practice, while 'reflexivity' refers to a stance of being able to locate oneself in the picture" (D'Cruz et al., 2007, p. 84). Reflexivity certainly involves locating the self, but also involves reflecting on oneself in relation to those we serve. Wehbi explains how she uses reflexivity when engaging in anti-oppressive practice by:

> . . . continually asking myself questions related to who I am in relation to the community I am working with: Am I an insider, outsider, expert? Do I own my privilege? Do I understand the complexity of my social location and its impact on my work? How did I come to this work?" (Wehbi, 2011, p. 138)

Although Wehbi is being *reflexive* by locating herself in a process, she is also *reflecting* on her practice, so it seems to us that in social work reflexivity and reflection are always merged. As a result, we use the terms interchangeably, and will delve into the essential aspects of both by using D'Cruz, Gillingham, and Melendez's (2007) concept of reflexivity, which they divide into three types.

## Three Types of Reflexivity to Consider Using

The first type of reflexivity is a considered response through which "an individual makes a personal choice by evaluating themselves and their individual response to his/her situation, particularly in terms of self-development and the choices available about the future course of his/her life" (D'Cruz et al., 2007, p. 75). You may have used this type of reflexivity in deciding to become a social worker. Perhaps you recognized you were good at helping others; maybe you recognized that you had a passion for social justice; maybe this helped you decide that social work might be a good fit for you. This type of reflexivity does not end when you enter a social work program or even begin practice. One has to continually revisit these reflections because your motivations will have implications for the ways you take up social work when you meet with a service user or community, and you need to be aware of the ways this might impact your work and how it is received.

The second form of critical self-reflexivity is a "self-critical approach that questions how knowledge is generated and, further, how relations of power operate in this process" (D'Cruz et al., 2007, p. 75). You have already been using this type of reflexivity throughout this book, because we have carefully taken you through processes in which you questioned issues of power and knowledge (especially in Chapters 2 and 3). All of this thinking needs to be drawn upon every time you engage with a service user or community. It is not enough to raise questions of knowledge and power in the abstract. The reason we have spent so much time critically reflecting on issues of knowledge and power in this text is so that you can do the same in practice. When you meet with a service user or community, ask who holds power and how it is being used; who defines the parameters and scope of the work you are doing together and for what purpose; whose knowledge, theory, and desires are driving the process and possibilities; and whose are not.

The third form of reflexivity is "concerned with the part that emotion plays in social work practice" (D'Cruz et al., 2007, p. 75). We have also addressed this throughout the book. In Chapter 2 we spoke of how your feelings need to be your teacher. This imperative not only applies when reading this text; it also applies when engaging with persons and communities.

## How the Anti-Oppressive Worker Uses Reflection and Reflexivity in Practice

All of these reflective and reflexive abilities have to be used when working with service users and communities. As mentioned above, the two anti-oppressive leaders from the field who took part in the 2012 "Looking for Anti-Oppression" study raised the need for critical self-reflection. These participants were interviewed together. One of these participants began by explaining that in the field:

> . . . [f]or anti-oppression to work, the practitioner or the service provider is thinking about the identities at play; they are thinking about their own identity, they are thinking about the identities of the service users and the family. . . . They are thinking about those identities in the context of how those identities are taken up in society; so not randomly thinking about them, like . . . listing off demographic stuff about people, [but instead] looking at identity in relation to context and who we are to that person, and understanding that the context is based on social division . . . so how is that identity responded to socially?
>
> And I would also say it's the slowing down of thought and so we are using a critical reflective practice framework here. So it's talking about critical reflective practice as a defining practice and approach that causes you to stop and think about what you're thinking: What's my identity? [and] What's the so what?

[i.e., What are the implications for our work]? What's their identity? How do I come to define that as their identity? What's the "so what" in how I define them and what's informing my thinking? (Participant in "Looking for Anti-Oppression" study; this interview excerpt has not been previously published.)

The other participant added that we also need to recognize that:

. . . [w]e are actually located within systems of power and privilege. So who might I be to them [the service user or community I am working with]? Who might they be to me? And then the critical reflective practice is what are also my assumptions that are informed by my social location, as well as the systems around me, such as child welfare or the school system. And so critical reflective practice is looking [and] thinking about my thinking, and thinking about the impact I might be having on the situation. So they see me as a White worker and then they become defensive and I might see them as non-compliant or distant or withholding right, rather than . . . [understanding that] they've got good survival strategies, [which is] fantastic you know [because] we can build on this [survival skills] right? And then how do I negotiate my Whiteness in relation to the social meaning of it to them to create an engagement with them? . . . So how do I as a White worker negotiate my Whiteness in that space so that I could invite conversations about the impact of racism and perhaps their fear of me right, so that we're not pretending [that] we don't realize what's going on.

[Social work takes place in] a history, a historical [context of] power relations and then my body adds to it. But you can also have a body, a same community member but still be part of a system that's been harmful to the community, so it's like how do we acknowledge that and allow the person to speak about their truth, about . . . their experience of oppression within the systems and their fear of us. (Participant in "Looking for Anti-Oppression" study; this interview excerpt has not been previously published.)

It is important to recognize that the points above were made by people in the field, not by people in academia. This is the type of deep analytical thinking that agencies committed to anti-oppression are engaging in, and the type of reflexive and reflective abilities that they are looking for when hiring social workers. There are no pre-set answers to any of the reflective and reflexive questions raised by the workers above—because the questions these participants raise involve issues that Schön (1983) says cannot be addressed with social work practice that relies on technical pre-packaged answers and solutions. This is why we said, in Chapter 1, that social workers have to "create anti-oppression in the moment," and every moment is potentially different. We have attempted to provide in the previous chapters of this book some of the understanding and knowledge needed to answer the questions the participants ask above, and to develop anti-oppression in the practice moments you will encounter. But having knowledge and understanding, and even answering reflective and reflexive questions, is not anti-oppression. For anti-oppression to occur, action needs to happen.

# The Need for Action

A social worker can be critically self-reflective and reflexive, caring and have a heart, and have the best anti-oppressive analysis, but none of this is of any use unless the social worker has the knowledge and skills to take or facilitate action that helps service users.

## Why Action Is Needed

During the time we were finalizing this book, June needed help herself. June's aging mother encountered a number of health issues, and June managed the logistics and paperwork of her mother's multiple clinic appointments and surgery bookings. She also attended to most of her mother's personal care needs. Doing this work without inside knowledge of medical systems, or any personal nursing care experience, and while also maintaining her own full-time job, became so demanding that June eventually got to the point where she needed help.

June did not need help with an anti-oppressive analysis. She already understood that there was a gendered expectation in society that she as a daughter would step up and do the caring despite having a full-time career. June also understood that there were language barriers between her mother and the medical system that were not easily bridged. As well, June noticed how some doctors and nurses did not respond well to her questions as a young Asian woman, and she also recognized that the medical staff simply could not understand the cultural need for her entire family to be involved in some of the decisions.

June wanted a worker who had a heart, a caring attitude, and some critical self-reflection skills, but these qualities were not her main priority. She simply wanted someone to get the medical system to meet her mother's needs. June did not want a worker on a mission to bring long-term fundamental systemic change to the health-care system. She simply needed a worker to get the system to work the best it could for her mother right now.

## Key Concept

Having a heart, and also good anti-oppressive analysis, is essential in social work. But unless you can turn this into action, your heart and your analysis are not going to be much help.

June got the help she needed by working with a person who had the expertise to understand, navigate, and organize the health-care system around her mother's needs. This person was an insider to that system with specialized knowledge, spoke the language of the system, and understood how it worked from a medical and an administrative perspective. The person also knew exactly what nursing and other supports June's mother was entitled to and was able to ensure that she got them. A part of what made this person so effective was that she not only had expertise, but also had the interpersonal skills to make her knowledge count by getting everyone to work together to meet clearly defined objectives that met the needs of June's mother. When this person started work, June emailed Gary and said, "Thank goodness help has arrived!"

## Anti-Oppression Needs More Than Analysis and a Heart

In many ways social work needs to be exactly the same as the help June obtained. Social workers ought to arrive with a full range of interpersonal and reflective skills. But unless they also come with the skills and ability to resolve problems, there is no point in social workers coming at all. We hear echoes of "thank goodness help has arrived" in the reactions of service users in the "Looking for Anti-Oppression" study. These service users regarded their workers as godsends. We described above how such service users' reactions were evoked initially by the worker's attitudes, having a heart, caring, or being different in some way. But in each case, the worker having an array of specialized skills and knowledge that were used to make a difference sustained this positive view.

We emphasized the need for social work skills because, in a book on anti-oppression, we naturally talk mostly about oppression and anti-oppression. As a result, one could easily misunderstand and think that social work undertaken from an anti-oppressive perspective rests only on the type of critical analysis outlined in this book. It does not. Instead anti-oppression rests on, complements, and often complicates the basic social work theories, knowledge, and skills you learn in other social work texts. If you only come with an anti-oppressive analysis and a desire to change the world, but cannot help remedy the everyday troubles that bring service users to social workers, you are a part of the problem service users face. Indeed, if you have analysis but no other knowledge or skills, all you can do is analyze and interpret. If all you are doing is analysis, you are actually appropriating service users' troubles to fuel your analysis and further your ideological ideals. In this manner the social work process becomes all about you and the social change you want, and not about what service users think, want, or need.

## Making the "Magic" of Social Work Happen

In the previous chapter we spoke of service users' knowledge and theory, but social workers have (or should have) their own knowledge, theory, and skills too. Social workers need to be clear about what they bring to the service users or communities they work with, because it is the mix of knowledge, theory, and skills that both workers and service users bring to this encounter that makes the real "magic" of social work happen.

Figure 11.3 portrays what occurs when a worker and service user meet and begin work together. The figure shows two circles, one representing the social worker's knowledge, theory, and skills, and the other representing the service user's knowledge, theory, and skills. Some purpose or need always brings these together—this can be a trouble that a service user or community faces, a proposed policy change, or a program development idea. Whatever the cause, there is always a purpose that has to be identified, and always a direction that has to be found.

The two circles not only represent worker and service users' knowledge, theory, and skills, but also differing perspectives, which include the differing ways they understand and experience issues, and what they see as solutions. In most situations there are not just two perspectives, because different workers, service users, and community members all have their own views and opinions, so do not take Figure 11.3 literally. It is an ideal type (mentioned in Chapter 1) that provides a simplified representation of the process as an entry point for understanding.

In Figure 11.3, the overlap between the circles is what makes social work possible. If the service user wants something that the worker feels unable to provide, the worker will usually resist, and if the worker wants something that the service user does not want, the service user will usually resist. The overlapping area is sometimes called **congruence**, which is the extent to which the worker and service user's ideas about the problem and solution overlap (Dumbrill, 2011, 2017). For social work to happen, complete overlap does not have to occur, but enough overlap is needed to open the possibility of **alliance**, which is the social worker and service user working together toward the same objective. Alliance is essential in any form of social work, because without it change is unlikely to occur (Dumbrill, 2011, 2017). Considerable work is usually needed to establish congruence and alliance, and doing so is a social work skill in itself, although achieving alliance also involves service users' work and skill (Damiani-Taraba et al., 2017; Gladstone et al., 2012).

## Congruence and Alliance Are Radical Ideas

The search for congruence and alliance is the starting point of all social work, and this builds on the principle of reciprocity that underpins the concept of Ubuntu that Desmond Tutu (Battle, 1997; Tutu, 2007) describes. Indeed, for the service user to become "all they

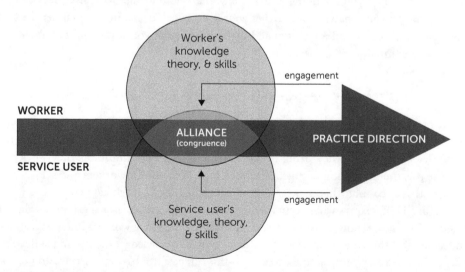

**Figure 11.3** The social work process
Source: Dumbrill, 2011, p. 57

can be" (by resolving the issues they face) and for the social worker to be "all they can be" (as a facilitator of change), a reciprocal relationship is required. In other words, in the process of achieving alliance (the overlap shown in Figure 11.3), the worker and service user depend on each other. Of course, it is not the service user's role to serve the worker, it is the role of the worker to serve, but this takes place in a context of each depending on the other. We have drawn on Tutu's teaching to explain this reciprocity, but Cabati makes the same point by drawing on Emmanuel Levinas:

> . . . the relational method is counterintuitive and disruptive. In many respects, it lies within the mainstream of Levinasian philosophy and takes a divergent point of view from the tacit foundations of conventional social work. The reciprocity of help—letting the helpee be an equal and help us—is a radical liberation because if it is absent—that is, that helpees do not reciprocate help to their helpers—the "help" withers and dies. (Cabiati, 2016, p. 250)

We discussed Levinasian ideas and their relationship to those of Tutu and other thinkers in previous chapters. These ideas, and the principle of reciprocity they embody, mean that "terms like 'workers' and 'users' are misleading categories in social work, because in a true 'helping relationship' each human being simultaneously gives and receives help" (Cabiati, 2016, p. 250). Although true, one needs to be careful with these ideas, because although reciprocity occurs, it is the social worker's job to meet the needs of service users and not the other way around. Consequently, in the casework relationship, you need to centre your purpose as the one who serves. If you view the way you serve as emerging from you being more expert and knowing than those you serve, rather than serving through an expertise and knowing that exists in reciprocity to the knowledge and skills of those you serve, you may find it difficult to build the type of relationship and knowledge needed in anti-oppression.

## Case Example: Finding Congruence— and Moving From Alliance to Action

A case in the "Looking for Anti-Oppression" study demonstrates successful congruence and alliance. A mother in that study faced racism, disability, was living with HIV, living in poverty, had children with complex medical needs, and had other issues that marginalized her. This mother's frustration levels reached a high at the same time that her coping mechanisms reached a low. As a result, the mother started to physically and emotionally abuse her son, and she was reported to child protection services by someone working in the medical system. The medical worker told the mother that she was reporting her to the CAS. This reporting and informing the mother about it did not seem to have been done in a hostile or punitive manner, but in the spirit of honesty and transparency that ought to define any helping relationship. Think about engagement in this case in Exercise 11.3.

We do not know how the worker managed to engage the mother in this case nor do we know the specific knowledge and skills they brought, but we do know that the

---

### Exercise 11.3

**Thinking about Engagement**

If possible, undertake this exercise in groups and consider:

1. What fears and hopes do you think might be going through the mother's mind knowing that child protection services are about to investigate her?
2. Which of these fears and hopes do you think are realistic?
3. What outcomes do you think the mother would be hoping for?
4. If you were the worker, what outcomes would you be hoping for?
5. If you were the worker, how would you approach this case, and how would you go about developing congruence and alliance?
6. What social work knowledge and skills could you bring to this mother that might help bring change?

---

mother said that what the worker did was "anti-oppressive" (which is why she asked to be in the study to talk about it). We also know about the mother's hopes and fears because she told us what she was thinking and feeling after being reported to the CAS. The mother said:

> Oh my gosh, I was really freaking out the ride back home I was freaking out. . . . On one hand I felt relieved because I didn't like smacking my son, I felt like I had lost control, I felt like it was this huge secret . . . [but now that the secret is out] maybe I can get help. But on the other hand I was freaking out because . . . it's those [CAS] people who take your kids away. (Dumbrill, 2012)

In the exercise we used the term "realistic" fears because sometimes fears are unfounded. We still take unfounded fears seriously—often they can be dealt with by reassurance—but in this case the mother's fears were absolutely realistic and based on sound knowledge. The child welfare system is known to blame mothers for the difficulties they face (Hughes, Chau, & Vokrri, 2015; Kellington, 2002; Swift, 1995), is more likely to remove Black children (OACAS, 2016), is more likely to judge parents living in poverty as "bad" and is more likely to remove their children (Pelton, 1989; Russell, Harris, & Gockel, 2008), is unlikely to understand the needs of mothers living with HIV and is likely to discriminate against them (Greene et al., 2016), and is more likely to remove the children of parents with disabilities (Booth, McConnell, & Booth, 2006; Callow, Tahir, & Feldman, 2017). Consequently, the mother "freaking out" at being referred to child protection services speaks to her astute awareness of these trends, and her concern for her children.

The anti-oppressive worker needs to not only understand the risk this mother's current behavior may pose to her children, but also to understand the risk the system presents to this family. The worker needs to guard against the risks the system poses, and to understand that if a parent appears hostile or "resistant," this does not necessarily indicate resistance to change, but may mean that the parent is doing what any parent ought to do: protect their child from the danger the social work system represents. This is where the worker's critical thinking and reflexivity are needed. Look back in this chapter and re-read the critical reflective thinking that the two anti-oppressive child welfare practice leaders said they expected workers to engage in. Did you engage in that type of thinking when you answered the questions in Exercise 11.3 above?

We do not know if the worker in this case engaged in critical self-reflection or reflexivity. The mother did not say, and she would not have known the answer because the objective of such thinking is not to share our analysis and thinking with the service user, but is to shape the way we are and act as social workers. Anyone who has been on the receiving end of oppression will be able to pick up subtle signs from a person that tells them whether the worker is on their side or not, and whether they understand how systems can operate to further tread down the oppressed. We believe that this mother had these abilities, and suspect this is why she said in the study that she hoped for a worker who:

> ... [would not] judge me and look at me like some kind of monster [for hurting my child]. . . . [I hoped for a worker who had] been through something [like this] themselves, or could imagine themselves going through something themselves . . . so when they meet their clients, they think, "Well, that could easily be me" . . . [they can put themselves] in the person's shoes. (Dumbrill, 2012).

Based on what the mother said about her worker, it seems that the worker had these qualities. Though we do not know all of the skills and knowledge the worker brought to this case, we can speculate about the worker's expertise. The child welfare system requires all workers in cases like this to formulate an immediate safety plan for the child with the parent. This is one of those instances where following the systemic requirement is imperative—and it also fits perfectly with this mother's wish to stop hurting her child. We can assume, therefore, that the worker knew about parenting strategies, had the skills to help the mother manage stress, and had the skills to help the mother to stop physically and emotionally harming the child right away.

Because the children remained at home, we can also assume that the worker had the skills and insights to recognize that the mother's goal was to stop hurting her son, and that the mother had the capability to achieve this. We can also assume that the worker, and the mother, had the skills to find congruence and engage in an alliance regarding this objective. The mother certainly spoke of how the worker helped her achieve this objective. The mother also spoke about how the worker, in the long term, addressed the stresses and struggles that impacted her parenting. The mother understood that these troubles had systemic causes, she understood how she was being trod down by isms and social inequalities, and it seems that the worker understood this too.

Although the worker did not bring systemic social change, the worker did support the mother in these struggles and was able to connect her with agencies that could provide additional support. The worker also seemed to understand that because of this treading down and the stress it caused, what might be a small matter for someone else might have larger significance for this parent (i.e., it would be a "mountain"). The mother described one of these "small matters" as running out of toilet paper and having no money to get more, and her worker coming to the rescue by delivering rolls of toilet paper. The mother laughed about this incident, and the laughter seemed to be from delight in a worker who really understood the issues that attempted to push her down. The mother explained,

> I had a lot of stress going on and I ended up taking it out on the kids, so they wanted to relieve some of that stress to help the situation. (Dumbrill, 2012)

The mother described what the worker did as anti-oppressive. The worker understood that big things were pushing this mother down, and knew that even pushing back at some of the little things could make a big difference in this mother's world. In this instance, the worker demonstrated that anti-oppression does not have to be as big as changing the world; it can be as small as bringing rolls of toilet paper!

## We Need Systemic Success

We have focused in this chapter mostly on stories and instances where workers got anti-oppression right, but social work does not always get it right. The theme in the "Looking for Anti-Oppression" study of social workers doing something "different" to get "anti-oppression right," implies that the "usual" thing social workers do is not regarded by service users as right. In all of our studies, several participants spoke of how social workers often got it wrong, which made it hard to trust the social work system to produce outcomes that help families or communities. Participants in the "Your Policies, Our Children" gave an example. A refugee parent explained that a teenage child was apprehended from their community by a Children's Aid Society to provide "protection."

> A child from our community was taken by Children's Aid—soon after she was with other children in government care who stole a car—they crashed the car and she died. Considering where I came from and what I had to do to take care of my child; to come to a land where you think everything will be ok and to then have a child die when they are healthy and not sick, that is sad. But then we can't do anything to stop this because we just came and we don't know our way around. Who will advise us? (Dumbrill, 2009)

The refugee participants were unsure whether social workers had the best interests of their children at heart. They spoke of advice their children were being given by school social workers:

> They [social workers] tell our children that they have a right to leave home at 16. What kind of future can a child expect if they leave home at 16? To say this to our children, social workers must either not care about them, or have very low expectations for their future. We have higher hopes for our children. Do social workers say this to their own children? (Dumbrill, 2009)

It was not just the wisdom of the child welfare system approaches that refugees were questioning, but the entire way social service "helping" and "caring" is conceptualized in a Western context. These questions resulted from participants discussing homelessness in Canada. They were aware of this Canadian problem because they saw it on the streets, and it came as a surprise to them because they could not understand how a country with so much wealth and stability (compared to the places they had escaped from) could have so much homelessness. In the context of these discussions a participant took the photograph shown in Figure 11.4 that shows a homeless man walking along a path, and a police SUV at the end of the path with officers watching him.

The participant explained the reason for the photograph.

> I took this picture because I saw on the news last week that some homeless people who were living in a Toronto neighbourhood were moved on by the police. The people in that neighbourhood wanted them driven away. The Salvation Army tried to help the homeless people and feed them and [wanted to] help them stay, but the government refused to listen and so the homeless people had to leave. . . . Some of these homeless people once were the same kids that the Children's Aid took and let go at 18; they have grown up and are homeless, and now the same government that took them from their homes drives them away. But where do they go? (Dumbrill, 2009)

The observations of this participant raise profound questions about social work. Why is it that when someone is below a certain age in Canada (usually 18), the state sends out social workers to help them, but once they are even a day over that age the state sends out the police to move them along? The study's participants recognized this as a contradiction, perhaps because they are new to Canada, and with fresh eyes they see the absurdity in what we have become too familiar with to notice.

Refugees in the study are asking why we send social workers out to care for someone in one moment, and as soon as they turn 18 we send the police out to move along in this next moment. A person does not change when they are 18, so if our caring changes simply

Figure 11.4 Homeless

*Photo by Gary C. Dumbrill. Reprinted with permission of Child Welfare Journal*

because a person reaches the age of 18, we have to ask ourselves whether we actually care about the person as a human being, or instead if we are actually "caring" for an idea, a philosophy, or an ideology. In other words, do we care because someone is human, or because they fit some arbitrary criteria such as "child" or some other socially constructed notion that marks them as deserving or not deserving? For refugee participants, "caring" was not something one switches on one day and off the next based on the idea of "deserving" or any other eligibility criteria, but is delivered simply because someone is human. As both Tutu and Levinas would contend, it is this type of caring that makes those who care human too. We suspect that the type of heart refugee participants said social workers should have, which we explored in Exercise 11.1, reflects this type of caring.

Despite refugee participants being skeptical about social work and social workers, they did have respect for the ideals of social work, and the core message they wanted delivered to social workers was that they wanted to work with social workers to make the social work system better. This thought brings us back to the idea that started this chapter: We cannot get to anti-oppression from here; we can only do so in partnership with service users and service user communities. For social work and social workers to become all that they can be requires a reciprocal relationship in which service users play a role in shaping the overall direction social work and social policy take.

## Chapter Summary

At the start of this chapter we said that by the end you will understand why social work cannot achieve anti-oppression from social work's current location. We have suggested that practice can be shaped by anti-oppression and we have based most of what we have said about how this can be done from the findings from our research that asked service users how social work, and particularly anti-oppressive social work, should be done. The suggestions service users made, such as the importance of caring and having a heart, may not be associated with the usual revolutionary ways anti-oppression is conceptualized, but we have argued that unless love and caring are the basis of revolution, revolution can never bring anti-oppressive change.

In this chapter we also emphasized issues such as congruence, engagement, and alliance, and although these are associated with regular social work more than anti-oppression, we contend that without them anti-oppression is impossible. We have also contended that unless the social worker brings concrete skills and expertise to service users, then no matter how sound their anti-oppressive thinking, nor how genuine their caring, workers will not be able to turn analysis and caring into action that helps.

We have also suggested that what helps is the small micro practical things that social workers do to support service users and push back at the way oppression treads service users down. The social worker does not have to set the bar of anti-oppressive success in their casework as changing the world—more often small things workers do can move what service users experience as mountains.

Finally, we considered how the theme that social workers who got anti-oppression right did something "different" has implications for the ways social work is imagined. Indeed, ideally we would want anti-oppression and good social work to not be something service users' experience as "different" (i.e., unexpected), but to be something they expect.

## Discussion Questions

In this chapter we said that if social work as an occupation gets anti-oppression right, we believe that instead of the trepidation, worry, and sometimes fear that some service users feel when social workers arrive, they will exclaim, "Thank goodness help has arrived." Consider the following.

1. What is the perception of social work in communities you are familiar with?
2. If you are not aware of any service user communities who are concerned by social work, or any that have no concerns about social work, what does this say about the circles you move within and the exposure you have had to the world?
3. How would you respond to a service user who felt concerned about your involvement with them, their family, or their community?
4. What do you plan to do to make it safe for all communities to engage with social work so that the reaction of everyone when a social worker comes to their door is, "Thank goodness help has arrived"?

## Activity

Visit the Social Work Education Participation (SWEP) YouTube channel and review their videos at http://www.youtube.com/user/SWEPTV/featured. Consider the benefits and limitations of the approach to social work education described in the video.

# Suggested Resources

Social Care Institute for Excellence. *Mo Robert's Interview* retrieved from http://www.scie.org.uk/publications/elearning/poverty/resources.asp

Baines, D. (2017). Anti-oppressive practice: Roots, theory and tensions. In D. Baines (Ed.), *Doing anti-oppressive practice: Social justice social work* (3rd edn., pp. 2–19). Halifax, Canada: Fernwood Publishing.

Fook, J. (2016). *Social work: A critical approach to practice* (3rd edn). London, UK: SAGE Publications Ltd.

Esquao, S.A. [J. Carriere] & S. Strega. (Eds). (2014). *Walking this path together: Anti-racist and anti-oppressive child welfare practice* (2nd edn). Halifax, Canada: Fernwood.

# References

Baines, D. (2011). An overview of anti-oppressive practice: Roots, theory, tensions. In D. Baines (Ed.), *Doing anti-oppressive practice: Social justice social work* (2nd ed., pp. 1–24). Halifax, Canada: Fernwood.

Battle, M. (1997). *Reconciliation: The Ubuntu theology of Desmond Tutu.* Cleveland, OH: The Pilgrim Press.

Booth, T., McConnell, D., & Booth, W. (2006). Temporal discrimination and parents with learning difficulties in the child protection system. *The British Journal of Social Work, 36*(6), 997–1015. doi:10.1093/bjsw/bch401

Cabiati, E. (2016). Teaching and learning: An exchange of knowledge in the university among students, service users, and professors. *European Journal of Social Work, 19*(2), 247–62. doi:10.1080/13691457.2015.1024615

Callow, E., Tahir, M., & Feldman, M. (2017). Judicial reliance on parental IQ in appellate-level child welfare cases involving parents with intellectual and developmental disabilities. *Journal of Applied Research in Intellectual Disabilities, 30*(3), 553–62. doi:10.1111/jar.12296

Crines, A.S., Heppell, T., & Dorey, P. (2016). *The political rhetoric and oratory of Margaret Thatcher.* London, UK: Palgrave Macmillan.

D'Cruz, H., Gillingham, P., & Melendez, S. (2007). Reflexivity, its meanings and relevance for social work: A critical review of the literature. *British Journal of Social Work, 37*(1), 73–90. doi:10.1093/bjsw/bcl001

Damiani-Taraba, G., Dumbrill, G.C., Gladstone, J., Koster, A., Leslie, B., & Charles, M. (2017). The evolving relationship between casework skills, engagement, and positive case outcomes in child protection: A structural equation model. *Children and Youth Services Review, 79,* 456–62. doi:10.1016/j.childyouth.2017.05.033

Dumbrill, G.C. (2009). Your policies, our children: Messages from refugee parents to child welfare workers and policymakers. *Child Welfare, 88*(3) 145–68.

Dumbrill, G.C. (2011). Doing anti-oppressive child protection casework. In D. Baines (Ed.), *Doing anti-oppressive practice: Social justice social work* (2nd ed., pp. 51–63). Halifax, Canada: Fernwood Publishing.

Dumbrill, G.C. (2012). Anti-oppressive child welfare: How we get there from here. *The Ontario Association of Children's Aid Societies Journal, 57*(1), 2–8.

Dumbrill, G.C. (2017). Emic and alliance: Anti-oppressive social work in child protection. In D. Baines (Ed.), *Doing anti-oppressive practice: Social justice social work* (3rd ed., pp. 57–69). Halifax, Canada: Fernwood Publishing.

Dumbrill, G.C., & Lo, W. (2008). *Your policies, our children: Refugee parents speak about the Impact of Canadian social policy on their families (a poster presentation).* Paper presented at the Symposium 2008: Cultural diversity and vulnerable families, a bias in favour of cultural competence, University of Quebec in Montreal, Canada.

Dumbrill, G.C., & Lo, W. (2009). What parents say: Service users' theory and anti-oppressive child welfare practice. In S. Strega & S.A. Esquao [J. Carriere] (Eds), *Walking this path together: Anti-racist and anti-oppressive child welfare practice* (pp. 127–41). Halifax, Canada: Fernwood Publishing.

Gladstone, J., Dumbrill, G.C., Leslie, B., Koster, A., Young, M., & Ismaila, A. (2012). Looking at engagement and outcome from the perspectives of child protection workers and parents. *Children and Youth Services Review, 34*(1), 112–18. doi:10.1016/j.childyouth.2011.09.003

Greene, S., O'Brien-Teengs, D., Dumbrill, G.C., Ion, A., Beaver, K., Porter, M., & Desbiens, M. (2016). A community-based research approach to developing an HIV education and training module for child and family service workers in Ontario. In H. Montgomery, D. Badry, D. Fuchs, & D. Kikulwe (Eds), *Transforming child welfare: Interdisciplinary practices, field education, and research* (pp. 163–185). Regina, Canada: University of Regina Press.

Guevara, C. (1965, March 12). From Algiers, for Marcha. *The Cuban Revolution Today.*

Havlin, N. (2015). "To live a humanity under the skin": Revolutionary love and Third World praxis in 1970s Chicana feminism. *Women's Studies Quarterly, 43*(3 & 4), 78–97.

Hughes, J., Chau, S., & Vokrri, L. (2015). Mothers' narratives of their involvement with child welfare services.

*Affilia: Journal of Women and Social Work, 31*(3), 344–58. doi:10.1177/0886109915574579

Kellington, S. (2002). *"Missing Voices": Mothers at risk for or experiencing apprehension in the child welfare system in BC.* National Action Committee on the Status of Women - BC Region, Vancouver, Canada.

King, M.L. (1967). *Where do we go from here: Chaos or community?* Boston, MA: Beacon Press.

King, M.L. (1994). *Letter from the Birmingham jail.* San Francisco, CA: Harper.

OACAS. (2016). *One vision one voice: Changing the Ontario child welfare system to better serve African Canadians. Practice framework part 1: Research report.* Retrieved from http://www.oacas.org/wp-content/uploads/2016/09/One-Vision-One-Voice-Part-1_digital_english.pdf

Pelton, L.H. (1989). *For reasons of poverty: A critical analysis of the public child welfare system in the United States.* New York, NY: Praeger.

Russell, M., Harris, B., & Gockel, A. (2008). Parenting in poverty: Perspectives of high-risk parents. *Journal of Children and Poverty, 14*(1), 83–98. doi:10.1080/10796120701871322

Schön, D.A. (1983). *The reflective practitioner: How professionals think in action.* New York, NY: Basic Books.

Swift, K.J. (1995). *Manufacturing "bad mothers": A critical perspective on child neglect.* Toronto, Canada: University of Toronto Press.

*The Globe and Mail.* (2001, October 17). Mike Harris's legacy. Retrieved from http://www.theglobeandmail.com/opinion mike-harriss-legacy/article763723/

Thompson, N., & Pascal, J. (2012). Developing critically reflective practice. *Reflective Practice, 13*(2), 311–25. doi:10.1080/14623943.2012.657795

Tutu, D.M. (2007). Ubuntu discussion with students during Semester at Sea 2007. Retrieved from http://www.youtube.com/watch?v=gWZHx9DJR-M

Tutu, D.M. (2011). *God is not a Christian: And other provocations.* J. Allen (Ed.). New York, NY: HarperOne.

Wang, C., & Burris, M.A. (1994). Empowerment through photo novella: Portraits of participation. *Health Education Quarterly, 21*(2), 171–86. doi: 10.1177/109019819402100204

Wang, C., Ling, Y.Y., & Ling, F.M. (1996). Photovoice as a tool for participatory evaluation: The community's view of process and impact. *Journal of Contemporary Health, 24*(3), 47–9.

Wehbi, S. (2011). Anti-oppression community organizing: Lessons from disability rights activism. In D. Baines (Ed.), *Doing anti-oppressive practice: Social justice social work* (2nd ed., pp. 132–45). Halifax, Canada: Fernwood.

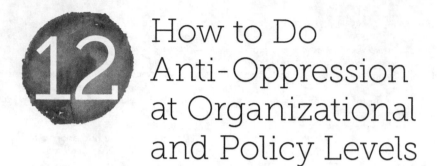

# How to Do Anti-Oppression at Organizational and Policy Levels

## In this chapter you will learn:

- Why organizational change is needed
- The challenges involved in bringing anti-oppressive change
- How to design and implement a process of anti-oppressive change
- Why clear change targets are important, what change levers are, and why outcomes need to be measured

## Introduction

A number of social work agencies that had been implementing anti-oppression for some time decided to hold a symposium to share with each other what they had learned so far. The agencies asked June and Gary to do a workshop—something to encourage participants in their anti-oppression journey—something different and unusual to appeal to their imaginations and open up new horizons.

Gary thought of doing an exercise with a donkey. June said that anything with a donkey was fine with her, because it was one of her favourite animals! Gary began to try and track down where he could borrow a real donkey but June, being more practical, brought a large cardboard image of a donkey with separate cardboard cutout donkey tails that had been designed for playing the childhood game of "pin the tail on the donkey."

At the symposium we pinned the cardboard donkey to the wall and said that it represented the participants' agencies. We distributed the cardboard donkey tails to groups of people attending and said that each tail represented a form of anti-oppression, and we asked them to write on each tail a form of anti-oppression that their agency was trying to implement. Luckily we had lots of tails, because the list was long and included anti-poverty work, anti-racism, anti-ableism, and many more, and some simply used the umbrella term "anti-oppression" to reflect their simultaneous focus on the intersection of multiple oppressions.

Next we asked groups to select a member, to cover that person's eyes with a mask that we provided, to spin them around, and for that person to try and pin the tail on the donkey. As all the participants selected were used to using eyesight as a means to find their way around, the results were hilarious. People were wandering all around the auditorium and pinning tails in the most unexpected places. Some participants laughed so much that they were close to tears.

Although the game generated laughter, we had a very serious point. The use of humour was strategic, because we find that people who can laugh and do silly things together are often more open to critically reflecting and doing serious things together too, and we were about to raise serious points for reflection.

We asked participants how they were implementing these forms of anti-oppression in their agencies and how they knew that they were working. In other words, how did they know that their anti-oppressive strategies were pinned in the right place? We asked deeper questions too. What anti-oppressive outcomes were they trying to achieve? Who got to decide that these outcomes were needed? How would these outcomes change the lives of service users for the better? How would they know when they achieved these outcomes? And most importantly, how were they going about achieving them? Participants immediately recognized the point of the donkey exercise, because anyone unable to answer these questions was metaphorically wandering around with their eyes closed carrying a donkey tail without knowing where to pin it.

All of the questions we were asking were about action. In the previous chapter we made it clear that anti-oppression cannot stop at rhetoric. It has to move to action that brings real change. So what was the action and what change were they hoping for?

By the end of this chapter, you will know how to move beyond the language of anti-oppression and, in an organizational context, bring change that is anti-oppressive. You will also know how to ensure that your goals and outcomes move beyond talk that sounds good to social workers, to become something that makes a difference in the lives of those the agency claims to serve.

# The Organizational Context

Anti-oppressive social work practice takes place primarily within the organizational context of non-profit social service agencies or human service organizations, such as child protection agencies, family service agencies, schools, shelters, mental health agencies, hospitals, and so on. These organizations, and the social work practised within them, exist to address specific social issues or needs, such as concerns about the welfare of children and families, education, violence against women, mental health, the well-being of people in hospital and how they will manage after discharge, and so on. Organizations like these are a part of an intricate network of agencies governed by an array of legislation and policies, which together help form Canada's welfare system—the means through which we try to ensure the well-being of citizens and others who live here (Turner & Turner, 2009).

Some services that maintain the welfare and well-being of the population are universal, such as the Canada child benefit, which parents receive regardless of need; the same is true of health-care services, which entitle everyone in Canada to see a doctor for free. Also, in Canada after meeting with a doctor, most forms of treatment will also be free, but to be treated a medical need will have to be established, and the type of treatment and its availability will be governed by an array of regulations. Social work is similar. In a variety of settings, social workers will meet with individuals and families to assess the need for service, but which service is then delivered, for how long, and in which forms will depend on an array of policies and procedures, and also on the way the agency envisions its mission and practice. If the government funds the agency, there is also likely to be a complex and detailed set of service eligibility regulations, along with government audits to ensure the agency follows these rules, especially if the agency offers any form of material help.

It is this context that social work organizations exist within. As such, the issue of anti-oppressive organizational change (or any other type of organizational change) is never simply a matter of an organization deciding to change and then doing so. It is a much more complex process in which things internal and external to the agency have to occur for change to happen.

# The Need for Organizational Change

Most social workers and agencies do not set out to practise in a way that treads people down or holds them back. Oppression occurs, however, because most social work agencies reflect and are governed by mainstream society, and as such reproduce the oppression that exists within broader society.

With the rise of anti-oppression, many social work organizations are critically examining their policies and practices, and are recognizing the ways that they either reinforce the oppression service users face, or fail to address the way oppression contributes to or sometimes causes the troubles that bring service users to their door. We refer to the process of trying to change this as anti-oppressive organizational change, and many social work agencies are engaging in this process (Barnoff, Abdillahi, & Jordan, 2017; Moffatt, Barnoff, George, & Coleman, 2017; Yee, Hackbusch, & Wong, 2015; Yee, Wong, & Schlabitz, 2014). Such change requires an understanding of how oppression operates in an agency through influences at the personal, agency, and societal levels.

## How Personal Attitudes, Prejudice, and Biases Can Cause Organizations to Be Oppressive

At the *individual level*, agency workers may have the type of personal attitudes, prejudices, and biases we discussed in Chapter 1 that allow oppression to operate. Because workers and managers are in a position of power in relation to service users, their prejudices are easily turned into oppression through the ways they work with various service users.

For instance, if a worker believes that everyone who lives in poverty is lazy and does not know how to manage money, the worker may communicate these beliefs in punitive attitudes toward service users living in poverty, and will likely only offer interventions that address a service user's personal motivation, rather than the structural causes of their predicament.

The same prejudices and biases that operate at a personal level can appear in the agency's goals, objectives, procedures, and culture. For instance, if a family needs financial assistance to buy food or other necessities, are they given funds to buy what they need, or are they given vouchers because the agency does not trust service users with money? Of course there may be times when restricting aid to the provision of vouchers is appropriate, but if an agency provides only vouchers because of a policy to never trust any service user with money, one has to ask questions about the agency's attitudes and beliefs in relation to service users.

Another example that some form of prejudicial attitude may exist toward service users is the disparity in the way child welfare agencies use funds and resources to meet the needs of children. Most child welfare agencies give higher levels of financial aid and support to foster families whom they recruit to look after other people's children than they give to people in the community whom they recruit to look after the children of kin. If child welfare is really about the welfare of children, why is there this disparity? We suggest that it results from prejudicial views about service users (and their kin) that have roots in the less eligibility attitude we discussed in previous chapters.

## How Societal Attitudes, Prejudice, and Biases Can Cause Organizations to Be Oppressive

At a *societal level,* social attitudes, prejudices, and biases also impact what the agency does and how it does it. Social workers are a part of broader society, and as such they reflect its values. But even if workers do not reflect dominant social values, social work organizations are hemmed in by broader social mandates and funding formulas, so that workers (or managers) may not have the power to change what the agency does and how it does it.

Although the attitudes, prejudices, and biases of those inside and outside the agency impact agency goals, objectives, policies, procedures, and culture, the agency as a corporate body also influences the attitudes of individuals and society. For instance, Gary was at a dinner event held by a child welfare agency and sat at a table with the agency's executive director, as well as politicians, journalists, and leaders of industry.

One of the leaders of industry said to the executive director, "You must see terrible things in your work."

"Yes," the executive director replied. "You wouldn't believe the terrible things we see. What some parents do to their children is heartbreaking."

Gary wondered why the executive director chose to portray child welfare in this manner.

## Exercise 12.1

### Agency Attitudes

If possible, undertake this exercise in groups:

1.  As a result of the executive director's comments, what type of "terrible" and "heartbreaking" things that parents do to their children come to mind?
2.  Review the Executive Summary of the Canadian Incidence Study of Child Abuse and Neglect (http://www.phac-aspc.gc.ca/cm-vee/csca-ecve/2008/cis-eci-04-eng.php) and note the proportion of all Canadian child abuse and neglect cases that match the type of incident the executive director's comments placed in your mind.
3.  Based on the data shown in the Canadian Incidence Study of Child Abuse and Neglect, does the type of incidents that the executive director's comments make you think of represent the vast majority of cases that child welfare services actually deal with?
4.  Why do you think the executive director said what he did?
5.  What social attitudes might the executive director's comments generate and what ideologies or purpose might these serve?
6.  What agency attitudes, policies, and procedures might this view promote, and what policies and procedures might this view prevent?
7.  What would you say if you were at the table and why?

## Pushing Back at Oppressive Agency and Societal Attitudes

The incident above is a little unusual. Few of the child welfare agency executive directors we know would characterize the complex work of child welfare with reference to the "heartbreaking" things that parents do to children. Quite the opposite, most child welfare leaders we know emphasize the way social inequalities and other forms of oppression present challenges to families, they discuss the need for social change, and they recognize how child welfare systems are implicated in many of these forms of oppression. For instance, David Rivard, the executive director of the Children's Aid Society of Toronto (known in that agency as a CEO), is on record as saying that the child welfare system as a whole, "including our own agency, has a long legacy of oppression and systemic racism" (Monsebraaten & Contenta, 2017). Rivard, and that agency's management and staff, seem intent on addressing the way oppression embeds itself in social work systems, and it appears that they are meeting with some success (Monsebraaten & Contenta, 2017).

This work of pushing back at social attitudes is complex and difficult because in most cases oppression does not appear in obvious and overt ways, but in more subtle ways that are hard to identify and challenge. What makes this pushing back process difficult is that, as mentioned above, the attitudes and culture of an agency are interconnected with the attitudes and culture of broader society, with both influencing each other. We show this interconnectedness in Figure 12.1.

Figure 12.1 shows how personal and societal attitudes shape the agency, and how the agency (and the way it talks about its work) also shapes individual and societal attitudes. These influences, in concert, shape agency goals, objectives, policies, procedures, and culture, and influence the attitudes of the agency toward its work. The confluence of these variables shapes agency outcomes, which in turn shape and reinforce social attitudes and biases. For instance, if Indigenous children, the children of parents living in poverty, or other marginalized groups are overrepresented in care, rather than seeing how the system treads these parents down to cause these outcomes, these outcomes can reinforce prejudicial views toward these groups and give rise to approaches that increase surveillance and punitive attitudes. In this manner an agency becomes locked in a vicious oppressive cycle. This makes anti-oppressive change difficult, because with so many influences interwoven, you cannot change the vicious cycle unless you change all these influences.

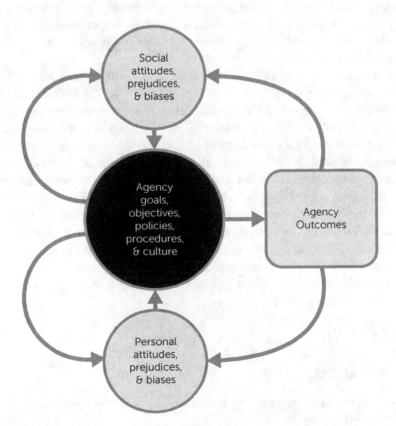

**Figure 12.1** Agencies and society

# The Problem of Whiteness and Dominance in Organizations

Most social work agencies are White (Grimes, 2001, 2002). We do not use the term "White" to refer to White people, but to the concept of Whiteness we spoke of in Chapter 4. We deliberately bring back and use the term "Whiteness" to remind you of the way Whiteness and the underpinning concept of White supremacy operate. Other terms we use interchangeably include "dominant space" or "the mainstream." We use terms from previous chapters because unless one brings all that knowledge into an understanding of how organizations operate and function, one will not grasp the challenge of organizational change.

As shown in Figure 12.1, an agency's goals, objectives, policies, procedures, and culture reflect the values and beliefs that come from dominant social space, which as mentioned before, is underpinned by Whiteness. As a result, Whiteness inform and shape the way organizations function and practice is undertaken. Put differently, every organization is a "socio-political system in which people act together under an imposed structure and ideology and use a specific set of technologies to achieve a specific objective" (Henry & Tator, 2010, p. 337). As such, all organizational policies and practices carry and impose a set of embedded ideological values and beliefs.

Unless an agency makes an effort to do otherwise, it will tend to reflect and maintain Whiteness and existing social relations (Grimes, 2001, 2002; Yee & Dumbrill, 2016). We suspect that this was in part why the first executive director we referred to above emphasized the threat "bad parents" pose to their children, and not the threat to children posed by poverty, racism, the legacy of residential schools and the Sixties Scoop, and the current disproportionate numbers of Black and Indigenous children being forcibly removed from their families and communities. The second executive director, however, publicly named the long legacy his agency and others have in playing a role in oppression and systemic racism. The first executive director reinforced Whiteness; the second said something to disrupt it. One might not think that naming something can disrupt it, but you will recall that Whiteness (and related oppressions) gains power by remaining unnamed. To name racism as operating removes its power to hide. Of course anti-oppression work does not stop with naming oppression, but it cannot start without it. Anti-oppressive organizational change has to start by naming issues.

## Key Concept

Anti-oppressive organizational change does not stop with naming oppression, but it cannot start without it.

# The Challenge of Change

Even if one names issues, it is difficult to bring anti-oppressive organizational change because, as mentioned in Chapter 11, oppression operates in largely undercover ways. Indeed, we are not aware of any social work organization that lists oppression, the preservation of Whiteness, maintaining the existing social order, or doing things the wrong way, as outcome objectives.

Despite social work agencies not declaring the maintenance of oppression as an organizational goal, social work organizations were designed to maintain and preserve the existing social order. Child welfare, for instance, was started not just to safeguard children, but to also protect society from the threat that children living in poverty might grow up to become. Karen Swift (1995) articulates this most succinctly:

"IMPLEMENTING THESE CHANGES WON'T BE EASY. WE'RE PRETTY SET IN DOING THINGS THE WRONG WAY."

**Figure 12.2** The challenge of change

> They believed that in "saving" neglected children, they also could save themselves and their positions of privilege. They most certainly hoped to help neglected children, but they wanted to reduce threats to the existing social order that they believed these children might come to pose. Their scheme was ingenious, providing themselves and their representatives with the authority of the state to intervene in and alter the private lives of those they saw as dangerous to their own interests. . . . This basic approach, with continual refinements, remains in place today. (p. 74)

It is not only child welfare services that maintain the existing social order. Scholars have developed in-depth critiques of the "different shades of social coercion" that social work organizations undertake to maintain the social order (Banakoda, Sinclair, Carniol, & Baines, 2017, p. 134). Instead of supporting service users by addressing the way inequalities within society contribute to the troubles that bring them to social work agencies, a type of social regulation takes place that holds service users responsible for their own troubles. An example given by Kennedy-Kish (Bell), Sinclair, Carniol, and Baines (2017) is **workfare**, which is a social policy used in Canada and around the world to require those who are unemployed to be available and willing to take any work that the government offers in order to receive social assistance. The entire project is based on the idea that the unemployed person rather than the labour market is the problem. Systems like this coerce people into low-paid precarious work that pushes them into poverty, which creates a whole range of other problems, many of which often create the need for yet more social work services. For instance, a person forced into a low-paying job where the hours and location do not fit their family schedules not only will be forced into poverty, but may also face issues of child care and transportation. If the stress and other problems this causes in a family result in the children being neglected (such as inadequate lunches and perhaps being picked up late from school) and conflict in the family (parents and children on edge and arguing), child welfare services are likely to be called. Unless practising anti-oppressively, the child welfare services will also see the parents, rather than the social conditions that have contributed to this downward cycle, as the problem. In this manner, welfare and social work systems can push service users further down rather than pushing back at the inequalities that cause these troubles. In other words, rather than helping service users with their troubles, social workers and social work systems become a part of those troubles.

## The Residual Model

Several mechanisms lock social work organizations into protecting dominant society by reframing social issues as personal problems. A primary means of achieving this is the **residual model** of welfare, which rests on the assumption that the social order works for most people, and as a result most services should only be provided as a last resort for those who have fallen between the cracks (Chappell, 2013). Embedded in the residual model is a belief that people should rely on savings, their own initiative, family, or the private market for their basic social welfare needs. Under this model the role of state-funded social work and state-funded benefits should be kept to a minimum. In many ways, the model is contradictory, because welfare payments and benefits are seen as "charitable" state support and a drain on taxpayers, but as noted in Chapter 7, the government giving tax breaks to those wealthy enough to put their surplus income into registered pension or educational funds, or the government giving bailouts to banks and corporations who have messed up their own finances, are not usually seen as charity or a drain on taxpayers.

The residual model results in social workers and social work organizations supporting the social order, rather than challenging it (Grant & Ojo, 2008). Many organizations and social workers understand this point, especially if they are engaging in the type of critical thinking we spoke of in Chapter 2, if they understand the way surveillance works that we spoke of in Chapter 4, and if they grasp the way the social order is held together as spoken of in Chapter 8. But it is often hard to develop this awareness, and rather than look at how we are implicated in oppression, it can sometimes be easier to look away. Smith (2017) refers to this as workers becoming "defended subjects", where rather than ask critical questions, social workers, ". . . defend themselves from complicity with harm done to service users" (Smith, 2017, p. 78).

## Key Concept

Do not let your commitment to social work result in you defending social work against critique. Instead let your commitment to social work result in you welcoming critique as a way to identify social work's mistakes and not repeat them.

Given the outside constraints placed on what social work organizations do, along with the constraints that can also come from inside the agency and inside ourselves, the challenge of anti-oppressive organizational change is enormous. But organizations are increasingly taking up this challenge (Barnoff et al., 2017; Moffatt et al., 2017; Monsebraaten & Contenta, 2017; OACAS, 2016; Yee et al., 2014; Yee et al., 2015). The key to responding to this challenge is recognizing that not only the organization, but also the people within it and the broader society that frames and mandates the agency's mission, need to change. In our work, we start this process of change with the people in the organization.

# Starting Where the Organization Is At

If an agency is at a point where it is seeking anti-oppressive change, then change has already begun. In most agencies we usually find that efforts to gain a social justice focus can be traced back long before the term "anti-oppression" was even coined. Such work may include an emphasis on structural social work (Hick, Peters, Corner, & London, 2009), feminist social work (Wendt & Moulding, 2016), anti-racist social work (Bartoli, 2013), and anti-poverty work (Schiettecat, Roets, & Vandenbroeck, 2017). Consequently, a good beginning point for anti-oppressive organizational change is to assess what an agency is already doing to embed a social justice perspective in its work and, if it is proving successful, to do more of the same.

Whatever form of social justice work an agency is already doing, we find that many agencies see anti-oppression as a way of enhancing that work because, as an umbrella term, anti-oppression brings together a number of social justice approaches in a way that better addresses multiple oppressions and the ways they intersect. Also, because students are graduating from social work and related disciplines with an understanding of anti-oppression, it makes sense for agencies to consolidate and expand their social justice efforts under this umbrella.

## Consolidating an Organization's Anti-Oppressive Vision

Even if an agency is already engaged in anti-oppression, this does not mean that everyone in the agency understands anti-oppression in the same way. Consequently, an important first task in the change project is to review how those in the organization understand anti-oppression.

Developing a shared understanding of anti-oppression in an agency can be quite difficult. In an agency that we helped with their organizational-change process, workshop participants raised the cultural practice of wishing everyone "Merry Christmas" during the December holiday season. Most participants understood that wishing someone "Merry Christmas," when this was not a part of the other person's cultural or religious tradition, might not be the most appropriate greeting to offer. In particular, they understood that in some circumstances the greeting might be outright offensive. For instance, imagine Indigenous parents who as children had been forcibly placed in a church-run residential school and abused in an effort to "Christianize" and indoctrinate them in Western culture. How would they experience that greeting, particularly if their child had now also been removed by the state as a result of troubles caused by generational and community trauma of residential school?

Of course many Indigenous people as well as people from a wide range of cultures celebrate Christmas and will not be offended by the greeting, but many do not. Most of the workshop participants understood this and were ready to think through the ways they might modify the greetings they offer to service users (and friends) who do not celebrate Christmas. Three participants, however, insisted that it did not matter how a person might receive or experience the greeting. These participants insisted that if the season was "Christmas," they had a cultural right to wish others a "Merry Christmas" and they intended to carry on this practice no matter how the other person received it.

In citing the example above, we want to be clear that Christmas is something we both celebrate, and we personally offer the greeting to others we know who celebrate this tradition, just like we offer greetings of Happy Hanukkah, Happy eid Mubarak, Happy Diwali, and similar greetings at the appropriate times to those who follow these traditions.

In our anti-oppression work we do not agree with regulating people by policing what they say, nor do we advocate banning any greeting. We believe, however, that people should be able to regulate themselves, and should be able to recognize that offering a "Merry Christmas" greeting to someone who may not appreciate it hardly reflects the Christmas spirit. Disregarding how this greeting might cause offence to some, and refusing to regulate one's own behaviour in instances where causing offence is likely, is indicative of a deeper problem that cannot be remedied by policing language.

## Grasping How We, and Our Organizations, Are Implicated in Oppression

As an agency moves forward in its change process, it would be easy to blame oppression on workers who insist on wishing "Merry Christmas" to people who do not celebrate it, or to blame any other individual who does not see oppression the same way we do. This is a mistake. If we blame these individuals, we make the political personal. We downgrade the structural problems of the agency to being simply a problem of a few oppressive individuals. If we understand anti-oppression as beginning and ending with individual workers or managers, we totally underestimate the challenge of anti-oppressive organizational change.

## Never Underestimate People or the Potential for Change

In addition, we may be underestimating the positive contribution these somewhat stubborn "oppressive" workers and managers bring to the agency. The fact that they disagree with one anti-oppressive issue at one point in time does not mean that they are not on board with anti-oppression at all. Perhaps they are way ahead of most in understanding and addressing oppression in another area, and perhaps their ability to "stubbornly" stick to a position is just the type of determination that an agency needs if it is to resist dominant social attitudes. Indeed, the three workers who struggled to grasp the problem with the indiscriminate use of the greeting "Merry Christmas" were leading an initiative to push back at the way the school system in their region was marginalizing refugee children. Consequently, never assume that, because a person fails to grasp one anti-oppression issue, they fail to grasp all issues. Do not write such people off as a "lost cause," because they may be way ahead of you in an area of anti-oppression where you are failing to grasp things. Work in partnership with them and move forward together.

Of course there are times when those who refuse to make any progress in understanding anti-oppression, and who also fail to implement even the simplest basics of anti-oppression, may have to be told that they are not aligned with the goals and objectives of the agency, which is a performance and competency expectation of the job. But be very slow to make this judgment, and be very quick to come alongside someone whom you disagree with to help them with their journey. Indeed, helping them in their journey will also help you in yours, because challenging oppression needs to be a social process, and the more different views that can be brought into this process, the stronger our anti-oppression will be.

## Find a Way to Identify the Way Oppression Operates in Your Organization

We discussed above how dominant societal attitudes and assumptions become embedded in an agency's goals, objectives, policies, procedures, and culture. Once an organization has developed a shared language and ability to talk about oppression, one way to tease out the ways the organization is implicated in oppression is to do an exercise where those in the agency try to design an agency that undertakes the work they do in a deliberately oppressive manner. Try this yourself in the exercise below.

## Exercise 12.2

### Designing an Oppressive Agency

If possible, undertake this exercise in groups.

Design a social work agency that is oppressive. We recognize that nobody wants to design such an agency, but for the purposes of this exercise, we ask that you do. The design, however, has to embed the oppression in the agency in a way that is not obvious or overt. The objective is to have oppression occurring, and to be able to also have plausible deniability, which means that you can deny that oppression is actually occurring. Build your organization using the following principles:

1.  Decide what type of social work your agency engages in. You could choose child welfare, school social work, mental health, violence against women, or some other type of social or social services work.

Continued

2.  Build oppression into your agency's policies, procedures, eligibility criteria, and the gender and racial composition of your staff. "Good" strategies to keep in mind are treating all service users and staff the same (even if they do not have the same needs), building your agency away from public transportation routes, delivering programs at times and locations where those who need them most cannot access them, and so on.

3.  Most importantly, ensure that your agency conceptualizes service user troubles as a personal problem, and does not look at or acknowledge any inequalities or structural causes of these troubles. Also make sure that your agency does not look for any structural causes of staffing inequalities built into the agency.

4.  Once you have done the above, write a brief overview of your oppressive policies, procedures, and practices on a flipchart or in your journal.

5.  Present your policies, procedures, and practices to another group, or if you have done it alone present to a friend. Then ask the group or friend to prove that your agency is oppressive. If you have done your work well, it ought to be difficult to prove that you are being oppressive. Even if someone can prove oppression is occurring, you should be able to deny that this was intentional.

6.  Conclude the exercise by reflecting on how many of the things you designed to be deliberately oppressive are already a part of the agencies that you know.

7.  List the things you learned (or were reminded of) in this exercise, and consider the implications for anti-oppression.

## Why Anti-Oppressive Change Is beyond Agency Control

One of the biggest challenges to anti-oppression is that the type of change needed to bring anti-oppression is beyond the control of most agencies. Gary Dumbrill and Winnie Lo (2015) have illustrated this elsewhere by contrasting two child welfare cases.

An Ontario child protection agency received a call reporting that a mother had been found unconscious in her apartment with twin infants left unsupervised. The mother was inebriated and had a history of alcoholism and drug use. A child protection worker was dispatched and arrived at the apartment to find paramedics taking the mother to hospital. The police were also on the scene; they handed responsibility for the safety of the unsupervised infants to the child protection worker.

At this point five men in business suits walked into the apartment, which, we ought to clarify, was a large penthouse suite of a luxury condominium. The man in front of the arriving contingent handed the worker his business card and introduced himself as the father of the infants and the partner of the mother. His business card identified him as the CEO of a multinational company. "I have the problem under control," the father said. "I am taking the rest of the week off work to look after the children. By the end of the week I will have my partner in rehab and I will have hired a live-in nanny. I will ensure the children are supervised at all times, and if you require more details of this plan please speak to these men who are my lawyers." He gestured to the other men in suits. (Dumbrill & Lo, 2015, p. 131)

The mandate of child protection agencies is to protect children, and wherever possible to do this without placing them in state care. This mandate worked perfectly in the scenario above, but not so well in an almost identical case that Dumbrill and Lo go on to describe.

Meanwhile, on the other side of town, another referral was made of a case with almost identical circumstances. In this case, however, the apartment was low-income housing, the parent lived in poverty with few resources, and there were no partner or family supports. The worker did not want to apprehend these children either but, unlike the first case, under the existing child welfare system there was no means to mobilize the resources and supports that would make it safe for the children to remain at home, so the worker had no choice but to bring the children into care. (Dumbrill & Lo, 2015, p. 131)

Explore the significance of these two cases and undertake the following exercise.

## Exercise 12.3

### How Would you Get to Anti-Oppression from Here?

If possible, undertake this exercise in groups:

1. In which of the above cases did oppression occur, and how would you describe the nature of that oppression?
2. If you were the worker in the case where this oppression occurred, what could you have done to be anti-oppressive?
3. If you were in charge of the child protection agency in the case where oppression occurred, what could you have done to be anti-oppressive?
4. Reflect on your answers and think through the implications for anti-oppression and anti-oppressive organizational change.

Oppression operates in the second case not as a result of the worker or the worker's attitudes, but because of the way the system works. The system works perfectly for the first family who are wealthy: their children remain safe at home, the mother receives treatment, and the children are not disrupted by a move away from home. The outcome in the second case is quite different, even though the case circumstances and the agency's mandate are the same. In this case, admission into care is necessary. Indeed, even if the mother going to private rehab and hiring a live-in-nanny were a cheaper option than bringing the children into care, the way services are imagined, funded, and delivered would prevent this option being used even though it might save taxpayers' money and would be in the best interests of the children.

In both cases, it took just over two years of treatment to resolve the addiction issues. Another disparity is that during this time the children in the first case remained at home, while the children in the second case remained in state care. Fortunately these cases took place prior to the reforms to Ontario's child welfare system that forces children under four to be made permanent wards of the state if they are in care for a period over 12 months. If this case happened today, the mother in the second case would lose her children forever, and the children would lose their mother forever too.

# A Model for Anti-Oppressive Organizational Change

It ought to be clear from previous chapters that any attempt at anti-oppressive organizational change has to involve service users. Unless agencies involve service users in these changes, they cannot be considered anti-oppressive.

Once an organization has developed a clear-enough consensus that change is needed, and once they are familiar with some of the ways that they may be implicated in oppression, the next steps in the change process involve service users. In Figure 12.3, we present a process that an agency might go through to initiate change. Service users must be involved in every step of this process.

## Step 1: Review Agency Goals, Objectives, Policies, Procedures, and Outcomes with Service Users and Stakeholders

The change model begins at step 1 in the centre circle. The agency meets with service users and stakeholders to review the agency's goals, objectives, procedures, and outcomes. *Goals* are a statement of the long-term purpose an agency is striving to achieve. For instance, a victim services agency might have goals that include supporting and ensuring the well-being of people who have been victims of crime. *Objectives* are the means to achieve the agency's goals. A victim services agency might offer crisis response, counselling, emergency accommodation, safety planning, legal representation, and so on.

*Policies and procedures* are the nitty-gritty of how the agency objectives are operationalized and achieved. These govern the everyday activities that social workers do to achieve

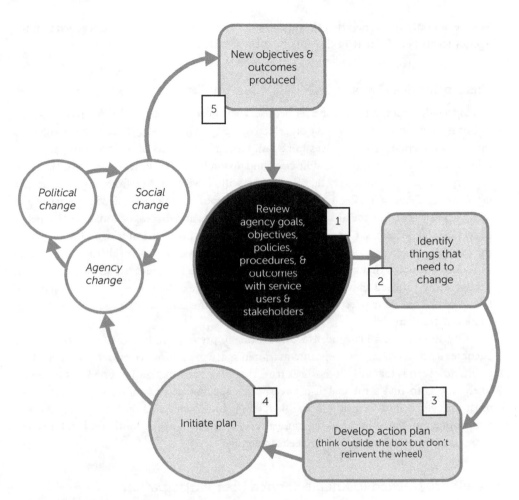

**Figure 12.3** An organizational change cycle

Source: Adapted from Dumbrill, 2012

agency objectives. For a victim services agency this may mean having a crisis-response worker or team on call 24/7, providing ongoing counselling as needed, providing emergency safe house or shelter accommodation, and having on-call legal staff. *Outcomes* are what the agency produces, and if the policies and procedures work as they should, the outcomes ought to be exactly the same as the agency's goals.

From an anti-oppressive perspective we constantly examine goals, objectives, policies, procedures, and especially outcomes through a critical lens. Mindful of the footprint oppression leaves on a community, we look for disparity in who gets served and disproportionality in who gets the best outcomes. We want to be sure that the agency's goals, objectives, procedures, and outcomes work equally well for the entire community the agency is supposed to serve, not just for those who fall inside the circle of first-class citizenship.

We are not only concerned that the outcomes are equitable; we are also concerned that the agency treats people fairly in the pursuit of those outcomes.

## Ensure Service Users from Multiple Marginalized Positions Are Involved

It is especially important to involve service users who occupy multiple marginalized positions in this review process, and in every other step of the change process. Indeed, one of the ways oppression operates is for services to be built around the needs of mainstream people. In other words, if you are White, middle class, and do not have disabilities or any other location of marginality, it is quite likely that the agency will be working fine from your perspective (as shown in Exercise 12.3). Such service users will not have the direct lived experience and direct knowledge of the racial, class, and other disparities and disproportionalities that occur in service and outcomes. Consequently, a principle of anti-oppression is to seek voices from the margins, and to develop and utilize knowledge and theory from outside the mainstream. This does not mean that an agency would exclude White middle-class service users from participating—indeed they will bring crucial knowledge of being on the receiving end of the system from their perspective—but if these are the only service users participating there is a problem.

Of course one could argue, as we have done in previous chapters, that as soon as one becomes a service user, one steps into marginal space in relation to service providers. Our point, however, is that although this is true, the more marginalization one faces the more likely one is to find a mismatch between one's specific needs and agency services. We must, therefore, look to multiple margins for the knowledge and theory needed to make anti-oppression work, because the more a service user is outside dominant locations, the more likely they are to know what needs to change.

## The Work Needed to Enable Service User Participation

Engaging the most marginalized service users in the process of change presents many challenges. Some of these challenges exist within ourselves, because we might privilege service users who have the social and cultural capital to seamlessly fit into an agency's planning events, and who hold ideas that will not upset an agency's practices too much. Tendencies to select service users who confirm what we do already were discussed in Chapter 10. We need to resist and disrupt this tendency.

Structural factors will also prevent the most marginalized service users from being able to participate. Those trod down by multiple forms of oppression, especially poverty, may face challenges to find the time to attend planning events and may not have the means to get there. To make participation possible, agencies need to provide financial compensation, babysitting, transportation, and other supports.

Even with all these measures in place, an agency may still find it difficult to get participation from all service user communities. Consider child welfare agencies as an example. Given that child welfare agencies have been removing children from marginalized communities in disproportionate numbers for generations, why would anyone from these communities believe that the child welfare system is open to change? Consequently, before step 1 can occur, bridges may have to be built and trust developed with service user communities.

## Step 2: Identify Things That Need to Change

Step 2 flows from and interacts with step 1. In step 1, the process of reviewing the agency's current goals, objectives, policies, procedures, and outcomes will invariably generate items for change. In identifying these areas, it is important to remember that oppression leaves a footprint because it occurs in patterns. We need to be on the lookout for those patterns and flag them for change, and this requires disaggregated data so outcomes for all the communities and groups an agency serves can be seen. In this process, agency administrators would be expected to bring all disparity and disproportionality data to the table, and expected to ensure that members of all communities reflected in these data are at the table.

Although disparity and disproportionality are measured in an organization's outcome data, oppression can also be felt in the culture of organizations through subtle attitudes. Because people can be trod down and pushed back in ways that do not always show up in hard outcome data, we have to pay attention to "softer" human relationship issues too.

## Step 3: Develop Action Plan

Once desired change is identified, a plan needs to be formulated to produce this change. Here it is important to be very specific about what the desired outcomes are and how an agency will know if they have been achieved. This stage can be difficult because agencies may not have the power to achieve the desired outcomes. For instance, suppose ending the overrepresentation in care or children living in poverty were set as an outcome. Exercise 12.3 showed how child welfare agencies have little power to gain different child welfare outcomes for those living in poverty. If you gained a different outcome when you undertook the exercise, excellent work, but we suspect that doing so required you to operate *outside* the policies, procedures, and budgets that govern that agency's work. Anti-oppression is about getting the type of things you did to bring that different outcome built *into* agency policies, procedures, and budgets.

## Key Concept

Anti-oppression is not finding ways to achieve anti-oppressive results by working *outside* agency policies and practices. It is about finding ways to build the means of achieving anti-oppressive results *into* agency policies and practice.

To bring anti-oppressive change to an agency requires work both inside and outside the agency. Shifts will be required in the political system (because government policy sets the framework for the agency's overarching goals and objectives), and in public opinion (because to some extent the government responds to the public, especially at election time). This is why, in Figure 12.3 above, in step 4 where we show the change plan being initiated, arrows in the figure show how change has to be brought at the agency, political, and societal levels.

## Understanding Targets and Levers

For anti-oppressive change to occur, the action plan needs to identify *targets* for change and *levers* that will be used to bring this change. Figure 12.4 below replicates Figure 12.3 above, but expands step 4 to show change targets (step 4A) and levers (step 4B).

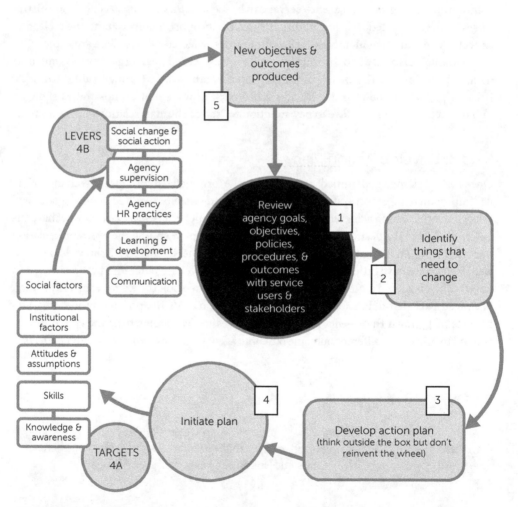

**Figure 12.4** Organizational change cycle and the strategies for change

Source: Adapted from figures based on Dumbrill, 2012, and Wong & Yee, 2010

*Targets* are the things that need to change for different outcomes to occur. A target is something that blocks anti-oppression from happening, and also a thing that can help make anti-oppression happen. For instance, workers' attitudes, assumptions, skills, knowledge, and awareness are all examples of targets.

*Levers* are the means used to achieve change in the target. Wong and Yee (2010) describe levers as "processes (formal and informal) that create the conditions for anti-oppression practice" (p. 21). For instance, if attitudes, assumptions, skills, and knowledge are targets for change, one has to identify the means to bring (lever) that change. Levers could include learning and development (training), the human resources department ensuring that desired changes are a part of worker evaluations, and so on.

The targets and levers shown in Figure 12.4 are based on Wong and Yee's (2010) anti-oppression framework for child welfare. This framework for child welfare is an organizational tool that can be used to undo oppression (e.g. racism, sexism, ableism, heterosexism, and other oppressions) in an organization's structure and practices. In 2010, the Ontario Association of Children's Aid Societies formally adopted this framework as a resource tool for child welfare agencies to develop and implement their own anti-oppression organizational change initiatives.

A model similar to the anti-oppression framework for child welfare is also used by Halton Region, a local government municipality, to engage in anti-oppression within all areas of that organization, including management, human resources, social work, health, accounting and administration, waste management, and more. In Halton Region, however, the term "anti-oppression" was not used because those working in the different departments were not familiar with the language of anti-oppression. As a result, Halton Region referred to their model as an "inclusion lens" (Yee et al., 2014), which is a term everyone could relate to. Although a different language than anti-oppression, this **inclusion lens** refers to the exact same thing, because to exclude is to push down and hold back so that people do not have the opportunity to fully participate—to include reverses that process.

The Halton Region project met with success because people could grasp the idea of inclusion and exclusion. This was a perfect entry point to focus on the processes and attitudes at the personal, systemic, and cultural levels that cause exclusion to occur. Halton Region even developed small cards for staff and managers with key inclusion messages on them, and a small lens in the middle as a reminder that unless you looked in the right way you might not even be aware that exclusion (oppression) was occurring. Everyone was taught how to use the lens and develop ways to stop it happening. The agency used the lens to examine the ways racism, sexism, ableism, heterosexism, and a number of other isms might be operating in their work at the personal, systemic, and cultural levels.

Although steps 4A and 4B in Figure 12.4 above are informed by the Halton and Children's Aid models, our Figure 12.4 model differs from these projects in one crucial way. The Halton Region and Children's Aid models involve service users at key stages, but our model involves service users in helping to govern the entire change process.

## Step 4: Initiate Plan

The next step is to initiate the plan. Let us imagine an agency that has identified the following things that need to change:

- Workers will understand and respond to the structural causes of service users' troubles.
- Workers will not have to pay in advance for their work-related expenses.
- Black and Indigenous children will no longer be overrepresented in care.

We can explore how each of these targets can be addressed.

### Workers Will Understand and Respond to the Structural Causes of Service Users' Troubles

Workers failing to recognize and respond to structural causes of service users' troubles is the opposite of anti-oppression. Consequently, ensuring that workers recognize and respond to service users' troubles at a structural level would be an anti-oppressive outcome. To achieve this objective we would need to understand why workers were not already recognizing and responding to structural causes. Many things could create this problem, so if this were a real scenario, we would have to spend time identifying the cause. But as our scenario is imaginary, we will identify a hypothetical cause, drawing from a real example found in the literature.

In a recent study into social work in Alberta and Ontario, McLaughlin, Gray, and Wilson (2017) found that experienced workers were more able than newer workers to understand and respond to the structural causes of service users' troubles. In addition, the experienced workers were able to practise in more flexible and collaborative ways with service users. The cause of this problem was found to be that, despite being trained in anti-oppression in social work school, new workers lacked the knowledge and experience needed to integrate a social justice focus in their work, and instead tended to more rigidly follow the bureaucratic rules and procedures of the organization.

We need to be cautious when applying research findings. Just because a study explains the cause of a problem somewhere else, do not assume that one's own similar problem have the same cause. This is particularly so with qualitative (non-numeric) findings, where the purpose of a research study is not to generalize (produce findings that can be broadly applied to a population), but instead to understand something in depth by focusing on a smaller sample. In real life this study might alert us to the possibility of what *might* be occurring in our agency, but we would want to look carefully at what actually was occurring in our own agency before we transferred these findings. Keep in mind, therefore, that only because our agency is imaginary can we assume that the issue identified by McLaughlin, Gray, and Wilson (2017) also identifies our cause.

With this cause identified, the target would become the worker's knowledge, skills, and confidence. We would delve deeper into the issue to identify the specific types of skills, knowledge, and confidence that were the issue, and specify in measurable terms the corresponding changes that were needed. The measures could be quantitative, qualitative, or a mix of both. The key is, however, to have a clear measure. There is little point in having a change goal unless one has a means to determine if it is reached.

Next, levers that can bring the desired changes are identified and used. In this case these would be a mix of supervision, learning, and development (which might include a mix of formal training and mentoring by veteran workers).

## Workers Will Not Have to Pay in Advance for Their Work-Related Expenses

Anti-oppression not only involves the way we treat and respond to service users; it also involves how we treat and respond to each other. This next example is a problem that arose in several agencies we worked with. Workers were expected to pay for their own gas mileage and all other work-related expenses in advance, which can be considerable, and retroactively claim for reimbursement, which sometimes took over a month to be paid. A number of workers said that they could not afford to make these payments and wait that long for reimbursement, and there was no way for them to be given these costs in advance.

This issue ought to be simple to resolve. The type of oppression occurring here is classism, the measurable anti-oppressive outcome is to have a system of cash advances for workers, and the target is agency policy and the HR department. Though an easy problem to solve, one might want to dig deeper. How was it that this was not recognized as a

## Exercise 12.4

### A Day of Golf

If possible, undertake this exercise in groups.

1. Discuss the golf-course team-building day mentioned on the next page. Do you consider this oppression? If yes, why? If yes, what type of oppression do you think is occurring? If you do not think oppression is at play, say why.
2. Who is likely to attend an event like this, who is not, and why?
3. Use some of the theoretical concepts discussed earlier in the book to unpack what is going on here. Especially consider a Bourdieuian analysis; what types of capital are at play?
4. Who is likely to get ahead in this organization and why? Who will be held back and why? If a person has characteristics (or capitals) that help them get ahead in this organization, are there also other social settings in which these capitals will help that person get ahead?
5. What would you target for change in this organization? What would your outcome measures be? What levers would you use to achieve these outcomes?

problem before? Staff had raised it as a problem before, but until the agencies began an anti-oppression process, nobody was prepared to do anything about it. Consequently, is the issue simply an HR policy that had not been thought through properly, or a whole system of thinking that enacted classism in the agency in other ways too? If the latter is the case, we might need to examine whether classism plays out in other ways in the organization.

Another example of oppression from the same agency that could be related to classism comes from the way the agency organized its team-development days. Team-building days took place at the local golf club and involved staff teams playing a round of 18 holes on the course. If a staff member did not want to attend this event, they could remain at the office and cover essential services while the rest of the agency played golf. There was always a small number of staff that chose to stay behind to cover essential services, and it always seemed to be the same people. What is occurring here?

## Black and Indigenous Children Will No Longer Be Overrepresented in Care

We have raised disproportionality issues in previous chapters. Consequently, it ought to already be clear why Black and Indigenous children no longer being overrepresented in care is an anti-oppressive priority. How to tackle this issue, however, is not so clear, because many causes need to be targeted for change. To complicate this issue further, the disproportionate numbers of Black children and Indigenous children in care have different histories and need to be addressed separately and in their own right. To make this example manageable, therefore, we will focus on Black children and families.

A plan has recently been developed to address the overrepresentation of Black children in care, and it provides an excellent example of what an anti-oppressive change plan looks like in real life. Examine this plan in Exercise 12.5.

## Exercise 12.5

### An Example of Organizational Change

This exercise will take at least two hours, so if there is not enough time to undertake this exercise now, return to it later. Consider reading the materials needed for this exercise as an individual, and then forming a group to address the questions the exercise poses.

To address the overrepresentation of Black children and youth in care, Children's Aid Societies in Ontario have developed a project called "One Vision One Voice." To orientate yourself to this project, watch Kike Ojo, project manager, describe the project and the issues that drive it on CityNews at http://www.citynews.ca/video/2016/09/29/video-systemic-racism-a-reality-ontarios-child-welfare-system-report-finds/.

Also read the One Vision One Voice project documents at http://www.oacas.org/what-we-do/government-and-stakeholder-relations/one-vision-one-voice/.

Next, if possible, undertake the following questions in groups. Identify and describe in your own words the following:

1.   How did the project involve service users and service users' communities?
2.   What outcomes does the project want to change?
3.   What are the targets of change?
4.   What levers will be used to bring change?
5.   How will those involved in the project measure change (outcomes)?
6.   What lessons stand out for you about organizational change based on this example?

It is too early to say whether the One Vision One Voice initiative is producing the outcomes it desires, but there is some evidence that this plan and related efforts are starting to bring change (Monsebraaten & Contenta, 2017). Of course there is much further to go not only in relation to race but also in relation to many other types of oppression. The task can at times seem monumental, but change is possible, and projects like One Vision One Voice can make it happen.

## Step 5: New Objectives and Outcomes Produced

In the organizational change process, this involves examining the changes that have occurred. This stage sets the agenda for the next turn around the change cycle beginning again with step 1. Questions asked in step 5, which set the stage for the cycle to begin again, include:

*   Has the plan produce the desired results?
*   How are changes to be sustained?
*   Do we need to modify the plan?
*   Are there other issues to be addressed?
*   What have we learned along the way?
*   Have we treated each other well and fairly in the change process?

These questions set the stage for the change cycle to begin again so that refinement is continuous and never ends. The process continuing is crucial because, as mentioned in previous chapters, Whiteness, or dominance, continually reinvents itself in an attempt to adapt to any challenge. As a result, anti-oppression has to continually adapt to stay ahead of oppression.

The step 5 question, "Have we treated each other well and fairly in the change process?" is also crucial, because sometimes in a change plan we replace one form of oppression with another, so it is important to be sure that this is not occurring. As well, one must not forget that an anti-oppressive plan is not only about treating the oppressed well. We also want to treat everyone well, and unless we do we will have forgotten what anti-oppression is about. Of course treating people well does not mean that we let people retain unearned privilege or that we accept them pushing others down and holding them back. We contend that we ought to treat everyone fairly, but in doing so we demand that others do the same.

## Chapter Summary

In this chapter we provided an overview of anti-oppressive organizational change. We explained how organizations, particularly mainstream organizations, tend to reflect and maintain Whiteness.

We provided a model for organizational change and gave examples of how it can be used. We gave you opportunities to use the model we presented, and in the exercise involving the One Vision One Voice initiative we gave you the opportunity to see a well-organized and well-thought-out real-life example of a change initiative.

We started the chapter with a story of a donkey and how we used the childhood game "pin the tail on the donkey" in an anti-oppression symposium workshop. The game enabled workers to think about and name specific types of oppression that needed to be targeted for change in their agencies. It also enabled workers to consider how they would lever these changes, and what anti-oppressive outcomes they would use to measure change. We hope that by now, at the end of this chapter, you know how to do that too.

## Discussion Questions

Share information in a group about an organization you have been involved with where issues of oppression have arisen. As a group, pick one of these examples and answer the following questions.

1. *Step 1 of the change process*: Which communities are impacted by this oppression, and how would you involve them in reviewing the organization's goals, objectives, procedures, and outcomes?
2. *Step 2 of the change process*: What things do you think those impacted by oppression will say need to change? Will different stakeholders have different opinions on what needs to change? What do you think would help them gain enough consensus to form a plan? Pick one small item that you think will make a difference, and move to the next question and stage.
3. *Step 3 of the change process*: If you were involved in the process, what type of plan would you suggest to address the issue you have identified?
4. *Step 4 of the change process*: In enacting the plan, what targets and levers will you use?
5. *Step 5 of the change process*: What outcomes do you anticipate? What issues will you flag for your next turn around the change cycle?

## Activity

It did not occur to us when we ran the donkey exercise at the workshop that we could have taken the donkey analogy further during that workshop. Donkeys are one of June's favourite animals for a good reason: they are smart and they have many other fine qualities. In keeping with the humour of our original donkey story, but at the same time making a serious point, research the characteristics of donkeys, and list those that might be useful for anti-oppressive social workers to emulate in their work.

Gary C. Dumbrill

**Figure 12.5** Thinking about donkeys

## Suggested Resources

Barnoff, L., Abdillahi, I., & Jordan, B. (2017). Building anti-oppressive organizations: Thoughts from a multi-dimensionally informed journey. In S. Wehbi & H. Parada (Eds), *Reimagining anti-oppression social work practice* (pp. 137–51). Toronto, Canada: Canadian Scholars' Press.

Cohen, M.B., & Hyde, C.A. (Eds), (2014). *Empowering workers and clients for organizational change*. Chicago, IL: Lyceum Books Inc.

Khan, J. (2016, May 14). *What our movements can learn from penguins*. Retrieved from https://www.youtube.com/watch?v=TQ707s2Xi7Q

Wong, H., & Yee, J.Y. (2010). An anti-oppression framework for child welfare in Ontario. Toronto, Canada: Ontario Child Welfare Anti-Oppression Roundtable. Retrieved from http://durhamcas.ca/wp-content/uploads/oacasaoframework.pdf

## References

Barnoff, L., Abdillahi, I., & Jordan, B. (2017). Building anti-oppressive organizations: Thoughts from a multi-dimensionally informed journey. In S. Wehbi & H. Parada (Eds), *Reimagining anti-oppression social work practice* (pp. 137–51). Toronto, Canada: Canadian Scholars' Press.

Bartoli, A. (Ed.). (2013). *Anti-racism in social work practice: Critical approaches to social work practice*. St. Albans, UK: Critical Publishing Ltd.

Chappell, R. (2013). *Social welfare in Canadian society* (5th edn). Toronto, Canada: Nelson Education.

Dumbrill, G.C. (2012). Anti-oppressive child welfare: How we get there from here. *The Ontario Association of Children's Aid Societies Journal, 57*(1), 2–8.

Dumbrill, G.C., & Lo, W. (2015). Adjusting a power imbalance: There is no anti-oppression without service users' voice. In S.A. Esquao [J. Carriere] & S. Strega (Eds), *Walking this path together: Anti-oppressive child welfare practice* (2nd ed., pp. 124–38). Halifax, Canada: Fernwood Publishing.

Grant, L., & Ojo, K. (Eds). (2008). *Anti-oppression in child welfare: Laying the foundation for change: A discussion paper.* Retrieved from http://www.oacas.org/wp-content/uploads/2017/01/Discussion-Paper-Anti-Oppression-in-Child-Welfare-Laying-the-Foundation-for-Change-Oct-2008.pdf

Grimes, D.S. (2001). Putting our own house in order: Whiteness, change and organization studies. *Journal of Organizational Change Management, 14*(2), 132–49. Retrieved from https://doi:10.1108/09534810110388054

Grimes, D.S. (2002). Challenging the status quo? Whiteness in the diversity management literature. *Management Communication Quarterly, 15*(3), 381–409. doi:10.1177/0893318902153003

Henry, F., & Tator, C. (2010). *The colour of democracy: Racism in Canadian society* (4th edn). Toronto, Canada: Nelson Education.

Hick, S.F., Peters, H.I., Corner, T., & London, T. (Eds). (2009). *Structural social work in action: Examples from practice.* Toronto, Canada: Canadian Scholars' Press Inc.

Kennedy-Kish (Bell), Sinclair, R., Carniol, B., & Baines, D. (2017). *Case critical: Social services and social justice in Canada* (7th edn). Toronto, Canada: Between The Lines.

McLaughlin, A.M., Gray, E., & Wilson, M.G. (2017). From tenuous to tenacious: Social justice practice in child welfare. *Journal of Public Child Welfare, 11*(4–5), 568–5. doi:10.1080/15548732.2017.1279997

Moffatt, K., Barnoff, L., George, P., & Coleman, B. (2017). Process as labour: Struggles for anti-oppressive/anti-racist change in a feminist organization. In H. Parada & S. Wehbi (Eds), *Reimagining anti-oppression social work research* (pp. 49–60). Toronto, Canada: Canadian Scholars Press.

Monsebraaten, L., & Contenta, S. (2017, June 30). Drop in number of Black children placed in care heralded as good start. *Toronto Star.* Retrieved from http://www.thestar.com/news/gta/2017/06/30/drop-in-number-of-black-children-placed-in-care-heralded-as-good-start.html

OACAS. (2016). *One vision one voice: Changing the Ontario child welfare system to better serve African Canadians. Practice framework part 2: Race equity practices.* Retrieved from Toronto, Canada: http://www.oacas.org/wp-content/uploads/2016/09/One-Vision-One-Voice-Part-1_digital_english.pdf

Schiettecat, T., Roets, G., & Vandenbroeck, M. (2017). What families in poverty consider supportive: Welfare strategies of parents with young children in relation to (child and family) social work. *Child & Family Social Work, 22*(2), 689–99. doi:10.1111/cfs.12285

Smith, K. (2017). A research design for the "messy actualities" of restructured social work. In H. Parada & S. Wehbi (Eds), *Reimagining anti-oppression social work research* (pp. 71–84). Toronto, Canada: Canadian Scholars' Press.

Swift, K.J. (1995). An outrage to common decency: Historical perspectives on child neglect. *Child Welfare, 74*(1), 71–91.

Turner, J.C., & Turner, F.J. (2009). *Canadian social welfare* (6th edn). Toronto, Canada: Pearson.

Wendt, S., & Moulding, N. (Eds). (2016). *Contemporary feminisms in social work practice.* New York, NY: Routledge.

Wong, H., & Yee, J.Y. (2010). *An anti-oppression framework for child welfare in Ontario.* Toronto, Canada: Ontario Child Welfare Anti-Oppression Roundtable. Retrieved from http://durhamcas.ca/wp-content/uploads/oacasaoframework.pdf

Yee, J.Y., & Dumbrill, G.C. (2016). Whiteout: Still looking for race in Canadian social work practice. In A. Al-Krenawi, J.R. Graham & N. Habibov (Eds), *Diversity and social work in Canada* (2nd edn, pp. 13–37). Toronto, Canada: Oxford University Press.

Yee, J.Y., Hackbusch, C., & Wong, H. (2015). An anti-oppression (AO) framework for child welfare in Ontario, Canada: Possibilities for systemic change. *British Journal of Social Work, 45*(2), 474–92. doi:10.1093/bjsw/bct141

Yee, J.Y., Wong, H., & Schlabitz, T. (2014). Beyond inclusion training: Changing human service and public organizations. In M.B. Cohen & C.A. Hyde (Eds), *Empowering workers and clients for organizational change* (pp. 135–55). Chicago, IL: Lyceum Books Inc.

# Where to from Here: Innovations and Hopes for the Future

**13**

## In this chapter you will learn:

- To review and reflect on the major lessons of this book
- More about the strengths and limitations of anti-oppression
- How to tell your own anti-oppression social work story

## Introduction

In previous chapters we always started with a story about oppression and anti-oppression that grounded the chapter in ordinary real-life events that we have encountered. As mentioned in the Preface, we did not share these stories to tell you about us, but to tell you something about the way oppression and anti-oppression operate in everyday life. In this final chapter we do not start with an introductory story, because what matters now is the story about how *you* understand anti-oppression and the ways you will address it. Only you can write that story.

We recognize that some of you already have long stories about oppression and anti-oppression work, and we hope this book has encouraged you on that journey. We also recognize that some of you are new to these ideas, and we hope this book has provided you with a good start to your anti-oppression story. Whatever stage you are at in your engagement with anti-oppression, we hope this book helps you to move forward in that work and make the world a better place.

At the end of this chapter we will ask you to think about your anti-oppression story, and where *you* will take anti-oppression from here. Before you do that, we will revisit and review some of the major lessons in this book, and we will make a number of new observations and suggestions for future directions.

## Looking Back: A Recap

We have covered much ground in this book. In **Chapter 1, What Are Oppression and Anti-Oppression?,** we looked at what oppression and anti-oppression are, and also what they are not. We said that in the dictionary sense of the term, the word "oppression" can be used to describe all manner of unfair and hurtful things that push people down and hold them back. Social work has a responsibility to oppose this type of unfairness, because social work attempts to make the world a fair and better place for everyone.

We pointed out, however, that in social work the term "oppression" is used for a very particular type of unfairness: the unfairness that operates through prejudices embedded in personal attitudes and acts, systems, and culture that push down and hold back the same groups of people time and time again in almost every aspect of their lives. We also explained that social work uses the term "unearned privilege" for the flip side of this phenomenon, which is the way an opposite set of biases embedded in personal attitudes and acts, systems, and culture privilege an alternate group of people by singling them out for positive treatment that moves them forward time and time again in almost every aspect of their lives (which is why this group becomes and remains dominant). The term "anti-oppression" is reserved for the way social work attempts to interrupt these processes. Such work is central in social work, because so many of the troubles that bring people to social work for help have roots in the inequalities and inequities caused by this pushing down and holding back.

In **Chapter 2, Thinking Critically about What We Know and How We Know It,** we began to explore the type of thinking needed to identify the ways oppression exists in society. We looked at how ideas and thinking that lead to oppression can be embedded in the assumptions we make about existence and the nature of the world (ontology), the ways we try to go about understanding the world (epistemology), the ways we explain the world of service users' troubles (theory), and the policies, programs, and remedies that social workers offer service users (practice). We suggested that unless we are able to engage in critical thinking and question the ontological, epistemological, and theoretical assumptions that our ideas and practice are based upon, we will not be able to tell whether oppression is operating in the ways we interact and relate to others and the way we undertake our practice.

In **Chapter 3, Thinking Critically about Power and Politics**, we took a deeper look at issues of power. We had already described in Chapter 1 how power is an essential component of oppression, because one cannot tread down and hold back entire groups of people unless one has access to power. In Chapter 3 we examined this power in more depth, especially how the type of power behind oppression is not simply individual power, but instead is embedded in systems and culture, which of course manifests at an individual level too.

But how did those with power gain it, and how did they make their culture and ways of being dominant? We began to explore this question in **Chapter 4, Whiteness: What It Is and Why We Need to Understand It.** This chapter was quite theoretical, and it needed to be, because it involved the deeper conceptual thinking needed to get to the ontological and epistemological roots of oppression. We looked at Whiteness, White supremacy, and also the racial contract, which is a type of societal understanding among those with power about who rules. We made no attempt to use concepts of Whiteness and the racial contract to explain all history, because White Europeans have only dominated the planet for a relatively short time. Although White supremacy helps us understand the power behind oppression for the past few hundred years, it does not explain oppression around the globe in ancient societies.

We also argued in Chapter 4 that Whiteness and White supremacy set the stage for understanding racism, which sets the stage for understanding most other isms and forms of oppression that operate today. We are not claiming that all oppressions are the same, but we are claiming that once one understands how White supremacy and racism work, it is easier to understand other isms.

In **Chapter 5, Isms and Intersectionality Part One: Racism and Sexism**, we looked at several forms of racism, including anti-Black racism, anti-Jewish racism, and anti-Muslim racism. We also examined sexism and intersectionality and the way oppressions overlap. In **Chapter 6, Isms and Intersectionality Part Two: Heterosexism and Cissexism, Ableism, and Sanism,** we looked at heterosexism, cissexism, ableism, and sanism. We also introduced the concept of performativity and the way it shapes society and people's lives. The isms we addressed in Chapters 5 and 6 are not all of the isms that could be addressed, but we trust that these are enough to give a fairly comprehensive view of some of the ways oppression operates and is resisted within society.

In **Chapter 7, From Colonization to Decolonization**, we spoke of how decolonization can refer to a "decolonization of the mind," which means using the type of critical thinking we spoke of in Chapter 2 to grasp how oppression operates, and to free our own thinking from the prejudices and attitudes that drive oppression. We argued, however, that in a Canadian context (and any other context where settlers have stolen Indigenous land), decolonization must refer primarily to a process that addresses issues of land and Indigenous sovereignty. We traced the history of colonization of what is now called Canada in some detail and examined the power relations that continue to hold colonization in place.

In **Chapter 8, The Problem of Poverty, Class, Capital, and the Social Order**, we built on the work of Chapter 4, which examined Whiteness and White supremacy, but here we delved back deeper into history, claiming that as far back as we can see in history, in most societies that social order has oppressed some and privileged others. We weaved into our understanding of oppression the way the existing social order creates enormous wealth for a few and poverty for many. We also explored how this could easily be fixed, because the wealth exists to end world poverty immediately, and all that is missing is the overarching human vision and will to make that happen. We spoke about our belief that ending poverty could actually happen, and about our rejection of the idea that poverty is an inevitable natural part of society that will always exist.

In **Chapter 9, Doing Anti-Oppression: The Social Work Dream,** we began to look in more detail at the place of anti-oppressive practice in social work. We outlined the theoretical roots of anti-oppression, and its strengths and limitations. In some ways this chapter returned to the proposition made in Chapter 1 that anti-oppression simply opposes oppression through the work that social workers do.

In **Chapter 10, Without Service Users' Theory There Is No Anti-Oppression,** we defined service users' knowledge and theory, and explained why it is essential in anti-oppressive social work. In **Chapter 11, How to Do Anti-Oppression with Individuals, Families, and Communities,** we talked about ways to engage in anti-oppressive practice at a casework level, and we drew extensively on what service users said about how they believed social work should be done with their families and communities. In particular we drew on examples they gave of workers getting anti-oppression right. In both of these chapters, we argued that unless service users have access to collective power, and have a real say in the way social work is designed and delivered, social work will never be anti-oppressive. We suggested that one way for service users to gain this power is through a service users' union.

In **Chapter 12, How to Do Anti-Oppression at Organizational and Policy Levels,** we examined anti-oppressive organizational change, how service users can be placed at the heart of the change process, and how social workers and service users together can leverage the type of agency, policy, political, and social changes to make anti-oppression possible. Finally, in this current **Chapter 13**, we consolidate these lessons and ask you to think about your story and where anti-oppression goes from here.

## Consolidating Lessons

You may recall that in Chapter 1 we said that anti-oppression was opposing oppression through the work that social workers do. This beginning definition of anti-oppression sounds very simple, but the knowledge needed to recognize and name oppression, and then oppose it through social work, is extremely complex.

Unless someone studies social work, oppression, and anti-oppression in some depth, like you have done by reading this book, they may find it difficult to grasp the complexities of doing social work in a way that is anti-oppressive. Indeed, sometimes friends we have in the natural sciences joke with us and say that social work is not "rocket science," because all social workers do is try to be kind and help people. We respond by pointing out that social work is actually far more complex than rocket science, because an astrophysicist simply needs a slide rule to plot a trajectory to the moon, but so far nobody has invented a slide rule to plot a trajectory to a poverty-free world, or developed a formula that produces social justice. Additionally, in the natural sciences, energy, which drives everything, is usually observable, predictable, and easily quantifiable. In social science, the equivalent concept to energy is power. In the social world power drives everything, it almost always masks itself, it constantly adapts to make itself fluid and unpredictable, and it can hardly ever be measured. Said differently, understanding social work, social science, and especially understanding anti-oppression, are extremely complicated. As a result, if you have gotten this far in this book, you have covered some highly complex ground.

# Key Concept

Social work is far more complex than rocket science, because an astrophysicist simply needs a slide rule to plot a trajectory to the moon. There is no slide rule to plot a trajectory to a poverty-free world, or to develop a formula that produces social justice.

Of course, complexity is of no use unless it can be operationalized, unless it helps us understand things better, and unless it helps us practise better. This is why we gave many practical examples of issues and cases related to oppression and anti-oppression, and gave you the opportunity to think them through. Now, in this final chapter, we give you an opportunity to see how far you have come. Think back to Chapter 1. You may recall that we gave you the following case study (see Exercise 1.3).

> A child protection worker apprehends a five-year-old from an Indigenous family living in poverty because the child was being left unsupervised, and because the conditions in the family home were a serious health hazard. The parents say that their child is being removed because of oppression and a racist child protection system.

You may recall that in Chapter 1 we asked you the following questions about this case:

1. Is it oppression, and if so why?
2. If it is not oppression, what is it, and why?
3. Regardless of what it is, if you were the worker, how would you deal with it, and why?

Now, some 12 chapters after first undertaking that exercise, we ask you to revisit the exercise and the answers you gave:

# Exercise 13.1

## Revisiting Earlier Decisions: Is This Oppression?

If possible, undertake this exercise in groups.

1. Review your Chapter 1 answers to Exercise 1.3, and consider whether you want to change any of the answers now that you are at the end of this book.
2. If your answers changed, reflect on why, and identify the information in this book that caused that change.

Continued

3.  If your answers did not change, reflect on why, and identify the information in this book that confirmed the position you took.
4.  Reflect on ways that the information in this book might have helped you to gain a better understanding, or to better explain to others, the historical, societal, political, and cultural context of this case.
5.  Finally, and this is the new and more complex question, if you were the worker or the executive director of the agency where this incident took place, map out a brief plan for anti-oppressive change that might have the potential to bring a different outcome and a different conversation with the family.

If your understanding has shifted since Chapter 1, consider revisiting some of the other exercises in this book and review them too, to see if your understanding in those has also shifted, especially ones that you were uncomfortable with or were not sure about at the time. As well, consider reviewing them a few years from now—we guarantee that your understanding will shift. Our understanding of anti-oppression will certainly shift. It will do so in response to continuing conversations with each other, with colleagues in the academy, workers in the field, service users and community groups, and also as a result of watching the way oppression changes and adapts to attempts to oppose it.

## Thank Goodness Help Has Arrived!

We spoke in Chapter 11 about the dream that, instead of the anxiety and concern that some service users feel when social work comes to their door, the reaction would be "thank goodness help has arrived."

One may associate the concern service users have about social work with only mandated services such as child protection or perhaps mental health. But such thinking avoids the issue on several levels. First, although most people might think that those who seek help from human service organizations are voluntary, in fact the idea of voluntary versus non-voluntary is a misnomer. Trotter (2015) argues that the majority of service users are involuntary, not only because of the presence of court orders or the threat of such orders if they do not comply, but because they are pressured into service use by partners, family, friends, or life circumstances. As well, even if someone voluntarily seeks help, we suggest that the stigma often associated with needing help means that the decision to get help may well be a last resort, and as such is not entirely "voluntary."

We are not suggesting that everyone has anxiety and concern when social workers arrive, but we are suggesting that this reaction may be more extensive than many social workers imagine. We also suggest that the existence of such fear is an indictment against the profession, and also an indictment against anti-oppression. Indeed, we have spoken about oppression being a system that treads people down, and anti-oppression being something that helps to push back. Yet Black parents talk about the fear they have when child protection social workers come knocking (Rankin, 2014), because they fear that rather than pushing back against oppression, social workers will push them down even further. Data proves that these fears are correct. News headlines confirm that the "child welfare system is rigged against black families" (Greenbaum, 2014). The system is not only rigged against Black families, it's also rigged against Indigenous families (Blackstock, 2009; Sinha, Trocme, Fallon, & MacLaurin, 2013), families living in poverty (Contenta & Rankin, 2016; Pelton, 1989; Russell, Harris, & Gockel, 2008), mothers living with HIV (Greene et al., 2016), and parents with disabilities (Booth, McConnell, & Booth, 2006; Callow, Tahir, & Feldman, 2017) —and these are just the treading-down instances we know about! If we got anti-oppression right, these would be the very service users who would be saying "thank goodness help has arrived," but the fact is that they are not saying this—they are saying the opposite.

Of course, there are service users who have said of social workers and the anti-oppressive practice they bring, "thank goodness help has arrived." As described in Chapter 11, Gary made efforts to interview such service users to find out what workers and agencies did to evoke this response, and we included these descriptions in the ideas we shared about how to do anti-oppression. But these practice responses were not the norm, and the evidence from the data we cite above (along with numerous similar studies), shows that for the most part social work has anti-oppression wrong.

We find that when anti-oppression is done right, it is often because of the ingenuity and creativity of the individual worker, not because of the system. This does not mean that workers who get anti-oppression wrong ought to be blamed for not getting it right. Indeed social work, particularly mandated services, are becoming increasingly regulated and bureaucratized. For instance, Esquao and Strega (2015) said that child protection social work is being transformed into "technologies of risk management" (p. 13) through which service users' troubles are conceptualized as personal problems and micro issues to be managed by workers, rather than understood as troubles shaped by broader social-political issues of inequality. We have emphasized how Canadian social workers have few practice options for switching off the pathologizing of service users and switching on a focus on the social inequalities that cause service users' troubles.

## Key Concept

Anti-oppressive social workers need to switch off the pathologizing of service users, and switch on a focus on the social inequalities that cause service users' troubles. Social workers cannot flip this switch on their own—they need the help of service users to do it.

The bureaucratization and regulation of social work we are experiencing in Canada is happening in other places too. In the United Kingdom, a national report on social services has raised the over-bureaucratization of UK social work practices as a problem, along with the corresponding inability of local authorities (agencies) to govern their own work in a way that meets service users' needs (Munro, 2011). If agencies are not allowed the autonomy to decide with service users the best service to deliver, and if the state locks what workers can do into a pre-set series of technical responses, none of which address structural inequalities, then anti-oppression is doomed. We may as well give up our dream of service users saying "thank goodness help has arrived," and ought to give up the idea that we could ever be a part of liberation, and instead simply accept that we are agents of social control.

## You Can't Get There from Here without a Service Users' Union

We have argued that, ironically, service users may have more power than social workers to shape the work that agencies do. We do not know how many social work service users there are in Canada, but the Canadian Association of Social Workers (CASW) estimate that in 2016 there were approximately 50,000 social workers in Canada (Canadian Association of Social Workers, 2017). We do not know the average caseload size of Canadian social workers, but depending on the nature of the agency and intervention, some workers will have small caseloads of perhaps 15 or even fewer, while some will have large caseloads of over 100. let's assume an average caseload of 30 service users. This means that at any time there will be 1.5 million people in Canada receiving social work services (50,000 × 30 = 1,500,000). These numbers represent considerable power. Indeed, in the last Canadian general election, Trudeau's Liberals won a "decisive majority government" on a margin of about 1.3 million votes (*CBC News*, 2015). Social work service users, therefore, have the power to decide who rules. Indeed, if we add those doing social work activities that might not be included in the CASW estimate of social workers in Canada, such as social service workers, child and youth service workers, and others, one might easily double the estimate of how many people do social work in Canada, and this will double the estimate of how many social work service users there are. This is a lot of voting power. Of course not all service users will agree on all issues, but with these numbers they would not need to. The political power this group could wield would be significant, and far more powerful than the power of social workers.

## Key Concept

If social work service users all got together, they would hold enough collective voting power to decide Canada's government at the next general election. If social workers are trying to advocate for service users, but are not advocating for service users to get together and use their own power, then social workers are going about anti-oppression the wrong way.

The reason we support the idea of a service users' union is not simply because of the political power they would wield, but because it is unethical for social work to have so much say in service users' lives without service users having a say themselves. We will not reiterate the arguments we made in earlier chapters for service users' power, but we remind you of those arguments. Until social work stops being something that is done without service users having much more of a say, it is never going to be anti-oppressive. And by "having a say" we do not mean inviting service users to take part in surveys, or inviting participation only from service users with the right kind of capitals (in a Bourdieuian sense) who will confirm what we want to hear. We are referring to a more complex and nuanced service users' voice: a voice backed by the power of a union so that it has to be heard and responded to.

## The Organizational Barriers to Service Users' Voice

In our efforts to help agencies move forward in their anti-oppression vision, we have noticed that agencies finding a way to take the initiative to engage with service users as a collective seems to be the biggest problem. Some agencies are taking this initiative, but not on the scale we envision within this book.

Agencies face many barriers in trying to involve service users. A major barrier is that there is simply no budget to free up staff to begin this liaison, let alone to cover the transport, child care, and other costs that service users will incur by taking part. In addition, we argue that service users need to be paid for coming to share their knowledge and theories, because they are doing so to help social workers get it right, and their labour in doing that should not be exploited.

Not only is there no existing budget in most agencies for service user engagement, most agencies will have trouble getting this type of initiative funded in future budgets. Indeed, we mentioned above how social work is becoming increasingly regulated and bureaucratized so that even if social work is ready to give service users a voice, the government that regulates the occupation and the public who puts the government in office may not be ready. This of course brings us back to the issue of the electoral power of service users as a collective, and also the power of this collective to change the public and political discourse on social welfare. You will recall from Chapter 10 that our recommendation is that this funding dilemma be solved by those who fund social work organizations being required to fund the development of a union that will give voice to service users. Indeed, we believe there is a case to be made that it is unfair to fund social work organizations to intervene in service users' lives, often against their will, without providing a part of that funding to enable those impacted by this intervention to have a voice. We are realistic, however, because we do not anticipate governments volunteering such funds. To gain this type of funding considerable political work and social action would be needed, and for us this is one of the places that anti-oppressive social work needs to focus its efforts.

## Are Agencies Really Ready?

Although we claim that funding formulas, regulation, and bureaucratization prevent social work organizations from engaging service users as a collective, we are not sure that agencies are actually ready to do this. Indeed, agencies have no problem finding funds to hire consultants, but they seem reluctant to use these funds to engage with service users. For instance, after Gary completed the "Our Families Your Policies" study with refugees, study participants volunteered to develop a one-day training workshop that would help social workers understand the struggles refugees face as newcomers, the ways these create issues that bring them to social workers, and the way social workers can work more effectively with their communities. Although Gary promoted this idea, and even though the service users and Gary were willing to do this free of charge, not a single agency took up this invitation; however, several agencies were willing to pay Gary to come on his own and explain these issues to them. Why is this?

## Exercise 13.2

### Why the Reluctance to Hear Service Users?

If possible, undertake this exercise in groups.

Consider why some agencies appear to be more willing to hire Gary or June to discuss anti-oppression and the ways to work with marginalized communities than to hire service user community members themselves to do this work.

1. Look back over previous chapters and draw upon some of the analytical frameworks we have discussed to explain this phenomenon.
2. List the frameworks you use. To start, we will name two—Bourdieu and Whiteness. If these are among the frameworks you choose, be sure to list the capitals you believe are involved, and also to explain how Whiteness advantages not only Gary, but also advantages June in this situation.

## Social Work and Uncomfortable Places

One reason agencies may prefer to have us rather than service users discuss anti-oppression with them is that agencies have a level of comfort with us. This may be true, but do not misunderstand the nature of this comfort. In the early days of anti-oppression, Gary was asked to help an agency on its journey. The first thing someone said in the workshop to Gary was, "Okay, do your worst." This comment revealed that the participants were expecting that the workshop was about to make them feel very uncomfortable, and of course they were right.

Neither of us set out to deliberately make anyone uncomfortable in anti-oppressive training, but discomfort comes with the territory. People cry, they get angry, they even shout at us, some storm out of workshops, others become argumentative in a manner designed to ridicule and put us down. Even in social work classes, where students come to learn anti-oppression, we sometimes face hostile reactions. Given these reactions, perhaps agencies in the field think it is better to hire us (fellow social workers) to suffer and respond to these staff reactions, rather than invite service users in to face these types of staff re-actions. If this is what agencies are thinking, we believe it is a mistake; service users have already been on the receiving end of social work's "bad behaviour" and are just as capable of addressing it as we are. If this is the concern, even though we disagree with it being a reason to not bring service users into agencies as trainers, we do appreciate why agencies are worried about the well-being of service users in this environment. Indeed, inviting anyone into an agency to help workers examine the way they are implicated in oppression is not always going to be a pretty process. Perhaps you felt some of this when you read this book. You should not have, because none of what we have said attacks you personally no matter what locations you occupy. Indeed, we see you as a part of the solution, not the problem. But even so, becoming a part of the solution requires examining how one is im-plicated in the problem, and that is hard and emotionally draining work. (Thank you for sticking at that work throughout this book.)

To be fair to social workers and agencies, the work they do is hard enough as it is. Adding the need for the level of reflexivity and critical self-examination we have called for in this book can make the work feel even harder. What other occupation do people join with the intent of helping others, only to suddenly be told that they have to first examine how they are a part of the problem? On top of this, anti-oppression is often framed as being achievable if workers simply practise in the right anti-oppressive way. As we made clear in Chapter 11, social workers cannot get to anti-oppression from here. Indeed, for the most part, social workers are locked into a practice that is almost entirely micro, and service users are locked out of having any real say in shaping the intervention they receive. In this environment, claiming that social workers can achieve anti-oppression if they simply do it right replicates what oppressive social work does to service users. It ignores the broader context and makes the political personal—the message is that if you try hard enough on the micro level you can do it. Of course you cannot, because it is a bigger social and political problem.

Another issue that makes the anti-oppressive activity of engaging service users diffi-cult to achieve is fear. The fear is not of the service users we have worked with and know, and likely not fear of most of the service users workers know on their caseloads. It is fear of some of the groups that have arisen and claim to represent service users. A number of online groups critique child protection services workers. Many of these groups make points that we fully support, but interwoven in the texts and comments of some of these groups are misogynistic, anti-LGBTTIQQ2S, and other comments that stand in direct op-position to the values of anti-oppression, of social work, and of a fair and just society. We know social workers who have received harassing emails from these groups. As a result, social workers and agencies are concerned about engaging with such groups.

It is not only workers who have concerns about some of these online groups, service users do too. Gary was doing research into service users' perspectives in a town where one such online group leader happened to live. The service users who attended Gary's research meeting said that they almost did not come, because they were worried that this man might show up, and they were scared of him. Herein is the complexity of oppression. The man running this online group may have at one time been a service user, and as such he would be in a marginal space and a position of non-dominance. But in his fight against child protection power, he seemed to be drawing on his Whiteness, on ideas of male dominance, and even concepts from White supremacy. It is understandable why social workers might be reluctant to engage with those from such online groups—but Gary's experience is that many service users are reluctant to engage with or be associated with some of the views expressed in some of these online groups too. This means that we must not let the attitudes of vocal online critics become an excuse for not engaging with service users as a whole. Indeed, failing to engage with service users for fear of some of the oppressive views and attitudes seen online may let these views and attitudes fester. Without any other service users' organization, online groups are one of the only platforms that give service users a voice. As shown in the town where Gary did his research, some of the views expressed in these online groups do not actually represent the views of all service users. We suspect that if agencies opened forums in which all service users could gain a voice, this would become evident.

## The Academy Must Change

We have critiqued agencies for not involving service users, but we need to critique the social work academy too. There is good reason to involve service users in helping the academy theorize, research, and teach social work, because "a fundamental requirement of social work theory is that it interacts with or is useful in some way in practice" (Payne, 2014, p. 5). Practice means nothing unless it is relevant to service users. There are, however, no institutional mechanisms in the Canadian social work academy to ensure that the work of academics is relevant to what social workers do or what service users need. Canadian social work schools are governed by an accreditation process, but this body and the regulations they develop are decided entirely by academics.

What service users say plays no formal role in accrediting Canadian social work programs and counts for little in the careers of social work academics. There is no requirement in the regulations for the tenure (permanence) and promotion of social work academics in the institutions that we are a part of, nor in other Canadian universities we know of, that requires social work academics to have an impact on policy, practice, or to produce anything that makes a difference in the lives of social work service users. There is, however, a very strict requirement that the work of academics has an impact on other academics. A primary means of measuring this impact is the number of publications the academic has in top-ranked, peer-reviewed journals. (A **peer-reviewed publication** is a paper reviewed and approved by other academics before it is published. **Journal rank** is determined mostly by the extent to which the journal is read and cited by other academics). These are very important indicators about the quality of an academic's work, but these are entirely inadequate indicators if the purpose of social work as a discipline is to benefit service users.

The problem above is compounded by the fact that peer-reviewed journals are hardly ever read by people in the field, and when they are read many in the field find them mostly out of touch and not relevant to the work they do. This is particularly so with much of the research social work academics produce; a review of studies on research utilization demonstrates that practitioners pay little attention to research published in journals, and that researchers do not communicate findings in ways that are useful or relevant to the field (Gray, Sharland, Heinsch, & Schubert, 2015). This is not surprising because, as mentioned above, there is no career incentive for academics to theorize and write for the field or to make a difference in the lives of service users. In fact, if academics spend too much time writing and disseminating their work in ways that impact the field, and less time on intellectualizing social work in journals that impact other academics, they risk never gaining the performance indicators required for tenure or promotion.

The work of academics being out of touch and irrelevant to what occurs outside the academy is not just a problem for the social work discipline. This issue was taken up in the national news in the UK, where it was suggested that linking academic success to publishing research in journals that are written for, edited by, and read by other academics creates universities that "... generate banal, wasteful research through the relentless focus on publications as a performance indicator" (Anonymous academic, 2017). Although we are critical of the social work academy, we do not go as far as this anonymous British academic with our critique, because we do believe that the academy does produce high-quality research that is useful in the field. But we do agree that the standards by which the work of the academy is measured need changing. The principle "nothing about us without us" that we have discussed throughout this book applies not only to practitioners, but also to schools of social work. It is inherently oppressive for academics to theorize about what service users need, and teach students how to meet these needs, without service users having any say. The social work academy in Canada needs to review and reorganize its goals, objectives, and procedures so that service users have a say.

One way the social work academy might become more responsive to service users and the field is through an initiative Gary has developed called the **principle of three voices**. The idea is that social work needs to be driven by three voices:

1. Academics (those who research, theorize, and teach social work)
2. Workers (direct-practice social workers, supervisors, managers, policymakers, and others on the delivery end of services)
3. Service users (anyone receiving or eligible to receive social work services)

The principle of three voices means that that the knowledge, theory, writing, and teaching that academics do, the programs that policymakers develop, and the practice that workers do have to be shaped by all three voices. Our reasoning is that if an idea or a program has those who research and teach social work, those who practise social work, and those who receive social work, all agreeing it is a good idea, then it probably is. The three voices principle (or what we like to call "3Voices"), is being used at McMaster University to develop teaching curricula in some courses, to develop target learning outcomes, and to develop a series of national conferences where all keynotes and workshops must be spoken with three voices.

## Key Concept

If those who theorize about social work and research it (academics), who do social work (practitioners), and who receive social work (service users) agree that a particular program, policy, or policy, or practice is good, then it probably is.

# The Need for Truth and Reconciliation

We addressed issues of colonization in Chapter 7, and we also spoke of the importance of Canada's Truth and Reconciliation Commission (TRC). Both need to be central in anti-oppression. The potential of truth and reconciliation is shown in South Africa. Apartheid, which is rule by minority Whites, began in South Africa in 1948. Racism and other forms of oppression existed previously in South Africa, but apartheid was different (Maylam, 2016). Think back to Exercise 12.2 where we asked you to design a covertly oppressive agency. Now think of doing that exercise but instead designing a country; instead of covert oppression, you design overt and obvious oppression; and you hold it in place by White uniformed government security forces using extreme violence and White undercover government security forces using torture and assassination. This will give you an idea of that regime and the deadly force it employed (Clark & Worger, 2016; Mandela, 1994; Maylam, 2016).

Apartheid ended in 1994 with free elections in which Nelson Mandela, leader of the opposition African National Congress Party, was elected president. With this election, everything changed in South Africa: power had shifted, freedom had come, and there were a lot of scores to settle.

After these changes, many feared that the country would devolve into even more violence, and in response Mandela asked Desmond Tutu to address in a non-violent way the wrongs that had been done. Tutu recognized that many thought the perpetrators of apartheid were monsters and demons, and he agreed that it was hard to imagine how a human could do the crimes they committed. Tutu claimed, however, that such thinking let the perpetrators off the hook because "monsters" have no real responsibility. Tutu argued that those who committed these crimes did have responsibility, and they needed to be held accountable for what they had done. He chose to hold them accountable through a process of truth and reconciliation (Tutu, 2011).

We could say much more about the historical backdrop to truth and reconciliation in South Africa, and you may want to consider researching that history, because it contains more lessons than the ones we are drawing out here. The lesson we are focusing on here is what truth and reconciliation did in South Africa so we can be aware of what it might do in Canada. Also, lest the brutality of apartheid distracts us from recognizing Canada's own need for truth and reconciliation, know that in the 1940s Canada's Indian Act and its reserve system helped inspire the way the South African government designed apartheid (Popplewell, 2010).

In South Africa, Tutu built truth and reconciliation on traditional African jurisprudence, which is non-retributive. Tutu (2011) explains, "When people quarreled in a traditional setting, the main intention was not to punish the miscreant but to restore good relations. . . . For Africa is concerned, or was concerned, about relationship, about the wholeness of relationship" (p. 32). Tutu's truth and reconciliation was also based on restorative justice. Again Tutu (2011) explains, "Restorative justice believes that an offence has caused a breach, has disturbed the social equilibrium, which must be restored, and the breach healed, in a process through which the offender and the victim can be reconciled and peace restored" (p. 42–3).

Tutu (2011) claims that restorative justice is always costly. He uses the example of a pen: one cannot steal someone's pen and expect reconciliation without giving the pen back. In South Africa, the primary restoration Tutu sought from the perpetrators of crimes was truth. He offered amnesty in exchange for telling the absolute truth about one's crimes to the public, to victims, and to the families of victims. By definition truth is always a part of truth and reconciliation, but in South Africa absolute truth was also seen as a type of restoration.

Canada has undertaken truth and reconciliation in a somewhat different context to South Africa. The most obvious difference is that, unlike South Africa, in Canada land and sovereignty have not been restored to the original people from whom it was taken. We addressed this issue in Chapter 7, and we suggest that the issue of decolonization mentioned in that chapter has to be central to truth and reconciliation.

The other difference between South Africa and Canada is that in Canada the full truth has not been told. Indigenous people told truth at the TRC, as did others too, but it seems to us that there is not a nationwide and especially not a government acknowledgement of truth. It is true that First Nations children on reserves receive less government services than all other children in Canada (Blackstock, 2009, 2011; Trocme, Knoke, & Blackstock, 2004). Yet the government spent $707,000.00 (CAD) on legal fees denying this truth, and once this truth was out the government still refused to right this wrong (Talaga & Ballingall, 2017). How can there be reconciliation with no truth?

Truth has to be central to not only formal TRC processes and responses to it, but to all anti-oppression. We travel to agencies and organizations all over Canada to speak on anti-oppression, and when we raise issues such as racism, we sometimes meet those who protest and say that this is not an issue in their communities. When we encounter this claim, we stop what we are saying, we ask people to pull out their cellphones, and do a search of their hometown name and the word "racism." We then ask them what the search brings up (try it yourself). Almost always it brings up dozens of articles about racism in their hometown. With this truth in hand, we ask them why they deny this truth and how they can hope to start anti-oppression, let alone reconciliation, without it. This Internet search can be done with other forms of oppression too. There can be no anti-oppression, no truth, no reconciliation, until people can be honest about the oppression that they and others are a part of.

## Grounding Anti-Oppression in Love

We mentioned in previous chapters, especially Chapter 11, that love has to be central in anti-oppression, but we have not defined love. We deliberately left defining the term to this final chapter to let the concept sit with you for a while—to allow you to develop your own understanding of what this means—before we more fully explain our understanding.

Although we say that love is important in anti-oppression, we have no right to tell the oppressed that they need to love. For us to do this would be offensive. We have no right to tell those on the receiving end of oppression what they ought to do. But we do not speak to you as someone who is oppressed, even though you may be; we speak to you as someone who is taking up social work (or a related discipline). As a part of your work as a social worker with and on behalf of others, it is important to speak to you in your role as a social worker about the need for love.

Love can be easily confused with a sentimental feeling, or as an effort to "be nice" and not offend, or to even suffer in silence, but these things are not what we have in mind when we use the term. Desmond Tutu (2011) grounds his social justice in a love that is confrontational, uncomfortable, and uncompromising in its pursuit of justice. This is the same love we spoke of in Chapter 11, which Dr Martin Luther King Jr spoke of from the Birmingham jail (King, 1994). This is nothing like sentimentality or passivity.

Love, according to Tutu and King, is confrontational and may at times require us to break the law (King, 1994; Tutu, 2011), but should never use violence. Others, like Guevara, argue that love can use violence to end oppression (Guevara, 1965). We are on the side of Tutu and King on this issue, but whatever side you fall on in this debate, we contend that the anti-oppression you engage in must be driven by love. Love is all about relationships—even relationships with oppressors. Love is also about truth. We have to be truthful about the oppression that exists and we have to be truthful about its impact. With love and uncompromising honesty about hard truths, we can find ways to work with one another. Without love and truth, anti-oppression will simply become oppression all over again, and the revolutionaries will simply become the new oppressors.

## Chapter Summary

In this final chapter, we have pulled together the major lessons of this book. We have also expanded some of the points, especially the central place that service users need to play in anti-oppression. We speculate about future development in anti-oppression and the ways anti-oppression needs to develop. We urge you as readers to be on the leading edge of this development.

In taking up the lessons of this book, it is not just your role as a reader to simply adopt all that we say. If you unquestioningly accept everything we say, you have not understood Chapter 2 where we cautioned you against accepting things at face value. Indeed, our ideas are always changing and what we understand today may change tomorrow. Take the ideas of this book, but do so critically and also adapt them to fit the way you work as a person, and adapt them to serve those you work with.

As mentioned at the start of this chapter, in all other chapters of this book we have always begun with a story—a story about something we have encountered or observed that related to the topic of that chapter. We used that story to ground the chapter in real life. In this final chapter, the story has to be about you and the way you make sense of and engage with the world. Before we ask you to develop your story, we will tell you one more story (in the Discussion Questions below), to set the stage for you telling your own story (in the Activity below).

At the start of this book we also said that there are no formulas or recipes that lead to anti-oppression. This means that one has to create anti-oppression in the moment. This creation has to be based on a deep understanding of how oppression is operating in that moment. We hope this book has helped give you the understanding to create anti-oppression in the moments you encounter. Aside from knowledge, we also hope that this book has strengthened or given you the hope and encouragement that is so needed in the work of anti-oppression. We thank you for staying with us in the narrative, and we wish you strength and success with whatever way you decide to take up anti-oppression and social justice. Go and make a good story—one that makes a difference.

## Discussion Questions

In the 1960s, there was a world-famous British music group called The Beatles. In 1969, group member John Lennon was in Canada, when a 14-year-old Canadian fan managed to get into John Lennon's hotel room with a tape recorder and ask several questions. At that time, Lennon had been making bold statements about the need for love, world peace, the end of war, and a focus on social justice. Also at that time, Lennon had been banned from entry into the United States. All of these issues are just as relevant now as they were in the 1960s. Lennon agreed to answer the 14-year-old Canadian's questions on these issues, and his questions about music, too.

Some 38 years later, the original soundtrack recording from this encounter was animated and made into a short film called, "I Met the Walrus." This animation won a 2009 Emmy Award. We do not agree with all Lennon says, but for us, some of his points resonate with points we have made in this book. In this final exercise, watch that film at https://youtu.be/jmR0V6s3NKk and reflect on the points that resonate for you from this film.

Discuss the following questions:

1. What points does Lennon make that you agree with and why?
2. What points does Lennon make that you disagree with and why?
3. Do any of the points Lennon makes resonate with ideas you read in this book? Do any clash with ideas you read in this book?

## Activity

Imagine yourself years from now toward the end of a social work career in which you have achieved much success. Now imagine a 14-year-old who hopes for a future in social work, who has heard of your reputation in anti-oppression, who asks to record your answers to questions. You agree. The interview begins:

- Hey, could you please tell me what is the situation with you and social work? What is it about you that made you decided to do social work?
- What did you do as a social worker to challenge oppression through your work?
- What are the main ways you changed things? And how did you figure out how to do that?
- What do you hope you will be remembered for the most?

Use the question above as prompts to write your own story—an imaginary story written by you in the future—a story that describes what you achieved, or more importantly helped others achieve, in anti-oppression. Articulate the way you imagine you would have lived and enacted your vision for social justice. Name the things (in your life, in this book, or elsewhere) that helped you refine and enact that vision.

After writing this story, keep a copy somewhere safe, add to the story as your ideas evolve, and most importantly go and make that story happen. Oh and of course, if long in the future a 14-year-old comes to you for words of wisdom about doing anti-oppression, don't forget to use the story you wrote, and maybe mention to them the book you read many years ago that gave you the idea of writing your story for just such a day.

## Suggested Resources

CBC. (2015, December 15). Truth and Reconciliation Commission final report. *The National*. Retrieved from https://youtu.be/lKKLgwlosaw

Paikin, S. (2016, June 2). TRC one year later: The path to reconciliation. *The Agenda*. Retrieved from https://youtu.be/_MhqF4yeSXo

Tutu, D. (2008). Reconciling love: Archbishop Desmond Tutu, University of California Television. Retrieved from https://youtu.be/iV2LURTu3eQ

# References

Anonymous academic. (2017, June 30). Pressure to publish in journals drives too much cookie-cutter research. *The Guardian*. Retrieved from http://www.theguardian.com/higher-education-network/2017/jun/30/pressure-to-publish-in-journals-drives-too-much-cookie-cutter-research?

Blackstock, C. (2009). Why addressing the over-representation of First Nations children in care requires new theoretical approaches based on First Nations ontology. *Journal of Social Work Values and Ethics, 6*(3).

Blackstock, C. (2011). The Canadian Human Rights Tribunal on First Nations child welfare: Why if Canada wins, equality and justice lose. *Children and Youth Services Review, 33*(1), 187–94. doi:10.1016/j.childyouth.2010.09.002

Booth, T., McConnell, D., & Booth, W. (2006). Temporal discrimination and parents with learning difficulties in the child protection system. *The British Journal of Social Work, 36*(6), 997–1015. doi:10.1093/bjsw/bch401

Callow, E., Tahir, M., & Feldman, M. (2017). Judicial reliance on parental IQ in appellate-level child welfare cases involving parents with intellectual and developmental disabilities. *Journal of Applied Research in Intellectual Disabilities, 30*(3), 553–62. doi:10.1111/jar.12296

Canadian Association of Social Workers. (2017). What Is Social Work? Retrieved from http://www.casw-acts.ca/en/what-social-work

*CBC News*. (2015, October 20). Justin Trudeau's Liberals to form majority government. *CBC News: Canada votes*. Retrieved from http://www.cbc.ca/news2/interactives/results-2015/

Clark, N.L., & Worger, W.H. (2016). *South Africa: The rise and fall of apartheid* (3rd edn). Abingdon, UK: Routledge.

Contenta, S., & Rankin, J. (2016, August 15). Report shines light on poverty's role on kids in CAS system. *Toronto Star*. Retrieved from http://www.thestar.com/news/insight/2016/08/15/report-shines-light-on-povertys-role-on-kids-in-cas-system.html

Esquao, S.A. [Jeannine Carriere], & Strega, S. (2015). Introduction: Anti-racist and anti-oppressive child welfare practice. In S.A. Esquao [Jeannine Carriere] & S. Strega (Eds), Walking this path together: Anti-racist and anti-oppressive child welfare practice (2nd edn, pp. 1–24). Halifax, Canada: Fernwood Publishing.

Gray, M., Sharland, E., Heinsch, M., & Schubert, L. (2015). Connecting research to action: Perspectives on research utilisation. *British Journal of Social Work, 45*(7), 1952–67. doi:10.1093/bjsw/bcu089

Greenbaum, B. (2014, December 11). Child welfare system rigged against black families. *Toronto Star*. Retrieved from http://www.thestar.com/opinion/commentary/2014/12/11/child_welfare_system_rigged_against_black_families.html

Greene, S., O'Brien-Teengs, D., Dumbrill, G.C., Ion, A., Beaver, K., Porter, M., & Desbiens, M. (2016). A community-based research approach to developing an HIV education and training module for child and family service workers in Ontario. In H. M. Montgomery, D. Badry, D. Fuchs, & D. Kikulwe (Eds), *Transforming child welfare: Interdisciplinary practices, field education, and research* (pp. 163–85). Regina, Canada: University of Regina Press.

Guevara, C. (1965, March 12). From Algiers, for Marcha. *The Cuban Revolution Today*.

King, M. L. (1994). *Letter from the Birmingham jail*. San Francisco, CA: Harper.

Mandela, N. (1994). *Long walk to freedom: The autobiography of Nelson Mandela*. London, UK: Little, Brown and Company.

Maylam, P. (2016). *South Africa's racial past: The history and the historiography of racism, segregation, and apartheid*. Abingdon, UK: Routledge.

Munro, E. (2011). *The Munro Review of Child Protection. Final Report: A child-centred system*. Retrieved from London, UK: http://www.gov.uk/government/uploads/system/uploads/attachment_data/file/175391/Munro-Review.pdf

Payne, M. (2015). *Modern social work theory* (4th edn). New York, NY: Oxford University Press.

Pelton, L.H. (1989). *For reasons of poverty: A critical analysis of the public child welfare system in the United States*. New York, NY: Praeger.

Popplewell, B. (2010, October 30). A history of missteps. *Toronto Star*. Retrieved from https://www.thestar.com/news/investigations/2010/10/30/a_history_of_missteps.html

Rankin, J. (2014, December 11). When CAS comes knocking. *Toronto Star*, p. A33.

Russell, M., Harris, B., & Gockel, A. (2008). Parenting in poverty: Perspectives of high-risk parents. *Journal of Children and Poverty, 14*(1), 83–98. doi:10.1080/10796120701871322

Sinha, V., Trocme, N., Fallon, B., & MacLaurin, B. (2013). Understanding the investigation-stage overrepresentation of First Nations children in the child welfare system: An analysis of the First Nations component of the Canadian Incidence Study of Reported Child Abuse and Neglect 2008. *Child Abuse Neglect, 37*(10), 821–31. doi:10.1016/j.chiabu.2012.11.010

Talaga, T., & Ballingall, A. (2017, June 2). Ottawa spent $707,000 in legal fees fighting decision that protects Indigenous children. *Toronto Star*. Retrieved from http://www.thestar.com/news/canada/2017/06/02/ottawa-spent-707000-in-legal-fees-fighting-a-rights-decision-that-protects-indigenous-children.html

Trocme, N., Knoke, D., & Blackstock, C. (2004). Pathways to the overrepresentation of Aboriginal children in Canada's child welfare system. *Social Service Review, 78*(4), 577–600.

Trotter, C. (2015). *Working with involuntary clients: A guide to practice* (3rd edn). New York, NY: Routledge.

Tutu, D.M. (2011). *God is not a Christian: And other provocations*. J. Allen (Ed.). New York, NY: HarperOne.

# Glossary

**ableism** The oppression of disabled people.

**absolute poverty** Not having one's basic human needs met, including food, safe drinking water, sanitation facilities, health, shelter, education, and information.

**additive model** A model of oppression that conceptualizes oppressions as separate, but that sometimes overlap, in which case they are "added" together so that a person can experience more than one oppression. This adding conceptualizes the overlaps as simply addition so that racism and sexism = racism + sexism. This model contrasts with the intersectional model, in which two oppressions such as racism and sexism combine to create a third space, which creates a unique mix that is more than the sum of their parts, and may not be addressed by existing anti-racism and anti-sexism efforts alone.

**aetiology** The cause of something—usually a disease or condition.

**agency** The power or capacity to do something.

**agender** Literally "without gender," which refers to a genderless or non-binary gender expression. For more see "Gender" in Chapter 6.

**alliance** A social worker and service user or community working together toward the same objective.

**ally** Someone who offers support or joins with another for some cause. In anti-oppression it usually refers to working with people to oppose an oppression they face, but that one does not face oneself.

**annihilation** The complete destruction or extermination of something. In this book we used the term to refer to attempts to destroy or exterminate (annihilate) specific peoples and their culture or ways of being.

**anti-Islam or anti-Muslim** Acts of prejudice directed toward those who are considered Muslim and/or a part of the Islam faith.

**anti-Judaism** Hatred and oppression of Jewish people based primarily on their religion.

**anti-Muslim or anti-Islam** Acts of prejudice directed toward those who are considered Muslim and/or a part of the Islam faith.

**anti-oppressive practice** The term "anti-oppressive practice" can be understood by breaking down the meaning of each word. "Anti" means it opposes, "oppression" is what it opposes, and "practice" is the context in which it operates. Anti-oppressive practice, therefore, opposes oppression through the practice (everyday activities) of social workers. For more see "What is anti-oppression" in Chapter 1.

**anti-psychiatry** Literally a critique of psychiatry, but used more broadly for a movement that also questions whether mental illness exists. For more see "Anti-psychiatry" in Chapter 6.

**anti-racism** Literally opposing racism. Although people have opposed racism ever since racism existed, the term is often used to refer specifically to a broad international social movement that began in the 1980s, comprised of activists, intellectuals, teachers, social workers, and everyday people committed to challenging racism in national and local contexts.

**anti-Semitism** The hatred and/or hostile attitudes or political acts toward Jewish people.

**appropriation** Taking something belonging to someone else and using it for one's own means.

**asexual** A person who experiences a low level or no sexual attraction to other persons.

**assigned sex** Usually refers to the sex one is assigned at birth.

**assimilation** Literally the process of taking in and absorbing something. In this book we use this word in relation to peoples and nations. We describe such assimilation as annihilation by other means, because it is the process of a dominant group absorbing another group into itself so that other group's distinctness is lost.

**austerity ailments** Mental suffering and distress caused by the impact of government cuts (austerity measures) to programs, services, and the social infrastructure.

**authoritative power** Getting one's own way by persuading others of one's legitimacy.

**bigender** The merging of male and femaleness in one's gender identity or expression.

**bisexual** Someone who is romantically attracted to both men and women.

**Biskaabiiyang** A return to one's self and a reinterpretation of traditional teachings in today's context. For more see "Do not confine decolonization to a metaphor" in Chapter 7.

**Black Lives Matter** A social movement that began in 2013 when George Zimmerman was acquitted for the killing of Black teen Trayvon Martin in Miami, Florida. It is now a worldwide chapter-based and member-led organization that engages in activism against anti-Black racism as an intervention to liberate Black lives from state violence and vigilantism.

**bourgeoisie** Marx referred to the ruling class in the age of capitalism as the bourgeoisie, which is a French term originally used to describe middle-class manufacturers and owners of industry. For more see "The ruling class" in Chapter 3.

**capitalism** A social system in which most people work producing things in factories, businesses, or some other setting owned by a proprietor or corporation.

**Charity Organization Society or COS** The COS was an early social work organization known most for bringing scientific logic and casework methods to help the poor become self-sufficient. It was founded in Britain in 1869 and expanded to Europe, Australia, and North America.

**cis**  See *cisgender*.

**cisgender**  A person whose sex matches their gender identity and gender expression. For instance, a cis male is someone with an assigned male sex, who regards themself as male, and who acts mostly in ways that society expects men to act. A cis female is someone with an assigned female sex, who regards themself as female, and who acts mostly in the way society expects women to act.

**cisnormativity**  The idea that assigned sex and gender align. For more details see "Gender" in Chapter 6.

**cissexism**  Oppression of those whose sex and gender do not align.

**class consciousness**  When people recognize that they are oppressed as a group (class).

**class struggle**  Literally a struggle or conflict between classes within society. In Marxist analysis, this struggle occurs between the ruling and working classes.

**coercive power**  Getting one's own way through the use of threat or force.

**colonization**  The process of conquering, occupying, and controlling a people's land or territory, or controlling the way they think and act.

**commodity fetishism**  The replacement of human relationships with the value of money and commodities.

**common sense**  A term seen by some as problematic from an anti-oppressive perspective because it is sometimes used as backlash against equity efforts. We think that scholars problematizing the phrase is a mistake, because efforts to achieve equity do make sense. In addition, we use the term "common sense" to refer to the wisdom on the street that sees through government excuses for not providing the public with adequate supports and services. For more see "The role of good casework and common sense" in Chapter 11.

**communism**  A form of socialism that produces a classless society with no private property and in which common interests and collaboration rather than competition drive the economy and relationships.

**communist society**  In Marxist theory, a period after revolution when the state fades away and there is no longer a need for any form of authoritative state control.

**community-based research**  Research in which community members (service users), organizations, and agencies become equal partners in designing, undertaking, and owning research that informs policy, practice, and social work education.

**confirmation bias**  A tendency for people to look for evidence that supports their ideas and ignore evidence that does not.

**conflict perspective** or **perspectives**  Theories that explain society and social relations as the result of conflict between groups, such as Karl Marx's ideas about class conflict. Those who hold a conflict perspective see society as being fundamentally unfair because those with power and resources tend to win conflicts and then structure and organize society in a way that favours their own group. For more see "Politics, paradigms, and self-reflection" in Chapter 2. Also see in this Glossary *consensus perspective*, which is the opposite of conflict perspective.

**congruence**  The extent to which a social worker's and service user's ideas about a problem and solution overlap.

**control**  In the literal sense means to influence, to direct, or to make or stop something from occurring. When used in relation to social work theory, control refers to an informed attempt to help someone—to gain control over a problem. For more see "Theory and understanding in social work" in Chapter 2.

**consensus perspective** or **perspectives**  Theories that explain society and social relations as the result of consensus and co-operation between groups. Those who hold this perspective see society as being fair. For more see "Politics, paradigms, and self-reflection" in Chapter 2. Also see in this Glossary the opposite term *conflict perspective*.

**coproduction**  Social workers and service users combining their knowledge to produce something together.

**corporate welfare**  The government using taxpayer's money to support the rich when they fall on hard times—such as bailing out bankers—but not doing the same for ordinary working people.

**corporeal standard**  The ideal physical body, as well as predominant mental, neuronal, cognitive, and behavioural norms.

**critical race theory (CRT)**  Theory about race and racism that builds on the insights advanced by critical legal studies and radical feminism movements and, more recently, that can be seen applied in the social sciences, political theory, and educational and ethnic studies. For more see "Critical race theory" in Chapter 5.

**critical self-reflection**  Questioning what we know and how we know it.

**cultural appropriation**  The process of someone (usually from the dominant culture) taking and using the symbols, art, and dress of another group for the benefit of the dominant group. For more see "Appropriation" in Chapter 4.

**cultural capital**  A source of power based on cultural assets such as academic credentials and etiquette. For a detailed description see "Pierre Bourdieu's view of power" in Chapter 3.

**cultural oppression**  The dominant group using their social influence to make the national culture follow their own norms, rules, traditions, and ways of being. For more see "Oppression through culture" in Chapter 1.

**culture jam**  A way of disrupting mainstream ideas embedded in everyday culture with the intent of revealing how domination is occurring.

**culture of poverty** The idea that poverty becomes a culture among the poor that contains defeatist attitudes that prevent the poor from getting ahead. See also *individual theories of poverty* and *systemic theories of poverty*.

**dead White men** or **man** A historical figure whose achievements may be over-rated or overstated as a result of them occupying a powerful or privileged social location.

**democracy** A political system in which, in theory, all citizens have a say in who rules and how they govern—in other words "rule by the people."

**deserving poor** Those who are poor because they are too ill or frail to work, and are therefore considered deserving of help. For more about deserving and undeserving poor see "Beliefs that the needy do not know best" in Chapter 10.

**description** When used in relation to social work theory, this means social workers gathering information and carefully describing it in ways that allows analysis to take place.

**developing or underdeveloped nations** A term used to refer to poorer nations that are mostly in the earth's southern hemisphere; alternate terms include Global South or the Third World.

**dialectic** A tension (such as a class conflict) between two opposites that interact with each other, which eventually results in a revolutionary change.

**difference** The process in which a dominant group separates itself from those they oppress. The dominant group perceives, constructs, and portrays those they oppress as "different" in some way. The dominant group then uses this "difference" to justify the oppression of another group. For more see "The basis of oppression" in Chapter 1.

**disability** The consequences of not meeting the corporeal standard, and being subjected to disablism. For more see "Ableism" in Chapter 6. Also see in this Glossary *corporeal standard* and *ableism*.

**dis-ability or dis/ability** Sometimes the parenthesis "dis" is split from the word "ability" to draw attention to the fact that "disability" cannot be understood without reference to "ability." For more see "Ableism" in Chapter 6.

**disabled peoples' movement** A movement of disabled people who developed the social model of disability. For more see "The social model of disability" in Chapter 6.

**disabled person** A person who has been "disabled" by ableism. For more see "Ableism" in Chapter 6. Also see in this Glossary *ableism*.

**disablement** The process of making someone disabled. For more see "Ableism" in Chapter 6.

**discourse** A way to organize, construct, and make meaning of something through the language that we use to talk about it. Power operates through the language that we choose to use about something. For more see "Postmodernism and power" in Chapter 3.

**discipline** A means to train or make people comply with rules and social norms.

**discriminate** To discriminate means to recognize difference, or to distinguish between things or people. In anti-oppression the term is often used to treat people differently in an unfair way on the basis of difference.

**discursive** The process and/or the act of creating a discourse.

**discursive technique** To construct ideas through discussion or talk. For more details see "Invisibility and exnomination" in Chapter 4. Also see in this Glossary *discourse*.

**disparity** Literally refers to a "great difference," and in social work is often used to refer to situations where such difference in service levels results from some form of ism or prejudicial treatment, or instance, First Nations children and families on reserves receiving less child welfare services and resources than other families and children.

**disposition** A way of being, but when taken up within the theories of Pierre Bourdieu, this is the way one's habitus embodies a field. For more see "Many fields and their relationship to habitus" in Chapter 8.

**disproportionality** Refers to something occurring within a group or population at a different rate to other groups or populations. Disproportionality is not calculated by comparing the total number of events occurring in differing populations, but is calculated by calculating the events as a ratio in relation to the numbers of people in each group or population being compared. Said differently, disproportionality refers to something being more likely, or less likely, to occur for you if you fall into a particular group or population, such as Black, White, Indigenous, refugee, employed, unemployed, and so on. An example is being pulled over by the police when driving a car—we know that Black drivers are more likely to be pulled over than White drivers and the extent of this disproportionality can be calculated.

**doctrine of discovery** An idea invented by Europeans that they had a legal right to own any land they could occupy.

**dominant discourse** The meanings that predominate within society and the things we accept as truth.

**dominant group** A term used for those who control most of society's capital, resources, and assets, and who have the ability to set society's norms and values.

**domination** A form of rule or control.

**doxa** A set of rules or protocols that can be written or unwritten.

**economic capital** The wealth (and power) that comes as a result of owning corporations, money, stocks, and other material assets.

**embodying** Internalizing something and taking on its characteristics.

**en vivo** A research term that means the code (a concept or theme) is based on an exact word or phrase a research participant used.

**epistemology** The theory of knowledge and how we know.

**equality** This term is usually understood as meaning things being equal, or as everyone being treated exactly the same. For more on equality, and how it differs from equity, see "Anti-oppression and human rights" in Chapter 1.

**equity** This term means to be fair or impartial, but is built on the recognition that people are not the same and have unique needs, so treating everyone the same is not always just or fair. For more on equity and how it differs from equality see "Anti-oppression and human rights" in Chapter 1.

**essentialist woman** A term used to describe an "imaginary woman" that is based on stereotypical features and thinking that all women are the same.

**essentialization** Literally the idea that everything has an essential nature or form. When used in this book it refers to the belief that someone's essential nature or being can be defined by their race, gender, sexuality, sex, or similar category.

**exnomination** The ability to not be named. For more details see "Invisibility and exnomination" in Chapter 4.

**explanation** When used in relation to theory, "explanation" is the way social workers "explain" the reason something is so. For more see "Theory and understanding in social work" in Chapter 2.

**exploitation** The process of gaining resources and advantage by treating someone unfairly.

**false consciousness** A concept Marx used to explain the way the oppressed fail to understand their own oppression. There is a false consciousness when a group (class) of people oppressed by an unfair system do not recognize that the system is unfair.

**falsification** An attempt to uncover truth and avoid one's own biases and beliefs by trying to prove one's own ideas wrong (as opposed to trying to prove them right). Also see in this Glossary *verification* and *confirmation bias*.

**feminism** A movement and perspective started and maintained by women that advocates for the rights of women.

**feudalism** A social system in which most people live and work on land owned by lords or barons appointed by a monarch.

**field** Bourdieu uses this term to refer to a setting in which power and influence are at play. A field can be a geographic region like a city or nation, or it can be a discipline like the legal profession, politics, the military, social work, or the corporate world. For more details see "Pierre Bourdieu's view of power" in Chapter 3.

**first dimension of power** A concept usually associated with Lukes that refers to power being exercised by a person or group using an ability to cause negative consequences for others to make others do something they would not ordinarily do, or to prevent them from doing something that they want to do. For more details see "Lukes's model of power" in Chapter 3.

**First World** Refers to nations that include Canada, the USA, Australia, New Zealand, the nations of Western Europe, parts of Asia, and a number of other nations with similar more developed economies. See "Poverty in the Global South" in Chapter 8.

**flight to innocence** Refers to the attempt to distance oneself from one's unearned privilege and to un-implicate oneself from the way oppression operates. For more see "Resisting racism" in Chapter 5.

**gay** Men who are romantically attracted to men.

**gender** A social construction that refers to the various expectations society has for the way men and women behave, dress, and even feel about themselves and their own identity.

**gender expression** The way one expresses one's gender (through behaviour, clothing, expression, etc.).

**gender identity** The way one perceives one's own gender (either as male or female, as a mix of these, or as no gender at all).

**gender non-conforming** Sexual identities and expressions that are not aligned with society's gender expectations.

**genderqueer** An umbrella term for sexual minorities.

**genocide** Defined by the United Nations as murder and the denial of a right to live, and also the denial of the right of existence as a human group.

**geocentric** Literally "earth centred," and used to refer to the idea that the planets and the sun rotate around the earth. The term is used in this book to explain paradigms.

**glass ceiling** A term used to refer to the sexism that prevents the advancement of women in work places.

**Global North** Refers to nations that include Canada, the USA, Australia, New Zealand, the nations of Western Europe, parts of Asia, and a number of other nations with similar more developed economies. See "Poverty in the Global South" in Chapter 8. Also see in this Glossary *First World*.

**Global South** A term used to refer to poorer nations that are mostly in the earth's southern hemisphere; alternate terms include *developing* or *underdeveloped nations*, or the *Third World*.

**globalization** An increasing connection between people, corporations, and nations around the globe. In the context of this book, the aspect of globalization that has been focused on is the way nation-states around the world are politically, economically, and socially interconnected in a worldwide market so that any decision made in one nation-state will have an impact on others.

**grand theory** A term coined by C. Wright Mills to describe attempts to explain all human history and the entire social order in one theory.

**habitus** A concept associated with the work of Pierre Bourdieu to explain the way we internalize structures, norms, and values of fields we operate within. The idea of habitus does not mean that we simply internalize and passively conform to any given field; rather it represents the ways we are shaped by fields and also the way we shape fields. For more on this concept see "Pierre Bourdieu's view of power" in Chapter 3.

**heliocentric** The idea that the planets and earth rotate around the sun and used in this book to explain paradigms.

**hetero** A word with Greek origins that means "different" and provides the prefix for words such as heterosexism, heterosexual, and so on.

**heteronormativity** The assumption that the human norm is opposite sex attraction.

**heterosexism** The oppression of those who do not comply with heteronormativity.

**heterosexual** Attraction to the opposite sex.

**heuristic device** A conceptual model that helps one figure out or visualize how things work. For more see "How social workers understand oppression" in Chapter 1.

**ideal type** Similar to a heuristic device, an ideal type is a conceptual model of reality. The notion of an "ideal type" is associated with the work of the sociologist Max Weber. These models are useful at a conceptual level to understand how things work, but they never represent the full complexity of reality.

**ideology** A set of guiding beliefs or ideas.

**impairment** Literally a "weakened" or "diminished" human being. For more on this term and how it is used in anti-oppression see "The social model of disability" in Chapter 6.

**imperialism** The process of governments and private companies building empires by taking over nations and the lives of the people who live there.

**inclusion lens** A way of looking at things such as programs, services, work activities, and so on, to examine whether anyone is being systemically excluded. For more see "Understanding targets and levers" in Chapter 12.

**Indian Act** Legislation that continues to define who an "Indian" is in Canada, and sets out the principles by which the Crown manages their lives. The Indian Act is regarded by many as racist, paternalistic, and built on the idea that Indigenous peoples are not capable of knowing or managing their own affairs.

**Indian agents** or **commissioners** A bureaucrat, who was usually White, or Whitened by years of working within the civil service, and who managed Indigenous peoples on behalf of the Canadian government.

**Indigenous knowledge** Knowledge developed by Indigenous peoples and often built on traditional teachings and ways of knowing.

**individual model of disability** Conceptualizing disability as an "illness" that exists entirely within the disabled person's body or mind, rather than existing as a result of our structuring society around certain types of bodies and minds.

**individual theories of poverty** The idea that the poor are responsible for their own poverty—that they make bad choices or are lazy and do not want to work. Also see in this Glossary *culture of poverty* and *systemic theories of poverty*.

**intellectual genealogy** The scholarly tradition and ideas that inform one's work.

**interest-convergence** The idea, or recognition, that advancements in Black rights only occur when this also benefits White people.

**internalized oppression** A concept used by some authors for the way members of oppressed groups sometimes internalize dominant ideas about their own group and oppress themselves. In this book we prefer the concept of habitus to explain the way each of us is implicated in oppression of others and sometimes people in the groups we ourselves are a part of.

**intersectional failure** Failing to recognize that a new form of oppression is occurring when two or more oppressions overlap, for example, failing to recognize that when racism and sexism overlap, neither anti-racism or anti-sexism can be relied on to address the type of oppression Black women will face in this intersection. For more see "Intersectionality" in Chapter 5.

**intersectionality** A term coined by Kimberle Crenshaw to identify what occurs when two forms of oppression intersect. Also see in this Glossary *intersectional failure*.

**intersex** Someone whose body does not conform to usual/stereotypical male or female anatomy.

**invisibility** Not being seen or recognized. We use this term in this book to refer to the invisibility of Whiteness, which has allowed Whiteness itself to continue to be an unnamed silent norm from which difference is defined and measured. For more details see "Invisibility and exnomination" in Chapter 4.

**iron cage of sex and gender normativity** A model developed by Dumbrill and Yee in this book to explain the oppression that occurs when people do not conform with normative sex and gender expectations. See Table 6.1 The iron cage of sex and gender normativity in Chapter 6.

**Islamophobia** A term sometimes used for or hatred of Muslims. Alternate terms are "anti-Muslim," "anti-Islam," or "anti-Muslim racism."

**ism** The suffix *ism* has origins in Ancient Greek language and is used to refer to either an ideology or a form of action. When used in anti-oppression it refers the way ideology or beliefs about differences, such as race, gender, etc., can lead to actions that oppress along these lines of difference. Such isms include racism and sexism. For more on isms see "Oppression through personal prejudice" in Chapter 1 and also the content of Chapters 5 and 6.

**Jim Crow laws** Non-federal state and local laws in the USA that enforced racial segregation.

**journal rank** A rating of the impact a journal has measured by such things as the extent to which the journal is read and cited by other academics.

**Kaswentha** A treaty that set out the relationship and sharing of space by the Haudenosaunee and the Dutch Crown, and also sets sovereign relations between later settlers and European governments.

**labour power** This concept has many meanings, but in this book we use this term to refer to the labour, or potential labour, of workers—particularly the working classes.

**laissez-faire** A lack of regulation—letting the market decide things.

**left political perspectives** or **the left** The political concept of the left originates in France when those in a lower social position sat to the left of the king. As a result, we use the term "left" today for perspectives informed by socialist ideas and the belief that the social order favours the elites on the right. For more about the terms "left" and "right" see "Politics, paradigms and self-reflection" in Chapter 2. Also see in this Glossary the opposite term *right political perspectives*.

**legitimacy** The literal meaning is that something is legal or valid. In this book the term is used to refer to a person of organization in a leadership position being accepted as having a right to lead or rule.

**lesbians** Women who are romantically attracted to women.

**less eligibility** An idea from the 1834 Poor Law Amendment Act built on the belief that poverty was a choice. The founders of the 1834 Act believed that if they could make poor relief uncomfortable—by making those who received "less eligible" (or worse off) than anyone else in society, this would cause those needing relief to go get a job and not be poor anymore. For more about this principle see "Beliefs that the needy do not know best" in Chapter 10.

**LGBTTIQQ2S** Lesbian, gay, bisexual, transgender, transsexual, intersex, queer, questioning, 2-spirit.

**liberal** or **liberal paradigm** In simple terms a liberal paradigm values equality and freedom of people and also the need for some government intervention to address social inequality. Of course the concept of liberal it is much more complex than this. For more details see "Politics, paradigms, and self-reflection" in Chapter 2.1

**liberalism** A word derived from "liberty." It carries connotations of freedom from oppression and freedom from the domination of the state or some other ruling mechanism.

**libertarianism** A political view that advocates a minimal role for the state in controlling and regulating citizens.

**limbos** A term coined and used by African American feminists who used their power and creativity to challenge and tear down the socially constructed idea of womanhood. See more in "First wave feminism" in Chapter 5.

**low income cut-off (LIC)** A calculation based on percentage of net income a person or family spends on shelter, food, and basic necessities compared to others in their community.

**macro** The word means very large, and in social science refers to anything that is large scale—for instance economics that operate at a national or international level (i.e. macro-economics) or the politics and social structures

that govern society such as macrosociology. In social work a macro-analysis would examine how these large structures and systems shape society and impact people and communities.

**mad pride** Mental health service users reclaiming the word Mad to resist the negative meanings connected with it.

**market basket measure** or **(MBM)** A measure of poverty based on funds needed to afford basic food, shelter, and living supplies in one's community.

**marginalization** The process of pushing people and groups to the edges of society where they are denied the opportunities and resources that those in the centre keep for themselves.

**matrix of domination** or **matrix of oppression** Rather than just looking at singular dimensions of oppression, the matrix of domination or matrix of oppression looks at the bigger context in which oppressions intersect by placing emphasis on the many sites of domination that drives oppression. For more see "A topography of domination" in Chapter 4.

**medical model** In relation to disability, the medical model is said to sometimes fall into the trap of framing and conceptualizing disability as an illness or abnormality in need of a cure.

**mental health** A psychological and mental state of well-being.

**mental illness** A condition that can be difficult to define, because unlike physical illness where a diagnosis is usually based on objective tests that identify bacteria, viruses, or physiological changes that cause the body to literally become ill, mental illness is mostly diagnosed through the symptoms one reports or the behaviours one exhibits. In broad terms, mental illness can be described as a lack of psychological or mental well-being, and the extent to which it interferes with one taking part in or enjoying everyday life.

**meritocracy** The belief that what separates those who get ahead from those who do not is hard work and intelligence, rather than the system the power group has instigated. For more see "Maintaining domination" in Chapter 4.

**metaphor** A phrase or word used in a non-literal way to imply a comparison.

**mezzo** Not large or small—this is the space between macro and micro. In social work this can include work and analysis at a neighbourhood or small institutional level.

**micro** The word means very small, and in social work refers to analysis and work at an individual or family level.

**microaggression** Multiple casual repeated commonplace acts that reoccur day after day that oppress. Microaggressions are usually considered to be unintentional—but we challenge the idea that these are truly unintentional. For more see "Oppression through personal prejudice" in Chapter 1.

**misogynist** A person who is anti-woman.

**mode of production** The way society produces what it needs to sustain itself and to also produce wealth.

**modernity** A period in history that emerged in the Enlightenment, and emphasized the importance of rationality, reason, and science. For more see "Postmodernism and power" in Chapter 3.

**naturalization** This term is used in this book in connection to Whiteness, and in this context the word refers to situating one's position as the natural or normal perspective. It is making one's way of being and understanding *the* way of being and understanding for everyone. For more see "How the dominance of Whiteness is maintained" in Chapter 4.

**neocolonialism** A type of colonization that is not maintained by military occupation, but through various aid and trade mechanisms.

**neo-liberalism** The idea that minimal government intervention and a free market produce an efficient and fair society.

**noble savage** A racist concept that represents Indigenous peoples before European contact as childlike, naive, and not corrupted by "civilization."

**normative** Literally the "norm," but in anti-oppression this does not mean "norm" as an average or what is most common, but as the way dominant society thinks *all* people *ought* to be. Being outside this norm does not simply mean becoming a numeric minority; it means being regarded as inferior, morally wrong, or defective in some way.

**nothing about us without us** A slogan developed by the Disabled Peoples' Movement that means social workers and others should not make decisions about or for disabled people without the direct involvement of disabled people themselves. In this book we have argued that this ought to apply to all social work service users.

**occupy movement** An international movement that protests economic inequality—especially the fact that most of the world's wealth is held by 1% of the population.

**old school tie** Literally a school tie worn by adults who attended the school associated with that tie, but used metaphorically to refer to the way those who attended an elite school recognize each other and help each other to gain social advantage. For more see "Buying even more advantage" in Chapter 1.

**ontology** Refers to beliefs about the nature of the world and its realities. Literally it means the study of existence—the process of attempting to understand what is "real."

**operating system** The term is commonly used for computer operating systems, but it can be used as an analogy for the social order. Also see in this Glossary *social order*.

**oppress** To press or tread someone down, usually in a way that holds them back in life. In anti-oppressive social work, the term is usually used to refer to the process of treading down and holding back entire groups of people, simply because they are members of that group. For more see "What is oppression?" in Chapter 1.

**oppression** See *oppress*.

**Orientalism** The word has several meanings, but is used in this text in the manner popularized by Edward Said. In this sense Orientalism is a patronizing or demeaning view of the East. It is imagining the East as inferior to the West. The purpose of viewing the East as inferior is so that the West can imagine itself as superior.

**Other** Used to refer to those defined by the dominant group as different. When used in this manner, the "O" is capitalized so that the word is rendered "Other." For more see "The basis of oppression" in Chapter 1.

**paradigm** A worldview. It is similar to the way ontological and epistemological perspectives mix to form understanding.

**patriarchy** A system of domination by men.

**people first language** See *people with disability* in this Glossary.

**people with disability** Language that is thought by some to be more respectful, because it emphasizes the person before the disability. This language has been critiqued, because it can mask the fact that people are disabled by a social-political process. For more see "Ableism" in Chapter 6.

**performativity** Enacting societal expectations in a way that reinforces those expectations.

**pluralism** The term has many meanings, but in this book we draw the term from political philosophy, where it refers to the idea that government is influenced by multiple groups. The theory is that the constant push and pull among competing interest groups attempting to influence government ensure that no one group dominates, and in this manner democracy works. In other words, the will of the people shapes government decisions through the power of interest groups. We have critiqued this idea; see "Who governs" in Chapter 3.

**poliarchy** A term used by Robert Dahl to refer to rule by many people.

**political colonization** The colonizer occupying and controlling a people's land or territory. For more see "The problem of science" in Chapter 2.

**positionality** A term used to refer to a relational position that arises from one's social location (such as race, gender, class, etc.). The concept is related to our social location—it is one's place or places in the social order and within society. Understanding this position (positionality) is important because it can shape the way we perceive others and the world around us. For more see subject-position in "How the dominance of Whiteness is maintained" in Chapter 4.

**positivism** A form of science that in its original form only accepted the observable as real (so recognizes no form of spiritual world). This form of science tends to break things into small elements to understand them (so it does not usually look at things in a holistic way). There are, however, many forms of positivism; some are less rigid than others. For more see "The problem of positivism" in Chapter 2.

**postcolonial** Literally "after colonial," but the term recognizes that even though colonialization may be officially over in a certain place, colonialism continues by other means.

**posthuman** Artificially enhanced human beings.

**postmodern** or **postmodernism** Refers to a historical period, said to have emerged in the late twentieth century, that rejects the premises of modernity, particularly the idea that science make human progress inevitable.

**power elite** A term used by C. Wright Mills, a sociologist at Columbia University, to define the dominant power group in society—he defined these as corporate, political, and military leaders whose interests are interwoven and who work together as a collective, mostly behind closed doors, to promote their shared interests and maintain their power position.

**power over** Usually thought of as a negative form of domination (rule or control) over people. Although power over is usually negative, at times power over can be used in a way that stops domination.

**power to** The use of power to enable another person to do something that they would not ordinarily be able to do.

**power with** A form of non-hierarchical power based on co-operation and collaboration in the context of relationship.

**peer-reviewed publication** A paper reviewed and approved of by other academics before it is published.

**photovoice** A participatory, community-based research method in which participants convey messages in words and pictures.

**practice wisdom** The wisdom or knowledge practitioners develop about ways of working from the experience of doing social work.

**prediction** This term refers to a forecast or estimation about something that will occur in given circumstances, or a prognosis. The term is not usually used in social work practice, but when used in relation to theory refers to the informed understanding social workers try to develop when examining the consequences of a problem or intervention.

**prejudice** To prejudge without being aware of facts; to discriminate based on one's personal biases.

**principle of three voices (3Voices)** The idea that social work needs to be driven by the knowledge and views of service users, service providers, and researchers/academics. For more on three voices see "The academy must change" in Chapter 13.

**privilege** A special advantage.

**profeminist** Activism led by men, in particular to help other men recognize their male privilege.

**proletariat** A French term used to describe the working class.

**protofeminist ancestors** Women who actively fought for women's rights before the term *feminism* was coined.

**quantitative data** Measurable data often represented in numeric values.

**queer** A collection of sexual identities or ways of being, and also to a process of challenging dominant norms and ideas. Indeed, at a theoretical level the concept of queer emphasizes that sex and gender cannot be categorized or framed. Said differently, queer, and the process of queering, break the power of what we consider "normal."

**queer theory** The rejection of traditional categories to question the way we understand sexuality, gender, and other related phenomena.

**racial contract** The racial contract is the idea that White should rule, or at the very least benefit the most from societal systems. As a type of social contract, the racial contract is not always written, but is instead embedded in the dominant culture and enforced in everyday actions at the personal, cultural and systemic levels. For more see "White supremacy The power behind Whiteness" in Chapter 4.

**racialization** The sorting of people based on the notion of racial difference.

**racialized** A person or group of people who have been socially constructed by the dominant group as "racially different" or Other, and then oppressed on the basis of this "difference."

**Rastafari** or **Rastafarianism** A religion/belief system developed in Jamaica with Ethiopian roots.

**reclaimed** A reclaimed word is a word that is usually offensive or derogatory, but has been "reclaimed" and used as a form of resistance by those the word is usually used against.

**reflexivity** and **critical self-reflexivity** Reflexivity is a person's ability to question their own pre-existing values, beliefs, and thoughts and to take action on them, while critical self-reflexivity describes a person's ability to use their self-awareness and emotions to self-implicate and challenge themself on their pre-existing values, beliefs, and thoughts. For more see "Politics, paradigms, and self-reflection" in Chapter 2.

**relative poverty** Having an income and resources that are significantly less than others in one's community.

**residual model** The idea that welfare services should only be provided as a last resort to people who have expended all other efforts to support themselves, such as the private market, savings, and family. For more on the residual model see "The residual model" in Chapter 12.

**resurgence or Indigenous resurgence** A reestablishment of Indigenous peoplehood, a reconnection to the land and traditions, and a reestablishment and renewal of what colonizers tried to take away.

**reverse racism** A rebuttal often used by people in a dominant racial position to deny the existence of anti-Black or other forms of racism. The person in the dominant position claims that they are the one that is actually experiencing racism and oppression.

**revolution** A fundamental change, often sudden, but that can also take place over time.

**right political perspectives** or **the right** The political concept of the right originates in France when those in upper elite social position sat to the right of the king. As a result, we use the term "right" today for perspectives informed by conservative ideas that favour social elites. For more about the terms "left" and "right" see "Politics, paradigms, and self-reflection" in Chapter 2. Also see in this Glossary the opposite term *left political perspectives*.

**ruling class** The class or group of people who rule.

**scientific colonization** The colonizer imposing their ways of thinking and understanding on those they have colonized. Political and scientific colonization have to be understood together, because they interact, with one process supporting the other. For more see "The problem of science" in Chapter 2.

**second dimension of power** or **power in the second dimension** Power exercised through manipulating agendas and decision-making processes. The idea is associated with Lukes's typology of power. For more details see "Lukes's model of power" in Chapter 3.

**Semite** A term that is hardly ever used nowadays except in linguistics where it refers to a family of languages. In earlier times it was inaccurately used to describe a "race," and as such provides a basis for understanding why anti-Jewish racism used to be called "anti-Semitism."

**service users' knowledge** The understanding and insight service users have into the troubles they face and services they receive. For more see "Service users' knowledge and theory" in Chapter 10.

**service users' theory** The refinement of service users' knowledge into theory. For more see "Service users' knowledge and theory" in Chapter 10.

**Settlement House Movement** An early social work organization founded in Britain in 1884 that went on to become a global movement. Settlement Houses are known primarily for having their workers and volunteers move into poor neighbourhoods in attempt to bring change through education, clubs for children and youth, and other social activities for the poor.

**settler colonialism** Colonization where the colonizers come and stay forever.

**sexism** Attitudes and processes that produce inequality for women; the oppression of women.

**sexual orientation** The sex one is attracted to.

**shadowboxers** A term developed by Black women and used to refer to Black women who refused to adhere to White middle-class norms. The efforts of these women are said to "preshadow" the Black feminism of third-wave feminism. In other words, do not think that Black feminism started in the third wave, because it has always been around.

**social capital** Any social connection (with an individual or institution) that gives a person prestige and power. In this book we have used Pierre Bourdieu's ideas to explain this concept. See "Pierre Bourdieu's view of power" in Chapter 3.

**social class:** Similar to SES, class represents one's position in society based on education, income, and employment. Class is usually divided into upper, middle, and lower levels, or upper, middle, and working class, with sometimes an "under class" being added. When using a Marxist analysis, class is also determined by one's relationship to the means of production, with the working class or proletariat selling their labour power, and the capitalist class or bourgeoisie owning the means of production.

**social contract** A contract, sometimes written into law or constitutions, sometimes not, in which people give up some of their freedom and liberty in exchange for following rules and regulations set by the state in exchange for the state providing some degree of safety, security, and stability.

**social construction** An idea people collectively believe and act upon.

**social exclusion** People being prevented from taking part in or enjoying events and activities in society that most others take for granted.

**social inclusion** The act of ensuring that social exclusion does not occur.

**social justice** A fundamentally fair society. There are many views of what is fair and what is socially just, but from an anti-oppressive perspective this tends to be conceptualized as people being treated according to their needs.

**social location** An aspect of identity, such as race, gender, age, or class, that situates one in specific locations in relation to society and the social order.

**social model of disability** Locates disabling conditions not in the bodies or minds of people, but in the tendency for the world to be structured to be navigable only for those with bodies and minds that meet ableist ideals.

**social order** or **the social order** The way institutions, organizations, government, culture, and so on hold together order within society—a social system. The concept is similar to a computer operating system. It is the way society works.

**socialism** A system in which most of the wealth-creating mechanisms are democratically owned and controlled by the people.

**socialist paradigm** In simple terms, a belief that it is best for the state to own or control the means of production and also services. For more details see "Politics, paradigms and self-reflection" in Chapter 2.

**social science** The science of human and human social relations, which includes disciplines such as psychology, sociology, politics, social policy, economics, law, and many more.

**socioeconomic status (SES)** A concept that refers to one's position in society based on variables such as education, income, and occupation.

**stigma** To be marked as "different."

**subject positions** The location of a person within a system or structure. For more see positionality in "Whiteness: The operating system at the centre of the circle" in Chapter 4.

**suffrage** The right to vote and the right to stand for political office. Sometimes "suffrage" is used to refer only to the right to vote, and "full suffrage" for the right to vote and stand for office.

**surplus labour** The labour over and above that needed to make a product, the profit from which usually goes to the person owning the means of production, not to the person undertaking the labour.

**surveillance** To watch or observe.

**symbolic capital** A concept associated with the work of Pierre Bourdieu, in which economic, cultural, and/or social capital are converted into another form of capital, which Bourdieu refers to as "symbolic." This capital can be further converted into a range of material benefits. To understand the concept fully, one has to grasp "Pierre Bourdieu's view of power" explained in Chapter 3.

**systemic oppression** The result of the prejudices of dominant groups becoming embedded in societal systems.

**systemic theories of poverty** Explaining poverty as the result of systemic inequalities. Also see in this Glossary *culture of poverty* and *individual theories of poverty*.

**terra nullius** A Latin term that means "nobody's land." It is a principle in law that allows a state to acquire land that does not belong to anyone. This principle was used to by settler governments to take the land of Indigenous peoples. For more see "What treaties mean today" in Chapter 7.

**the personal is political** A term coined in second-wave feminism to describe the way that what happens to women personally reflects politics, in particular the way that sexism operates at a societal level. The insight this slogan provides has become a bedrock for understanding all oppressions, because any process that holds entire groups of people back and does not give them rights that the dominant group takes for granted, is political.

**theories** or **theory** All social work helping rests on theories, which are sense-making mechanisms. These mechanisms help social workers figure out what is happening and then develop ways to help. For more on theory in social work see "Theory and understandings in social work" in Chapter 2.

**third dimension of power** or **power in the third dimension** A concept associated with the work of Lukes, in which power is exercised over others by controlling the way they see and understand the world. This is regarded as the ultimate form of power, because it is completely invisible—there is no need to coerce, control agendas, or to exclude anyone from decision making, because people will only pursue the possibilities that those with power allow them to imagine.

**Third World** A term sometimes used to refer to poorer nations that are mostly in the earth's southern hemisphere; alternate and preferred terms include the *Global South* and *developing* or *underdeveloped nations*.

**Third World women** A term used to describe all Third World women as the same and based on stereotypical features.

**topography** A map or bird's-eye view of something.

**trans** Literally means "across" or "the other side." Used as a prefix with words such as transsexual or transgender and sometimes as an abbreviation for either.

**transgender** Those who have or express a gender different from their assigned sex.

**transhumanization** An attempt to enhance and modify the species-typical human body through technologies.

**transitioning** A medical and surgical intervention to change a person's body to have their sex reassigned to better match their gender identity

**transsexual** Sometimes transsexual is used interchangeably with transgender, but it is probably best to use the term *transgender*, because some authors claim that transsexual is a derogatory term, which results from it being associated with a medical diagnosis that pathologizes transgender as a form of identity disorder. However, some people prefer to use the term *transsexual*, especially those who are transitioning through medical and surgical intervention to change their body to have their sex reassigned to better match their gender identity. Given the fluidity of language related to these concepts, we recommend doing what everyone ought to do in civil society: if one has to refer to a person's sex or gender, find out and use the term that a person themself prefers to be used.

**tsunami** A giant tidal wave.

**Two Row Wampum Treaty** A treaty that set out the relationship and sharing of space by the Haudenosaunee and the Dutch Crown, and also sets sovereign relations between later settlers and European governments.

**Two-Spirit (2-Spirit)** A term reclaimed by Indigenous peoples to describe those in their communities who are considered to have both male and female spirits, including the social roles they hold in the community. Two-Spirit is also an umbrella term used by Indigenous peoples to describe gender-diverse and sexually diverse people.

**Ubuntu** A word that comes from a Zulu phrase that a person only has existence as a person through relationship with other people. The term is taken up more broadly in parts of Africa as a philosophy about life, human relations, and the responsibility we have one for another. For more details see "The power of love" in Chapter 3.

**undeserving or undeserving poor** Those who are blamed for their own poverty. See also *deserving poor* and *less eligibility* in Chapter 10 and in this Glossary.

**unearned privilege** The advantage that those in the dominant group gain as a result of isms holding others back.

**unintentional prejudice** A person being unaware that they are being prejudicial.

**universalization** Thinking that one's own experience is everyone's experience—which results in one thinking that one's perspective is or ought to be everyone's perspective. For more see "Naturalization and universalization" in Chapter 4.

**verification** Trying to prove that one's ideas and conclusions are correct. Also see in this Glossary *falsification* and *confirmation bias*.

**waves of feminism** A way of conceptualizing the history of feminism.

**Weberian ideal type** See *ideal type*.

**White guilt** Feelings of guilt that are often immobilizing and that White people or others in a position of Whiteness sometimes feel when they develop an awareness of the way they are implicated in and benefit from certain types of oppression.

**White innocence** Those advantaged by their Whiteness denying the existence of this advantage and of corresponding processes that cause disadvantage (such as racism, sexism, etc.).

**White, male, rational subject** In this phrase, "White' describes this position as a part of Whiteness. "Male" emphasizes the male aspect of Whiteness (because, currently and historically, White men claim to produce most of what we regard as knowledge). "Rational" refers to this position producing what is regarded as rational facts. "Subject" is one's group's subjective perspective. For more see "White supremacy: The power behind Whiteness" in Chapter 4.

**Whiteness** A term used to relate to a position of dominance. The term builds on the idea of race, but Whiteness is not just about White people, nor is it just about race. It is about a collection of positions that dominate.

**White privilege** The unearned benefits and privilege a person with White skin gets from being White.

**wildcard** In the context of this book, we used the term "wildcard" to refer to someone who is unpredictable because they refuse to operate within the status quo—they think and act outside the box.

**womanism** A word originally coined by Alice Walker that describes a movement and perspective that advocates for the rights of Black women and how they face the complex intersectionality of race, gender, sexuality, and class oppression.

**women's lib** The short form for "women's liberation," popularized during second-wave feminism.

**word on the street** Knowledge and wisdom that circulates through communities by word of mouth.

**workfare** A social policy used in Canada and around the world to require those who are unemployed to be available and willing to take any work that the government offers in order to receive social assistance.

**workhouses** Residential institutions with brutish conditions and hard labour regimes.

**xenophobia** Fear or hatred of the Other. It comes from the Greek words "xeno" (stranger) and "phobia" (fear); thus, it is the fear of the stranger.

**xeno-racism** Racism not necessarily based on skin colour, but built on Otherness such as immigration status, culture, religion, etc. Also see in this Glossary *Other*.

# Index

1% vs 99%, 66, 67–8
1491s: *Geronimo E-KIA*, 98

ableism, 153–7, 356; devaluing of all human life, 154; medical model of disability and, 154–5; social model of disability and, 156
abortion, 154
Abu Rayhan Biruni, 45
action, 111, 222, 235, 239; love and, 80, 83; need for, 286, 297, 298–304; truth and reconciliation and, 191, 192–3; White guilt and, 187–9
Addams, Jane, 131, 132
additive model, 134–5, 356
aetiology, 162, 356
Africa: Band Aid representation of, 204–5; Christianity in, 38; poverty in, 205; Ubuntu in, 78
African National Congress Party, 350
agencies: society and, *315*; *see also* organizations
agency, 12, 356
agendas, 73; power and, 60, 65
agender, 149, 356
aging, 154
aid: Global South and, 204; Global North and, 205–6; personal needs of givers and, 206; tsunami in Sumatra (2004), 199, 206
Ali, Muhammad, 72
alliance (service user/social worker), 300, 301, 356
alliances, 245–6
ally (allies), 152, 356
alterity: of Third World women, 137
America: discovery of, 103
Americans, 99
"angels": social workers as, 288, 291–2
Anishinabek: Biskaabiiyang and, 184
Anishnawbe: on Seven Grandfathers'/Grandmothers' Teachings (Seven Sacred Teachings), 78, 79, 80
annihilation, 94, 356
anti-Black racism, 119–20, 119–22, 233–4; critical race theory and, 119–20; interest-convergence and, 120–1; manifestations of, 122; race line and, 121–2
anti-Islam (anti-Muslim), 124, 356; racism, 124–6
anti-Judaism, 123, 356
anti-Muslim (anti-Islam), 124, 356; racism, 124–6
anti-oppression, 227, 340, 353; in ancient societies, 228–9; dialogue and, 240–1; intellectual genealogy of, 234–5; shift from anti-racism to, 227, 235–7, 251; social justice and, 229–30; social work and, 231–2, 247–8; as term, 236, 338; as umbrella term, 229, 233–4, 235, 237, 319; *see also* anti-oppressive practice
anti-oppressive organizational change, 312–15, 334, 340; action plan, 327–9; anti-oppressive vision of, 319–20;

beyond agency control, 322–4; challenge of, 317–19; cycle of, *325*, 333; identifying what needs to change, 327; initiating action plan, 330–3; levers and, 328–9; model for, 324–33; new objectives and outcomes produced, 333; review goals, objectives, procedures, and outcomes, 324–7; starting point for, 319–21; strategies for change and, *328*; targets and, 328–9; underestimating people and potential for, 320–1
anti-oppressive practice, 1–2, 189–90, 339–40, 356; action and 240, 298–304; addressing all oppressions, 245–6; anti-racism and, 129–30; assigning blame and, 239–40; being "different," 287–9; broader political perspectives, 243; common sense and, 290; critical self-reflection and reflexivity, 294–7; in current social work environment, 282–3; decisions made by social workers and, 23–4; making a difference, 287–9, 292; fighting racism and other isms, 292–4; heart and, 284–6; love and, 80, 286, 352; moving mountains, 290–1; need for systemic success, 304–6; organizational context, 311–12; party politics and, 242; good casework and, 289–90; settler colonization and, 177; starting points for, 283–97; struggle and, 232
anti-psychiatry, 163–4, 356
anti-racism, 128, 233–4, 356; agenda of total transformation, 243; all talk, no change, 239–40; backlash against, 236, 251; dialogue and, 240–1; binaries and, 244–5; CCCS and, 234; challenges of, 227; cherry-picking oppressions, 245; decolonization and, 186; ideological dogma and, 240; intellectual genealogy of, 234–5; mistakes with, 237–47; ourselves as the system, 247; as party political divide, 241–2; service users' theory and, 259–61; shift to anti-oppression from, 227, 235–7, 251; theoretical inadequacy, 238–9; in UK, 235–6
anti-Semitism, 19, 20, 123–4, 356
"AOP" (anti-oppression), 189–90; *see also* anti-oppressive practice
apartheid, 350
appropriation, 95–6, 356; cultural, 95–7, 357
archetype, 40
Aristarchus of Samos, 45
asexual, 150, 356
assimilation, 94–5, 356
assumptions: theory and, 32–6
austerity ailments, 162, 207, 356
austerity measures, 264

Baines, D., 282–3
Baker, Ella, 132
"Ballad of a Hero" (Tempest), 162
Band Aid, 204
Barnes, Colin, 155

sanism, 158–64; anti-psychiatry and, 163–4; challenging, 162–4; oppression through psychiatry, 159–61; service user solutions, 164

Schön, D.A., 297

schools: private, 12–13; residential, 23, 94–5, 191

science: colonization and, 36; debunking fake, 42–3; imperial dreams and, 36–7; potential in social work, 40–4; as tool of colonization, 37–8, 40

Seidman, S., 40

Semite, 123, 364

service user involvement, 256, 277–8; discomfort with, 346–8; fear and, 347–8; organizational barriers to, 345; in organizational change, 326–7; things to avoid with, 262–8

service users: anxiety about social workers, 342–3; community-based research and, 261–2; guide for, 271, 272; number and political power of, 344–5; as oppressed group, 3; peer support and, 273, 274; primary reasons for, 230; service driven by need not ideology, 260–1; social location and, 90; thankfulness for help, 342, 343, 344; voice of, 282–3; voluntary vs involuntary, 342

service users' knowledge, 257–8, 340, 364; about dangers, 270; drawing upon, 261–2; examples in action, 269; helping to develop, 271; as less than social workers', 256–7; things to avoid when utilizing, 262–8; word on the street and, 268–71; of workers and systems, 270

service users' theory, 257–8, 340, 364; drawing upon, 261–2; essential in anti-oppression, 259–61; examples in action, 269; helping to develop, 271; things to avoid when utilizing, 262–8; word on the street and, 268–71

service users' union, 273–5, 340, 344–5; child protection, 276; for foster parents, 274–5; funding for, 277; helping social workers, 276; plans for, 276–7

Settlement House Movement, 248, 249, 250, 266, 364

settler, as term, 185

settler colonialism (colonization), 172, 175–7, 364

settler nativism, 186–7

Seven Grandfathers'/Grandmothers' Teachings, 78

sex: assigned, 146, 148, 356; normative rules of, 146; as term, 146

sexism, 8, 130–1, 364

sexual attraction, 149–50

sexual orientation, 149, 364

shadowboxers, 132, 364

Shakespeare, T. and N. Watson, 155

Sharma, N. and C. Wright, 184

Simpson, L., 193

Sinclair, Raven, 8

Sixties Scoop, 23, 191

slavery, 101, 119, 121, 188

slaves: "problem" of, 48, 49, 51

Smite, 123–4

Smith, A., 244

Smith, K., 318

social class, 92, 212, *212*, 364; *see also* class

social construction, 364; of gender, 146; race and, 100, 102

social contract, 101, 201–2, 364

social exclusion, 4, 95, 364

social inclusion, 4, 364

socialism, 201, 364; reverse (for the rich), 68, 220

socialist paradigm, 364

social justice, 4, 221, 364; fourth-wave feminism and, 137; social work and anti-oppression, 229–30

social location, 88, 364; flower exercise, 111–12; internal divisions and, 92; locating one's own, 110–11, 244

social media: fourth-wave feminism and, 137

social order (the social order), 200, 222, 339, 364; child welfare and, 317; exploring, 201–2; problem of existing, 221–2; production of poverty and, 202–3; progression and, 212–13

social science, 32, 37, 364

social work: academic-practice divide, 238–9; attitudes towards, 340; as danger to service users, 270; determined by wealthy, upper-middle-class, White people, 250–1; exploitation and, 78; field placements, 81; immediate need and, 230–1; individual orientation and societal orientation, 249–51; integrating anti-oppressive perspective into, 231–2; "magic" and, 299–300; mental health services and, 160; "mothers of," 131–2; need vs ideology, 260–1; as oppressive, 259; on origins of oppression, 76; power and, 64–5; primary reasons for, 230; process of, *300*; reflection and reflexivity and, 296–7; regulation and bureaucratization of, 343–4, 345; ruling relations and, 75–8; science in, 40–4; service users' knowledge and theory and, 258; as the system, 247; uncomfortable places and, 346–8; *see also* anti-oppressive practice; practice

social work academy, 348–50

"social work dream," xi, 228, 247–8, 276, 277

social workers: as "angels," 288, 291–2; expenses and, 331–2; human rights work vs, 4; as "Indian Agents," 181–2; as knowing best, 257; knowledge and, 259–60, 272; number of, 344; power and, 273; removal of children from homes, 22–3; social location and, 90; structural causes of service users' troubles and, 330–1; theory and understanding in, 31–2, 259–60; understanding of oppression, 2–3; use of term "oppression," 5–7

social work students: host families and, 264–5

societal attitudes: organizations and, 312–13; pushing back at, 314–15

society: agencies and, *315*

socioeconomic status (SES), 212, 364; *see also* class

Socrates, 30

South Africa: truth and reconciliation in, 350–1

Stenberg, Amandla, 96

Stewart, Maria W., 132

stigma, 158, 257, 364

storytelling, 120

subject positions, 101, 103, 365; *see also* social location

subjects, defended, 318

subjugation, problem of ongoing, 39–40

subsistence level, 204